Law and the Administration of Justice

Administration of Justice Series

INTRODUCTION TO THE ADMINISTRATION OF JUSTICE

Robert E. Blanchard, Volume Coordinator
Riverside City College and the American Justice Institute

PRINCIPLES AND PROCEDURES IN THE ADMINISTRATION OF
JUSTICE

Harry W. More, Volume Coordinator
San Jose State University, San Jose

LAW AND THE ADMINISTRATION OF JUSTICE

Vernon Rich, Volume Coordinator
Southern Illinois University, Carbondale

EVIDENCE AND PROCEDURE IN THE ADMINISTRATION
OF JUSTICE

Kenneth Katsaris, Volume Coordinator
Tallahassee Community College, Tallahassee

COMMUNITY RELATIONS AND THE ADMINISTRATION
OF JUSTICE

David P. Geary, Volume Coordinator
University of Wisconsin, Milwaukee

Law and the
Administration of Justice

VERNON RICH
Volume Coordinator
Southern Illinois University
Carbondale

John Wiley & Sons, Inc.
New York London Sydney Toronto

Library of Congress Cataloging in Publication Data:

Rich, Vernon, 1939-
Law and the administration of justice.

(Administration of justice series)
Includes bibliographies.
1. Criminal Law—United States. 2. Criminal
justice, Administration of—United States.
I. Title. II. Series.
KF9219.R5   347′.73   74-17322
ISBN 0-471-71915-3

Printed in the United States of America

10 9 8 7 6 5 4 3 2 1

Contributors

Volume Coordinator:
Vernon Rich

Rewriter:
Charlotte Shelby

Barry S. Brown
Bloomington, Indiana

Neil C. Chamelin
Institute of Government
University of Georgia,
Athens, Georgia

Patricia Constance
Center for the Study of Crime,
Delinquency, & Corrections
Southern Illinois University,
Carbondale, Illinois

Frank Dell'Apa
WICHE Corrections Program
Boulder, Colorado

Kent B. Joscelyn
School of Public and Environmental
Affairs
Indiana University,
Bloomington, Indiana

Jacquelyn Jurkins
Multnomah Law Library
Portland, Oregon

Jonathan Lindberg
Department of Political Science
University of Wisconsin,
Oshkosh, Wisconsin

Roger I. Purnell
Center for the Study of Crime,
Delinquency, & Corrections
Southern Illinois University,
Carbondale, Illinois

Constance M. Rigsby
Center for the Study of Crime,
Delinquency, & Corrections
Southern Illinois University
Carbondale, Illinois

David P. Skelton
Attorney-at-Law
Bloomington, Indiana

Introduction to the Series

Wiley has undertaken a significantly different approach to the development of five textbooks. The "Administration of Justice" series responds to the belief that teachers should be given an opportunity to state their textbook needs and to define how the organization and contents of a textbook can best serve these needs. Although teachers are generally asked to react to a book after it is published, we sought advice before final decisions were made.

Traditional textbook publishing has assumed that an author is all-knowing about the content of his book and how the content should be organized. The results often have been disappointing for the following reasons.

1. Some books are very long because they attempt to ensure that there will be something for everyone in the text.
2. Some books are written with one type of student or one section of the United States in mind.
3. Other books reflect an author's strengths and weaknesses; they are sound in some areas (where the author is strong) and superficial in other areas.

We began by working with five tentative outlines that were sent to hundreds of educators and professionals within the criminal justice system. Feedback on the outlines—on how they could be strengthened and improved—was excellent and encouraged us to sponsor a series of meetings throughout the United States. Many participants helped us to synthesize the comments received on the outlines, and each participant prepared revised outlines based on the responses evoked by questionnaires. We especially thank the participants. The books could not have been produced without the help and enthusiasm of Bernard Barry, Scott Bennett, Bob Blanchard, John Boyd, Wordie Burrow, Tom Cochee, Bill Cusack, Stan Everett, Matt Fitzgerald, Ed Flint, Jack Foster, George Gaudette, Dave Geary, Henry Guttenplan, Karl Hutchinson, Keith Jackson, Ken Katsaris, Art Kingsbury, Roger Kirvan, Martha Kornstein, Harry More, and Vern Rich.

Several sets of new outlines resulted from the regional meetings, and these outlines were further expanded and refined at a final meeting. Responsibility for the final outlines was placed with the following educators, who managed the process of evolving the outlines into books with great care, professionalism, and perseverance.

Robert E. Blanchard, Riverside City College and the American Justice Institute, *Introduction to the Administration of Justice.*

Harry W. More, San Jose State University, *Principles and Procedures in the Adminstration of Justice.*

Vernon Rich, Southern Illinois University, *Law and the Administration of Justice.*

Kenneth Katsaris, Tallahassee Community College, *Evidence and Procedure in the Administration of Justice.*

David P. Geary, University of Wisconsin, Milwaukee, *Community Relations and the Administration of Justice.*

Volume coordinators identified leading national figures whose area of particular competence is represented by a chapter in each volume. Specialists throughout the United States brought their insight and experience to bear on the writing of individual chapters, which met the goals and requirements of our advisory groups. These chapter authors are listed on page v. Thus, five highly authoritative, highly current, exceptionally interesting textbooks have resulted.

Individual chapters were examined by the volume coordinator and then were assigned to professional writers. Joseph Schott, Jim George, Charlotte Shelby, Irvin Lee, and Betty Bosarge worked hard and well on homogenizing the volumes. In addition to the responsibility of rewriting two volumes, Charlotte Shelby devoted considerable effort, imagination, and skill to enhancing the clarity and excitement of the other volumes.

Our approach to the development of this series, I believe, has resulted in five important textbooks. It will be for the students and instructors to determine how well we have done. Write to me and tell me how the books might be made even more useful to you.

Alan B. Lesure, Editor
John Wiley & Sons, Inc.

Preface

Law and the Administration of Justice is not a law book. Instead, it is an accumulation of basic concepts drawn from history, anthropology, sociology, psychology, law, and philosophy to form a foundation for law as it undergirds the administration of criminal justice. It is written not for the student of law, but for the student of justice administration—the police officer, the security representative, the criminal investigator, the correctional institution employee, the parole or probation officer, and the person seeking an understanding of the law as a foundation of the justice system.

Criminal justice personnel in nonattorney positions need a working acquaintance with the substantive criminal law of the political subdivision by which they are employed, and with all superior levels of government. A student of law prepares himself to be a specialist in law, but a student of justice administration studies law alongside the behavioral sciences, including topics such as group dynamics, community development, cross-cultural relations, crisis intervention, management, counseling, security, behavior modification, and criminology. The latter student—for whom this text is intended—must be able to integrate the law with the many other bodies of knowledge that he should acquire in order to practice justice administration successfully.

Probably the most significant impetus to a broad conceptual approach of the criminal law has been the trend toward recognizing discretion as essential for modern-day social control. To be able to justify the trend toward the increased use of discretion by law enforcement, security, and correctional personnel, the men and women serving in these roles must be capable of coping with frequently complex philosophical, political, legal, and sociological problems. The law provides a distinct dynamic set of standards for exercising discretion, but the law is simply one ordering device among many recognized as instrumental in maintaining social control in our nation's communities and states.

Chapters 1, 2, and 3 provide a behavioral, philosophical, and historical setting for the Anglo–American criminal law. Chapter 1 attempts to place law into the larger social-ordering context by identifying the fundamental concepts by which change in law is guided and against which it is constantly measured. Chapter 2 is a comparative study of criminal law contrasting the basic substantive law and, to a limited sense, the procedural law of several cultures and nations. To compare one nation's system with another tends to facilitate identification of the fundamentals of each system. Chapter 3 emphasizes the historical contributions to our present Anglo–American system of criminal law.

Its author provides some major philosophical underpinnings to key historical events.

Chapter 4 develops the rationale for how and why society attaches criminal liability to certain prescribed acts that are deemed harmful to society. Key principles begin to emerge that can be termed basic principles of criminal law, which have remained fairly stable for several generations.

Chapters 5 through 8, the central focus of the text, provide the basic substantive law emphasizing the common law, but also provide a broad view of some of the major deviations from the common law by statutes. Chapter 5 deals with *Offenses Against Persons* followed by *Offenses Against Property* (Chapter 6), *Offenses Against Habitation and Occupancy* (Chapter 7), and *Miscellaneous Offenses* (Chapter 8).

Parties to a Crime, Chapter 9, establishes criminal liability on the basis of the roles played by various parties to a crime, such as principals, or perpetrators, and accessories. It also examines the role of witnesses.

In *Defenses: Capacity and Responsibility*, the most frequently used substantive defenses to charges of criminal liability are examined, as well as are provisions in the criminal law that excuse liability even though the criminal act is established.

Most treatments of the criminal law tend to overlook the crime victim. Chapter 11 stresses the substantive rights of the victim to aid, self-defense, restitution, and payment for damages suffered. Sharply contrasting these rights are the rights of the person confined for perpetrating the criminal act, discussed in Chapter 12. This chapter illustrates the more significant rights of the confined, but it does not provide an exhaustive treatment of the rapidly developing case and statutory law in this area.

Chapter 13 also looks at the rights of a special group—juvenile offenders. It, too, does not pretend to be an exhaustive or definitive study but merely provides an overview.

The major theories of justice: the positive law theory, the natural rights theory, and the social good theory are examined to provide a broad view of jurisprudence in Chapter 14.

A rapidly developing body of law for the criminal justice agency administrator is administrative law, which is examined in Chapter 15. The impact of the courts via administrative law is perhaps one of the major change forces in the criminal justice system.

Chapter 16, *Discretion and the Law*, takes a positive view of the open recognition of the use of discretion and advocates the development of a sound rule-making procedure firmly recognized in administrative law to provide structure to guide its exercise. The recommendations of the American Bar Association and the National Advisory Commission on Criminal Justice Standards and Goals are described.

Appendix A is a major feature of the text. It exposes the student to a thorough study of the method by which law evolves, is researched, and becomes precedent for future legal decisions. The ability to use a law library is probably a law student's most helpful skill in law school, and this need is equally valid for the nonlegal student of criminal justice who must search case law, identify relevant statutes, and present an accurate statement of the "law" in a given political subdivision.

Probably the most unique contribution of the text is its diversity of knowledge bases. A sole-author text cannot achieve the necessary breadth to provide such a text. It represents an extensive effort to balance several writers' ideologies that were shaped by diverse experience, education, and training patterns.

Vernon Rich

Contents

Law and the Administration of Justice

The study of this chapter will enable you to:

1. Describe how criminal law changes to help achieve the social ordering goals of our society.

2. Provide four examples of the application of the exclusionary rule of evidence.

3. Describe how due process requirements tend to balance rights of the individual with the rights of society.

4. Define the "police power" of a government.

5. Contrast the rehabilitation theory of punishment with the deterrence theory.

6. List the three characteristics common to every criminal law.

7. List the major subfunctions of adjudication.

8. List and define the four major reasons that most people observe folkways, mores, and laws.

9. Describe how the U.S. Supreme Court can "alter" the law.

10. Describe how discretion is used by the police officer in the enforcement of laws.

1
The Role of Criminal Law in Social Order

Introduction

Law and order.
Innocent until proven guilty.
Equal justice for all.
Crime does not pay.
Pay his debt to society.

These are the phrases commonly used to describe the role of criminal law in the American social order. They derive from the traditional view of the criminal law as that body of rules and procedures that requires that every person who breaks a law will be arrested by the police; tried in a court of law before a jury of his peers; convicted of his crime; sentenced to prison; rehabilitated; then returned to society—the debt for his transgression paid. This so-called protection from the transgressions of the criminal few permits the vast majority of law-abiding citizens to go about their daily tasks in peace.

Police corruption.
Mafia.
The guilty go free on technicalities.
The police are handcuffed by the Supreme Court.
Death penalty.
The poor and the black cannot get a fair trial.
Pigs.

This is the language of American criminal law in turmoil. The role of the criminal law in our society, which seems so clear in its traditional form, has come into serious question. Uncertainty prevails, and questions go unanswered:

Why are men who are obviously guilty of serious crimes set free by the courts?

Why do the poor and ethnic minorities complain that they are treated unfairly by the criminal law?

Why do the vast majority of persons released from prison commit other crimes and return to prison?

Why do some groups of people demand that drug use, abortion, and sexual acts be decriminalized, while others argue for harsher penalties for the same acts?

Why are some acts crimes in some states and not in others?

Why are some defendants set free on probation for the same crimes for which others serve 20 years in prison?

The list of questions is endless. The law appears to be unequal in the land of equal justice for all. We know that the majority of crimes go unreported to the police, and that the majority of those crimes reported to the police go unsolved. We know that prisons do not rehabilitate and, in all probability, they produce a class of criminals more skilled in crime when they leave prison than when they went in. We know that courts are crowded and that in too many areas of our country the idea of a fair trial for a poor or minority defendant is relatively novel.

In the face of all this uncertainty, in light of the glaring deficiencies of the American sytem of criminal justice, why then do we persist in the traditional beliefs of a fair system of arrest–trial–rehabilitation? Is there any hope that our criminal law will fulfill its traditional role of protecting us from the criminal few? Or is, in fact, the traditional definition truly descriptive of the role of the criminal law in social order? In order to begin to answer these questions, we must examine the sources of the criminal law. We must also learn something of the way in which the criminal law is enforced and administered. Finally, we must examine the process of criminal justice and the way in which the criminal law changes to meet new social needs.

The Sources of Law

Social Ordering

Because men live in groups, they have laws. A hermit has no need of laws. He lives outside the society of men, and he may engage in any pattern of behavior that he wishes, for there are no rules, no customs, no statutes to govern his actions. When people live in daily contact with one another, however, they need some means of regulating their behavior in order to be able to predict how others will behave in relation to themselves and to understand the limits placed on their own behavior for the benefit of others. This concept of behavior regulations may be called social control, or *social ordering*.

Social ordering must be accomplished in any society because human interactions often result in conflict. Humans compete for economic resources. It does not matter if the resources are the prey of a primitive hunting tribe or the stock that controls a giant international corporation. Humans compete for esteem and power, whether the esteem and power result from membership in a secret tribal society or election to the presidency of the United States. And, given the observable nature of human behavior, they will compete with violence, with deceit, with avarice, and with callous disregard for others. Such behavior potentials clearly require some ground rules, unless human society is to be ruled by the strongest and most ruthless.

These ground rules need not, however, be laws. Social ordering can be accomplished in ways other than through a legal system. In every society, from the most primitive to the most complex technological systems, there exist certain societal ground rules, called *norms* by social scientists.[1]

Consider all the words we use to describe the phenomena we call norms: customs, mores, folkways, rites, rituals, regulations, rules, laws, statutes, routines, canons, etiquette, ceremonies, conventions, habits, ethics, fashions, taboos, maxims, styles. All these synonyms for norms can be classified conveniently under the three major headings: (1) folkways, which may be viewed generally as customs, or generally accepted ways of doing things or "getting along" with others; (2) mores, those moral or ethical rules that, if violated, may be injurious to society; and (3) laws, those formal rules of behavior issued by the government and, if violated, result in the violator's being punished by the government. In each of these three categories of norms, there is some definition of behavioral standards and some sanction for violating the norm. In violations of folkways, the sanction for violating the norm might be merely to be con-

---

[1] Robert Bierstedt, *The Social Order* (New York: McGraw-Hill, 1957), pp. 174–189.

sidered eccentric or odd. For example, the person who insists on wearing an overcoat in the summer or who keeps a hundred cats as pets certainly violates the folkways or customs of our society but suffers only the sanction of being thought a little "crazy." In the case of violations of mores, the sanction is more severe. Society labels the individual "immoral" or "unethical." The person who commits adultery or who submits a false job application to an employer is considered not merely eccentric, but actually a threat to social stability, and is therefore considered immoral. But the violation of a criminal law results in the sanction of fine, imprisonment, or even death. The threat to society is considered so great that a law violation is treated harshly compared to the violations of folkways or mores.

Societies (in a primitive state of development) that lack either the institutions of government or a written language also lack any norms that may be called laws. Some anthropologists believe that such societies have something called *primitive law,* a system of formal enforcement of sanctions for the violation of some customs that have developed an "official" status. But, for the purposes of studying American law, we must use a different definition. Laws, in the contemporary sense, are written expressions of the enactment or decree of legitimate governmental authority, which formally define standards of behavior and provide for punishment by the government for those who disobey.

Critical to an understanding of this concept of law is the realization that any legal system, including our system of criminal law, does not stand alone. The law of a given society is the official mirror of the economic, religious, political, philosophical, moral, and social make-up of that society. Laws in complex societies such as ours are, to some extent, the formal enactment of the mores of society. The law supports the mores considered most important or critical to societal survival by an additional sanction for breaking them—the infliction of punishment by the state. Thus, as society changes over time, so also does the criminal law, to help achieve the social ordering goals of our society.

The Police Power
The rationale for each criminal law in our society is basically the same: to prevent harm to the public interest. The ability of government to create criminal laws is called its *police power.* Police power has nothing directly

to do with the police, but is rather a technical, legal term that describes what most lawyers and political scientists believe to be a basic characteristic of a state: the power to regulate its public health, safety, welfare, and morals. Essentially, the exercise of police power provides for the prohibition of that private conduct which is deemed harmful to the society as a whole. The exercise of police power is intended to channel human conduct away from the undesirable conduct that causes harm to society, and toward the desirable conduct that is beneficial to society. This goal is thought to be attainable by the operations of the criminal law and the imposition of criminal punishments on the violators.

Characteristics of Criminal Law
Every criminal law has the following three characteristics:
    1. It is a written enactment of the government.
    2. It provides for the regulation or channeling of human behavior.
    3. It provides punishment for violators.[2]
If any of these three characteristics is missing in a statute (that is, a written law passed by a legislature), that statute is not a criminal law. Thus, there can be no crime unless there is a written law defining it.[3] Similarly, even if a statute defines the behavior expected of citizens, it is not a criminal law unless violators are punished according to a statutorily defined punishment.

An example of these characteristics of criminal law may be found in the criminal code of the state of Indiana. Before 1969 in Indiana, any one could carry a pistol aboard an aircraft. He would not have committed a crime and he could not be punished. In 1969, airplane hijackings were a major public concern. Public opinion in Indiana demanded that the legislature take action to reduce the harm to society caused by these hijackings, and, accordingly, the legislature enacted the following statute:

[2] Jerome Hall, *General Principles of Criminal Law* (Indianapolis: Bobbs-Merrill, 1969); Wayne LaFave, *Handbook on Criminal Law* (St. Paul: West, 1972).
[3] In the historical development of American law, there are common law crimes inherited from England, but only a few American states retain these, and in no American state are common law crimes of any great significance.

Indiana Code, Title 35
Article 23. Weapons.
> *Chapter 1. Firearms Aboard Aircraft.*
> *Section 1. It shall be unlawful for any person to board or attempt to board any commercial or charter aircraft having in his possession any firearm, explosive of any type, or other lethal or dangerous weapon.*

The statute went on to provide punishment of fine and imprisonment for anyone who was convicted of the acts prohibited in Section 1 of the statute. Therefore, after 1969, anyone who carried a pistol aboard an aircraft in Indiana was a criminal. The act of carrying the pistol aboard an aircraft became criminal conduct because the legislature declared it to be so in a written law, defined the exact behavioral standards expected of each citizen, and provided punishment for those who did not obey.

No matter what the crime, the above three elements must be present in order for a criminal law to exist. Any human conduct that is labeled criminal must have been defined as such by a legislature, whether the crime is first degree murder or overtime parking. The behavior prohibited must be defined with such precision that there can be no doubt as to what the legislature meant. The violation of a legal norm in our society is viewed as such a serious event, and the imposition of punishment by the government is thought to be such a drastic measure, that the greatest care must be taken to define and to channel behavior in a fundamentally fair and open fashion.

Crime and Punishment

Conformity

The central question that faces social scientists and lawyers who are concerned about the problem of crime is: Why do people commit crimes in the first place? The next obvious question is: How can our society prevent the commission of crimes? There is general agreement that not only do most people observe the bulk of our folkways, customs, mores, or ethical standards, but they also observe most of our laws. The reasons for the conformity to societal norms are many, but there are at least four elements motivating this compliance.[4]

[4] Bierstedt, *The Social Order,* p. 195.

1. There is great *utility* in observing the law and other norms. Society functions better when everyone knows what to expect from everyone else. Consider the nature of the society we might have if we did not know from day to day that everyone would pay his bills, would drive on the right side of the road, and would refrain from shooting a rifle in our direction.

2. A sense of *group identification* satisfies our psychological need to belong to a group, which causes us to conform to its norms. We all tend to dress in similar fashion, to eat the same foods, and to speak the same language. These things identify us as Americans both to outsiders and to ourselves.

3. We tend to conform to norms through *habituation,* or force of habit. If we cover our mouths when we cough or stop at stop signs ten thousand times in a row, it becomes difficult for us not to do the same thing when we cough or see a stop sign again. Once habituated to conformity, we must make a conscious effort to violate a norm.

4. We conform to societal norms because of *socialization,* or indoctrination into the "correct" way of doing things. We are taught by our parents to conform to societal norms, including laws. Our parents teach us to look both ways before crossing streets, to respect our elders, and to consider the policeman our friend. This phenomenon of socialization is particularly important in understanding criminal behavior, for consider what happens to the child whose parents do not "socialize" him to obey the law. Such a child may not, in his later life, view the law as a norm to be observed; he may become a criminal.

Punishment

Criminologists and sociologists, psychologists and psychiatrists, lawyers and policemen—all have their theories of what causes people to commit crimes. Theories range from mental illness as a cause of crime to crime caused by the conscious, willful plan of evil men. Many persons believe that crime is a result of poverty or ethnic discrimination; to others crime is merely another manifestation of the moral decline of our society. But, whatever the cause or causes (and no one is certain of the causes of crime), there is general agreement in our society that the enforcement of the criminal law is the proper way to prevent and to correct criminal activity.

Theories of Punishment

Many theories explain the existence of criminal law and punishment. They can be conveniently categorized in general terms to include the theories of *deterrence, isolation, rehabilitation,* and *retribution.* The *deterrence* theory of crime and punishment is twofold: first, the punishment of the individual offender should specifically deter him from future bad acts; and, second, the threat of punishment combined with the actual punishment of offenders will educate noncriminals in the consequences of bad behavior, thus providing a general deterrence to those who might commit future crimes. There is little scientific evidence to prove or disprove the theory of deterrence.

The *rehabilitation* theory (also called the corrections theory) of crime and punishment is that the criminal law serves as a selection device to determine those to be punished. Punishment under the rehabilitation theory is the giving of appropriate therapy to the convict in order to return him to society. The rehabilitation theory of crime and punishment has been of only recent application, and there is little evidence that it has, as yet, been of any benefit.

The *isolation* theory of crime and punishment is that the criminal law is a device for identifying persons dangerous to society who are then punished by being isolated from society as a whole, so that they cannot commit other antisocial acts. The isolation theory is used to justify the death penalty and long-term imprisonment. Obviously, this theory is effective in preventing criminal acts by those executed or permanently incarcerated.

The *retribution,* or vengeance, theory of crime and punishment is of ancient origin. It is, in essence, a form of retaliation best expressed by the phrase, "an eye for an eye."

All of the variations of these theories of crime and punishment attempt to explain the rational basis for the exercise of the police power by the state. Each theory finds some support in the current application of the criminal law in American society. The ultimate rationale of the criminal law, however, is simply that the criminal law provides a highly specialized form of social ordering for those acts officially considered to be severe violations of normative behavior. When certain kinds of behavior are viewed by a society as so bad that folkways and mores are insufficient to control them, the law is used—with its inherent threat of punishment—to prevent the bad behavior for the protection of the whole society.

The Criminal Justice System

We have seen that the criminal law is a highly specialized social ordering mechanism by which the government regulates behavior and punishes disobedience, and that the ultimate purpose of the criminal law is the prevention of harm to society. We also know that, despite the threat of punishment and despite the obvious benefits of obedience to the law, many people nonetheless disobey and become criminals. We shall now examine the method by which the criminal law is applied to these law-breakers. Just as a football game would make little sense if there were no rules of the game, so would a society make little sense if there were no norms or laws. And just as the game of football has people who write the rules of play, referees who enforce the rules, and coaches who teach proper ways of playing within the rules, so too does society have its people who make, enforce, and interpret the criminal law. These people are legislators, policemen, prosecutors, judges, correctional officers, and administrators. Together, these people and the jobs they perform are called, in their aggregate, the *criminal justice system.*

System Definition

The criminal justice system is that collection of functions performed by the legislators, police, prosecutors, courts, probation and correctional personnel, private security personnel, and other related agencies both within and outside of the government; for the purpose of enforcing, administering, and adjudicating the criminal law. Each entity or agency with criminal justice responsibility has its own function, and taken together, these functions form a *system*, or coherent grouping of functions and agencies, for the delivery of criminal justice services. The ultimate objective of the delivery of these services is to ensure that the criminal law performs the function of social ordering. The criminal justice system has four primary functions: lawmaking, law enforcement, adjudication, and corrections.

The process of operating the criminal justice system in order to work toward social ordering objectives may be termed the administration of justice. Criminal justice agencies operate to channel, to control, and to set standards for behavior in both official and unofficial ways. The key to understanding how the system works is to understand the concept of discretion on the part of each member of the criminal justice system.

As each official plays his role in the administration of justice, the criminal law (which seems so clear and precise on paper) evolves as a flexible standard of conduct that differs from state to state and city to city in its substantive provisions, its procedures, and its enforcement as each policeman, judge, and correctional officer exercises his discretionary judgment of how best to perform his job in the social ordering process.

Lawmaking

The function of lawmaking is performed primarily by state legislatures and Congress, and to a lesser degree by city and county councils. The lawmaking function is performed as a part of the legislative process whereby a theoretically representative assembly debates and adopts laws for the definition of behavioral standards. The laws for which punishment is provided by the state are criminal laws. They are assumed to be reflective of a popular consensus, derived from commonly held attitudes, beliefs, and opinions.

The function of lawmaking serves the objective of social ordering by defining the standards of behavior to which each member of society must adhere. Legislators have great discretion in making laws, because they are limited only by the requirements of the federal and state constitutions in their ability to create legal rules. This ability causes differences in the criminal law from state to state and allows change in a given state at varying times. The law is not rigid but, by its nature, must be flexible enough to accommodate changing social conditions.

Law Enforcement

Federal, state, local, and private police agencies perform the law enforcement function in the criminal justice system. Theoretically, the police enforce all laws uniformly by arresting all violators, but there are more law violations than the police can possibly handle. Thus, they are required to use discretion in the selective enforcement of criminal laws. Other duties, which may range from traffic control to rescuing cats from trees, leave even less time for criminal law enforcement.

When the legislative body has created a criminal law, it has spoken the theoretical will of the people. But often we know that laws are unpopular or are geared to affect only a small group. Thus, a law against gambling may prove unpopular in a community where poker is the principal Saturday night recreation. In such a community the police might not enforce the antigambling law. Similarly, a law prohibiting the use of an American flag as a decoration on clothing might be enforced against a long-haired holder of radical ideas, but not against the policeman who has a flag sewn on his shirt sleeve, or the president of the local chamber of commerce who wears a flag in his lapel.

Each police officer must decide when and if he will enforce the law. No matter what the legislature says the law is, and no matter how the statute in the law book reads, the process of criminal law is ineffectual if the policeman does not arrest the violator. The arrest however, is not enough to ensure the enforcement of the law. It must be made in such a way as to enable the prosecutor to secure a conviction; that is, according to proper constitutional procedures, for if the policeman violates the rights of the accused, the court will probably set the accused free. The arrest must be accompanied by sufficient evidence, for without evidence the prosecutor cannot prove that the accused committed the crime.

The law enforcement function serves the objective of social ordering in two primary ways. First, the actual enforcement of the law (by arresting offenders) triggers the "official" sequence of arrest–trial–punishment, thus maintaining social order by channeling and correcting the behavior of individual offenders. Second, the mere presence of law enforcement personnel has a preventive effect. People are deterred from criminal acts by the presence of the police, or, more often, by their own belief that the police will arrest them if they commit a crime. The police exercise their discretion in the maintenance of social order by choosing to intervene or not in disputes, by choosing to arrest or not upon witnessing crimes, and by choosing either to solve problem themselves or, by arresting, to let others in the system solve the problems of social ordering.

Adjudication

The function of adjudication in the criminal justice system is performed by prosecutors, judges, and related judicial personnel. The adjudicative process is divided into three major subfunctions that are closely related: (1) the prosecution, (2) the determination of guilt, and (3) the imposition of sentence.

The prosecutor decides when and if to pursue the conviction of those arrested by the police. He has the choice of declining to prosecute, of prosecuting on a lesser charge, or of pursuing the maximum possible punishment. Often, he will reduce the charge for which the offender was arrested to a lesser offense in exchange for a plea of guilty. This practice is called *plea bargaining*. If the prosecutor is unable to dispose of the charges by guilty pleas, he must present the state's case against the accused at a criminal trial. During the trial the prosecutor offers the evidence gathered by the police and the testimony of police officers and other witnesses, as proof that the accused committed the crime for which he was arrested. The lawyer for the accused offers evidence to the court in an attempt to prove that the accused is not guilty of the specific charge brought by the prosecutor. The burden of proof in a criminal trial is severe: The prosecutor must prove beyond a reasonable doubt that the accused actually committed the acts of which he is accused.

In a criminal trial, the judge is the *trier of law* and the jury, when there is one, is the *trier of fact*. This means that the vote of the jury is based on only the facts presented at the trial by the prosecution and the defense. The judge, and only the judge, decides what law applies to the facts of the case. In the absence of the jury the judge also decides the facts of the case; that is, what evidence and statements presented by both sides at the trial are true.

If the court finds the accused innocent, he is set free. If the finding of the court is that of guilty, the judge must then decide on an appropriate punishment for the defendant. Even when the punishment is clearly prescribed by statute, the judge may (except in very unusual cases) exercise his discretion to suspend the sentence, to place the defendant on probation, to give less than the maximum sentence, or otherwise to apply a punishment that is geared to have an impact on the individual offender. In serious cases, the judge usually avails himself of a presentence investigation report prepared by the probation department, which gives the judge the information he needs to make the best decision for the sentencing of each defendant.

Corrections

The function of corrections in the criminal justice system includes the activities of penal institutions, parole and probation agencies, and related social service and mental health agencies. The general objective of all these agencies is to rehabilitate the offender in order to return him to a normal and productive life. The measure of success for corrections is *recidivism*; that is, the commission of a crime by one who has committed it before. The *recidivism rate* is a percentage measurement of the repetition of crime by previously convicted criminals. Modern correctional institutions and programs seek not only to prevent recidivism, but also to modify behavior so that the offender makes positive changes in his life style to enable him to observe societal norms in the future.

Correctional officials have broad responsibility to decide whether the probationer or parolee is obeying the conditions of his release, and they have the power to petition the court to revoke probation or parole and to return the parolee to prison for infractions. Conditions of probation and parole are typically defined so that they can be revoked with some ease. Correctional officials also decide what course of rehabilitation convicts in prison are to have (if any). They determine whether the prisoners under their charge need medical or psychiatric care or counseling; if prisoners and parolees are to receive treatment for alcohol and drug addiction; and if their charges will receive job training and job placement assistance upon release.

The role of correctional officers in the social ordering process is to provide rehabilitative services to channel the behavior of convicted felons and misdemeanants into endeavors that are more productive than is crime. Too often, however, this effort is doomed to failure because the caseloads of correctional officers are too great, their levels of training and competence are too low, or their knowledge of successful techniques of criminal corrections is too sparse.

Administration of Criminal Justice Services

Although the various agencies of the criminal justice system seem to be working at odds, the long-range objectives of the agencies are the same. When the policeman works for the arrest and conviction of a felon, and the correctional officer works for the release and rehabilitation of the same felon, they are both actually working toward the same goal— social ordering. The mere existence of the criminal justice system prevents most potential violators from transgressing; thus the persons actually processed through the system are that smaller percentage of individuals who engage in antisocial behavior.

The administration of criminal justice services requires that those persons in executive positions be sensitive to public opinion. In a democratic society, the criminal justice system must be responsive to the people or it is doomed to failure. Citizens must perceive that the system is operated fairly, efficiently, and with due regard for the rights of individuals. The social, psychological, and moral benefits that accrue to the law-abiding citizen can be realized only if the nonlaw-abiding citizen has his behavior modified and channeled into generally acceptable patterns of appropriateness by the criminal justice system.

Criminal Procedure

Due Process of Law

We have seen how each component of the criminal justice system performs a definite role in the application of the criminal law to social ordering objectives. This process is governed by special rules of law called *criminal procedure*. Criminal procedure refers to the constitutional, statutory, and judicial limitations placed upon the application of the substantive criminal law. Such limitations are necessary because, in the United States, we have a government of laws and not of men. The concept that no one is above the law and that the law is applied to everyone in a fundamentally fair manner is critical to an understanding of the meaning of the term *due process of law*. Due process is of two types: substantive and procedural.

Substantive due process, a constitutional requirement that applies to all criminal laws, means that no criminal law may contain any provisions contrary to the Constitution. Thus, a criminal statute that permits the police to search houses without a warrant on suspicion only, would violate the requirements of substantive due process. The government cannot, by statute, authorize something prohibited by the Constitution. Procedural due process means that not only must the substantive criminal law conform to constitutional requirements, but that the manner in which the substantive criminal law is enforced and applied must also conform to constitutional requirements. Thus, a warrantless search of a house on mere suspicion by a public officer would violate the requirements of procedural due process. In its essence, due process means simply that those who make, enforce, and apply the criminal law must themselves obey the law. Due process will not permit the violation of one part of our law in order to enforce another part.

The Exclusionary Rule

The requirements of due process, both substantive and procedural, are most often raised at the time of a criminal trial. A criminal defendant will ask the court to exclude some piece of evidence against him on the grounds that it was illegally obtained (i.e., obtained in violation of the requirements of procedural due process) or will ask the court to dismiss the charge against him on the ground that the statute under which he is accused is itself illegal (i.e., unconstitutional because it violates the requirements of substantive due process). In either event, the violation of due process requirements will result in the freedom of the accused.

If the statute itself is unconstitutional, the result is most probably just. A severe problem of social ordering arises, however, if the accused is released because of a procedural due process violation. Such a circumstance means that the accused goes free, not because he is innocent or because the statute is unconstitutional, but because the evidence of his guilt is excluded from consideration at his trial. The ultimate result is that a guilty person is free. The practice of not considering evidence illegally obtained is called the *exclusionary rule* of evidence and is the subject of one of the central debates of contemporary criminal law.

The issue concerning the exclusionary rule is as follows: Is it better to let the guilty go free or to encourage the police to violate constitutional rights by admitting evidence at trial that has been illegally obtained? The issue is significant because it is central to the criminal process—the way we prove guilt or innocence.

The manner in which the judge and jury determine if the accused is guilty or innocent is to consider the evidence presented at the trial by the prosecution and the defense. Often the evidence takes the form of statements made by the accused or of property taken from the possession of the accused. If these statements or property are obtained from the accused in a manner that violates his constitutional rights, he has been denied procedural due process. In this event, the judge is bound to exclude the illegally seized evidence from consideration at the trial. Often the result of this action is that the prosecution lacks evidence sufficient to prove the guilt of the accused beyond a reasonable doubt. In this event, the court must find the accused not guilty, and he goes free.

Developing Criminal Law and Rights of the Accused

The criminal law, most particularly the law of criminal procedure, underwent great changes in the decade of the 1960s, when the U.S. Supreme Court restructured the manner in which the criminal law is written, enforced, and applied in America. The key to what has been called the American "criminal law revolution" is found in four amendments to the Constitution:

Amendment IV
The right of the people to be secure in their persons, houses, papers, and effects, against unreasonable searches and seizures, shall not be violated, ...

Amendment V
No person . . . shall be compelled in any criminal case to be a witness against himself, nor be deprived of life, liberty, or property, without due process of law; . . . .

Amendment VI
In all criminal prosecutions the accused shall enjoy the right . . . to have the Assistance of Counsel for his defence.

Amendment XIV
Section 1. . . . No State shall make or enforce any law which shall abridge the privileges or immunities of citizens of the United States; nor shall any State deprive any person of life, liberty, or property, without due process of law; nor deny to any person within its jurisdiction the equal protection of the laws.

These amendments are at the heart of the theory that has come to be called the "incorporation doctrine." The incorporation doctrine describes the rationale used by the Supreme Court to apply the Bill of Rights guarantees of the U.S. Constitution to the states. Essentially, the rationale is that the "due process" required of the states by the Fourteenth Amendment means that the states must apply the due process requirements of the Constitution. The Bill of Rights is "incorporated" in the Fourteenth Amendment as applied to the states. The various justices of the Court disagree as to the extent of this incorporation (and a pure incorporation theory has never commanded a majority of the court), but there has been majority agreement that the Fourth, Fifth, and Sixth Amendments to the Constitution are such fundamental requirements of due process of law that they now apply to the states as well as to the federal government.

The Supreme Court must have a case before it to effect the criminal law. The court cannot "make" law; only the legislature can do that. What the Supreme Court does do, however, is to rule on the constitutionality of appeals brought before it. The Court enforces the requirements of substantive and procedural due process. When a person is convicted of a crime, he has a right to appeal that conviction. He may try to convince a higher court that some error of law has been made at his trial. If either the criminal statute under which he was convicted or the methods of gathering evidence and prosecuting him used by the police and prosecutor violated due process requirements, the defendant is entitled to be found not guilty—or at least to get a new trial. Typically, a person will be convicted in a state court at the county level. He then appeals his conviction to higher state courts. If the highest state court rules against him, he then appeals to the U.S. Supreme Court to argue his federal rights. These federal rights, in order to apply to a state court conviction, must be included in the Fourteenth Amendment requirement of due process.

The Supreme Court hears only a fraction of criminal appeals; most are disposed of at lower state court levels. The power of the Supreme Court is severely limited, because it can decide only those cases that come before it. When the Court does decide a case and announces a rule of constitutional law, it creates an impact in every area of the criminal justice system.

The Court decides cases by the majority vote of its nine members, each of whom has his own philosophy of criminal law, his own opinions of how the criminal justice system should function, and his own "liberal" or "conservative" bias in terms of his general political outlook. Each justice is also aware of the political and emotional mood of the country. The Court seems to be responsive to both public opinion and the changing needs of the criminal justice system.

The interrelationship between the developing criminal law and the Supreme Court is best illustrated by the way in which the court has interpreted the Fourth, Fifth, and Sixth Amendments in the past decade. It has restricted the police in the manner in which they may search for evidence and secure confessions. It has placed a requirement on the states that they must provide counsel for every defendant who cannot afford to hire his own lawyer. These developments in the criminal law are the center of the contemporary debate about the proper role of the criminal justice system and criminal law in our society.

Fourth Amendment Rights. The historical origins of the Fourth Amendment are found in colonial American objections to legal devices called "writs of assistance," by which British soldiers were empowered to conduct general searches of colonial houses to enforce unpopular tax laws. The British right to be free from searches and seizures without warrant had been established well before the American Revolution, and the writs of assistance would not have been permitted in England itself. After the Revolution, the new Constitution included in its first ten amendments the right to be free from unreasonable searches and seizures. Such a right means that a policeman may search one's home only with a warrant, and he may search only for items specifically listed in the warrant. Issued by a judge, a search warrant is a document that is proof that the policeman seeking to make a search has satisfied the judge that there is *probable cause*; that is, that a reasonable man would have good reason to believe that a crime has been committed and that evidence of the crime is located in the place to be searched

In order to enforce the right to be free from unreasonable searches and seizures, the courts applied the exclusionary rule and prevented the introduction of evidence that had been obtained in violation of the Fourteenth Amendment. Thus, the issue for the courts in each case was the "reasonableness" of the search. This rule was enunciated in *Weeks* v. *United States* in which the Supreme Court held that, in federal prosecutions, the use of evidence secured through an illegal search was barred by the Fourth Amendment.[5] The right did not, however, apply to the evidence in state prosecutions. In *Wolf* v. *Colorado,* the Court held that, in a prosecution in a state court for a state crime, the Fourteenth Amendment does not extend the Fourth Amendment prohibition against the admission of the illegally obtained evidence to the states.[6] At the time, about 30 states permitted the use of illegally obtained evidence. During the 1950s, many states changed their rules of evidence and adopted the federal rule of exclusion.

In the 1960–1961 term, the Supreme Court decided *Mapp* v. *Ohio,* the landmark Fourth Amendment case that changed the criminal

[5] 232 U.S. 383, 34 S.Ct. 341 (1914).
[6] 338 U.S. 25, 69 S.Ct. 1359 (1949).

law to the present rule.[7] In that case, the police were observing Miss Mapp's house in the belief that a wanted criminal was hiding inside. They once went to the door and sought permission to search the house and were refused. Three hours later, they broke into the house and began a search. When Miss Mapp demanded to see their search warrant, they showed her a piece of paper that they later admitted was not a search warrant. The police searched the house from top to bottom, finally breaking into a chest in the basement. In the chest, they found obscene materials and arrested Miss Mapp for possession of pornography. Miss Mapp was convicted and appealed to the Ohio Supreme Court, which affirmed the conviction. She then appealed to the U.S. Supreme Court, which reversed the Ohio decision and in the process reversed its own decision in *Wolf*, by extending the Fourth Amendment right to the states.

Mapp required of state prosecution an exclusionary rule that had generally already been adopted.

> *The ignoble shortcut to conviction left open to the state tends to destroy the entire system of constitutional restraints on which the liberties of the people rest. Having once recognized that the right to privacy embodied in the Fourth Amendment is enforceable against the states and that the right to be secure against rude invasions of privacy by state officers, is, therefore, constitutional in origin, we can no longer permit that right to remain an empty promise.*

The Court decided that the right to privacy is more important than the control of crime.

Fifth Amendment Rights. The historical origins of the Fifth Amendment lie in the British court of Star Chamber where supposed enemies of the king were taken without having been charged with a crime, were tortured, and were made to confess to criminal acts. This practice was so repugnant to any concept of fairness or objectivity in determining guilt that is was finally abandoned in Great Britain. It became basic to British jurisprudence that no person should be compelled to be a witness against himself. The right was embodied in the Fifth Amendment of the U.S. Constitution.

American police had repeatedly and obviously violated the Fifth Amendment rights of the accused. This problem was particularly acute in areas where racial bigotry was strong, and minority defendants were

[7] 367 U.S. 643, 81 S.Ct. 1684 (1961).

beaten into confessions—the "third degree" was a commonplace experience. The Wickersham Commission, in 1931, reported that the practice of police brutality to coerce confessions from the accused was widespread.

Perhaps the single most important change in American criminal procedure since the adoption of the Bill of Rights is the decision in *Miranda* v. *Arizona*.[8] This decision banned the "third degree" and the coerced confession and required the police to give each accused a warning of his constitutional rights. This decision is the single most debated case in police circles, because, by arming the accused with the knowledge that he need not be cooperative, nor even talk to the police in the course of an investigation, it is felt that it is the police who are "handcuffed."

Obviously, the best source of information about the accused's involvement in a crime is the accused himself. If he will give evidence of criminal activity or confess to the crime, the police job becomes quite simple. Conversely, if the accused remains silent, the police often are unable to obtain any evidence of the crime. In the *Miranda* opinion, written by Chief Justice Warren, the Court examined some of the techniques used by the police to coerce confessions from the accused, concluding that in the 1960s the third degree had been replaced by less obvious psychological tricks of interrogation, so that there was little evidence of physical brutality in contemporary interrogations. Nonetheless, the Court found that psychological intimidation is as bad as physical intimidation and is not permissible under the Fifth Amendment. Accordingly, any confession obtained in such a way is, by definition, "involuntary" and must be excluded from evidence. The *Miranda* decision imposed procedural safeguards upon the police in the following language:

> *Prior to any questioning, the person must be warned that he has a right to remain silent, that any statement he does make may be used as evidence against him, and that he has a right to the presence of an attorney, either retained or appointed. The defendant may waive effectuation of these rights, provided the waiver is made voluntarily, knowingly, and intelligently.*

Sixth Amendment Rights. The origin of the Sixth Amendment lies in the fact that even the educated layman is at a tremendous disadvantage in defending himself against criminal charges because of the complexities of the criminal law and procedure. The Bill of Rights clearly provides

[8] 384 U.S. 436, 86 S.Ct. 1602 (1966).

the right to counsel. The Court in *Johnson* v. *Zerbst* held that, at least in federal prosecutions, a court must appoint counsel for a defendant who cannot afford to retain counsel of his own.[9] The federal rule did not apply directly to the states, and many states did not provide counsel to poor defendants. Without a lawyer the accused did not often know his rights. The constitutional rights available to the defendant were useless without counsel to assert them for the accused.

In the landmark case of *Gideon* v. *Wainwright,* the Supreme Court held that the right to counsel is a fundamental requirement of due process under the Fourteenth Amendment, and thus applies to state as well as federal prosecutions.[10] The state of Florida did not provide counsel to indigent defendants except in cases in which there might be a death penalty. The Court reversed a conviction where the accused did not have court-appointed counsel at trial. To underscore the importance of this right, note that when the case was tried again, this time with Gideon represented by a lawyer, he was found not guilty. In 1972, *Argersinger* v. *Hamlin* extended the right to counsel of the Sixth Amendment to all cases, felony or misdemeanor, in which there is any possibility of a jail sentence.[11] Even for traffic tickets, the court must appoint counsel for those defendants who cannot afford to hire their own lawyers.

The Role of Criminal Law in Social Order

The role of criminal law in social order is multifaceted, confusing, and complex. There are many acts labeled crimes in our society that generate high emotions, moral indignation, and psychological outrage. The criminal law constantly walks a tightrope between the necessity of controlling the threat of crime and the necessity of maximizing the freedom of the individual in a democratic society. The criminal law and the people who operate the criminal justice system are caught in the dilemma of reconciling crime control and due process, social ordering and fundamental fairness.

In a fundamental sense, the criminal law is a society's system of

9 304 U.S. 458, 58 S.Ct. 1019 (1938).
10 372 U.S. 335, 83 S.Ct. 792 (1963).
11 407 U.S. 25, 92 S.Ct. 2006 (1972).

self-defense that controls those disruptive individuals whose behavior threatens the fabric of society itself. The manner in which the criminal law deals with the behavior of these people mirrors the attitudes of the general public as to what is wrong (as well as what is right) with our society and our way of life.

Student Checklist

1. Can you describe how criminal law changes to help achieve the social ordering goals of our society?
2. Are you able to provide four examples of the application of the exclusionary rule of evidence?
3. Can you describe how due process requirements tend to balance rights of the individual with the rights of society?
4. Do you know how to define the "police power" of a government?
5. Are you able to contrast the rehabilitation theory of punishment with the deterrence theory?
6. Can you list the three characteristics common to every criminal law?
7. Can you list the major subfunctions of adjudication?
8. Are you able to list and to define the four major reasons that most people observe folkways, mores, and laws?
9. Are you able to describe how the U.S. Supreme Court can "alter" the law?
10. Can you describe how discretion is used by the police officer in the enforcement of laws?

Topics for Discussion

1. Discuss the concept of a criminal justice *system*.
2. Discuss the meaning of criminal law as a social ordering device.
3. Discuss the use of discretion in the administration of justice.

4. Discuss four theories of punishment and their impact on the criminal law.

5. Discuss the exclusionary rule and its impact on the criminal justice process.

ANNOTATED BIBLIOGRAPHY

Berman, Harold J., and William R. Greiner. *The Nature and Functions of Law*. Second Edition. Brooklyn, N. Y. Foundation Press, 1966.

Bodenheimer, Edgar. *Jurisprudence*. Cambridge, Mass.: Harvard University Press, 1962. A historical, philosophical treatise of the role of law in social order. It focuses on the synthesis of social order and justice.

Derrett, J. D. M. *An Introduction to Legal Systems*. New York: Frederick A. Praeger, 1968. A descriptive view of seven major cultures of the world in terms of their legal systems.

Mueller, Gerhard O. *Crime, Law and the Scholars*. Seattle: University of Washington Press, 1969. A broad survey of criminal law, jurisprudence, criminology, and the behavioral sciences woven in such a fashion to create an impression of harmony, controlled growth, and balance between law and social order.

Pospisil, Leopold. *Anthropology of Law: A Comparative Theory*. New York: Harper & Row, 1971. A comparative analysis of several cultures in terms of their legal systems. Emphasis is given to the cross-cultural dimensions of the study in an effort to highlight those behavioral factors common to all legal systems.

The study of this chapter will enable you to:

1. Describe how codes or systems of law are responsive to the social ordering requirements of the culture they serve.
2. Define "arrest with judicial permission."
3. Contrast the European provisions for arrest with those in the United States.
4. Contrast the objectives or goals of the Soviet system of law with those of France and the United States.
5. Describe how the role of the investigating magistrate in France differs from that in the United States.
6. Define the origin of civil, or civilian, law.
7. Describe how the common law of England evolved to current law in the United States.
8. Contrast the roles, duties, and powers of the prosecutor in three different legal systems.
9. Compare four nations' use of the exclusionary rule of evidence.
10. Describe how punishment varies among four different countries.

2
Comparative Criminal Law

Legal Systems of the World

Historical Legal Traditions

Codes of law are found among the earliest historical documents. The Ten Commandments of the Bible comprise a legal system with clearly defined social ordering objectives. The Babylonian Code of Hammurabi and the Code of the Twelve Tables of early Rome are other examples of ancient legal systems. These early systems had many things in common, such as the retributive justice of "an eye for an eye" and a strong religious and moral basis for their existence. They differed, however, in the same ways that modern codes of law differ; each legal system was a mirror of the society that it served. The moral and legal requirement of monotheism found in the Ten Commandments could never have been the law of the Rome of the Twelve Tables, which marked the earliest division between law and religion. The Babylonian Code of Hammurabi would have been completely alien to the social ordering requirements of the ancient Hebrews of the Bible. Just as the language, culture, architecture, and governments of ancient peoples differed dramatically, so too did their systems of law.

With the millenium-long consolidation of political rule of the West by the Roman Empire came the first opportunity for a worldwide legal order to develop. The greatest contribution of the Roman Empire to history was its development of a coherent legal system and an efficient government administration, which brought stability and order to the world. With the fall of Rome in the West and the decline of Byzantium in the East, the world once again fell into disorder, and the long Dark Ages descended on Europe—the rule of law gave way to the rule by the

27

strongest and most ruthless. In other parts of the world, such as China and India, other legal institutions developed which had a lesser influence on the modern world than did the development of the Western legal systems.

The Renaissance, which ended the Dark Ages, was responsible for the rediscovery of the Roman law. In the universities of Italy, France, Spain, and Germany, Renaissance legal scholars began the systematic study of the ancient Roman law which had once unified the world. The influence of these scholars was so great that the developing countries of modern Europe adopted the form of Roman law which was created by these university scholars. Local custom, although remaining important, ultimately gave way to the new Roman law of the universities. By the time of Napoleon, the legal systems in virtually all the countries of Europe were based upon the Roman law traditions of the universities. As the Roman Emperor Justinian had done 1500 years before, Napoleon codified the Roman law of France into the Code Napoleon, which became the basic influence on contemporary European law. Today the legal systems of European countries are referred to as Roman, or civilian, after the civil codes which embody their law. The civilian legal systems of the world, based upon Roman law, comprise one of the three major legal families of the world today.

During the same period that European law was undergoing its transformation to its modern form through the adoption of Roman law, quite a different pattern emerged in England, but with results just as important. The consolidation of government in England coupled with the rise of the judiciary to create the common law of England. This lengthy historical development resulted in a uniformity of law throughout the realm. Rather than rely on the Roman law as a guide, the common law relied on the value of precedent and consistency of decision by its judges for the development of a legal philosophy and system. Common law rules that are now 700 years old are still applied in some Anglo-American jurisdictions. The common law of the English-speaking peoples is the second great family of legal systems in the world today.

As England and the countries of continental Europe expanded their colonial empires beginning in the fifteenth century, they imposed their legal systems onto their colonies and their native populations. Thus, almost the entire world had imposed upon it either the legal system of England, based on the common law, or the legal system of a European country, based upon the Roman law. Local legal systems of the conquered peoples were either destroyed or changed to conform to the requirements of the new imperial powers. Even countries that never suffered colonial rule, such as Ethiopia and Thailand, have adopted Western legal systems. Except for the most primitive of countries, virtually every government in the world today has either a common law or a civil law legal system. The notable exceptions are those countries ruled by Communist governments. Although it is argued that Communist governments have a form of civil law legal system, most comparative law scholars recognize the legal systems of Communist countries as the third major family of legal systems: socialist law.

The socialist legal system originated with the Russian Revolution of 1917. Since the Communist take-over of Eastern Europe and China in the 1940 and its later domination of other countries, such as Vietnam and Cuba, the socialist law family has grown to include about one-third of the people of the world. The socialist systems are also based on Roman law, but differ greatly from the civil law systems, because they are legal systems subordinate to the state, which, in turn, is subordinate to the directions of the Communist party and its philosophy of Marxism-Leninism. The basic premise of socialist law is not the achievement of social ordering through the operation of law, but rather the achievement of an ideal Communist society that will function without the necessity of law or government.

Almost every legal system in the world today can be classified in one of three groups: common law, civil law, or socialist law. The common law countries are typically English-speaking former British colonies, such as the United States, Canada, Australia, and India. The civil law countries are those countries of Western Europe and their former colonies, who share the Roman law historical tradition, such as France, Germany, Spain, Italy, Latin America, much of Southeast Asia, and much of French-speaking Africa. The socialist law countries are those ruled by Communist governments, such as the Soviet Union, Eastern Europe, and China, where traditional civil law has been modified to meet the requirements of Marxism-Leninism. There exist, of course, mixed systems of law. The state of Louisiana, for example, has a French civil law tradition even though it is a part of the larger American common law system. Many African legal systems are based either on English or French law, but have very strong components derived from their own ancient tribal law. Both Japan and Turkey have adopted civil law systems based on European experience, but heavily flavored with their own traditions.

Indian law, based upon the law of England, bears elements of Hindu religious law. Although legal systems of the world can be readily classified into three major families, the law of each country must be viewed individually, because the law is both a reflection and a definition of the kind of society that exists within the borders of the unique legal system of each country.

Governments and Their Legal Systems

To understand foreign legal systems, we must look behind the written law of a country, to the government that administers the law, for there is often a great difference between the written law and the practices of legal administration. The law is meaningless without administration. Criminal law in Nazi Germany or Stalinist Russia compared favorably, on paper, with the law of the United States or any other democratic country. But the administration of that law bore no relationship to the written word. The worst of totalitarian excesses can occur in a country with the most liberal of laws—if those laws are not fairly and conscientiously administered. Too often, dictatorships use the law—not as a guide to action—but as a weapon of propaganda.

One measurement of the nature of a legal system is to examine who makes the laws. In the United States laws are made by elected representatives and are reflections of public opinion. In Saudi Arabia the king makes the law according to the Koran of his Islamic faith. In the Soviet Union the laws are made by those Communist party members whose purpose in serving in Soviet legislatures is to perpetuate the Communist state.

Another measurement of the nature of a legal system is the position of the judiciary. In France the judge is an independent public official answerable only to higher judges. In the Soviet Union the judge is an employee of the government, who can be overruled by the executive. In Saudi Arabia the king who makes the laws is also the chief judge. In the United States there is a complete separation of powers, with the judiciary as an equal branch of government: the judge in criminal trials shares his power of decision with a jury. In India there are no juries. In France and Germany jurors sit with the judges and jointly hear the evidence. Each system defines its own roles for judges and juries, and these roles profoundly effect the administration of the substantive law. Identical laws might produce differing results depending on the independence of the judge or the presence of an impartial jury.

Criminal Law Objectives

A common objective of all systems of criminal law seems to be social ordering. Its rationale differs widely from system to system and from government to government. In the United States our criminal law system gives attention to the necessity of due process as well as crime control. In France crime control seems more important than the protection of individual rights. In the United States and most of the rest of the world crimes of violence are thought to be a greater problem than are economic crimes. In the Soviet Union economic crimes, which are viewed as crimes against the state, are considered the more serious offenses. The social ordering objectives of the criminal law vary in detail according to the law family to which the system belongs, the nature of the government that administers the law, and the severity of the crime problem sought to be controlled.

Fundamental Rights of the Accused

In the United States the power of the government over individual citizens is severely limited by the Constitution. When an American is accused of a crime, he has many rights that he may exercise to protect himself from conviction. He need not give evidence that would incriminate him; he need not even talk to the police. He may retain a lawyer, but, if he does not have enough money to hire a lawyer, the government must hire one for him. He has the right to confront the persons accusing him and to cross-examine witnesses against him at trial. He has the right to a speedy trial and the right to be free on bail pending trial. He also has the ultimate right of due process of law, which means that the government itself must obey the law in enforcing it against the accused. These rights, embodied in our Bill of Rights, seem so fundamental to ordered liberty that we might assume their necessity in the operation of any fundamentally fair system of criminal justice. Although the United States is not unique in the rights afforded the accused, we are not typical of legal systems where fundamental human rights are an issue.

In India, a country with an English colonial history and common law legal traditions, the constitution is patterned in large measure on the U. S. Constitution. There are similar citizens' rights, such as the presumption of innocence until proven guilty, the right to bail, the right to counsel, the right to a public trial, and the right not to testify against oneself. India, however, because it has experienced severe problems of maintaining public order in its vast and complex country, has abandoned the right to trial by jury altogether, has severely limited the right not to incriminate oneself, and has substantially lessened the right to be free from unreasonable searches and seizures. Although Indian legal history is similar to that of the United States because of our common history of British colonial domination, the contemporary law of the two countries differs in important aspects because of the differing social ordering needs.

In Peru, a country with a civil law system, there is a strongly different conception of fundamental rights. The discovery of the truth of a criminal accusation is more important than the rights of the accused. The dwelling house, made inviolable from unreasonable searches and seizures in the United States, may be searched by the government in Peru with little necessary justification. In some Peruvian trials the accused has no right to have public proceedings, nor to cross-examine certain witnesses (for example, government officials, who may give evidence by filing depositions with the court). The judge, after he has completed his investigation of a case but before trial, can presume the guilt of the accused and deny him bail. Many guarantees of the fundamental rights of the accused may even be suspended for 30 days at a time by executive order.

In the Soviet Union the constitution provides many of the rights found in the U.S. Constitution, in addition to other rights. The exercise of these rights is quite limited, however, because rights are often ignored when the government determines that the interests of advancing communism are threatened by the exercise of individual rights. The Soviet Union also lacks the right of *habeas corpus* and any right to be free from both double jeopardy and *ex post facto* laws. There is no formal concept of due process in the Soviet Union. Many basic rights, such as the right to a speedy trial, the right to confront witnesses, the right to know the nature of the accusation, and the right not to be a witness against oneself—although available by statutory enactment—have no constitutional basis in the Soviet Union.

The Investigation of Crime

The investigation of serious crime to prepare evidence of guilt or innocence for presentation to the court (during a criminal trial) is a universal problem. Each family of legal systems has evolved its own characteristic approach to the solution of the problem. The Anglo-American legal systems use the adversary system of unsupervised police investigation of crime followed by the criminal trial. The civil law systems generally use the pretrial investigation of crime by an investigating magistrate who is a member of the judiciary and who supervises the police. The socialist law systems tend to follow the Soviet model, and the investigations of crime are conducted by police, examining magistrates, and prosecutors; all of whom are under the direction of the branch of Soviet government known as the Procuracy. Each system offers certain advantages and disadvantages, and each ultimately seeks to ascertain the truth.

In the United States, the police gather all evidence of the crime, which is held by them until it is presented to the prosecutor. The prosecutor then decides if the evidence is sufficient to secure a conviction. If so, he proceeds to file an information, or he seeks an indictment before a grand jury. There is little judicial control over this process, and the record of the investigation generally remains secret until the time of trial. This American system is completely alien to both civil law and socialist law systems of criminal investigation. In Europe, the Soviet Union, and most of the rest of the non-common law world, the judiciary enter the investigative process almost as soon as an arrest is made or suspicion focuses on the accused.

The first stage of a criminal investigation in any legal system is always conducted by the police. The "probable cause" required before American police can arrest a suspect is matched by the "strong" or "grave" suspicion required in the civil and socialist law worlds. The distinction between the systems, however, is that American police may proceed to arrest, to search, and to interrogate upon their own initiative in the presence of probable cause, while their European and Soviet counterparts must seek judicial permission to perform these same functions. The only time that a European policeman can arrest without judicial permission is when there is serious danger that delay will cause the escape of the accused or the destruction of evidence.

Although non-common law arrest standards appear to be higher, the converse is true of the ability of European and Soviet police to question suspects, to search for evidence, and to summon witnesses to answer inquiries. Outside the common law system, searches are less objectionable than arrests, and they may be ordered by judges on "suspicion" only, rather than on "grave suspicion." When persons are arrested under civil or socialist law systems, they must generally be presented to the custody of an investigating magistrate within 24 hours of their arrest. This rule is designed to prevent police abuses in interrogating the accused to coerce his confession.

Abusive police interrogation is universally outlawed. In Sweden the accused may demand the presence of a trusted person at his interrogation, and any police "trickery" in questioning the suspect is prohibited by statute. West Germany has adopted the essence of the American *Miranda*-type warnings, which its police must give to suspects prior to interrogations. Yugoslavia, a socialist law country, has banned police interrogations of suspects altogether. There is apparently good reason for this concern over police interrogation abuses. In France, for example, there is a 24-hour maximum period of police detention permitted, and the accused has the right to remain silent and not to cooperate with the police. But the police in France never warn the accused of his rights. In Spain the police often exceed the 24-hour limitation on detention. The reason that the police temptation for abusing interrogation rules is so strong is that in civil law and socialist law countries the police forever lose custody of the suspect once he is presented to the official called the *investigating magistrate.*

The investigating magistrate is a judge who is trained as a criminal investigator with command power over the police. He combines the integrity and impartiality of the judiciary with the powers of the prosecutor and grand jury—plus the investigative expertise of the police. His sole function is to ascertain the complete truth about the accusations against the suspect. The investigating magistrate inquires into every aspect of the case to determine whether there should be a criminal trial or the charges should be dismissed. The magistrate interrogates the accused, the witnesses, and the arresting police officers; he examines evidence, the crime scene, and any other relevant sources of information. He examines the opinions of expert witnesses and seeks other professional advice about the case. All of this information goes into a case file, in France called the *dossier,* which is delivered to the prosecutor at the conclusion of the investigation along with the investigating magistrate's recommendation as to the disposition of the case.

In France, the investigating magistrate, called the *juge d'instruction,* takes charge of the accused from the police when the accused first appears before him. After that time, the investigating magistrate has complete charge of the investigation. He may delegate tasks to the police, but the police no longer have any responsibility or right to continue the investigation independent of the magistrate. At the first appearance, the accused is told the charges against him and advised of his rights to remain silent and to retain counsel. If the police have interrogated the accused before his appearance before the judge, the record of this interrogation goes into the *dossier*. If the defendant refuses to participate in the subsequent investigation or if he exercises his right against self-incrimination by refusing to answer the magistrate's questions, this, too, is noted in the *dossier,* and will later influence the trial court. The French have great confidence in their judiciary to seek the truth and to do justice in a fair and impartial manner. The investigating magistrate in France is not working for the defense or the prosecution, not for the accused or the state, but rather is making a completely independent inquiry into the facts of the case in order to determine the truth.

In the Soviet Union the same general form of investigation of serious crime is followed as in Europe, for the socialist law system evolved from the civil law tradition. In the Soviet Union (and in other socialist law countries) there exists an institution of government unique to Russian historical development. This institution is called the *Prokuratura,* or *Procuracy.* It is, in essence, a fourth branch of government independent of the executive, legislative, or judicial (but still directly responsible to the Supreme Soviet, for even the law in the Soviet Union is subordinate to the will of the Communist party). The Procuracy is an institution that has officials throughout the Soviet government, from the highest levels down to the village councils. Its primary function is to supervise the legality of the operations of the entire government, including the workings of executive and administrative bodies, the police, the agencies of criminal investigation, and the system of criminal corrections. The Procuracy has the power to direct the police to arrest suspects, to appoint examining magistrates (comparable to the civil law investigating magistrates), and to prosecute accused persons at criminal trials. The closest example to the Soviet Procuracy in the American system would be an office that combined features of the U.S. Attorney General, congressional investigating committees, local grand juries and prosecutors, and the FBI.

The power and the influence of the Procuracy in the Soviet system are incredibly broad, but it can best be understood by examining its four principal functions: the conduct of pretrial investigations and indictments; the prosecution of crimes; the supervision of the legality of judicial acts; and the supervision of the legality of administrative acts. The conduct of pretrial investigations and indictments and the prosecution of crimes follow civil law systems, except that both pretrial investigations and prosecution are carried out by the same agency. The function of supervising the legality of judicial acts allows the Procuracy to protest and to appeal both convictions and acquittals of criminal cases. The function of supervising the legality of administrative acts allows the Procuracy to protest and to appeal the actions of the police. The Procuracy, in short, has the power to influence the entire criminal justice process in the Soviet Union from arrest through prosecution, trial, and criminal corrections.

The same procedure is followed basically in the Soviet Union as is followed in France after an arrest for a crime. The accused is immediately presented to an examining magistrate (appointed by the Procuracy), who conducts a preliminary examination of the accused, interrogates witnesses, and examines evidence prior to preparing an indictment. The indictment is a detailed written statement of the charges and evidence against the accused. The accused is informed of his right not to cooperate with the investigation, to state his side of the case in the pretrial investigation, and to examine the whole record of the case against him. Disclosure to the accused is so complete in the Soviet Union that the prosecutor cannot introduce evidence not previously disclosed to the defendant (at the pretrial investigation stage) at the criminal trial.

Although superficially similar to the civil law system of criminal investigation, the socialist law system differs in three basic essentials.

1. The only appeal of the accused from abuses of his rights that might occur during the pretrial investigation is to the Procuracy, which has appointed and directs the examining magistrate in the first place.
2. The accused has no right to counsel until the pretrial investigation is completed and the indictment is presented to the trial court. By this time there is little that counsel can do to protect the rights of the accused.
3. Detention for investigation, which is usually a short period in Europe and normally limited to one month in the Soviet Union, may be extended for up to nine months by order of the Procuracy.

The Decision to Prosecute

Evidence of crime comes to prosecutors in the Anglo-American legal family from the investigation of the accused by the police. Once this information is transmitted to the prosecutor, the police role (except to appear as witnesses at the criminal trial) ends. The prosecutor then decides whether or not to proceed with the prosecution of the accused, whether to reduce the charge, or whether to dismiss entirely. Often in the American system, the prosecutor will plea-bargain with the defendant, exchanging a reduced penalty or a reduced charge for a plea of guilty. Such a system of prosecutorial discretion is also found in many parts of Canada. The Anglo-American prosecutor is an independent public official with broad discretion.

By contrast, the West German prosecutor has no discretion at all in his decision to prosecute. He is obligated to proceed when he has evidence of crime presented to him as a result of the pretrial investigation of the accused. He may not even discuss a plea-bargained disposition with the accused or his attorney. The German prosecutor is viewed as an objective "guardian of the law," who must bring charges when presented with evidence of crime, even if he feels that he cannot secure a conviction at trial. His conduct is governed by the "principle of legality," requiring the vigorous prosecution of all serious crimes (although petty offenses, juvenile offenses, and other offenses specifically exempted from this principle may be disposed of at his discretion). If the German prosecutor fails to bring appropriate charges, any citizen can petition his superiors to bring the charges, and any victim of crime in Germany can, himself, bring charges if the prosecutor does not.

In Japan, which has basically a civil law system of criminal law, the prosecutor has the broadest of discretion. He may abstain from prosecution at all for petty crimes, and he may exercise his power of "suspension of prosecution" for good cause. By statute, he must consider the character, age and environment of the offender along with the circumstances and gravity of the offense. If, in consideration of these elements, he determines to his own satisfaction that the "social defense" policy of the Japanese law is fulfilled, he may suspend prosecution.[1] A part of the

---

[1] "Social defense" means that the criminal law should be concerned with the protection of society as a whole from the dangers of crime by either isolating the dangerous criminal in prison or modifying his behavior in such a way that he is no longer dangerous. This disposition of criminal cases for social defense purposes is more important than the retributive punishment of criminals or the strict application of the criminal law.

decision to suspend prosecution is usually the agreement of the accused to seek some kind of after-care treatment in order to rehabilitate himself. Japanese courts periodically review prosecutors' records to provide judicial supervision of the use of the suspension of prosecution power. Belgium has a similar system of suspension of prosecution in the interest of social defense.

In France the decision to prosecute is more complex, for private parties may join their civil action for damages with the public prosecution. If the victim of the crime brings a private prosecution, the state counsel (prosecutor) is obligated to prosecute the public charge as well. The state counsel is a judicial officer and not a mere advocate for the prosecution of offenders. When the investigating magistrate, who has directed the investigation of the accused, presents the facts in the *dossier* to the state counsel for prosecution, the state counsel must review the facts to determine if the prosecution can meet the heavy burden of proof, and if the prosecution of the accused will serve the interests of justice. The French state counsel also concerns himself with the individualization of punishment for offenders to achieve social ordering objectives.

In the Soviet Union the prosecutor is an official of the Procuracy. The Soviet prosecutor not only makes the decision to prosecute but also is the official who conducts the pretrial investigation of the accused. He combines the functions of the French investigating magistrate and state counsel in a single office, and has great control over the course of the trial. Despite this control, the Soviet prosecutor appears at trial on an equal footing with the accused, and Soviet courts do not infer guilt from the mere fact of indictment. At the trial stage (even though the judge participates actively in examining witnesses and evidence), the Soviet procedures shift from a civil law style inquisition to a common law style adversary proceeding.

Determination of Guilt

In every legal system the guilt of the accused is determined through the criminal trial. The most critical factor influencing the outcome of the trial is not the structure of the court, nor the skill of the attorneys, nor the presence or absence of a jury. It is rather the evidence presented to the court for the purpose of proving guilt or innocence. Each of the three families of legal systems has well-developed rules of evidence designed to maximize the probability that the trial court will discover the truth about the guilt of the accused. These rules of evidence cover three main areas: the "burden of proof," the kinds of witnesses permitted to testify, and the admissibility of certain controversial kinds of evidence.

In every system of modern criminal law, the burden of proof is on the prosecution with the assumption of the innocence of the accused. The accused is not deemed guilty until the prosecution proves him guilty, and he need not prove his innocence. It is the prosecution who must carry forward evidence of his guilt to convince the court. The distinction between common law burden of proof and civil and socialist burden of proof is that the Anglo-American burden of proof "beyond a reasonable doubt" seems, at least in theory, more severe than the civil law burden of proof, which requires the prosecutor to "convince" the court of the truth of the accused's guilt. The difference between the two burdens is, however, more apparent than real. Because the Anglo-American system of evidence is adversary, the court seldom goes beyond the evidence presented by the prosecution and defense. Accordingly, because the parties control the availability of evidence, the burden must be absolutely on the prosecution to assure that all relevant facts come before the court. In the inquisitorial civil and socialist systems, the court itself can go beyond the pleadings of the parties to ascertain all facts relevant to the case. In France, for example, the judge must make up his own mind and arrive at a "profound personal conviction" of the accused's guilt. The prosecution not only must produce sufficient evidence of guilt, but also must convince the court that there are no circumstances that might excuse the application of the criminal law, such as insanity or incapacity. Under any modern system, the evidence of criminal guilt must be complete and convincing; merely presenting more evidence for guilt than against it is not sufficient to convict in any modern legal system.

The burden of proof in criminal trials is satisfied by the introduction of evidence for the consideration of the court. This evidence comes in two forms: the testimony of witnesses and the presentation of physical evidence. In some law systems, certain kinds of witnesses either are privileged not to testify or are prohibited from testifying, thus preventing whatever evidence they might be able to give from coming before the court. The net result of this is that less than the whole truth is discovered.

This situation is tolerable because the benefits of the exclusion are thought to be more important than is the gap in the truth that the exclusion causes.

An example of this kind of testimonial exclusion is the American right not to incriminate oneself by being a witness at one's own trial. In the United States, this Fifth Amendment right may be exercised not only at criminal trials, but in every other kind of proceeding. Americans are absolutely privileged not to incriminate themselves: the American belief is that the integrity of the person is more important than the evidence he could give which might incriminate him. In Indian law, the same privilege not to testify at one's own trial prevails, but the right does not extend as broadly as the American right. In a civil trial, or at the trial of another, Indian law compels self-incrimination. The Indian viewpoint is that, although it is not right to force one to testify at one's own trial, it is permissible, in order to ascertain the truth if there is no direct injury to the witness' interests.

Most legal systems do not require husbands and wives to testify against one another. Some criminal codes, such as those of Spain and Peru, extend this privilege to close relatives and, in some instances, even to cousins and relatives by marriage. The privilege is designed to protect the relationships of the family and is based on the assumption that close relatives might not tell the truth about their relative's criminal activity in any case! Similarly, most systems have evidentiary privileges that apply to communications with doctors, lawyers, and clergymen.

The Anglo-American law of evidence also excludes evidence called "hearsay," which is an out-of-court statement introduced in court for the purpose of proving the truth of the statement. Such evidence is excluded in common law jurisdictions because it may be untrue and might unduly prejudice the jury. Furthermore, hearsay is evidence offered by a witness who does not have first-hand knowledge of the facts to which he is testifying and he might not know the truth. The civil law and socialist law systems do not exclude hearsay (or any other evidence for that matter), because the common law objections to such evidence do not exist. In systems where there are no juries (or where juries and judges deliberate together), there is little chance that hearsay will unduly prejudice the proceedings. The court seeks the whole truth and can ascertain for itself whether the hearsay statement is true. The European and Soviet courts would rather hear all the evidence than risk missing the truth.

Because these courts admit all evidence that they deem relevant, the exclusionary rule of evidence, which is such an important aspect of American criminal procedure, is virtually unknown in the rest of the world (including other common law jurisdictions). The American rationale for excluding illegally obtained evidence from criminal trials is that this is the only way in which the police can be controlled and prevented from violating the rights of the accused. The rest of the world's legal systems view the problem differently. In Canada and England, illegally obtained evidence is admissible with the discretion of the trial judge. Persons whose rights are violated by the police may bring private lawsuits to recover damages for the violation of their rights, but the criminal court will not ignore evidence of crime merely because it was gathered improperly.

Similarly, evidence offered in French courts is supposed to be legally obtained, but France permits proof by any means. So long as the French judge does not base his personal conviction of guilt totally on illegally obtained evidence, there is no objection to its introduction. West Germany also allows "free evaluation of evidence." The German judge has the right to an unlimited access to all evidence of crime, the Germans viewing truth as more important than individual rights. To temper the effects of this viewpoint, however, Germany has (by statute) adopted a *Miranda*-type standard for its police, to prohibit coerced confessions. In Israel, Japan, and the Soviet Union, the admissibility of evidence is within the discretion of the trial judge. Israeli courts will inquire into the voluntariness of confessions but otherwise do not inquire into the legality of procedure for obtaining evidence. Japanese courts feel that it is better to punish the police officer who violates the rights of the accused or to compensate the accused for the violation, than to let the accused go free for the technical violation of his rights. In the Soviet Union, the Procuracy has the function, not only of prosecuting criminal cases, but also of overseeing that the Soviet police gather evidence according to law.

Despite the wide variations in the rules of evidence followed by the various legal systems of the world, they share the same basic purpose—to provide for a fundamentally fair way of determining the guilt of the accused. No one way is necessarily more fair than another. The demands of justice are universal; only the methods of achieving it vary from nation to nation.

Civil and socialist law courts tend to assess harsher penalties upon conviction than do American courts. Although the worldwide trend seems to be the liberalization of criminal corrections, the legal systems of Europe seem to be more concerned with the protection of society as a whole and with the rights of the victim of crime specifically, than with the rights and rehabilitation of the offender. In the United States, the priorities seem to be the opposite. Accordingly, the death penalty (except in France) has disappeared in Europe and has been replaced by sentences of life imprisonment for crimes such as murder. The same pattern has occurred in the United States, but the essential difference between the systems is that life imprisonment in Europe really means life imprisonment, but American life sentences make murderers eligible for parole after a relatively short period.

Serious crimes of violence carry relatively longer sentences in Europe than in the United States, and the maximum sentences are actually imposed by European courts. The purpose of these longer sentences is the protection of society through the lengthy incarceration of people who have demonstrated violent tendencies. For similar reasons, the defense of insanity is seldom used in Europe because most European criminal codes provide for long mandatory periods of confinement in mental hospitals for defendants found not guilty by reason of insanity. In the case of perpetrators of violent crimes, an insanity plea could result in a life-long confinement in a mental institution. The American treatment of insanity pleas is much more liberal than the European system. In Italy, for example, a defendant found not guilty by reason of insanity, of a crime that carries a punishment of life imprisonment, must spend at least 10 years in a mental hospital for prisoners. The mandatory period cannot be shortened, and the prisoner can be released after that time only when he is declared sane by the court and dangerous neither to himself nor society. In Germany, Austria, and Spain, the person found not guilty by reason of insanity is confined in a hospital and may not be released until the court so orders.

The American system of probation and parole is also much more liberal than its European counterpart. Almost all but the most dangerous criminals are eligible for probation upon conviction in the United States, but in Europe persons convicted of the more serious crimes are not eligible for probation. Generally, only minor offenses in Europe result in probation for first offenders. In France probation is available only to those not previously convicted and who have been convicted of an offense carrying a penalty of less than five years. In Italy and Spain the conditions are the same, except that the penalty for the offense must not exceed one year. In Germany the term must not exceed nine months. Generally, European courts also require that the offender make restitution for any damage he has caused by his offense. He must also appear unlikely to commit any other offenses before probation is considered.

Parole availability is also more liberal in the United States than in Europe. In America parolees become eligible for release usually after serving one-fourth to one-third of their sentences. In Europe parole usually does not occur until one-half to three-fourths of the sentence has been served. In France and Italy a prisoner must serve one-half, in Spain three-fourths, and in Germany two-thirds of his sentence before he is eligible for parole. Recidivists must serve even greater portions of their sentences before becoming eligible. Parole in Europe is the exception rather than the norm, and parolees are released only with great caution, to provide protection to the public.

European punishments are harsher than American ones, and Soviet punishments are harsher than European ones. The rationale for this is found in the Soviet belief that criminals not only threaten the social order, but also impede the progress of the socialist state toward its goal of attaining a pure Communist society. The criminal damages both the present society and the future society. The Soviet criminal law uses punishment not only to isolate criminals from society and to deter others from bad behavior, but also to educate the Soviet people to a Communist social consciousness. In order to perform this educational as well as legal function, the Soviet judge has broad sentencing powers, including: (1) penalties of public censure; (2) confiscation of property; (3) a money fine of a percentage of the defendant's salary; (4) a prohibition from practicing a trade or profession; (5) exile from the city; (6) banishment to a remote area; (7) assignment to a corrective labor camp; and (8) imprisonment. The judge may choose a severity of the punishment from minimum to maximum sentences or impose no punishment at all if he deems the defendant to be not socially dangerous at the time of sentencing. The attention paid to the reformation of the defendant's attitude and life style in the Soviet criminal court is very similar to the juvenile court in the United States. It is not enough in the Soviet Union that the criminal be punished; he must also become a useful, productive member of the Soviet society.

Conclusion

In the three major families of legal systems: common law, civil law, and socialist law, there are striking similarities and profound differences in the manner in which the problem of crime is solved. These great legal systems are the product of centuries of historical development and are reflective of the societies that they serve. The legal system of each society tends both to preserve and to promote the basic political and economic philosophies of the government that administers the law. Thus, democratic ideas of personal freedom are stressed in civil law and common law jurisdictions, whereas communistic ideas of the importance of freedom from economic exploitation are emphasized in socialist law systems.

Many fundamental legal rights are universal in their existence, but vary widely in their application. The right not to be a witness against oneself means very different things depending on whether the right is exercised in the legal system of the United States, France, India, or the Soviet Union. Many rights considered fundamental in the American law system are totally absent in other systems. India has no juries and Sweden does not allow release on bail, yet both legal systems appear to administer justice fairly and impartially. On the other hand, many legal institutions considered critical to ordered liberty in other countries are unknown in the United States. In Japan a criminal court, upon the acquittal of the accused, also formally and officially restores the social reputation of the accused. This practice is fundamental in Japanese jurisprudence because of the high value of "face" in Eastern society.

The mechanics of criminal investigation vary from system to system, and the discretionary powers of criminal justice officials present a bewildering array of variations to the student of comparative criminal law. The investigative and jurisprudential methods by which the guilt or innocence of the accused is determined seem equally diverse and contradictory. The philosophies of crime, punishment, and corrections show dramatic variation among common law, civil law, and socialist law systems. The central theme that unites all these diverse systems of criminal law, however, is that of social ordering. The social ordering objectives of any society dictate the kind of criminal justice system and the kind of criminal law it shall have. The American system of criminal law and criminal justice has many good and some bad features, but the same may be said for any other system. The true measurement of success is whether or not the criminal justice system of a given country functions in such a manner as to achieve the social ordering aspirations of its people. If a foreign law system can achieve this goal, then it is not better or worse than the American system, but only different from it.

Student Checklist

1. Can you describe how codes or systems of law are responsive to the social ordering requirements of the culture they serve?
2. Are you able to define "arrest with judicial permission"?
3. Do you know how to contrast the European provisions for arrest with those in the United States?
4. Are you able to contrast the objectives or goals of the Soviet system of law with those of France and the United States?
5. Are you able to describe how the role of the investigating magistrate in France differs from practices in the United States in performing an investigation?
6. Can you define the origin of civil, or civilian, law?
7. Can you describe how the common law of England evolved to current law in the United States?
8. Are you able to contrast the roles, duties, and powers of the prosecutor in three different legal systems?
9. Can you compare four nations' use of the exclusionary rule of evidence?
10. Can you describe how punishment varies among four different countries?

Topics for Discussion

1. Discuss the differences between the three major families of legal systems.
2. Discuss the similarities among the three major families of legal systems.
3. Discuss the mechanics of criminal investigation as used in the several nations covered.
4. Discuss the variations in the use of discretionary powers by criminal justice officials in the nations covered in this chapter.
5. Discuss the commonality of the social ordering goal among the three major families of legal systems.

ANNOTATED BIBLIOGRAPHY

Dando, Shigemitsu. "System of Discretionary Prosecution in Japan," 18 *Am. J. Comp. L.* 518 (1970). An excellent descriptive article on the use of "suspension of prosecution" by the prosecutor in Japan. It is a form of diversion from the system to be utilized by the prosecutor in his exercise of discretion.

Glos, George E. "A Study in the Treatment of Crime and Law Enforcement in the United States as Compared to the European Countries," 3 *St. Mary's L.J.* 177 (1971). A contrast of the criminal law of several nations of Europe with each other and the United States. In addition to the substantive law differences, emphasis is also given to differences in insanity provisions to determine criminal provisions.

Grosman, Brian A. "The Role of the Prosecutor in Canada," 18 *Amer. J. Comp. L. 498* (1970). A description of the history and contemporary role of the prosecutor in Canada. The use of discretion is a major topic in the description. The article emphasizes the need for an analytical comparison of the prosecution function in several nations to understand fully the function of prosecution in society.

Hrones, Stephen. "Interrogation Abuses by the Police in France—A Comparative Solution," 12 *Crim. L.Q.* 68 (1969). This article contrasts the U.S. system of criminal justice with that of the French with major emphasis on interrogation practices. It examines the hypothetical impact of *Miranda* on the French system and suggests that the *Miranda* remedy for abusive practices would tend to make France's system more adversary in nature.

Towe, Thomas E. "Fundamental Rights in the Soviet Union: A Comparative Approach," 115 *U. Penn. L.R.* 1251 (1967). A detailed, analytical view, by a comparative method, of the fundamental rights of citizens in the Soviet Union. The constitutional guarantees are the primary source, but the article also stresses that these guarantees must be viewed in the context of socialist legal philosophy. For example, great importance is placed on economic goals of society whereas less importance is given to ethical and moral values against violating the law.

Vouin, Robert. "The Role of the Prosecutor in French Criminal Trials," 18 *Amer. J. Comp. L.* 483 (1970). A description of the role of the prosecutor in France as contrasted primarily by the English prosecutor. Stress is given to the prosecution's use of discretion and his role in criminal trials.

The study of this chapter will enable you to:

1. Describe how law tends to be flexible to meet the contemporary needs of society.
2. Contrast four dominant philosophies of law throughout history.
3. List the general social function of any system of law.
4. Identify the role of discretion in justice administration.
5. Define "law."
6. List the major periods in the history of English law.
7. Discuss how the present state of law was achieved; recognizing mores, customs, common law, statutes, case law, and administrative law.
8. Identify the major philosophers who contributed to Anglo-American jurisprudence.
9. Explain the concept of precedence, or *stare decisis*.
10. Describe how common law emerged in the United States.

48

3
Anglo-American Criminal Law: Origins and Premises

Introduction

The novice criminal justice student generally has a burning interest in the criminal law. He approaches the study of "law" with the belief that it is something that can be learned once and then applied forever after.

Unfortunately for the student, this cannot be done. Law is a changing, dynamic process that reflects the constant change and growth within a society. It is this ability of the law to change that allows it and our institutions—our very society—to survive.

Traditionally, we think of laws as being made by legislators or judges. We fail to realize that acts of discretion by the individuals who make up our criminal justice system also make and define law. For example, the decision of a police officer to make an arrest for some new breach of the peace, or the decision of a parole officer to establish some new condition of parole, also makes law. Thus, new law is made every day.

Frequently, such actions have more impact on society than did the original enactment of the law, because they reflect the actual implementation of law. Unfortunately, the history of our criminal law is replete with examples in which discretion was either improperly used or abused. Often the decision that produced the abuse was in conflict with our basic philosophy of law and its institutions.

A system evolves on the basis of past experience. It makes decisions on new needs in light of past successes and failures. The future evolution of our system of justice depends upon the decisions of the individuals involved in the administration of justice. Such decisions represent an exercise of discretion. The proper exercise of discretion can flow only from an understanding of the origins and premises that underlie our system of government, its institutions, and its laws.

To provide an understanding of the nature of law, this chapter briefly outlines the concepts and philosophies that have contributed to our system of law and government. The origins of our criminal law are identified, and the basic premises of our criminal law are set forth. The objectives of the chapter are twofold: to provide the student of criminal justice with an understanding of how we reached the present state of law, and to develop insight for the future use of discretion.

A warning must be offered. This chapter represents a summary of history. Because brevity dictates that generalizations be made, they should be accepted with caution. In addition, legal historians disagree on many simple facts relating to specific events, although such disagreements seem petty compared to the arguments raging over interpretations of legal philosophy and its impact on our law. This chapter should, therefore, be thought of as an artist's rough sketch that hints at the dimensions and composition of a painting; the subject and theme can be seen, but the details are still to be painted by the student through further study of the law.

The Nature of Law

An examination of the early writings on the development of law reveals that most authors discussed law in the context of the development of formal society. Law was seen as part of the fabric of government. Often the authors were concerned with the appropriate form of government, and in particular the authority for government and the law. Because the criminal law bears a close relationship to the formulation and maintenance of order in a society, these early discussions often dealt specifically with acts now known as crimes.

As a whole, these writings reflect a recognition that individuals banded together to form a society with formal institutions because of basic rewards, such as division of labor, security, and social cooperation. That such group functioning placed some limitation on individual action was also recognized in these early works.

Therefore, formative writings on the philosophy of law and the role of the state tend to focus on the nature of individual rights or freedoms and the duty and authority of the government. It is both interesting and useful to understand and appreciate the historical period in which the authors wrote. One might even generalize that authors writing in times of relative peace tended to favor freedom for the individual; those writing in times of war tended to favor the authority of the state or government.

Our present system of criminal law has its roots in these early writings. The positions of selected authors and schools of thought are discussed in the following pages. Although the authors presented are not an inclusive list, most scholars agree that each of them has directly influenced the development of our legal system. Therefore, further study of their works is suggested for the student of criminal justice.

Early Philosophers

The Sophists. The Sophists were itinerant teachers in Greece in the fifth century B.C. They taught that man was naturally selfish: if man follows his true nature, he acts in a manner that he perceives to be in his own best interest. The Sophists saw law as an artificially created convention designed to control the individual in the interest of those who ran the government. This represented an early expression of the nature of law in the Western World as the will of the state, the sovereign, or those in power.

Plato. Plato (427–347 B.C.), the noted Greek philosopher, wrote in the fourth century B.C. He thought of man as a rational being in a rational universe. Plato's concept of the law was stated in his work, *The Republic.* He believed law to be based on custom and convention, reflecting only an opinion of truth. In his model of a state, the rulers were scientists, not lawmakers, and political authority was based on the precise knowledge of the scientist rulers. Although Plato concluded later in his life that his ideal could not be achieved, his work reflects one of the early statements that law is drawn from custom.

Plato not only formulated the theoretical aspects of the law, but also commented on specific crimes. For example, he addressed the question of criminal attempt by saying:

One who has a purpose and intention to slay another who is not his enemy, and when the law does not permit him to slay, and he wounds him, but is unable to kill him, he should be regarded as a murderer, even though out of respect for "fortune and providence," the death penalty should be remitted and banishment for life, together with compensation for the victim should be substituted.

Aristotle. Aristotle (384–322 B.C.) was a famous pupil of Plato. He perceived man as political by nature and that man achieved his innate potential by taking part in the affairs of the state. Although he believed in the exercise of governmental power by a ruling class, he opposed arbitrary rule. He believed that the governing class must rule according to law. In his opinion, law reflected a collective wisdom embodied in custom, tradition, and usage, which created the basis for political authority.

Cicero. The Roman orator, politician, and philosopher Cicero (106–43 B.C.) believed that all men possess reason and can distinguish between good and evil. He was influenced by the Stoic doctrine of brotherhood and equality of man, a doctrine we find reflected in the Declaration of Independence. Cicero thought of a state as a "partnership in law." He believed that man had an existence before states existed. Thus, man could be perceived apart from the state, and he possessed rights not dependent upon the state. This philosophy represents an early statement of the rights of the individual.

Jean Bodin. The work of the French social and political philosopher Jean Bodin (1530–1596) represents a transition from the medieval concept of law based on custom to that of law as a directive made by the sovereign of ruling power. In 1576 he declared that he had discovered the supremacy of the sovereign within the state. Actually, laws were made long before the creation of the national monarchies, which formed the basis for Bodin's commentaries. Although he stressed the authority of the sovereign to make law, he also noted that such authority was limited by "fundamental law." Therefore, the power of the sovereign was not absolute.

Thomas Hobbes. The British philosopher Hobbes (1588–1679) wrote during the troubled years of the Commonwealth period of England. Untrained in the law, he was primarily a political philosopher. His view of society was one of the first based on psychology or a behavioral approach. He pictured man as basically "selfish, cruel, covetous, and vainglorious." He believed that government must be established because only the force of the state could restrain man from evil.

His writings were among the first to raise the "social contract" theory of law and government. He saw the individual as agreeing or contracting with other individuals to obey the will of one—the sovereign or king. In his chapter entitled "Of Civill Lawes" from the book *Leviathan or the Matter, Forme and Power of a Commonwealth* (1651), he defined law as a command of the sovereign, whose power was not subject to the law.

The philosophy of Hobbes, often labeled positivist, has not attracted many adherents through the passage of time, although his analytical style, with its emphasis on the precise definition of terms, has continued to appeal to many jurists. Even though his view of individual rights was limited, Hobbes spoke forcefully on the subject of punishment and set forth concepts later incorporated into our Constitution and Bill of Rights. He believed that a person found guilty of a crime should not be punished by a penalty greater than that provided for at the time of its commission, nor should any penalty be inflicted for an act not illegal at the time of its performance. These ideas have evolved into the constitutional prohibition against *ex post facto* laws.

John Locke. Locke (1632–1704), the philosopher who founded the school known as British Empiricism, also used the concept of a "social contract" to explain the role of the state and the nature of law. But his views differed sharply from those of Hobbes. He saw man as sociable and peaceable. He, therefore, saw the creation of a "social contract" that formed the basis for the state, flowing from convenience and the desire to create a society. In his treaties on civil government in 1690, he stated that natural law was the foundation of legal order. He believed that certain rights naturally belonged to man, and that these natural rights were more valid than law created by man. Furthermore, these rights should be the basis for the system of government. This approach has served as a foundation for many concepts of constitutional government.

Locke had a strong influence on the creation of our government. He was quoted frequently during the Constitutional Convention. The phrases "no taxation without representation" and "the right to life, liberty, and estate" are from his writings. The latter phrase was echoed in Thomas Jefferson's famous words, "life, liberty, and the pursuit of happiness."

Legal historians believe that Locke did not have a strict social contract in mind, but rather the legal idea of a trust. However, such a distinction does not change Locke's basic tenet: man makes an agreement to live in a society and to create a civil government with the power to make laws in the interest of public welfare, laws that do not violate the natural rights of man. When the sovereign violates this social agreement, he forfeits his right to office. This concept formed the basis for the American Revolution.

Locke's concept of a social agreement still exerts influence today. It is reflected in the acts of civil disobedience designed to test legally the reasonableness and constitutionality of various laws. Recent examples of this are the acts of disobedience that led to the judicial decisions striking down the laws that had been the basis for segregation.

Montesquieu. The French political philosopher Montesquieu (1689–1755), in an unusual work, *The Spirit of the Laws* (1748), continued the philosophical development of the rationalist approach of Hobbes and Locke. His legal philosophy is buried in a maze of political, sociological, and historical detail that includes, among other things, a chapter on classification of crimes. He turned away from the tradition of natural law and declared that every community must solve the task of lawmaking in response to its own particular spirit. This includes the historical, sociological, political, and economic conditions prevalent within that particular community. Similarly, he sought to explain law within the context of a particular cultural system.

His most important contribution to our system of law was the concept that liberty and justice can best be secured under a constitution that separates governmental power into three branches: legislative, executive, and judicial. This concept of government included the theory of checks-and-balances among the three branches of government. This theory has been applied in our federal and state governments.

Rousseau. In 1762 the French philosopher Jean Jacques Rousseau (1712–1778) published *The Social Contract.* The title is misleading, for his concepts were radically different from those of Locke. His work has been described by some as a multicolored scarf, in which one can find any color by looking at different parts; it has been cited by spokesmen from all portions of the political spectrum to support their causes.

Rousseau believed that it was feeling, not reason, that motivated man to form a society. He believed the community to be the force that made man a moral being. Property rights, freedom of speech, freedom of religion, and other human rights were created by society and were not a state of nature. The term "social contract" in Rousseau's philosophy was little more than the recognition by man that he has interests in common with other individuals. He saw the individual interests merging to create a "general will," and he believed that the state represented the exercise of this general will. The concept that the general will comes from the people and is the ultimate law in society grew into the doctrine of popular sovereignty. Many modern societies (including our own) have based their systems of government and law on this idea of democracy. The concept is demonstrated by the phrase, "democracy is government of the people, by the people, and for the people."

Schools of Legal Philosophy

The preceding paragraphs sketched some of the concepts of key men whose thoughts influenced the creation of our system of law and government. Many other individuals, including those who have written much more recently, have also shaped our system of justice. Legal scholars tend to group philosophers into three basic traditional schools. As in any element of the law, scholars disagree in either the grouping or the definitions. Nevertheless, Berman and Greiner identify the following schools of thought.[1]

The *philosophical* school adheres to the natural law theory. It takes the view that law originates in the nature of man as a creature capable of reason. This perspective contrasts sharply with the view of Hobbes, who saw law as a command of the sovereign.

The school of *analytical jurisprudence* perceives law as distinct from morals. It argues that, at any given moment, the existing law is analytically separate from any moral ideas of what the law should be.

[1] Harold J. Berman and William R. Greiner, *The Nature and Functions of Law* (Brooklyn: Foundation Press, 1966).

Law is essentially a body of technical rules and concepts to be analyzed.

The *historical* school sees law as evolving from the traditions, customs, and character of the community. Some proponents of the historical approach have sought to link the evolution of law with the social history of man as he evolved from the primitive family group to the modern territorial state.

In the nineteenth and twentieth centuries, various sociological approaches to jurisprudence in Western civilizations developed which blended the earlier concepts of analytical and historical jurisprudence. The development of law through legal decisions is seen as a process that involves the weighing of the social consequences of alternative courses of action and a balancing of various kinds of interests. In the the 1920s and 1930s a movement called "legal realism" enjoyed brief popularity. It viewed what was done by officials (judges, sheriffs, clerks, jailers, lawyers, and others) as the law itself.

In recent years, legal philosophers have tended to synthesize the thought of the various schools and move toward the concept of law as a process. In doing so, the law is thought of in terms of functions, not in terms of its origins or sanctions.

Berman and Grenier set forth three general social functions of any system of law:

1. The function of restoring equilibrium to social order when that equilibrium has been seriously disrupted.
2. The function of enabling members of the society to calculate the consequences of their conduct, thereby securing and facilitating voluntary transactions and arrangements.
3. The function of teaching people right belief, right feeling, and right action—that is, to mold moral and legal conceptions and attitudes of society.

Our criminal law can be seen as fulfilling these functions. The legal system provides a forum for the resolution of disputes. One need not carry on a private feud because the sovereign, acting through the courts, will punish the wrongdoer. The criminal laws provide clear guidelines for behavior. They not only proscribe wrong behavior, but prescribe right behavior. We drive on the right side of the highway expecting others to do the same. The law has facilitated our private conduct (in this instance, the operation of a motor vehicle). Other laws formally set forth societal standards of conduct. They assist in the communication of the moral standards of a society from generation to generation. More particularly, new law helps establish clearly the standards for conduct expected in new situations created by the ever-increasing complexity of society.

What Is Law?

The previous section has discussed how the conceptual framework of our system of law has developed, to aid the student in understanding why law exists. Emphasis has been placed on understanding that law is a process with certain basic functions, a dynamic process that is constantly changing. However, one may well ask: What is law?

Because there are as many answers as there are men who have thought about the question, no single answer can be given. It is critical that the student grasp the sense of the art of law, which allows room for variation in thought; at the same time, he should sense the common themes and areas of agreement. It is also necessary to recognize that when one speaks of the law many different concepts may be involved. The reference may be to a particular law that can be discussed with specificity. The word "law" is also sometimes used to refer to the legal system or to the entire process of law within our society.

If one thinks of the Law (with a capital L) as referring to the process, and law (with a small l) as referring to a particular rule or regulation, one of the best responses to the question "What is the Law?" is given by Berman and Grenier's definition.

> *Law is an institution in the sense of an integrated pattern or process of social behavior and ideas. What goes on inside courts, legislatures, law offices, and other places in which law-making, law-enforcing, law-administering, and law-interpreting is carried on, together with what goes on inside the minds of people thinking with reference to what goes on in those places, forms a law way of acting and thinking, which overlaps but is not identical with economic, religious, political, and other social ways of acting and thinking.[2]*

The utility of this definition lies in its creation of a framework for the study of law (the process). Although not everyone agrees with it, its value to a student of criminal justice lies in its provision of a starting point—and not an end—for the study of law.

[2] Ibid.

Development of Anglo-American Criminal Law

The previous section of this chapter focused on the development of the theoretical concepts and philosophy underlying our system of law. This section examines the development of American criminal law and, to a lesser extent, the role of the institutions that create and administer criminal law.

When we speak of criminal law, we are generally speaking of two kinds of law. The first is substantive law which sets forth the actual rules or regulations governing conduct. For example, this body of law includes the actual definitions of crimes and is usually what the lawman refers to when he speaks of the law.

The second type of law is procedural, or "adjective," law. It deals with the procedure by which disputes are resolved. When the history of our criminal law and procedure is examined, more change is noted in the development of the procedural aspect of criminal law. Changes in procedure accompany (or are accompanied by) changes in the institutions of government and the structure of the legal system. The actual acts that are prohibited, the crimes, remain remarkably the same throughout the passage of time. Frequently, the same misconduct is a crime in legal systems having significantly different procedures for dealing with such acts.

The procedural base and much of the substantive criminal law of the United States have evolved from the English law and are shared with other English-speaking nations of the world. The roots of our laws lie in the English common law. Thus, it is necessary to grasp the development of the common law to understand our present law.

British Law

There are four principal periods in the history of British law. The first is that before the Norman Conquest of 1066. Little is known of British history before 600 A.D. England was inhabited by tribal groups. The predominant law was tribal custom, which was strongly influenced by the Germanic origin of many of the tribes. The main sources of information concerning the Anglo-Saxon law prior to 1066 are ecclesiastical documents, wills, charters concerning grants of land, and the proclamations or dooms of the Anglo-Saxon kings. Written law was scarce and extremely terse. For example, the laws of Ethelbert, King of Kent, drafted in about the year 600 A.D., contained 90 brief sentences.

During the period from 600 to 1066 A.D., England was moving from a tribal toward a feudal state. The courts of the time were local in nature and they applied local custom. As custom varied from location to location in England, so did the law.

The second period stretches from 1066 to the time of the Tudors (1485). During this time the common law of England developed. The Norman Conquest of 1066 brought William the Conqueror to the throne of England. He created a centralized government with a system of royal courts. Originally, these courts did not interfere with the local courts. However, a system of procedures developed allowing appeals from the decisions of the local courts to the royal courts. In time the royal courts tended to supercede the local courts. These royal courts came to be known as the Courts of Westminster after the name of the place where they sat from the thirteenth century on.

The decisions of these courts formed the basis for the English common law. The name stems from the fact that the law was "common" to all of England. The law was "common" because the courts developed and followed the doctrine of "precedence." Simply stated, this doctrine states that once a given fact situation is decided, all similar cases will be decided in the same manner. The first decision is referred to as the precedent and the judge deciding the case is said to "discover" the law on the subject. In general, the more cases following the earlier case, the stronger the precedent becomes. This concept of precedence, or *stare decisis* (a Latin phrase meaning "let the decision stand"), has been incorporated into our legal system.

The major principles of law that form the basis of our system of criminal law and that of the English-speaking nations developed from the judicial decisions of this period and the period from 1485 to 1832. This latter time period is referred to as the third period of English legal history and represents a further evolution of the common law.

The history of the period from 1066 to 1832 is a rich one for the scholar of law. The origins of our forms of procedure and practice, the language of the law, and its customs flow from this time.

Although this short discussion does not allow adequate treatment of all the factors that created our law, two significant developments are worthy of brief discussion. The first deals with the role of the judge.

Earlier mention was made of the role of the judge in the discovery of the law and the application of precedent to shape the common law of England. The manner in which this function was performed deserves further consideration. The English system depended upon the *accusatorial*, or *adversary*, system of judicial discovery rather than the *inquisitorial*. The basis of the adversary system is the concept that the responsibility for the development of the facts lies with the parties to the case, not with the judge who renders the decision. The judge does not take an active role in the questioning of witnesses nor the search for facts, but instead he adopts the passive role of an impartial referee. The judge then reaches his decision by applying the appropriate precedent to the facts as presented. The inquisitorial system, on the other hand, relies on the active participation of the judge or judges to search for the truth by extracting information from witnesses or other evidence. Our legal system in both the criminal and civil aspects is based on the accusatorial concept, and the judicial role is defined accordingly.

The second significant concept evolved during the development of the common law was the distinction between a "crime" and a "tort." The early Anglo-Saxon law was limited in its approach to wrongs of the type we now perceive as crimes. Such acts were regarded as essentially private disputes to be resolved between the parties. If the dispute reached a court, the wrongdoer would, in some cases, be required to atone for his act by the payment of a sum of money to the injured party or his relatives. In some cases, where this was considered inadequate justice, a "blood feud" was allowed. This was controlled vengeance, allowing the avenging of a wrong upon the wrongdoer.

However, if the wrongdoer committed an act against the king or his royal household, a breach of the "king's peace" occurred. In such cases any monetary damages would be paid to the king, and any other punishment would be administered in the name of the king. As the governmental structure of England grew more centralized, the concept of the "king's peace" was expanded. The first expansion cited by many was along the great roads, in essence following the territory of the king. As time passed and the centralized government grew stronger, the concept expanded throughout all England. Acts previously considered private disputes between individuals now included the king as a passive party, if the act constituted a breach of the peace. The definition of these "breaches of the king's peace" constituted an early definition of criminal law. One of these early statements was set forth by King Henry I in *Leges Henrici*, which placed prohibited acts in two classes: felonies and misdemeanors. This classification is still commonly used today.

However, the judges of the royal courts were the primary sources of the definitions of substantive crimes. By 1600 the felonies of murder, suicide, manslaughter, burglary, arson, robbery, larceny, rape, sodomy, and mayhem; and such misdemeanors as assault, battery, libel, and perjury had been identified.

The courts continued to recognize private wrongs (torts) and to award money damages to the injured party. The distinction between crimes and torts lies in the fact that a crime must involve a wrongful act breaching the public peace. Although many criminal acts also constitute torts, allowing private claims for damages as well as criminal prosecution, there are also many acts that constitute only private wrongs.

The fourth period in English legal history stretches from 1832 to the present. It is characterized by the adaptation of the common law to legislative change. The adaptation of, and interaction between, judicial discovery of the law and legislative expression of the law actually started much earlier. Royal proclamations and parliamentary acts formed a part of the law of England long before 1832. However, the role of the judiciary in incorporating the edicts and acts to actually create and to implement the law was dominant before that time. Since 1832 the role of the legislature in England has significantly increased, particularly in the last 30 years.

A practical fact about the common law in its early period must be noted. Although the doctrine of precedence was established and followed, the lack of simple methods for the reproduction of writings limited the dissemination of information on the law. To find the "law" on a particular subject, one had to turn to a skilled legal practitioner familiar with the various documentary sources that contained the relevant decisions on the point in dispute. Some of the royal proclamations, parliamentary acts, and legal writings of the period therefore had as their objective not the making of new law, but the codification or restatement of existing law as "discovered" by the courts. The objective of this process was to facilitate commerce and public life through a wider understanding of the law.

For example, *Blackstone's Commentaries,* a famous statement of the law with great impact on early colonial law, was not written for the use of the legal profession. The *Commentaries* comprise Blackstone's lectures given in 1758 at Oxford University to students of the liberal arts, not to prospective lawyers.

It is important for the student of criminal justice to recognize that our present criminal laws evolved from the common law of England, as did our criminal practice and procedure. Significant features of the common law adopted by our legal system include the principle of precedence, or *stare decisis*, the *accusatorial* approach to trial practice, and the distinction between private and public wrongs. In addition, the actual definitions and titles of much of our substantive criminal law have been drawn from the English common law.

The American Experience

The development of our legal system dates from the seventeenth century. Independent colonies were created in Virginia in 1607, at Plymouth in 1620, in Massachusetts in 1630, and in Maryland in 1632. The Dutch colony of New York became English in 1664; the colony of Pennsylvania, originally Swedish, became English in 1681. There were 13 separate colonies by 1722.

Although the law of these colonies clearly had its inception in the English common law, a point-for-point transfer did not occur. First, the common law as it existed in the early 1600s had been developed to fit the needs of a feudal society, a society quite remote in nature from that found in the American settlements. The problems facing the colonists were frequently new and not covered by existing common law.

Second, the common law of the seventeenth century was complex and deeply bound to archaic procedure that required skilled legal technicians to implement adequately. Such individuals were not present in sufficient numbers in the colonies to effectively implement the English common law system.

The early law applied in the colonies was therefore fairly primitive. Judicial decisions were based on what knowledge existed of English law, local custom, the Bible, religious belief, and on the few existing local legislative acts. At best the law amounted to little more than the exercise of judicial discretion.

This same judicial discretion, which had previously led to the shaping of the English common law, produced an unfavorable reaction in the colonies. Several colonies undertook the drafting of codes to avoid arbitrary judicial decisions: Massachusetts (1634) and Pennsylvania (1682) are two examples. Their approach was quite different from the English law approach, which, at this point in time, looked upon statutes as a threat to liberty—a perspective derived from the many years of judicial discovery of the law, an established judiciary, and an established body of common law. Therefore, these early colonial codes reflect the origins of the divergence between American and English views over the proper source of law: the legislature versus the judiciary.

During the eighteenth century, as the colonial societies became more developed and commerce flourished, the courts frequently applied the common law to resolve disputes not covered by code or statute. In the same sense, disputes involving statutes were frequently interpreted in the light of prior common law decisions.

American independence was proclaimed in 1776 and became a fact in 1783. This formative period, extending through 1787 when the Constitution and the Bill of Rights were adopted, was a significant time in the development of our law. The battle with England had created a spirit that fostered the concept of a separate American law. Relationships with France, a nation of codified law, were by contrast friendly. The general concept of the United States as a republic with the authority of government flowing from the general will of the people tended to encourage the concept of legislative establishment of law.

The basic framework of the United States government, with three equal branches (legislative, executive, and judicial), created relationships distinct from those of English government, and, in particular, placed the courts in a different role. The Constitution clearly vested the lawmaking role in the Congress, subject to judicial review. Although the Constitution and the Bill of Rights are unique in the explicit statements of the roles of the branches of government, the reservation of powers to the several states and the people, and the identification of basic individual rights; the Constitution limited rather than abolished the rights of the courts to discover law. The Constitution favored a system of codified law but did not abolish the common law approach.

During the nineteenth century, several states moved toward the development of comprehensive codes to replace the common law. A Massachusetts law commission in 1836 proposed the drafting of a code, and the New York Constitution of 1846 provided for the drafting of a comprehensive "written and systematic" code. However, even these approaches tended to include "reception" statutes allowing incorporation of the common law when appropriate. During the eighteenth and nineteenth centuries most of the states incorporated the basic principles of the common law, either through their constitutions or by legislative and judicial acts. The extent of the common law adopted was usually dependent upon its appropriateness to local requirement.

Most of the states cited the common law crimes at the outset. However, the enactment of criminal statutes was initiated almost immediately, and by the nineteenth century a number of states has enacted comprehensive criminal codes covering the common law crimes as well as new crimes unknown to the common law. In some cases, the statutes expressly provided that there would be no crimes except as found in the code. In other states that did not have such an express provision, the courts held that the comprehensive code abolished the common law crimes by implication. Although some states at this time do not have a comprehensive criminal code, the clear trend in the twentieth century is to enact criminal codes abolishing the common law crimes.

A careful distinction must be made at this point. When we say that common law crimes have been abolished, reference in most cases is actually made to a point of procedure. The majority of the acts that were common law crimes continue to be crimes because they are now expressly prohibited by statute. A few common law crimes have not been incorporated into statutory law, so one may say that they are abolished. However, the critical point is that, in those jurisdictions that have abolished common law crimes, a person cannot be tried for an act unless it is specifically defined as a crime by a statute. This is a sharp distinction from the common law procedure, whereby a judge could determine whether an act was criminal, even though previous cases did not identify that particular act as prohibited.

A word of caution must be noted. Many criminal codes contain catchall statutes designed to make harmful behavior illegal—behavior that may not have existed at the time of legislative enactment. In many jurisdictions that abolished common law crimes these catchall statutes have been used by judges to define new crimes. Even under a criminal code some latitude exists for judicial discovery, yet the trend in recent years is to require clarity and specificity in criminal statutes, and thus to narrow the latitude for judicial discovery.

The present criminal laws of the United States (the federal jurisdiction) and the law of the states are found in several forms:

1. Primarily in statutes enacted by the legislatures.
2. In administrative regulations passed pursuant to legislative delegation of authority.
3. In the Constitution of the United States and its amendments, and in the constitutions of the states.
4. To a limited extent, in the common law of crimes.

The trend today is to require statutory definition of criminal acts; therefore, behavior not forbidden and punished by statute is not a crime.

It is critical that the student comprehend the fact that there is not a single body of "American criminal law." The Constitution clearly recognized the separate sovereignty of the states. Thus, a federal criminal code exists that represents federal criminal law, applicable to all persons within the United States no matter where they may be; and each state has a separate body of criminal law applicable within that state. There is a high degree of commonality among the state criminal laws, but there is not uniformity. Thus, one cannot speak of a single body of American criminal law. In addition, a person can, by a single act, violate both a state and a federal law, as in kidnapping. Theoretically, this could result in dual prosecution. In practice, one jurisdiction (federal or state) usually defers to the other.

As the society within the United States has grown more homogeneous, there have been efforts by legislators, judges, and practicing lawyers to instill more commonality in the laws of the several states. The most significant of these efforts is reflected in the development of the Model Penal Code by the American Law Institute, a private organization. The Model Code reflects the efforts of legal scholars and practitioners to re-examine systematically the substantive criminal law and then to set forth alternative ways of dealing with basic issues that should be considered by legislatures. The emphasis of the Model Code is not on uniformity, for the appropriateness of criminal law applicable to local needs is recognized. The primary concern lies with the necessity to develop a current restatement of the law in the many states not possessing comprehensive criminal codes.

The Model Penal Code, the Uniform Rules of Criminal Procedure developed by the National Conference of Commissioners on Uniform State Laws in 1952, the American Law Institute's Model Code of Pre-arraignment Procedure, and the American Bar Association's Project on the Minimum Standards for Criminal Justice represent significant sources on recent developments in our criminal law and procedure and are of interest to students and practitioners.

A primary fact for the student of criminal justice to remember about our present system of criminal law is that its basis is statutory law. Although the concepts and principles of the common law have often been incorporated in statutes, the role of the judiciary in the *discovery* of law has been limited to the interpretation of law established by the legislature in most jurisdictions.

Principles of Criminal Law

Professor Jerome Hall has set forth six basic premises that underlie the criminal law.[3] These premises are reflected in our current criminal law, and the trend of current judicial interpretation and legislative action appears to reinforce their conceptual validity.

The first premise is often identified by the Latin phrases *nullem crimen sine lege, nulla ponna sine lege* (no crime without law, no punishment without law). This reflects the concept of fairness; that there should be some advance notice or warning to an individual that a particular act is criminal, and how it will be punished. The implementation of this premise is reflected in the present trend toward elimination of common law crimes and reliance on statutes that constitute express notice to the public.

The second premise is based on the concept that an individual should not be punished for his thoughts. For criminal liability to exist there must be some act. This is sometimes referred to as the requirement for an *actus reus,* or guilty act.

The third premise is the converse of the second. Criminal liability requires more than an act. Some sort of *mens rea,* or guilty mind, must also exist. This premise has been perhaps the most ignored, in that criminal statutes have made certain conduct by itself sufficient for criminal liability. Recent decisions have tended to limit the "strict liability"

[3] Jerome Hall, *General Principles of Criminal Law* (Indianapolis: Bobbs-Merrill, 1960).

theory. Frequently, statutes that impose "strict liability" provide for only minimal punishment (usually a monetary fine).

The fourth premise sets forth the concept that the guilty mind and guilty act must concur. The act forming the basis for criminal liability must have been committed as a result of guilty intent.

The fifth premise focuses on the requirement of causation. The result that is prohibited must have arisen from, or have been caused by, the combination of the accused's guilty mind and guilty act. Acts of omission as well as commission are sufficient to be considered causative. Difficult problems arise when a harmful end result differs from the result that the accused expected, or occurs in a different way than the accused planned. An unplanned homicide that occurs in the course of a burglary would be such an example. Such a case is easily resolved, but it is easy to see that more complex cases can arise.

The sixth premise, the most basic and perhaps the most important, is the concept of harm. Criminal law exists to prevent harm to the public. If there is no public harm, there can be no crime. Unfortunately, the criminal law has been seen as a convenient way to regulate human conduct. Many acts have been declared crimes, even though they present little risk to society. Often such acts involve private conduct that may be labeled immoral by the majority. The enactment and enforcement of laws labeling criminal certain behavior that is not a risk to society waste the resources of the criminal justice system, undermine our system of law, destroy the faith of the public in the fairness of our institutions of justice, and treat cruelly those convicted.

It is critical for the survival of our system of justice, and perhaps our society, that the criminal law and the activity of the criminal justice system be limited to, and focused on, the management of behavior that is an actual risk to society.

Summary

The goal of this chapter has been to trace the origins and premises underlying Anglo-American criminal law, to provide the student of criminal justice with an understanding of the present state of the law. Such an understanding will, in turn, give him a strong basis for future professional decision-making, especially in the exercise of discretion.

Our system of laws is based on the general will of the people. This fact is shown by the works of those philosophers most influential in the development of that system. For this and other reasons, law in this country is a dynamic process, adjusting to the various needs of society as they arise.

England has had the strongest influence on the American system of law. As the society of England became less tribal and more centralized, the courts also centralized and developed the common law, based on the principle of *stare decisis*. Other products of the increased sophistication of the English legal system were its accusatorial trial and the development of the distinction between crimes and torts. In the last few centuries the English common law has been increasingly displaced by the development of statute law.

Although much of American law is based on English law, it is distinctive in a number of ways. Notable among these distinctions are the stronger role of the legislature in lawmaking, the more distinct separation of powers, and the accent on codes to replace the common law. The displacement of the common law by statute has happened often in the United States, particularly in the area of criminal law.

To aid in understanding the underlying themes of criminal law, Jerome Hall has made one of the best distillations of its trends and premises available. Briefly stated, these principles should be present in all situations where the criminal sanction is invoked: legality, *actus reus, mens rea,* act and mind concurrence, causation, and harm.

Student Checklist

1. Can you describe how law tends to change to meet the current needs of society?

2. Can you identify and contrast the dominant philosophies of law throughout history?

3. Are you able to list the general social functions served by any system of law?

4. Can you identify the role of discretion in justice administration?

5. Can you define "law"?

6. Are you able to list the major periods in the history of English law?
7. Can you provide a general picture of how the present state of law was achieved?
8. Can you identify the major legal philosophers in history?
9. Are you able to explain the concept of *stare decisis*?
10. Can you describe the evolution of common law in the United States?

Topics for Discussion

1. Discuss what is meant by "judge-made law" in contrast with statutory law.
2. Discuss the social utility of strict liability statutes in determining criminal liability.
3. Discuss the social value of *stare decisis*.
4. Discuss the relationship between a moral, a social standard, and a law.
5. Discuss how the theory of "social contract" relates to law as a means of social control.

The study of this chapter will enable you to:

1. Define and give three examples of strict liability offenses.
2. Describe how negligence may constitute the intent element of a criminal offense.
3. Contrast "transferred intent" with "specific intent."
4. Explain how an omission to act may create criminal liability.
5. Define *mens rea*.
6. Define *actus reus*.
7. Distinguish *mala in se* offenses from *mala prohibita* offenses.
8. Describe the felony-murder rule and how the intent element of murder is established.
9. Explain the requirement for concurrence of act and intent to have criminal liability.
10. Describe the importance of the causation principle.

4
Elements of Criminal Liability

Chapter 4 deals with the basic question: "To whom do criminal sanctions apply and why?" Study of the "rules" or substantive offenses is meaningless without some attention to this question.

We must first consider the basic principles of criminal law, which have been mentioned in Chapter 3. These principles are applicable to all types of criminal and quasicriminal laws. It makes no difference, for the purpose of this chapter, whether one considers statutes, common law rules of law, administrative regulations, or any other criminal sanction. If the laws are not in agreement with the general principles of criminal law, they are improper.[1]

Principles of Criminal Law

These principles of criminal law contain the following key concepts:[2]
1. *Mens rea* ("guilty mind"), or intent
2. *Actus reus* ("forbidden act"), or act
3. Concurrence of intent and act
4. Social harm
5. Causation

[1] For a full discussion, see Jerome Hall, *General Principles of Criminal Law,* 2nd ed. (Indianapolis, Ind.: Bobbs-Merrill, 1960).
[2] Hall, *General Principles of Criminal Law*; Rollin M. Perkins, *Perkins on Criminal Law,* 2nd ed. (Mineola, N.Y.: Foundation Press, 1969); Wayne R. LaFave and Austin W. Scott, Jr., *Criminal Law* (St. Paul, Minn.: West, 1969).

6. Punishment

7. Legality

Before examining in detail each of these concepts and the principles of law that they reflect, it is appropriate to consider Jerome Hall's statement combining the principles:

> *The harm forbidden in a penal law must be imputed to any normal adult who voluntarily commits it with criminal intent, and such a person must be subjected to the legally prescribed punishment.*[3]

Each of the concepts and their associated principles of law will be defined and elaborated on, following a definition of *"corpus delicti,"* in order to place the concepts into better perspective.

Corpus Delicti, "Body of the Crime"

The student invariably asks why *corpus delicti* is not listed as a general principle of criminal law. Briefly, it is a rule of evidence, not properly considered as a principle. This rule of evidence is a legal conclusion that there has, in fact, been a crime.

In order to establish this legal conclusion, it is necessary to show that there has been a socially harmful occurrence and that it was the result of someone's criminal act or omission. Alternatively stated, the *corpus delicti* rule of evidence requires adherence to the first five listed principles of criminal law when the criminal sanction is invoked and it is part of the seventh principle.[4]

The "body of the crime" is *not* the dead body of a person in a murder or manslaughter case. The rule can be applied just as well to any other crime, although its most popularized application is in murder cases. This fact seems to stem from a fear that someone may be convicted and punished for a crime that never occurred.[5] The rule requires that there be independent evidence to establish the fact that all the elements of a crime are present. It is a limitation on the use of the out-of-court confessions, or confessions made to police officers or prosecutors outside of court. A confession alone will not establish the guilt of an accused person.

---

[3] Hall, *General Principles of Criminal Law,* p. 18.

[4] For a more comprehensive discussion of the rule, see Perkins, *Perkins on Criminal Law,* pp. 97–106. Several interesting examples are cited.

[5] LaFave, *Criminal Law,* p. 17.

The purpose of the rule, as with all rules of evidence, is to test the reliability of elements of proof. The student should be aware of the fundamental mistrust of out-of-court confessions.

In a sense, the requirement that *corpus delicti* be established is an expression of a belief in the principles of criminal law. If there is no *corpus delicti,* it is inappropriate to apply criminal sanctions. Failure to show the existence of behavior that falls within the definition of crime leads to the legal conclusion that there has been no crime.

Mens Rea

In establishing that there has been a crime, one basic element is intent, or *mens rea.* An element of an offense is no more than a fact. Various types of evidence may be used to establish such facts, and there is no best form of proof for all cases. Care should be exercised to avoid confusion of "fact," which is a legal conclusion, with "evidence," which tends to prove those legal conclusions.

The intent element varies with different types of crimes, but the basic notion is that people will not be subjected to the criminal process unless they have entertained thoughts of an "evil" nature. It is the concept of *mens rea* that forms the cornerstone for various special defenses, such as insanity, intoxication, or infancy. In the absence of the intent, no matter how harmful an act is, it may well be found to be noncriminal. This statement does not mean that negligence will excuse harmful acts, because it will not. Civil liability may result from the negligence whereby a court may require the wrongdoer to pay for damages caused, or to otherwise make the injured party whole again. Depending on the level of neglect involved, an act may still be a crime even though it results from negligence.

In speaking of intent, it is useful to consider two types of offenses: *mala in se* and *mala prohibita. Mala in se* offenses are "wrongs in themselves"; the latter are "wrongs by statute, but not otherwise." This division is a type of classification of offenses by moral turpitude involved in the offense. Division of offenses in this manner may help for the purpose of understanding intent elements of offenses.

Many *mala prohibita* offenses do not require proof of intent. These are called "strict liability" statutes. Examples are plentiful—one of the clearest is parking in a "no parking" zone. But, even in cases of so-called strict liability, an accused must be generally aware of his actions. This aspect of general awareness will be discussed further under "voluntariness" in the section of this chapter dealing with *actus reus.*

In cases of *mala in se,* the requirement of proof of intent remains.[6] The distinction lies in historical development rather than in some notion of relative seriousness of offenses. The decision implicit in imposition of strict liability is that certain acts must be subject to criminal law regardless of why they were done. In cases of *mala in se* offenses, even though the harm may be great, there is no offense without intent because intent is simply one of the elements of the offense, and without proof of *all* elements there is no offense. Statutes that include an element of knowledge, even though they are *mala prohibita,* also require proof of a type of intent for conviction.

Assignment of strict liability is an expression of a change in attitude about the necessity of proof of an "evil mind" in all criminal cases. One possible explanation of the increasing number of offenses not requiring proof of intent lies in the difficulty of proving intent. It amounts to destruction of a possible defense that would be essentially the same as "ignorance of law." As this discussion concerns acts that are wrong only because they are so designated by statute, it would be simple for an accused to allege ignorance of the law, and thus no evil intent, thereby providing a basis for acquittal for lack of *mens rea.* No one but the accused himself would ever actually know the extent of his knowledge. This situation may be what the legislators wish to avoid by assigning strict liability.

In some cases, intent is inferred from circumstances. This type of intent is called "presumed," or "constructed," intent, which leads to a legal conclusion that some acts, by their very performance, necessarily include an evil intent. LaFave has criticized this position as being a strained reasoning process in an attempt to retain the intent element in all offenses. Recognition of some offenses as being crimes without intent will, he maintains, remove the need for such reasoning.[7] At the same time, one's sense of justice is not offended by such a proposal if one

---

[6] Morissette v. United States, 342 U.S. 246, 72 S.Ct. 240, 96 L.Ed. 288 (1952), is a case that demonstrates the requirement of proof of intent. The Court held that the traditional type of intent required for a theft-type offense must be proved to sustain a conviction, even in a case in which there is a statute covering the actions, and that statute is silent on the topic of intent.

[7] LaFave, *Criminal Law,* p. 200.

keeps in mind that the offenses that are complete without intent often relate to matters of great social concern that did not conceptually exist at common law. Add to that consideration the difficulty of proof, and there is substantial cause to accept LaFave's preference for elimination of the element rather than creation of a presumption.

Some offenses require proof of a particular type of mental state, usually called "specific intent." In such cases, conviction for an offense requires proof of what may be considered a more serious level of evil intent than is required for other offenses. Failure of such proof would not necessarily mean acquittal, however, but might result in conviction of a lesser included offense. A lesser included offense is one that is "merged," or part of an offense, but that requires one or more fewer elements of proof for conviction. As an example, the offense of desertion under the Uniform Code of Military Justice consists of absenting oneself from one's unit *with intent to remain permanently away*. If the prosecution fails to prove that intent, it may still be able to get a conviction for absence without leave, which consists of absenting oneself from one's unit without lawful authority. Thus, there is an element of intent involved in the lesser offense, but it is only of the nature of general awareness.

Negligence does not necessarily preclude criminal liability. Indeed, a certain level of neglect may satisfy even a specific intent requirement. For example, consider the case of murder. Murder is the killing of one person by another *with malice aforethought* and without justification or excuse. (See Chapter 10 for a fuller discussion of justification and excuse.) This specific intent element may be supplied by a level of neglect which amounts to a conscious disregard of human safety. Other commonly required particular or specific states of mind or intent are "corrupt," "willful," and "wantonness." An act such as voluntarily discharging a firearm into a crowd (without a particular target and with no conscious desire to kill or injure anyone) would support a finding of the required malice aforethought. It is an act so dangerous and so likely to produce the death of another that one may be said to have intended the reasonable consequences of his act. An accidental discharge, in contrast, would not have the same legal consequences but would not necessarily exclude criminal liability.

Sometimes an intent to do one act will establish the intent element for another offense, even though the act that was intended did not occur. This is called "transferred intent." Criminal liability may attach for acts that are inherently dangerous. The law, in effect, holds that one who is engaged in a dangerous activity is liable for the reasonable consequences of his act. Perhaps the best study of the doctrine of transferred intent can be found in the felony-murder rule. A felony-murder, briefly, is a homicide in the course of a felony offense involving threat of bodily harm. The intent to commit a felony is deemed sufficient to supply the *mens rea* for murder. (See Chapter 5 for a fuller discussion of felony-murder.)

The concept of transferred intent is useful because it provides a rationale for matching an intent to do one thing with an entirely different prohibited result. Thus, the criminal sanction may be applied to situations in which harm was done in a different way than anticipated. As a matter of proof of crime, it is conceptually easier to show intent to do one thing and then to "transfer" that intent to another result, than it would be to show that the actual result was a clearly predictable result of the evil mind. This concept should also be considered in light of the later discussion of concurrence of act and intent.

Motive is frequently confused with intent, yet it has little to do with establishing legal liability for an act or omission prohibited by statute. The distinction between the two is that proof of motive may be used to help establish intent. Motive amounts to a reason or explanation for certain behavior. Just as proof of motive does not establish intent, proof of no motive cannot establish lack of intent. Motive may seem to have great significance and may have a practical effect on the question of sentencing, but it is limited as a matter of evidence toward establishing guilt.

Actus Reus

Some sort of prohibited act or omission must be performed or there is no crime. No matter how evil one's thoughts might be, criminal sanctions will not be applied to those having thoughts alone. In cases of strict liability crimes, it is the act alone that determines whether there is a crime.

There is a sort of mental awareness involved in the act that must not be confused with *mens rea*. An act, in order to provide the basis for criminal prosecution, must be voluntary. Persons are not held criminally liable for involuntary acts or results that are beyond their control. A muscular spasm or seizure would not be considered a voluntary act. Even in cases of strict liability offenses, there is no crime in such circumstances. An overpowering physical force that causes one to do something removes the aspect of the voluntary act. No crime will be charged to an unconscious person who plays the role of a puppet, or someone who attempts to resist but is nevertheless forced to enact a crime. In effect, such persons' acts are not their own.

The student must be careful to distinguish cases in which there is only a threat of force or violence. In such cases, the defenses of necessity, duress, coercion, or compulsion may be raised, but there still exists a voluntary act. The individual has weighed alternatives and chosen a particular course of voluntary action. The law recognizes such situations as defenses, but such recognition does not imply the absence of a voluntary act.

The general rule that there must be an affirmative, voluntary act has an exception. For purposes of many criminal statutes, an omission to act is sufficient to establish the *actus reus*.[8] Or, alternatively, a failure to act can be considered the same as an act.[9]

Not every failure to act will be so considered by the criminal law. Omissions are only "acts" when there is a duty to act affirmatively which is imposed by law and a subsequent failure to perform that act. An example of such a duty is the requirement to file federal income tax returns. A failure to file the required return constitutes the *actus reus* of the offense. Note that none of this discussion concerns the existence of an intent element or proof of such an element.

The accused party must also have the ability to fulfill the duty imposed upon him. If, for example, an individual were charged with failure to file an income tax return and that person did not have the capacity to comply with the law, there would be no offense. This offense must be distinguished from the recognition of limited mental capacity, for it is a physical inability that concerns us here. (See Chapter 10.) Suppose that the person charged with failure to file an income tax return had suffered a stroke while preparing his return and was completely paralyzed. If the effects of the physical inability prevented any possibility of filing, there would be no basis for a successful prosecution.

[8] See Perkins, *Perkins on Criminal Law,* p. 592, for a distinction between a forebearance to act and an omission. Here, both are called omissions.
[9] A good example of legislative treatment of this topic is found in Chapter 38, Illinois Revised Statutes: " 'Act' includes a failure or omission to take action." (§2–2, Article 2 is "General Definitions.")

The same conclusion can be reached by applying the concept of voluntariness to the omission to act. If a failure to fulfill a legally imposed duty lies beyond the control of an individual (no capacity), it is also involuntary. However, the reason for not relying on this approach will become apparent in the subsequent discussions of criminal negligence.

Conviction for an offense involving an omission to act often requires proof of knowledge of facts. This requisite is not the same as is proof of knowledge of the duty. The duty is imposed by law; ignorance of the duty, then, amounts to ignorance of law. But ignorance of factual matters is another thing entirely. Suppose, for example, that a statute requires reporting of any automobile accident by the owner of any automobile that is damaged. Further suppose that the owner of an automobile leaves it parked and departs the area for a time; during his absence, another automobile accidentally collides with the parked vehicle and inflicts minor damage. If, because of not being aware of the fact that his auto was damaged in an accident, the owner fails to report, he cannot be successfully prosecuted. In this case, the individual cannot be held liable because he does not know the facts out of which his duty arises.

In imputing criminal liability where a lack of facts is established, the law examines whether a duty was imposed by the law to make oneself aware of the facts. Generally, a lack of knowledge of facts will excuse the omission. However, there is another type of case in which part of the duty imposed by law is to make oneself aware of the facts. In such cases a failure to notice these facts, in itself, serves as a basis for criminal liability. Of course, the result of the failure must be harmful. Such a failure is called "criminal negligence," "recklessness," or occasionally "gross negligence."

The concept of negligence is a difficult one and must not be oversimplified. Figure 4–1 clarifies the use of negligence as a basis for assigning criminal liability.

Let us consider a continuum of all behavior. Some behavior is completely acceptable, and there are degrees of acceptability of others. As far as the criminal law is concerned, some behavior is acceptable, although it is unacceptable in the broader social sense. These cases involve tort liability. Note that civil sanctions may be imposed on behavior that falls within the legitimate sphere of criminal law. For example, one who is properly convicted of involuntary manslaughter may also be held liable for damages in a wrongful death action; or one who is convicted of

Figure 4-1. Intent-sanctions continuum.

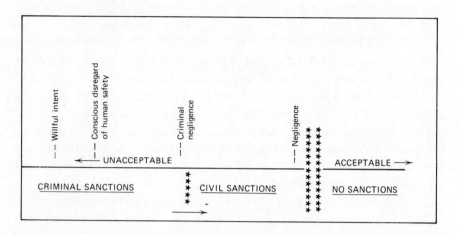

assault may be liable for money damages for the intentional tort of assault.

Generally, there is some sanction for all socially harmful behavior. At a certain level of seriousness of the danger, the sanction can be criminal. As a rule of thumb, criminal negligence involves activities that are inherently dangerous. Examples are blasting, handling firearms, burning, and operating a motor vehicle. When one is engaged in such activities, failure to take notice of facts can result in serious injuries to persons or property. The application of criminal sanctions to failures to exercise due care is an expression of the perceived seriousness of the potential social harm involved in such activities.

The student should take care, in studying various offenses in which the *actus reus* is an omission, not to be misled by the name of the offense. For example, "child neglect" seems to imply an element of negligence. However, it is clear that an element of carelessness or recklessness is not necessarily involved; the violation can be from an intentional omission to provide required care for a child. This is only one illustration that all omissions to act are not negligence, but it shows the necessity of reading criminal statutes carefully to comprehend their full meaning.

Concurrence of Act and Intent
Some offenses, as indicated above, require no proof of *mens rea*. In such cases, there is no requirement of concurrence. However, in all cases in-

volving intent, or *mens rea,* there must be concurrence. This principle is an expression of the basic belief that an evil mind must accompany a prohibited act. Either one, without the other, does not constitute an offense under criminal law.

First, consider the situation of presence of intent but absence of an act. In such a case, there is no offense because one of the essential elements is missing. Then, consider a slightly altered situation in which the intent exists for a limited time but then disappears. Subsequently, an act occurs that constitutes the fulfillment of that earlier intent. Is there an offense? The answer to this question depends on whether the act and intent are concurrent. Concurrence does not always mean that both exist for exactly the same period of time.

For example, suppose that one person decides to murder another but takes no action toward fulfillment of that desire. If, at some later date after the intent to murder has been abandoned and forgotten, the death of the intended victim occurs as a result of the actions of the person who once had intended that result, there is no offense of murder. The result would be different if there had been an action concurrent with the intent. Once a plan has been put into action, abandonment of intent may not operate as a defense. Also there could be criminal liability based on an act that falls into the category of criminal negligence.

Consider the situation of an act occurring without intent. Again, one element of the offense is missing and no crime has taken place. Altering this situation somewhat, suppose that the intent is formed after the act is completed. In another homicide case, if a death results from innocent or justifiable acts of an actor and that actor subsequently forms an "evil mind" that would provide the intent element for murder, there is no offense for lack of concurrence of act and intent. Homicide is not always criminal. (See Chapter 5 for a discussion of this.) For present purposes, consider homicide as one person killing another.

The requirement of concurrence of act and intent is an expression of a belief that neither the act or the intent is sufficient to warrant invoking the criminal process.

Social Harm

Without an injury to society, there can be no crime. This is *not* a requirement that there be harm to an individual before there can be a crime.

The so-called victimless crimes still involve an element of social harm.[10]

The perception of social harm is the foundation of the notion of crime. So far as injury to individuals is concerned, remedies can be found entirely outside the criminal courts. But these civil court or private remedies are considered inadequate to make society whole again after it has experienced injury. Thus, a "crime" is a wrong done to a people as a group, the result of an evil intent and a prohibited act working together.

Current Anglo-American concepts of crime are based on the development of certain attitudes following the Norman invasion of England.[11] As the English common law developed, the party who was injured was the monarch. The monarch was the state and represented "society" personified. The captioning of cases "*Rex* v. _____" or "*Regina* v. _____" demonstrated the relationship of the monarch to the crime. Contemporary attitudes express the belief that a crime is an injury to society. Again, an indication of that attitude can be found in the case captions "*State* v. _____" or "*People* v. _____."

One limitation to this notion is the concept of victimless crime. The arguments for decriminalization of certain acts are that they harm only their perpetrators and are not, themselves, socially harmful. Others hold that there is a legitimate social interest in the protection of each member of a group (from himself, if necessary). Even victimless crimes are thought to have a victim—society.

All crimes involve an element of social harm. The sources of judgment as to what is harmful are many and include legislatures, courts (acting in the common law tradition), and administrative authorities. Whatever the basis for their judgments, they are deemed, in law, to be competent to declare an activity socially harmful.

There may be various levels of perceived social harm in particular acts, and differences are usually reflected in the process of sentencing.

---

[10] For a detailed discussion, see Edwin M. Schur, *Crimes Without Victims* (Englewood Cliffs, N.J.: Prentice-Hall, 1965).

[11] An excellent source on this topic is C. Ray Jeffrey, "The Development of Crime in Early English Society," *Journal of Criminal Law, Criminology, and Police Science* (March–April 1957), 47, 647–666.

But some social harm must result, or the acts are not properly called crimes.[12]

Causation

The causation principle requires that the evil intent and the prohibited act, working together, produce the social harm that is called a crime. Such terms as "proximate cause," "legal cause," or "cause in fact" are frequently used to describe causation. The essential idea is that the law recognizes logical cause and effect, but with limitations.

The issue to be resolved is that of responsibility. The criminal sanction may be invoked only if the criminal activity (act and intent) is shown actually to produce a social harm. As already indicated in the discussion of transferred intent, the result need not necessarily be the same as that intended. And, as will be demonstrated in the discussion of attempt, neither must the criminal activity proceed to its planned or reasonable conclusion. What is really at issue here is the extent to which the criminal sanction may apply. Without a close, factual relationship between criminal activity and *some* social harm, there is no crime. Similarly, social harm that is not caused by concurrent act and intent is not a crime. The concept of causation limits criminal liability.

Some of the most interesting problems in the area of causation are found in situations in which more than one person engages in criminal activity at the same time. Suppose, for example, the following:

Wells determined to kill Poole. Knowing that Poole was about to go out into the desert, Wells placed deadly poison in Poole's canteen of water, Rivers saw Wells handling the canteen but thought it belonged to Wells. Assuming that Wells was about to go into the desert, and intending to kill Wells, Rivers made a hole in the canteen so that the water would leak out (without Well's knowledge). Poole went out into the desert with the poisoned and leaking canteen and died. Who killed (caused the death of) Poole?

Wells would be expected to raise a defense that Rivers' action was an intervening cause that factually resulted in the death of Poole. There

---

[12] We do not intend to overlook the social impact of private wrongs, but the concern of this book is with the criminal law, rather than the law of torts. Nor do we suggest that perceptions of social harm do not or should not change.

is no question that he could be convicted of at least an attempted murder. Whether his act of poisoning the canteen caused the death is a question of fact that would be determined by the jury. The jury might easily find him guilty of murder on that basis.

Rivers would gain nothing by admitting that his intent was to kill someone other than Poole. A defense that his act was beneficial to Poole by saving him from death by poisoning would not succeed. There is little question that his action caused Poole's death.

The student is urged to work out his own answers to this problem after studying offenses against persons, and again after looking into matters of defense.

Causation is the last element that must be proved to establish that there is a crime. Attention should be given to what happens after the legal fact of crime has been established.

Punishment

Punishment is the sanction imposed when liability for a crime is established. It must be imposed, just as guilt must be established, in a legally prescribed manner. The concept of punishment involves several objectives, and the student should avoid considering any one of those objectives exclusively. Although there are greater or lesser emphases on particular aspects from time to time and from place to place, the student must not ignore those that receive less emphases.

The purposes served by the imposition of punishment are many and subject to considerable dispute. In summary, the purposes can be divided into those emphasizing the offender and those emphasizing the community. All stated purposes seem to share the same fundamental notion that punishment for crime is a social benefit.[13]

The purpose that focuses attention on the offender is called rehabilitation or correction. The offender, after punishment, is supposed to be reformed and unlikely to engage again in criminal activity. Another means of keeping the offender out of trouble is incapacitation or prevention. It is presumably to the benefit of the offender that he is kept out of

[13] For a comprehensive treatment of this topic, see LaFave, *Criminal Law*, pp. 21–25.

trouble, usually in confinement. The direct or immediate benefits to society are readily apparent, but the long-range benefits are rather doubtful. The offender-oriented theories of punishment do not consider capital punishment as an alternative.

Punishment theories that are socially oriented can be divided into revenge and crime prevention types. Crime prevention can be further subdivided into restraint, deterrence, and education. Revenge, also called "retribution," is aimed at inflicting injury on the offender to approximately the same extent as the injury he inflicted. "An eye for an eye" is probably the most morally and emotionally influenced theory of punishment.

Restraint is the other aspect of incapacitation, imposed to protect society rather than to prevent the offender from further criminal activity. And deterrence may be one of the most overtaxed theories of punishment. Essentially, punishment of one offender is supposed to prevent others from engaging in similar behavior.

Education is a function of punishment closely related to deterrence, because both involve informing the public that certain behavior is unacceptable. But the educational effects are supposedly more general in nature. Although only potential offenders can be deterred, all members of the group can be informed as to what behavior is unacceptable. Education, in addition, need not affect the audience deeply or personally in order that its objective be met.

Given these myriad and self-contradicting purposes, it is impossible to generalize effectively about the purposes of punishment. For a particular offense, the punishment may vary with the perceived needs of various offenders, or with the perceived dangers to society from individual offenders. Over a period of time, ideas as to proper focus of attention in punishment may vary considerably among virtually identical cases: the identity of victims or offenders may weigh heavily in the question of punishment. The seriousness or the type of the offense may have considerable impact. The only safe generalization is that the matter of punishment will be determined by the circumstances of each case.

Legality

The principle of legality of criminal law is the basis for the framework of procedural rules governing the criminal process. The one phrase that can be used to summarize this topic is *due process of law*. The whole body of American constitutional law (regarding criminal matters) is involved in the concept of legality.

More than mere procedural rules are involved in this topic. The procedural rules are representations of expressions of the principle, they do not define its entire scope. The phrase *nulla poena sine lege* ("no penalty without law") is perhaps more expressive of the principle than due process of law, but it is really too broad in meaning for present purposes.[14]

Professor Hall indicates that the true issues are the power of the state and the limitations on that power.[15] The requirements of due process are manifestations of the principles of individual rights and powers versus the authority of the state. (See Chapter 3 for a more detailed discussion of the origins of law.) Essentially, it is a sense of justice or fairness that is expressed by due process of law. In terms of absolute standards, these concepts are difficult to measure—and to indicate, when achieved.

The Constitution and its interpretations provide the most nearly complete definition of due process. A periodic reading of this document will provide continued interest and frequent new insights.

Summary

The student is reminded of the combined generalizations regarding the principles of criminal law that were discussed at the beginning of this chapter. They should be kept in mind along with some points raised in discussion, in further studies of criminal justice.

One of the most useful questions to raise in attempting to discover the pattern of criminal laws is: "Why is this a crime?" Careful consideration of the principles of criminal law may help provide the answer to that question.

[14] Hall, *General Principles of Criminal Law*, Chapter 2.
[15] Professor Hall's discussion reaches various aspects of rule of law, and identifies that concept as a fundamental limitation on the power of the state. Rule of law is really closer to the meaning of *nulla poena sine lege* than due process. His argument should be considered carefully.

Student Checklist

1. Can you define and give three examples of strict liability offenses?
2. Do you know how to describe how negligence may constitute the intent element of a criminal offense?
3. Can you contrast "transferred intent" with "specific intent"?
4. Are you able to explain how an omission to act may create criminal liability?
5. Are you able to define *mens rea?*
6. Can you define *actus reus?* .
7. Do you know how to distinguish *mala in se* offenses from *mala prohibita* offenses?
8. Are you able to describe the felony-murder rule and how the intent element of murder is established?
9. Can you explain the requirement for concurrence of act and intent to have criminal liability?
10. Can you describe the importance of the causation principle?

Topics for Discussion

1. Discuss the "poisoned canteen" example.
2. Discuss the role of the state in criminal offenses.
3. Discuss the overlap between civil and criminal law for injuries or damages between individuals.
4. Discuss the major approaches to punishment as provided in all criminal statutes.
5. Discuss the differences between "transferred intent," "specific intent," "general intent," and "presumed intent."

ANNOTATED BIBLIOGRAPHY

Hall, Jerome. *General Principles of Criminal Law*. Indianapolis: Bobbs-Merrill, 1960. A major textbook covering the basic underlying principles of our criminal law. It provides a good balance between common law and statutory law.

Perkins, Rollin M. *Perkins on Criminal Law*. Mineola, N.Y.: Foundation Press, 1969. One of the more comprehensive textbooks on criminal law with primary emphasis on common law, but with adequate coverage of statutory law to enable the student to identify the differences.

Schwartz, Louis B., and Stephen R. Goldstein. *Law Enforcement Handbook for Police*. St. Paul: West Publishing, 1970. A recruit-level handbook of criminal law from a layman's perspective. It attempts a nonlegal approach to the study of the criminal law. Numerous realistic field problems and examples illustrate points.

Weinreb, Lloyd L. *Criminal Law*. Mineola, N.Y.: Foundation Press, 1969. A casebook approach to criminal law and the inherent problems associated with administering the law. Several problems are posed by the author along with case commentary. Sample legal forms and several supportive articles provide depth to the topic and some direct application of the criminal law, by using legal forms and sample data.

The study of this chapter will enable you to:

1. List three classifications of criminal offenses.
2. Contrast homicide with murder.
3. Identify the reason why suicide was a criminal offense in old common law.
4. Contrast "specific intent" with "general intent" as an element of an offense.
5. Distinguish between assault and battery as offenses.
6. Define the elements of the offense of rape.
7. Contrast assault and battery with the offense of mayhem.
8. Distinguish voluntary manslaughter from involuntary manslaughter.
9. Contrast false imprisonment, kidnapping, and abduction in terms of the social harm they prohibit.
10. List five examples of manslaughter identifying each as either voluntary or involuntary.

5

Offenses Against Persons

Introduction

A criminal offense is any social harm defined and made punishable by law by a governmental unit (the federal government, a state, a city, or a village). Although the common law has been followed by a majority of the states for defining criminal offenses, numerous states have moved from the common law to statutes. Some of these states, which are known as "code states," have specified that common law will no longer be recognized in their state.

The primary difference between common law–defined offenses and statutory law is that the statutes reflect contemporary problems and current social values in determining what acts are prohibited and what acts must be proved by the state for the conviction of a person accused of committing a crime. Generally, however, the differences between common law and statutory law are slight in terms of the elements, the conduct that is prohibited, and the penalties.

The classification of offenses as crimes against persons or crimes against property is arbitrary, but it does allow for some division of offenses based on the nature of the elements involved. Offenses against persons are generally those offenses that regulate the conduct of one person against another person. Offenses against property are usually those offenses primarily concerned with property. The social harm resulting from offenses against property directly affects the owner or possessor of the property, but the offense is usually deemed to be less harmful than those offenses against a person.

Other classification schemes of offenses are used; a brief review of those classifications follows. One such scheme divides all crime into the three major groups of: (1) treason, (2) felony, and (3) misdemeanor. When these groupings were identified in common law, treason was judged to be a serious crime—an offense that attacked the security of the kingdom, or its contemporary counterpart, the government of a nation. It was soon subdivided into high treason and petit treason, a distinction between being very serious and less serious. The other two groups—felony and misdemeanor—are still used today in law and in the administration of justice.

Offenses are also divided into two groups based on their reference to moral turpitude. The more serious group consists of offenses that are considered inherently evil or bad in themselves. The other group consists of offenses that are deemed bad or evil because a government or legislature determines that the offense is contrary to the good of the public. In Latin, these groups of offenses are called *mala in se* and *mala prohibita*. *Mala in se* refers to the offenses that are inherently bad or evil. *Mala prohibita* refers to offenses that are bad because they are prohibited.

Some jurisdictions distinguish offenses on the basis of: (1) felony–capital offenses, (2) felony–noncapital offenses, (3) high misdemeanor, and (4) low misdemeanor. In a majority of the states, the practice appears to be that they subdivide or group their criminal offenses into three to five categories, using some of the distinctions or groupings cited here.

States that have recently revised their statutes or are currently in the process tend to distinguish or group their offenses in terms of the social harm involved in the offense. In addition, police departments, courts, and social service agencies in larger jurisdictions are moving toward subdividing their services by using the same criterion of social harm. For example, the investigation units of the larger police departments are frequently dividing their personnel into work units known as "offenses against persons," "offenses against property," and "offenses against morality."

This chapter will cover those offenses deemed to be crimes against persons. Although the title of an offense and some of the terms used in specifying it and its elements and sanctions may vary, there is usually a thread of commonality between offenses among the various states. This chapter focuses on those crimes common to most states. A word of caution is necessary for the practitioner in criminal justice, however. Although most states have a thread of commonality to their offenses, a practitioner should carefully study and analyze the relevant state statutes and case decisions for his jurisdiction. Second, practitioners should be exposed to a formal training program that covers the law of his particular state before practicing.

Homicide

Homicide is generally defined as the killing of a human being by another, which excludes suicide (the killing of a human being by himself). Homicide is often mistakenly equated with murder. Although homicide is the killing of one person by another person, in many cases such action is not deemed criminal. These cases of noncriminal homicide are usually termed justified or excused for purposes of determining criminal liability. An example would be the execution of a person legally sentenced to death. This is not to say that noncriminal homicides are without sanctions in the law. For example, a death due to negligence on the part of another person could render the person responsible for the death liable for civil damages for a wrongful death, yet not criminally liable.

Criminal homicides are our primary concern in this chapter. They are usually subdivided into groups, using either degrees or specific offenses requiring different elements. Examples of the latter grouping are: (1) murder, (2) voluntary manslaughter, and (3) involuntary manslaughter. Examples of the degrees subdivision are first degree, second degree, and third degree.

Murder

Murder is usually defined as "a homicide without justification or excuse and with malice aforethought." Under common law, murder is deemed to be a general intent crime; however, specific intent to kill any particular person, although not required, was adequate to satisfy the general intent requirement. The key element in murder is the intent element, and it is usually described as being "with malice aforethought." The malice may be either expressed or implied and can usually be described as coming from one of five intents as follows:

1. An intent to kill. A general intent to kill any person or a specific intent to kill a specific person is adequate. Either intent may be transferred if a third person or bystander is unintentionally killed.

2. The intent to inflict great bodily harm. If the person intends to inflict great bodily harm that could reasonably be interpreted to result in death, even though the death was not intended, this fact would be adequate to constitute the required element of intent.
3. Intent to commit a felony. This form of intent is usually known as the felony-murder rule. If, in the commission of a dangerous felony, a person is killed, whether intentionally or not, the perpetrator is as guilty as if he had intended the death of the person killed.
4. Resisting lawful arrest with force. If the perpetrator intends to resist lawful arrest and kills the arresting officer, the intended resistance would generally be adequate to constitute the intent necessary for murder.
5. The commission of a willful act exhibiting a wanton disregard for the lives of others. Whenever the willful and wanton disregard of human life is exhibited in an act and the consequences are reasonably foreseeable, the act will be adequate to constitute a general intent—the general intent necessary for murder.

In some states, murder is broken down into degrees. Common law had no degrees of murder; therefore, wherever murder is identified in degree form, it is done by statute. First degree murder is usually identified as all killings with "malice aforethought", which means "willful, deliberate, and premeditated." This would include murder perpetrated by poison, torture, or ambush; or in the perpetration of a felony, such as arson, robbery, rape, or other serious felony. Second degree murder would include all killings with malice aforethought other than those classified as first degree murder. These may be murders associated with abortion, aggravated assault, or any other crime that is considered an inherently injurious felony.

Sample Statutes

782.01. Homicide Generally.
The killing of a human being is either justifiable or excusable homicide, or murder or manslaughter, according to the facts and circumstances of each case.

782.02. Justifiable Homicide.
Homicide is justifiable when committed by public officers and those acting by their command in their aid and assistance, either in obedience to any judgment of a competent court, or when necessarily committed in overcoming actual resistance to the execution of some legal process, or

in the discharge of any other legal duty, or when necessarily committed in retaking felons who may have been rescued or who have escaped, or when necessarily committed in arresting felons fleeing from justice.

Homicide is justifiable when committed by any person in either of the following cases:

1. *When resisting any attempt to murder such person, or to commit any felony upon him, or upon or in any dwelling house in which such person shall be; or*
2. *When committed in the lawful defense of such person of his or her husband, wife, parent, grandparent, mother-in-law, son-in-law, daughter-in-law, father-in-law, child, grandchild, sister, brother, uncle, aunt, niece, nephew, guardian, ward, master, mistress, or servant, when there shall be a reasonable ground to apprehend a design to commit a felony or to do some great personal injury, and there shall be imminent danger of such design being accomplished; or*
3. *When necessarily committed in attempting by lawful ways and means to apprehend any person for any felony committed, or in lawfully suppressing any riot, or in lawfully keeping and preserving the peace.*

782.03. Excusable Homicide.

Homicide is excusable when committed by accident and misfortune in lawfully correcting a child or servant, or in doing any other lawful act by lawful means with usual ordinary caution, and without any unlawful intent, or by accident and misfortune in the heat of passion, upon any sudden and sufficient provocation, or upon a sudden combat, without any dangerous weapon being used and not done in a cruel and unusual manner.

782.04. Murder.

The unlawful killing of a human being, when perpetrated from a premeditated design to effect the death of the person killed or any human being, or when committed in the perpetration of or in the attempt to perpetrate any arson, rape, robbery, burglary, abominable and detestable crime against nature, or kidnapping, shall be murder in the first degree, and shall be punishable by death.

When perpetrated by any act imminently dangerous to another, and evincing a depraved mind regardless of human life, although without any premeditated design to effect the death of any particular individuel, it shall be murder in the second degree, and shall be punished by imprisonment in the state prison for life, or for any number of years not less than 20 years.

When perpetrated without any design to effect death, by a person

engaged in the commission of any felony, other than arson, rape, rob-
bery, burglary, the abominable and detestable crime against nature, or
kidnapping, it shall be murder in the third degree, and shall be punished
by imprisonment in the state prison not exceeding 20 years.

Assisting Self-Murder
Every person deliberately assisting another in the commission of self-
murder shall be guilty of manslaughter.

Murder
(a) A person who kills an individual without lawful justification commits
murder if, in performing the acts which cause the death:
1. *He either intends to kill or do great bodily harm to that individual*
   or another, or knows that such acts will cause death to that in-
   dividual or another; or
2. *He knows that such acts create a strong probability of death or great*
   bodily harm to that individual or another; or
3. *He is attempting or committing a forcible felony other than volun-*
   tary manslaughter.

Manslaughter
Manslaughter is usually defined as "the unlawful killing of one human
being by another *without* malice aforethought." Manslaughter is charged
when homicide occurs under circumstances not severe enough to be
murder and not mild enough to constitute excusable or justifiable homicide. Manslaughter is usually separated into. voluntary and involuntary
manslaughter.

Voluntary Manslaughter. To constitute voluntary manslaughter there
must be adequate provocation by the victim "to arouse a furious passion
in a man of ordinary temper so as to cause him to act in a rash manner
without reflection." In this case, the objective test of a "reasonable man"
standard is used to determine whether the provocation is adequate to
constitute provocation. Circumstances that are usually deemed adequate
to constitute provocation are:
1. Assaults and batteries.
2. Unlawful arrest.
3. Insulting words or gestures coupled with some other conduct, such
   as a slight battery.
4. Sex crimes involving female relatives.

5. A wife's adultery.

6. A mutual quarrel or combat situation.

Another element for voluntary manslaughter is that the killing must be in the heat of passion. The only question involved here is: "Was the accused, in fact, sufficiently enraged to cause a heat of passion?" The "reasonable man" test is not used here. The killing must be sudden and without an opportunity to cool off. This also is an "in fact" test. It does not utilize the "reasonable man" test. Assuming that there was adequate provocation, causal connection must be established between the heat of passion and the cause of the fatal act.

Involuntary Manslaughter. This category is an unintentional killing, committed without excuse or justification, and not under circumstances constituting malice aforethought. Involuntary manslaughter covers unintentional homicides in the doing of an inherently dangerous or unlawful act. Involuntary manslaughter can also be extended to cover homicides that are the result of criminally negligent acts. Many states further provide for a degree of manslaughter known as vehicular homicide. Usually, this offense is subdivided on the basis of the amount of negligence involved in the act leading up to the homicide.

Sample Statutes

Manslaughter.
The killing of a human being by the act, procurement or culpable negligence of another, in cases where such killing shall not be justifiable or excusable homicide nor murder, according to the provisions of this chapter, shall be deemed manslaughter, and shall be punished by imprisonment in the state prison not exceeding 20 years, or imprisonment in the county jail not exceeding one year, or by fine not exceeding $5000.

Unnecessary Killing to Prevent Unlawful Act.
Whoever shall unnecessarily kill another, either while resisting an attempt by such other person to commit any felony, or to do any other unlawful act, or after such attempt shall have failed, shall be deemed guilty of manslaughter.

Voluntary Manslaughter.
(a) A person who kills an individual without lawful justification commits voluntary manslaughter if at the time of the killing he is acting

under a sudden and intense passion resulting from serious provocation by:

1. *The individual killed, or*
2. *Another whom the offender endeavors to kill, but he negligently or accidentally causes the death of the individual killed.*

   Serious provocation is conduct sufficient to excite an intense passion in a reasonable person.

Involuntary Manslaughter and Reckless Homicide.

(a) A person who kills an individual without lawful justification commits involuntary manslaughter if his acts whether lawful or unlawful which cause the death are such as are likely to cause death or great bodily harm to some individual, and he performs them recklessly.

(b) If the acts which cause the death consist of the driving of a motor vehicle, the person may be prosecuted for reckless homicide or if he is prosecuted for involuntary manslaughter, he may be found guilty of the included offense of reckless homicide.

Infanticide and Feticide

Criminal statutes concerned with the death of unborn and newly born children vary widely in terms of their coverage, just as do the various interpretations of the common law in this area. Furthermore, the recent concern with abortion and the subsequent actions by legislatures across the nation have tended to leave this area of homicide greatly unsettled. The major issue involved with offenses in this category is: "At what time does the fetus become a living human being?" or in the alternative: "Does the statute regulate the intentional interruption of a fetus in development?"

Suicide

Under common law, suicide was a felony providing for the forfeiture of property if the suicide was successful. Under statutory legislation, suicide is seldom a felony and has generally been ignored as a crime in the majority of states. Still another group of states continue to treat suicide or attempted suicide as a misdemeanor.

Frequently, the liability of an accessory to suicide is questioned. Some states provide a specific statute to punish the person assisting suicide, whereas other states treat it as murder or manslaughter, depending on the causal connection between the assistance given and the act causing death. For states that have abolished suicide as a crime, there is no liability under accessory principles, which hold that an accessory in a felony is charged as a principal. An interesting situation arises when a person, in attempting to kill himself, kills another. These cases are normally resolved on the basis of whether the essential intent element is fulfilled.

Assault and Battery

In common law, battery was the unlawful touching of one person by another. Battery has always been and remains an offense distinct from assault, even though some statutes have used the phrase "assault and battery" or have used the word "assault" to describe battery, which tends further to confuse the issue. A common law assault was a lesser included offense of battery.

The prohibition of battery is among the clearest examples of the concept of the sanctity of the person. Any unauthorized touching establishes the offense: there need be no weapons or particular level of violence.

Statutes have produced a variety of "aggravated" battery, in which the crime is rendered more serious by various circumstances, such as use of weapons, status of the victim, or other special threats to peace and security. And the punishment is relatively more severe for these more serious forms of battery. Without a statutory distinction, an unlawful touching with a feather is indistinguishable from an unlawful touching with a dangerous weapon.

The word "unlawful" should provide a clue to the most readily available defense to battery—consent. (See Chapter 10 for a detailed discussion of consent in excusing criminal liability.) Briefly, consent is limited in two ways. First, consent may only be given by one who is legally competent to do so. Second, there are certain acts to which a victim cannot lawfully consent. In a sense, the victim is protected from certain physical abuses even against his own wishes.

A common law assault was an attempted battery, which cannot

exist once the battery is complete. The law of torts, which may exist in statute form, contains an explanation in the definition of assault as "placing in fear or apprehension of receiving a battery." In such cases, assault may be established with proof of a threat to commit a battery accompanied by the ability to make good the threat.

In essence, the offense of assault consists of an apparently real threat of battery, which produces a reasonable apprehension that the battery will be completed. An assault need not result in a battery, and a battery is possible without an assault having preceded it. Criminal sanctions for assault appear to be based on the same considerations as those for battery. Both are the essence of breach of the peace.

Sample Statutes

Punishment of Assault.
Whoever commits a bare assault shall be punished by a fine not exceeding $100.

Punishment of Assault and Battery.
Whoever commits assault and battery shall be punished by imprisonment not exceeding six months, or by fine not exceeding $500.

Aggravated Assaults.
Whoever assaults another with a deadly weapon, without intent to kill, shall be guilty of an aggravated assault, and shall be punished by imprisonment in the state prison not exceeding five years or in the county jail not exceeding one year or by fine not exceeding $3000, or by such fine and imprisonment.

Assault With Intent to Commit Felony.
Whoever commits an assault on another, with intent to commit any felony punishable with death or imprisonment for life, shall be punished by imprisonment in the state prison not exceeding 20 years. An assault with intent to commit any other felony shall be punished to an extent not exceeding one-half the punishment which could have been inflicted had the crime been committed.

Assault.
(a) A person commits an assault when, without lawful authority, he engages in conduct which places another in reasonable apprehension of receiving a battery.

Battery.
(a) A person commits battery if he intentionally or knowingly without legal justification and by any means,
1. *Causes bodily harm to an individual; or*
2. *Makes physical contact of an insulting or provoking nature with an individual.*

Aggravated Assault.
(a) A person commits an aggravated assault, when, in committing an assault, he:
1. *Uses a deadly weapon;*
2. *Is hooded, robed or masked in such manner as to conceal his identity;*
3. *Knows the individual assaulted to be a teacher . . . ;*
4. *. . . a park district employee . . . ;*
5. *. . . a government social worker . . . ;*
6. *. . . a peace officer or correctional officer performing official duties . . . ;*
7. *. . . a fireman . . . ;*
   etc.

Aggravated Battery.
(a) A person who, in committing a battery, intentionally or knowingly causes great bodily harm, or permanent disability or disfigurement commits aggravated battery.
(b) A person who, in committing a battery either:
1. *Uses a deadly weapon;*
2. *Is hooded, robed, or masked, in such manner as to conceal his identity;*
3. *Knows the individual harmed to be a teacher; etc.*
(c) A person who administers to an individual or causes him to take, without his consent or by threat or deception, and for other than medical purposes, any intoxicating, poisonous, stupefying narcotic, or anesthetic substance commits aggravated battery.

Reckless Conduct.
(a) A person who causes bodily harm to or endangers the bodily safety of an individual by any means, commits reckless conduct if he performs recklessly the acts which cause the harm or endanger safety, whether they otherwise are lawful or unlawful.

Written Threats to Kill or Do Bodily Injury.

If any person writes or composes and also sends or procures the sending of any letter or inscribed communication, so written or composed, whether such letter or communication be signed or anonymous, to any person, containing a threat to kill or to do bodily injury to the person to whom such letter or communication is sent, or a threat to kill or do bodily injury to any member of the family of the person to whom such letter or communication is sent, the person so writing or composing and so sending or procuring the sending of such letter or communication, shall upon conviction be fined not more than $2000 or be sentenced to the penitentiary for a period not exceeding 10 years.

Mayhem

Mayhem is a battery that mutilates or causes permanent loss of the use of part of the body of the victim. Mayhem may easily be feared as much as murder—perhaps even more.

The common law offense was directed at those losses that rendered the victim less able to fight in self-defense. Such an injury might be relatively less important at a time when people are not required to rely heavily on their own skills and abilities to protect themselves. Perhaps the safest conclusion about the seriousness of mayhem is the social context in which it occurs. This assumes that increasing the severity of the punishment or sanction causes deterrence of criminal acts.

The injury need not amount to a physical severance of the affected part of the body. Loss of use amounts to the same thing.

Sample Statute
Mayhem
Whoever, with malicious intent to maim or disfigure, cuts out or maims the tongue, puts out or destroys an eye, cuts or tears off an ear, cuts, slits, or mutilates the nose or lip, or cuts off or disables a limb or member of any other person, and whoever is privy to such intent, or present, aiding or abetting in the commission of such offense, shall be punished by imprisonment in the state prison not exceeding 20 years or by fine not exceeding $5000.

Note: See also Sample Statute, **Aggravated Battery,** under **Assault and Battery.**

Rape

In a sense, rape is an aggravated form of battery. Common law rape was "unlawful sexual intercourse with a female without consent." Statutes have not altered the material elements of the offense but have caused some variations from the common law requirements.

It may help to understand the common law prohibition of rape if one considers the concept of women as property. Whether the property interest infringed by this form of battery was that of the father, who thus lost substantial value in the "market" for chaste daughters; or that of the husband, who lost his property right to exclusive possession of the woman; there was something more at stake than a battery to the person of that man. This statement does not suggest that the sanctity of the woman's person was not important in arrival at the rules concerning rape: it only suggests a basis for the more serious nature (in earlier times) of the offense—its being an infringement of property rights (including casting doubt on inheritance) as well.

It is difficult to imagine any act, short of homicide, that is more violative of a person's right to personal security than is rape. This concept has apparently been applied in the relatively few jurisdictions whose provisions for rape can apply to a male victim as well as a female. The crime of rape is essentially an offense against the person. The common law elements of rape are: (1) the unlawful (2) carnal knowledge (3) of a female (4) by force (5) against her will.

Unlawfulness refers to the fact that the intercourse takes place without the victim's consent and that the person accused of the rape is not the victim's husband. Common law provides that a man cannot rape his wife even though physical force was used to accomplish the act. One viewpoint is that the woman could be said to have consented to all acts of sexual intercourse at the time of marriage. The second viewpoint is that such acts are lawful. Given a lawful act, consent or lack thereof is meaningless. A man may be found guilty of rape upon his wife, however, when he acts as an accessory to another man performing the act of carnal knowledge.

Carnal knowledge is the legal term meaning sexual intercourse, and common law usually required that penetration be established or proven, however slight. The element "female" needs little discussion, because under common law it was generally deemed that a man could not be the victim of a rape. An important exception to this principle should be noted under statutory law, since many states now provide that a male can, in effect, be raped. These statutes are frequently termed sexual assault rather than rape. A female can also be charged with rape, using the accessory principle noted earlier under the first element of rape.

The element of "by force" is usually met by proof of a threat of force or violence, and by the fact that the threat must be of immediate personal injury, rather than at some future time. A threat to the victim's property will not meet this element. A frequent problem with this element is whether the victim provided any resistance and if so, in what amount. Generally, it is deemed that, if no resistance is offered, it cannot be said that the intercourse was forced. Today, the majority interpretation of resistance is that each victim will be measured according to her ability considering age, strength, health, and other circumstances surrounding the act.

The element of "against her will" is generally established or proven by showing that the act did not involve the consent of the victim. Consent may be a defense to the charge if the victim is of legal age and has the mental capacity to give consent. Numerous problems are encountered with this element, based on local interpretations by the courts of statutes in a particular jurisdiction.

Consent is important, though, in cases of so-called statutory rape. This is an example of a law protecting a victim from herself. Statutes provide a legal capacity to consent to sexual intercourse at a particular age: the specific age varies widely among jurisdictions. Essentially, the age of consent statute deprives a person of the very ability to permit this form of touching. All acts of sexual intercourse with a woman below the age of consent thus become rape. These remarks should be considered further in connection with the defense of consent in Chapter 10. Such a defense is unavailable to one who has sexual intercourse with a person under the legal age of capacity to consent to that particular act.

Statutory rape is an offense that was not recognized at common law, because common law recognized that a female under the age of ten was deemed incapable of consenting to an act of intercourse. Under statutory rape, as generally defined by statute, the major elements of force and consent are not important. Consent by a female victim under the age specified in a state's statute cannot constitute a defense to the charge of statutory rape. Frequently a defense of mistake of fact is raised by the defendant, but generally the defendant is held to act at his own peril regardless of the apparent age of the victim.

Sample Statutes

Rape and Forcible Carnal Knowledge.
Whoever ravishes and carnally knows a female of the age of ten years or more, by force and against her will, or unlawfully or carnally knows and abuses a female child under the age of ten years, shall be punished by death, unless a majority of the jury in their verdict recommend mercy, in which event punishment shall be by imprisonment in the state prison for life, or for any term of years within the discretion of the judge. It shall not be necessary to prove the actual emission of seed, but the crime shall be deemed complete upon proof of penetration only.

Carnal Intercourse With Unmarried Person Under Eighteen Years.
1. *Any person who has unlawful carnal intercourse with any unmarried person, of previous chaste character, who at the time of such intercourse is under the age of eighteen years, shall be punished by imprisonment in the state prison for not more than ten years, or by fine of not exceeding $2000.*
2. *It shall not be a defense to a prosecution under this section that the prosecuting witness was not of previous chaste character at the time of the act when the lack of previous chaste character in the prosecuting witness was caused solely by previous intercourse between the defendant and the prosecuting witness.*

Carnal Intercourse With Unmarried Female Idiot.
Any male person who has carnal intercourse with an unmarried female, with or without her consent, who is at the time an idiot, lunatic, or imbecile, shall be deemed guilty of a felony, and, on conviction shall be punished by imprisonment in the state prison at hard labor for not exceeding ten years.

Rape.
(a) A male person of the age of 14 years and upwards who has sexual intercourse with a female, not his wife, by force and against her will, commits rape. Intercourse by force and against her will includes, but is not limited to, any intercourse which occurs in the following situations:
1. Where the female is unconscious; or

2. Where the female is so mentally deranged or deficient that she cannot give effective consent to intercourse.
(b) Sexual intercourse occurs when there is any penetration of the female sex organ by the male sex organ.

Deviate Sexual Assault.
(a) Any person of the age of 14 years and upwards who, by force or threat of force, compels any other person to perform or submit to any act of deviate sexual conduct commits deviate sexual assault.

Principal in the First Degree.
Whoever commits any criminal offense against the state, whether felony or misdemeanor, or aids, abets, hires, or otherwise procures such offense to be committed, is a principal in the first degree and may be charged, convicted and punished as such, whether he is or is not actually or constructively present at the commission of such offense.

Seduction
Seduction has developed as an offense by statute. The elements tend to vary for the offense, but they generally involve the enticing of an unmarried female to engage in sexual intercourse by some false promise, such as a promise to marry her. Usually the statutes require that the unmarried female be of a previous chaste character. It is usually required that the victim place some reliance on the false promise. Some of the states provide as a defense to the charge the fact that the parties subsequently married (if marriage was the originally false promise).

Incest
Incest is the act of sexual intercourse between persons related by blood. The offense is a crime in all states, and varies somewhat in terms of the closeness of the relationship prohibited. Sexual intercourse between immediate family members such as father–daughter, brother–sister, and mother–son are consistently prohibited.

Sample Statutes
Incest.
(a) Any person who has sexual intercourse or performs an act of deviate

sexual conduct with another to whom he knows he is related as follows commits incest:

1. Mother or son; or

2. Brother or sister, either of the whole blood or the half blood.

Aggravated Incest.

(a) Any male person who shall perform any of the following acts with a person he knows is his daughter commits aggravated incest:

1. Has sexual intercourse; or

2. An act of deviate sexual conduct.

(b) "Daughter" for the purposes of this section means a blood daughter regardless of legitimacy or age; and also means a stepdaughter or an adopted daughter under the age of 18.

Incestuous Marriages Prohibited.

A man may not marry any woman to whom he is related by lineal consanguinity, nor his sister, nor his aunt, nor his niece. A woman may not marry any man to whom she is related by lineal consanguinity, nor her brother, nor her uncle, nor her nephew.

Sodomy

Sodomy is defined at common law as being a sex act between a human being and an animal, or anal intercourse between human beings. These acts are popularly termed "crimes against nature."

Sample Statutes

Crime Against Nature

Whoever commits the abominable and detestable crime against nature, either with mankind or with beast, shall be punished by imprisonment in the state prison not exceeding 20 years.

Unnatural and Lascivious Act.

Whoever commits any unnatural and lascivious act with another person shall be punished by fine not exceeding $500 or by imprisonment not exceeding six months.

Abortion

Broadly speaking, abortion is a form of battery. Its specific aim is miscarriage, or the killing of a fetus. This is an offense that is difficult to discuss without confusion arising as to the identity of a victim. However, such concerns are unimportant in studying the offense. If the law has determined that intentional miscarriage is generally unacceptable, regardless of who the victim is, there can be an offense. Again, the offense is against a person because the expectant mother is unlawfully touched in some manner in the process.

A woman who aids another in performing an abortion on her own body may be guilty of abortion herself, through application of the law of parties. (See Chapter 4). This is another clear indication that the law will not recognize rights of the fetus in arriving at this result.

Some statutes have made the attempt to produce a miscarriage a substantive offense of abortion. This produces a situation in which it may be impossible to sustain a conviction for attempted abortion, which elevates an incomplete criminal activity to the status of a completed offense. If nothing else, this is an indication of the perceived seriousness of the offense. When even the attempt is treated as a complete offense, the behavior has considerable social disapproval.

Several states have recently passed legislation making certain types of abortion legal. Other states have reduced the sanction.

Sample Statutes

Abortion; Death of a Child.

Every person who shall administer to any woman pregnant with a quick child any medicine, drug, or substance whatever, or shall use or employ any instrument or other means, with intent thereby to destroy such child, unless the same shall have been necessary to preserve the life of such mother; or shall have been advised by two physicians to be necessary for such purpose, shall, in case the death of such child or of such mother be thereby produced, be deemed guilty of manslaughter.

Performing Abortion.

Whoever with intent to procure miscarriage of any woman unlawfully administers to her, or advises or prescribes for her, or causes to be taken by her, any poison, drug, medicine, or other noxious thing, or unlawfully uses any instrument or any other means whatever with the like intent, or with like intent aids or assists therein, shall, if the woman does not die in consequence thereof, be punished by imprisonment in the state prison not exceeding 7 years, or by fine not exceeding $1000.

Killing of Unborn Child by Injury to Mother.

The willful killing of an unborn quick child, by any injury to the mother of such child which would be murder if it resulted in the death of such mother, shall be deemed manslaughter.

Abortion.

Every person who shall administer to any woman pregnant with a quick child any medicine, drug, or substance whatever, or shall use or employ any instrument or other means, with intent thereby to destroy such child, unless the same shall have been necessary to preserve the life of such mother, or shall have been advised by two physicians to be necessary for such purpose, shall, in case the death of such child or of such mother be thereby produced, be deemed guilty of manslaughter.

Abortion.

(a) A person commits abortion when he uses any instrument, medicine, drug, or other substance whatever, with the intent to procure a miscarriage of any woman. It shall not be necessary in order to commit abortion that such woman be pregnant or, if pregnant, that a miscarriage be in fact accomplished. . . . (c) It shall be an affirmative defense to abortion that the abortion was performed by a physician licensed to practice medicine and surgery in all its branches and in a licensed hospital or other licensed medical facility . . . necessary for the preservation of the woman's life.

Fornication and Adultery

Although both offenses have greatly grown into disuse, many states still carry these offenses on their statute books. Fornication is defined as being sexual intercourse between two unmarried persons; adultery is usually defined as intercourse between a male and a female with at least one being married to someone else. States vary as to which party needs to be married to sustain the charge; as to whether both parties must be married; and as to whether the unmarried partner, if applicable, is liable to the charge of adultery. At common law, adultery was considered a serious offense because of the social harm caused by jeopardizing others' rights of inheritance.

Sample Statutes

Adultery.

(a) Any person who cohabits or has sexual intercourse with another not his spouse commits adultery, if the behavior is open and notorious, and

1. *The person is married and the other person involved in such intercourse is not his spouse; or*
2. *The person is not married and knows that the other person involved in such intercourse is married.*

Living in Open Adultery.

Whoever lives in an open state of adultery shall be punished by imprisonment in the state prison not exceeding two years, or in the county jail not exceeding one year, or by fine not exceeding $500. Whether either of the parties living in an open state of adultery is married, both parties so living shall be deemed to be guilty of the offense provided for in this section.

Fornication.

(a) Any person who cohabits or has sexual intercourse with another not his spouse commits fornication if the behavior is open and notorious.

Fornication.

If any man commits fornication with a woman, each of them shall be punished by imprisonment not exceeding three months, or by fine not exceeding $30. (The statutes make both parties equally guilty in fornication.)

Lewd and Lascivious Behavior.

If any man and woman, not being married to each other, lewdly and lasciviously associate and cohabit together, or if any man or woman, married or unmarried, is guilty of open and gross lewdness and lascivious behavior, they shall be punished by imprisonment in the state prison not exceeding two years, or in the county jail not exceeding one year, or by fine not exceeding $300.

Indecent Exposure

Indecent exposure is usually defined as the act of exposing oneself in an indecent manner in a public place. Local standards of indecency guide the enforcement of such a statute.

Sample Statutes

Exposure of Sexual Organs.

It shall be unlawful for any person to expose or exhibit his sexual organs in any public place or on the private premises of another, or so near thereto as to be seen from such private premises, in a vulgar or indecent manner, or so to expose or exhibit his person in such place, or to go or be naked in such place. Provided, however, this section shall not be construed to prohibit the exposure of such organs or the person in any place provided or set apart for that purpose. Any person convicted of a violation hereof shall be punished by a fine of not more than $500 or by imprisonment in the county jail for a period of not more than six months, or by both such fine and such imprisonment, in the discretion of the court.

Public Indecency.

(a) Any person of the age of 17 years and upwards who performs any of the following acts in a public place commits a public indecency;
1. An act of sexual intercourse; or
2. An act of deviate sexual conduct; or
3. A lewd exposure of the body done with intent to arouse or to satisfy the sexual desire of the person; or
4. A lewd fondling or caress of the body of another person of either sex.
(b) "Public place" for purposes of this section means any place where the conduct may reasonably be expected to be viewed by others.

Prostitution

Prostitution under common law is "the offering by a female of her body for sexual intercourse with men for gain." Some states have deviated from this common law definition and attempt to prohibit any indiscriminate sexual activity with several men regardless of the gain element. Offenses associated with prostitution are pandering; pimping; operation of bawdy houses; and the white slave traffic, or Mann Act. Only the latter offense is regulated at the federal level and is, in essence, a prohibition against "the interstate transportation of females for the purpose of prostitution or other immoral purposes." The other offenses are provided for at the state or local level. Pandering and pimping are usually defined as being synonymous and involve the procuring of females to work in a house of prostitution. The offense of operation of a bawdy house is the operation of a house of prostitution, which is deemed a public nuisance under common law. Most statutes today require that proof be obtained showing that the house involves several acts of prostitution.

Sample Statutes
Prostitution.
(a) Any person who performs, offers or agrees to perform any of the following acts for money commits an act of prostitution:
1. *Any act of sexual intercourse; or*
2. *Any act of deviate sexual conduct.*

Pandering.
(a) Any person who performs any of the following acts for money commits pandering:
1. *Any act of sexual intercourse; or*
2. *Arranges or offers to arrange a situation in which a female may practice prostitution.*

Pimping.
(a) Any person who receives money or other property from a prostitute, not for a lawful consideration, knowing it was earned in whole or in part from the practice of prostitution, commits pimping.

Keeping a Place of Prostitution.
(a) Any person who has or exercises control over the use of any place which could offer seclusion or shelter for the practice of prostitution who performs any of the following acts keeps a place of prostitution:
1. *Knowingly grants or permits the use of such place for the purpose of prostitution; or*
2. *Grants or permits the use of such place under circumstances from which he could reasonably know that the place is used or is to be used for purposes of prostitution; or*
3. *Permits the continued use of a place after becoming aware of facts or circumstances, from which he should reasonably know that the place is being used for purposes of prostitution.*

Procuring Female Under Age of Sixteen for Prostitution.
Whoever procures for prostitution, or causes to be prostituted, any unmarried female who is under the age of sixteen years shall be punished by imprisonment in the state prison not exceeding ten years.

Keeping House of Ill Fame.

Whoever keeps a house of ill fame, resorted to for the purpose of prostitution or lewdness, shall be punished by imprisonment not exceeding one year.

Soliciting for a Prostitute.

(a) Any person who performs any of the following acts commits soliciting for a prostitute:
1. *Solicits another for the purpose of prostitution; or*
2. *Arranges or offers to arrange a meeting of persons for the purpose of prostitution; or*
3. *Directs another to a place knowing such direction is for the purpose of prostitution.*

Patronizing a Prostitute.

(a) Any person who performs any of the following acts with a person not his spouse commits the offense of patronizing a prostitute:
1. *Engages in an act of sexual intercouse or deviate sexual conduct with a prostitute; or*
2. *Enters or remains in a place of prostitution with intent to engage in an act of sexual intercourse or deviate sexual conduct.*

False Imprisonment

False imprisonment, unlawful restraint, or false arrest are all essentially the same offense. The thrust of the offense is the thwarting of an individual's wishes to be or go where he wishes. Physical restraint of an individual is violative of personal interests, but other forms of restriction are not always so clear. A person is arrested when his freedom of movement is significantly restricted (when there is no physical restraint) and there is knowledge of that restraint on the victim's part.

The key to this offense is authority to keep the person restrained. Law enforcement officers have the clearest power to arrest, but even they may violate a false imprisonment statute if they exceed the authority granted.

Sample Statutes

Unlawful Restraint.

(a) A person commits the offense of unlawful restraint when he knowingly without legal authority detains another.

False Imprisonment and Kidnapping.

Whoever without lawful authority forcibly or secretly confines or imprisons another person within this state against his will, or confines or inveigles or kidnaps another person, with intent either to cause him to be secretly confined or imprisoned in this state against his will, or to cause him to be sent out of this state against his will; and whoever sells, or in any manner transfers, for any term, the service or labor of any other person who has been unlawfully seized, taken, inveigled or kidnapped from this state to any other state, place or county, shall be punished by imprisonment in the state prison not exceeding ten years.

Kidnapping

Kidnapping is a more serious form of false imprisonment. At common law, the aggravation consisted of removing the victim from his own country. In an era of relatively free international travel and passport protections, perhaps such an occurrence does not seem serious. However, the concept was developed before the citizen of one country had much protection of the laws of a foreign state.

Modern statutes designate kidnapping in a variety of ways. False imprisonment aggravated by youth of the victim, secret methods, demands for ransom, and use of weapons are some of the provisions used. Kidnapping was a misdemeanor at common law but is a felony under most statutes. The so-called Lindbergh Law provides federal criminal sanctions for kidnapping that involves or assumes interstate movement of the victim.

Sample Statutes

Kidnapping for Ransom.

Whoever, without lawful authority, forcibly or secretly confines, imprisons, inveigles or kidnaps any person, with intent to hold such person for a ransom to be paid for the release of such person, or any person who aids, abets or in any manner assists such person in the confining, imprisoning, inveigling or kidnapping of such person, shall be guilty of kidnapping a person and shall be punished by death, unless a majority of the jury shall recommend the defendant to the mercy of the court, in which event the punishment shall be by imprisonment for life in the state prison.

Kidnapping.
(a) Kidnapping occurs when a person knowingly:
1. *And secretly confines another against his will, or*
2. *By force or threat of imminent force carries another from one place to another with intent secretly to confine him against his will, or*
3. *By deceit or enticement induces another to go from one place to another with intent secretly to confine him against his will.*
(b) Confinement of a child under the age of 13 years is against his will within the meaning of this section if such confinement is without the consent of his parent or legal guardian.

Aggravated Kidnapping.
(a) A kidnapper within the definition [of the above statute] is guilty of the offense of aggravated kidnapping when he:
1. *Kidnaps for the purpose of obtaining ransom for the person kidnapped or from any other person, or*
2. *Takes as his victim a child under the age of 13 years, or*
3. *Inflicts great bodily harm or commits another felony upon his victim, or*
4. *Wears a hood, robe or mask or conceals his identity.*
As used in this Section, "ransom" includes money, benefit or other valuable thing or concession.

Abduction

The term "abduction" is used to cover a variety of activity and tends to be sometimes confused with kidnapping. Most legal historians identify the origins of the English statute as being for the protection of property interests from fortune-seekers.

The status of women as property, and the limited possibilities for their placement in the social structure if they did not marry, made it important that they be protected for prospective bridegrooms. A reputation for chastity was an important aspect of the economic worth of a woman. Thus, if a man took a woman away from her parent's custody and kept her away, he could effectively force her to marry him because she would not be suitable for another. An attempt to control such practices apparently spurred the passage of the original statute dealing with abduction.

Offenses of this nature are, in large part, a violation of property rights. But more than that, they protect an individual who is weak and must rely on the protection of another. By depriving a young woman of her parents' custody, one would deprive her of her own personal security. This, then, is the focus of such offenses.

Student Checklist

1. Can you list three classifications of criminal offenses?
2. How does homicide relate to murder?
3. Why was suicide a criminal offense in old common law?
4. How does "specific intent" contrast with "general intent" as an element of an offense?
5. Can you distinguish between assault and battery as offenses?
6. Are you able to define the elements of the offense of rape?
7. How do assault and battery contrast with the offense of mayhem?
8. How do you distinguish voluntary manslaughter from involuntary manslaughter?
9. Can you contrast false imprisonment, kidnapping, and abduction in terms of the social harm they prohibit?
10. Are you able to list five examples of manslaughter, identifying each as either voluntary or involuntary?

Topics for Discussion

1. Discuss the differences between the sample statutes on manslaughter.
2. Discuss the differences between assault and battery.

3. Discuss the intent element required for the various offenses against the person.

4. Discuss the five types of intent listed in the section on murder.

5. Discuss the differences between kidnapping, false imprisonment, abduction, and unlawful restraint.

ANNOTATED BIBLIOGRAPHY

Belli, Melvin. *The Law Revolution.* Vol. 1: *Criminal Law.* Los Angeles, Calif.: Sherbourne Press, 1968. The famous attorney presents a tour of American criminal law as viewed by a colorful practitioner. He contends that we are in a major revolution of the law and attempts to identify the trends of change.

Inbau, Fred E., and James R. Thompson. *Criminal Law and Its Administration.* Mineola, N.Y.: Foundation Press, 1970. An excellent casebook approach to criminal law with adequate commentary and analysis to serve the nonlegal student of the administration of justice.

Inbau, Fred E., James R. Thompson, and Claude R. Sowle. *Criminal Justice.* 3rd ed. Mineola, N.Y.: Foundation Press, 1968. A thorough, two-volume treatise of criminal law and criminal justice. The extensive experience of the authors is evident by their broad, comprehensive coverage of the foundation topics as well as of the contemporary issues facing the field today.

Klotter, John C., and Jacqueline R. Kanovitz. *Constitutional Law for Police.* 2nd ed. Cincinnati, Ohio: W. H. Anderson, 1971. A major resource for constitutional law issues associated with police practices. The text emphasizes procedural law but also serves as a foundation for substantive criminal law.

The study of this chapter will enable you to:

1. Distinguish real property from personal property.
2. List and define five elements of larceny under the common law.
3. Contrast the offense of robbery with the offense of larceny in terms of the elements required for each.
4. Describe how forgery varies from the offense of obtaining property under false pretenses.
5. Define the offense of embezzlement.
6. Describe the social utility of receiving and concealing stolen property statutes.
7. Identify differences between robbery and larceny from the person.
8. Describe the offense of counterfeiting.
9. Describe how modern-day statutes for larceny and theft vary from their common law predecessors.
10. Contrast the offense of extortion with robbery.

6

Offenses Against Property

A discussion of property offenses should properly begin with the distinction between real and personal property. *Real property* is land, buildings, and other things that are permanently attached to land. A tree, for example, is real property. Once a tree has been cut or removed from the land, it becomes firewood or lumber (forms of personal property). But it is real property as long as it remains literally attached to the land. Real property is *not* simply any property that is tangible or "real"; instead, it is realty or land. *Personal property* is all property other than real property; it need not have any particular monetary value or form. It is not all property in which there is a personal interest.

Occasional confusion stems from the nature of property rights. Because an interest in real property belongs to an individual, there is a tendency to mislabel such interests as personal property. But it is the nature of the property itself, and not its ownership, that is significant in distinguishing between real and personal property.

Mineral rights are real property interests. When oil is still underground, it is part of the land and subject to control by whoever owns the rights to use the land. When the oil is pumped out of the ground, it becomes the personal property of whoever owns the right to possess and enjoy the goods—in this case, oil. Although both mineral rights and the product itself may be bought and sold, the former is real property and the latter personal property.

Ownership of personal property may be shared by more than one person. Again, the nature of the property is described by the term "per-

117

sonal." This fact does not mean that it must be the exclusive right of any one person. Several people may share ownership of personal property.

Because of the differences in the nature of real and personal property, differences in the laws protect the various interests associated with the two types of property. Chapter 7 illustrates the law regarding those particular portions of real property used as dwellings. For the most part, other transgressions against real property rights are settled in civil courts rather than criminal courts.

Offenses against property are offenses against the rights of individuals to that property. This does not mean, as indicated previously in Chapter 5, that property crimes are against persons simply because interests are personal or because there is a victim. The point is that the offense is not strictly against the *article of* property itself, but against an interest or right in that property. It is the right to the person's use and enjoyment that is violated.

A property crime may be committed against one who has only a temporary interest in the article. Consider this example:

> *Paines rents an automobile to Byrd for a period of 24 hours. During the rental period, Smith steals the car. There is an offense against the property interest (rental agreement) of Byrd. Even if the car is returned before the end of the rental period, the offense against property can be sustained. If Smith keeps the car beyond the expiration of the rental period, there is an offense against the property rights of Paines as well.*

Property, therefore, is more a matter of rights than a description of goods. The offenses against property are directed against the interests of lawful possession as well as against ultimate ownership.

It is the nature of interest protected by crimes against property that provides a most persuasive reason for the existence of such crimes. The law provides a measure of predictability to those who wish to preserve interests in goods. Business and commerce are protected by property crimes. To some extent, social order is provided by legal devices that make an individual secure beyond his own ability to protect the fruits of his efforts. Here, it may be wise to recognize private property as a concept not shared by all groups of men. But, where private property is recognized, it is given legitimacy by the laws regarding property crimes. As each separate offense is examined, remember that it is personal property that is protected by these offenses.

Larceny is the taking and carrying away of property with intent to permanently deprive the owner of it. It was a felony at common law. All elements must be established or there is no larceny. These elements are: (1) A taking (2) and carrying away (3) of the property of another (4) with the intent (5) to permanently deprive.

The taking element must not be confused with the carrying away element. Taking is nothing more than the exercise of control over an article without authority, and in conflict with the rights of another to possession. Thus, merely laying hands on an article may establish the taking. But there need not be a direct physical contact; a taking could also be accomplished by covering the article with another article, such as a garment. An example would be the following:

> In a public washroom, Lamb removes his wristwatch and washes his face and hands. As Lamb turns and reaches for a towel, Trapp drops another towel over Lamb's watch with intent to steal the watch when he picks up the towel. This act would be sufficient to establish a taking, although it would not yet amount to theft because there is no carrying away. Trapp has exerted his own control over the property of Lamb.

Some actual movement of the goods is required for the element of carrying away to constitute larceny, regardless of how slight. In the example cited, if Trapp pulled the towel toward himself and thus moved the watch, however slightly, the larceny would be complete. Problems of proving intent and practical considerations might preclude a prosecution for larceny if Lamb then removed the towel and recovered his watch, but the offense would nevertheless be complete and could be successfully prosecuted.

One student reaction to the example might be: "What if Trapp said he thought it was his watch or that he did not know it was under his towel?" The student is referred to Chapter 10 regarding mistake-of-fact defenses, with the suggestion that a dishonest mistake, no matter how reasonable, will not excuse.

Proof of intent is always a difficult problem. In the absence of a confession or admission, intent must be established by circumstantial evidence and remains a question of fact for the jury. If a reasonable inference from the surrounding factual circumstances can be drawn, and if that inference is intent to permanently deprive whoever is lawfully in possession of his goods, there is a larceny (provided that taking and carrying away are also established).

An intention to temporarily use goods and return them to the owner will not provide the basis for a larceny prosecution. Although there was no similar lesser included offenses at common law, the taking with intent to temporarily deprive the owner may be made a criminal offense by statute. However, when the intended deprivation essentially contradicts the rights of ownership or possession, intent to permanently deprive may be found.

Sample Statutes

Theft.

A person commits theft when he knowingly obtains or exerts unauthorized control over property of the owner and

1. *Intends to deprive the owner permanently of the use or benefit of the property; or*
2. *Knowingly uses, conceals, or abandons the property in such manner as to deprive the owner permanently of such use or benefit; or*
3. *Uses, conceals, or abandons the property knowing such use, concealment, or abandonment probably will deprive the owner permanently of such use or benefit.*

Theft of property not from the person and not exceeding $150 in value is a Class A misdemeanor. A second or subsequent offense after a conviction of any type of theft is a Class 4 felony. Theft of property from the person or exceeding $150 is a Class 3 felony.

Larceny.

1. *A person who, with intent to deprive or defraud the true owner of his property or of the use and benefit thereof, or to appropriate the same to the use of the taker, or of any other person:*
   (a) *Takes from the possession of the true owner, or of any other person; or obtains from such person possession by color or aid of fraudulent or false representations or pretense, or of any false token or writing; or obtains the signature of any person to a written instrument, the false making whereof would be punishable as forgery; or secretes, withholds, or appropriates to his own use, or that of any person other than the true owner, any money, personal property, goods and chattels, thing in action, evidence of debt, contract, or property, or article of value of any kind;*

2. *If the property stolen is of the value of $100 or more, the offender shall be deemed guilty of grand larceny, and upon conviction thereof shall be punished by imprisonment in the state penitentiary not exceeding five years, or in the county jail not exceeding 12 months, or by fine not exceeding $1000.*
3. *If the value of the property stolen as mentioned in the preceding section is less than $100, the offender shall be deemed guilty of petit larceny and upon conviction, shall be punished by imprisonment in the county jail not exceeding 6 months or by fine not exceeding $300.*

Larceny from Persons

An aggravated form of larceny exists when property is taken from the person of the victim or from his immediate area of control. Pickpockets are the clearest examples of cases covered by this offense. As with all aggravated forms of offenses, the penalty is usually greater for larceny from the person.

In our example of larceny in a public washroom, it is possible to argue that the taking was from the person of Lamb, but the example would be much clearer if Trapp had severed the band while the watch was on Lamb's wrist or if he had taken the watch from Lamb's pocket.

Robbery
A more serious form of larceny is robbery. Robbery is a larceny from the person by means of force or violence. The elements of robbery are usually identified as: (1) a larceny (five elements) (2) from the person of another (3) by force or threat of force.

To establish robbery it is not necessary that a deadly weapon be used. Larceny from the person is accomplished in secret or by stealth; robbery is an open and violent transgression of one's property rights. Therefore, it is a mistake to consider robbery a crime against persons. Its essence is the violation of property rights, and the property crime is aggravated by what might be an assault or a battery.

If a robbery is accomplished with use of certain deadly weapons, it may be subject to even more severe punishment as "armed robbery." Other forms of aggravation that are frequently considered by statute to compound the offense are concealment of the perpetrator's identity and the status of the victims. Care must be exercised to avoid confusion of armed robbery with so-called strong-arm robbery. The latter is simple robbery.

In all cases of robbery the fundamental offense is larceny, and the offense is deemed more serious because of attendant circumstances or means by which the larceny is accomplished.

Sample Statutes

Robbery.

Whoever, by force, violence, or assault or putting in fear, feloniously robs, steals, and takes away from the person or custody of another, money or other property which may be the subject of larceny, shall be punished by imprisonment in the state prison for life or for any lesser term of years, at the discretion of the court.

Robbery.

a. A person commits robbery when he takes property from the person or presence of another by the use of force or by threatening the imminent use of force.
b. Sentence.
Robbery is a Class 2 felony.

Armed Robbery.

a. A person commits armed robbery when he violates Section 18–1 while armed with a dangerous weapon.
b. Sentence.
Armed robbery is a Class 1 felony for which an offender may not be sentenced to death.

Extortion

Extortion was a common law misdemeanor, directed more at public officials' conduct than at protection of property rights, but statutes have provided expansions to make the offense a property crime. One crime ordinarily contemplated by extortion statutes is blackmail. Another crime is larceny by means of an implicit threat, which does not amount to a robbery.

A threat to expose something about an individual that would prove embarrassing to him is deemed blackmail. The threatened exposure may or may not be of something illegal, and the individual threatened may or may not actually be guilty, or the facts be true. The law represents a protection of property against larceny by means of threats to character or reputation.

Extortion under common law consisted of the following elements: (1) An unlawful fee (2) collected (3) under cover of office (4) by a public official (5) with intent to be corrupt.

Under statutory provisions, the usual elements are simply the obtaining of money or something of value under a threat. The threat is usually less than the threat necessary for robbery.

Similarly, communications that only imply threats may be covered by extortion statutes. A statement such as: "Accidents sometimes happen. It would be too bad if you had an accident. Don't you think you should have insurance?" is perfectly innocent on its face. But, under certain circumstances, it can produce fear or apprehension, and result in a payment for "protection." Thus, two areas not specifically covered by robbery prohibitions are called extortion and made crimes.

Sample Statutes

Extortion.

Whoever, either verbally or by written or printed communication, maliciously threatens to accuse another of any crime or offense, or by such communication maliciously threatens an injury to the person, property, or reputation of another, or maliciously threatens to expose another to disgrace, or to expose any secret affecting another, or to impute any deformity or lack of chastity to another, with intent thereby to extort money or any pecuniary advantage whatsoever, or with intent to compel the person so threatened, or any other person, to do any act or refrain from doing any act against his will, shall be punished by imprisonment in the state prison not exceeding 10 years.

Theft (common law extortion).

A person commits theft when he knowingly obtains by threat control over property of the owner, and:

1. Intends to deprive the owner permanently of the use or benefit of the property; or

2. *Knowingly uses, conceals, or abandons the property in such manner as to deprive the owner permanently of such use of benefit; or*

3. *Uses, conceals, or abandons the property knowing such use, concealment, or abandonment probably will deprive the owner permanently of such use or benefit.*

(e) Sentence.

1. *Theft of property not from the person and not exceeding $150 in value is a Class A misdemeanor. A second or subsequent offense after a conviction of any type of theft is a Class 4 felony.*

2. *Theft of property from the person or exceeding $150 is a Class 3 felony.*

"Threat" means a menace, however communicated to do one of the following:

1. Inflict physical harm on the person threatened or any other person or on property.
2. Subject any person to physical confinement or restraint.
3. Commit any criminal offense.
4. Accuse any person of a criminal offense.
5. Expose any person to hatred, contempt, or ridicule.
6. Harm the credit or business repute of any person.
7. Reveal any information sought to be concealed by the person threatened.
8. Take action as an official against anyone or anything, or withhold official action, or cause such action or withholding.
9. Bring about or continue a strike, boycott, or other similar collective action if the property is not demanded or received for the benefit of the group which an individual purports to represent.
10. Testify or provide information or withhold testimony or information with respect to another's legal claim or defense.
11. Inflict any other harm which would not benefit the offender.

Embezzlement

Our discussion has centered on the wrongful taking of goods. But what of cases in which property is lawfully in the temporary possession of a person, but is kept from its rightful owner when that temporary possessory right expires? One such case is embezzlement.

Embezzlement is the wrongful appropriation by a person to whom property is entrusted, an act which might be larceny except that there was no wrongful taking. It is a statutory offense only; it was not a crime at common law. (It first appeared in statute form in 1529.)

Embezzlement usually consists of the following elements: (1) The fraudulent conversion (2) of personal property of another (3) by a person entrusted with the property.

Creation of the crime of embezzlement is a recognition that an owner of property cannot be fully aware of the character and background of everyone to whom he entrusts property. It is one thing for a property owner to entrust goods to his own servant who is more or less under complete control; but it is another matter to impose liability for loss to an owner who relies on employees, in large organizations where there is relatively little direct control. As an example, compare the case of a farmer who entrusts a flock of sheep to a hired man with the case of a stockholder in General Motors who essentially entrusts funds to all the employees of the firm. The greater the complexity of economic relationships, the greater the need to protect interests of those whose goods are involved in productive activities.

Embezzlement is still an offense against property. Thus, no offense occurs until the person to whom the property has been entrusted actually withholds it from the rightful possession of another. An example might be the following:

> *John Carlson is an employee in the business of Henry Worth. Carlson receives all cash in behalf of the firm and accounts for it at the end of the day. One day, Carlson decides to pocket $500. He does so, but he changes his mind before the end of the day and replaces the $500 in the till. He is not guilty of embezzlement because he did not retain possession after his employer's demand for surrender of the funds.*

As a practical matter, it is difficult to establish a wrongful withholding of funds until the time for accounting. Some classes of persons, such as bank employees or public officials, may be specially treated by embezzlement statutes. Such treatment is merely a reflection of the relatively greater trust placed in such persons.

Sample Statutes
Embezzlement.

> *If any factor, commission merchant, warehouse keeper, wharfinger, wagoner, stage driver, or other common carrier on land or on water, or any other person with whom any property that may be the subject of larceny is entrusted or deposited by another, shall embezzle or*

fraudulently convert the same, or any part thereof, or the proceeds, or any part thereof, to his own use, or otherwise dispose of the same, or any part thereof, without the consent of the owner or bailor and to his injury, and without paying to him on demand the full value or market price thereof; or if, after a sale of any of the said property with the consent of the owner or bailor, such person shall fraudulently and without consent as aforesaid convert or embezzle the proceeds, or any part thereof, to his own use and fail or refuse to pay the same over to the owner or bailor on demand; and if any person borrows or hires property aforesaid and embezzles or fraudulently converts it or its proceeds, or any part thereof, to his own use, he shall be punished as if he had been convicted of larceny.

Secreting with Intent to Embezzle.
Whoever secretes with intent to embezzle or fraudulently conceals for his own use any property delivered to him which may be the subject of larceny, or any part thereof, shall be punished as if he had been convicted of larceny.

Fraudulent Sale of Personal Property by Lessee.
If the lessee of personal property sells or conveys it without the written consent of the owner or lessor, and without informing the person to whom it is sold or conveyed, that it is so leased, he shall be punished as if he had been convicted of larceny.

Embezzlement by Officer, Clerk, Agent, Servant, or Member of Company or Society.
If any officer, agent, clerk, servant, or member of any incorporated company, or if any officer, clerk, servant, agent, or member of any co-partnership, society, or voluntary association, or if any clerk, agent, or servant of any person embezzles or fraudulently disposes of, or converts to his own use, or takes or secretes with intent so to do, anything of value which has been entrusted to him, or has come into his possession, care, custody, or control by reason of his office, employment, or membership, he shall be punished as if he had been convicted of larceny.

Theft (common law embezzlement).
A person commits theft when he knowingly obtains or exerts unauthorized control over property of the owner and
1. *Intends to deprive the owner permanently of the use or benefit of the property; or*
2. *Knowingly uses, conceals, or abandons the property in such manner as to deprive the owner permanently of such use or benefit; or*
3. *Uses, conceals, or abandons the property knowing such use, conceal-*

ment, or abandonment probably will deprive the owner permanently of such use or benefit.

False Pretenses

If dishonest persons to whom goods are entrusted are to be punished, it is reasonable to punish those who engender a sense of trust by means of deception, who thereby induce owners to part with property. Essentially, such statutes prohibit obtaining property by lying or misrepresentation.

Obtaining property under false pretenses usually includes the following elements: (1) Knowingly (2) and designedly (3) obtaining the property of another person (4) by false representations (5) with intent to defraud.

Possibly the most significant area covered by this type of statute is the "bad check" case. In other ways, people may be protected against other fraudulent practices that deprive them of property, such as "confidence games" or "bunco." Examination of the bad check case may be useful, because practices are frequently misunderstood.

The check represents an order to a bank directing payment of funds on deposit to a designated person. A check that is written in excess of the amount on deposit (if that situation is known to whoever draws the check) amounts to a misrepresentation as to the funds on deposit. Even though the "float" is a very widely recognized source of short-term credit, checks written without sufficient funds on deposit are technical violations of many statutes covering this topic. Any misrepresentation of fact, if made with fraudulent intent, will establish such offenses whether the lie is in writing or oral. Fraud requires a misleading of the victim. If the person to whom the false representation of fact is made is not actually misled, there is usually no basis for prosecution under this class of statutes.

Sample Statutes
Obtaining Property by False Personation:
Whoever falsely personates or represents another, and in such assumed character receives any property intended to be delivered to the party so personated, with intent to convert the same to his own use, shall be punished as if he had been convicted of larceny.

Theft (obtaining property by false pretenses).
A person commits theft when he knowingly obtains by deception control over property of the owner and
1. *Intends to deprives the owner permanently of the use or benefit of the property; or*
2. *Knowingly uses, conceals, or abandons the property in such manner as to deprive the owner permanently of such use or benefit; or*
3. *Uses, conceals, or abandons the property knowing such use, concealment, or abandonment probably will deprive the owner permanently of such use or benefit.*

Forgery

Another part of the "bad check" problem is that of forgery. Forgery can be accomplished by misrepresentation of identity or by alteration of an existing check. Check cases do not exhaust the scope of forgery, but are illustrative. Generally, forgery is applicable more widely than false pretenses. This is not because forgery applies to more types of documents, but because forgery also applies to documents affecting more than property interests.

Forgery, as a common law offense and a statutory offense, usually includes the following elements: (1) The making of a false writing or materially altering a document (2) having apparent legal significance (3) with intent to defraud.

When an individual draws a check, part of the representation is that he is who he purports to be. Someone who lies about his identity by signing someone else's name to a check is a forger. Similarly, if a genuine check is altered by one other than the drawer, to an amount greater than that for which is was drawn, there is a forgery. There is considerable public interest in suppression of forgeries because of the impossibility of investigating the truthfulness of all documents. "Uttering" (passing) forged instruments knowingly and fraudulently is discouraged for the same reasons.

Sample Statutes
Forgery.
Whoever falsely makes, alters, forges, or counterfeits a public record, or a certificate, return, or attestation of any clerk or register of a court,

public register, notary public, justice of the peace, town clerk, or any public officer, in relation to a matter wherein such certificate, return, or attestation may be received as a legal proof; or a charter, deed, will, testament, bond, or writing obligatory, letter of attorney, policy of insurance, bill of lading, bill of exchange, or promissory note, or an order, acquittance, or discharge for money or other property, or an acceptance of a bill of exchange or promissory note for the payment of money, or any receipt for money, goods, or other property, or any passage ticket, pass, or other evidence of transportation issued by a common carrier, with intent to injure or defraud any person, shall be punished by imprisonment in the state prison not exceeding ten years, or in the county jail not exceeding one year, or by fine not exceeding $5000 or by both such fine and imprisonment.

Forgery.
(a) A person commits forgery when, with intent to defraud, he knowingly:
1. *Makes or alters any document apparently capable of defrauding another in such manner that it purports to have been made by another or at another time, or with different provisions, or by authority of one who did not give such authority; or*
2. *Issues or delivers such document knowing it to have been thus made or altered; or*
3. *Possesses, with intent to issue or deliver, any such document knowing it to have been thus made or altered.*
(b) An intent to defraud means an intention to cause another to assume, create, transfer, alter, or terminate any right, obligation, or power with reference to any person or property,
(c) A document apparently capable of defrauding another includes, but is not limited to, one by which any right, obligation, or power with reference to any person or property may be created, transferred, altered, or terminated.

Counterfeiting

Counterfeiting is not properly classified as an offense against property; it is briefly presented here only to distinguish it from forgery. Counterfeiting the lawful money of a country was originally considered high treason. One who makes false money is undermining confidence in the government by creating a danger that lawful currency will be considerably devalued, even to the extent of becoming virtually worthless. In such extreme cases, economic chaos would result and the government itself could fail. This example is, of course, based on the assumption that a money economy exists and that the advantages of a single legal tender are recognized.

Sample Statute

Counterfeiting Coin; Having Ten or More Such Coins in Possession with Intent to Utter.

Whoever counterfeits any gold, silver, or any metallic money coin current by law or usage within this state, or has in his possession at the same time ten or more pieces of false money, or coin counterfeited in the similitude of any gold, silver, or metallic coin; current as aforesaid, knowing the same to be false and counterfeit, and with intent to utter or pass the same as true, shall be punished by imprisonment in the state prison for life, or for any term of years.

Theft Statutes

Without belaboring the historical development of the common law, common law larceny did not cover all of the situations regarding property misappropriation which have already been discussed. After considerable development of a patchwork set of offenses against property interests, some jurisdictions have combined all such offenses under statutes prohibiting theft, stealing, or larceny. Such efforts were aimed principally at the simplification of prosecutions by reducing the risk of errors in pleadings or evidence.

Grand theft is another statutory modification. Even in jurisdictions that do not separate most offenses by degrees, this sort of distinction is often drawn. The effect is to provide a more serious punishment for the more serious degree of theft. The distinction between grand theft and theft is the value of the property taken. A fair comment on the value is that it reflects no uniform figure but depends on the value considered important to those drafting the statute. For some items of property that are the frequent target of theft, such as automobiles or horses, specific auto theft or horse theft statutes provide that these acts are grand theft without consideration of value.

A deviation from common law provisions for theft is the state of Illinois's provision for "Theft of Labor or Services or Use of Property." This statute provides, in part, "A person commits theft when he obtains the temporary use of property, labor, or services of another which are available only for hire, by means of threat or deception or knowing that such use is without the consent of the person providing the property, labor, or services." Such a statute provides for a large gap in common law which normally recognized a cause of action in civil law for the theft of services.

Sample Statutes

Larceny of Hogs.
Whoever commits larceny by stealing any hog, the property of another, shall be punished by imprisonment in the state prison not less than two years nor more than five years.

Larcency of Automobiles.
The larceny of any automobile, motor truck, motorcycle, or motor scooter shall be deemed a felony and any person convicted thereof shall be punished by imprisonment in the state prison for a term not exceeding five years or by fine not exceeding $5000.

Theft of Lost or Mislaid Property.
A person who obtains control over lost or mislaid property commits theft when he:
1. *Knows or learns the identity of the owner or knows, or is aware of, or learns of a reasonable method of identifying the owner, and*
2. *Fails to take reasonable measures to restore the property to the owner, and*
3. *Intends to deprive the owner permanently of the use or benefit of the property.*

Receiving or Concealing Stolen Property

Statutory provisions dealing with knowingly receiving or concealing stolen goods are not strictly offenses against property interests. They are, however, aimed at the protection of property interests by reducing traffic in stolen goods, and making the fruits of theft more difficult to enjoy.

Receiving stolen property statutes usually require the following elements: (1) The property must have been stolen by another person (2) and must retain its character of stolen property at the time it is received, and (3) it must be received (4) with knowledge or wrongful intent.

The receipt of stolen goods is more commonly known as "fencing." It is not necessary to be involved in such traffic on a large scale to be guilty of such an offense. And knowledge of the stolen character of the goods may be inferred from various circumstances, such as missing serial numbers, bargain prices, and the like. Furthermore, payment for the stolen goods may not be required for conviction.

"Concealing" does not necessarily mean "hiding." It is the stolen character of the goods that is being concealed, and such concealment may occur in the open. The act of concealment is an exercise of control over the goods to tend to keep the goods out of the lawful owner's control.

Sample Statutes

Buying, Receiving, Concealing Stolen Property.
Whoever buys, receives, or aids in the concealment of stolen money, goods, or property, knowing the same to have been stolen, shall be punished by imprisonment in the state prison not exceeding five years, or by fine not exceeding $500.

Theft.
A person commits theft when he knowingly obtains control over stolen property knowing the property to have been stolen by another or under such circumstances as would reasonably induce him to believe that the property was stolen, and
1. *Intends to deprive the owner permanently of the use or benefit of the property; or*
2. *Knowingly uses, conceals, or abandons the property in such manner as to deprive the owner permanently of such use or benefit; or*
3. *Uses, conceals, or abondons the property knowing such use, concealment, or abandonment probably will deprive the owner permanently of such use or benefit.*

Destruction of Property

The offense of destruction of property is directed at an article of property itself as well as at the rights of possession. When property is destroyed or damaged, the value of possession is impaired. It would be absurd to suggest that the property itself is the focus of the law's protection, but there is physical damage, too.

Malicious mischief was the common law offense covering destruction of property. Some of the property that would be covered by such provisions is now within the scope of statutes, such as arson (see Chapter 7). If one takes the position that there is a legitimate social interest in the total resources of the community, it would be possible to punish this variety of "mischief," even without impairment of personal property rights.

Provisions to punish property destruction also afford a measure of security that would be missing from prohibition of misappropriation only. That is, the loss of use of property is to be discouraged even if it results in no benefit to whoever is responsible for the loss.

Sample Statutes

Criminal Damage to Property.

Any of the following acts shall be a Class A misdemeanor and any act enumerated in subsection (1) or (6) when the damage to property exceeds $150 shall be a Class 4 felony;

1. *Knowingly damages any property of another without his consent; or*
2. *Recklessly by means of fire or explosive damages property of another; or*
3. *Knowingly starts a fire on the land of another without his consent; or*
4. *Knowingly injures a domestic animal of another without his consent; or*
5. *Knowingly deposits on the land or in the building of another, without his consent, any stink bomb or any offensive smelling compound and thereby intends to interfere with the use by another of the land or building.*

Injuring Public Buildings or Structures.

Whoever wantonly, willfully, or maliciously shall mar, deface, injure, or mutilate the capitol, or any other public state, county, or municipal building or structure, or any church, synagogue, or any building used by a civic or charitable organization, or the contents or the walls thereof, or the fence, or the trees, or the grounds, or shall cause same to be done, shall be punished by imprisonment not exceeding 12 months, or by fine not exceeding $500.

Throwing Noxious Substances Against Buildings.

Whoever willfully and maliciously throws into, against, or upon any dwelling house, office, shop, or other building or vessel, or places therein or thereon any oil of vitriol, coal tar, or other noxious of filthy substance, with intent unlawfully to injure, deface, or defile such dwelling house, office, shop, building, or vessel, or any property therein, shall be punished by imprisonment not exceeding six months, or by fine not exceeding $300.

Student Checklist

1. Can you distinguish real property from personal property?
2. Do you know how to list and define five elements of larceny under the common law?
3. Are you able to contrast the offense of robbery with the offense of larceny in terms of the elements required for each?
4. Are you able to describe how forgery varies from the offense of obtaining property under false pretenses?
5. Can you define the offense of embezzlement?
6. Do you know how to describe the social utility of receiving and concealing stolen property statutes?
7. Do you know how to identify the differences between robbery and larceny from the person?
8. Can you describe the offense of counterfeiting?
9. Can you describe how modern-day statutes for larceny and theft vary from their common law predecessors?
10. Are you able to contrast the offense of extortion with robbery?

Topics for Discussion

1. Discuss the intent element required for each of the offenses against property.
2. Discuss the differences between larceny, larceny from the person, and robbery.

3. Discuss the differences between real and personal property in terms of how these differences affect what is required for the various property offenses.

4. Discuss evolutionary changes between common law larceny and modern-day theft or larceny statutes.

5. Discuss the problems of enforcement associated with each of the offenses covered in this chapter.

ANNOTATED BIBLIOGRAPHY

Chamelin, Neil C., and Kenneth R. Evans. *Criminal Law for Policemen.* Englewood Cliffs, N.J.: Prentice-Hall, 1971. An introductory level coverage of criminal offenses for the new or practicing officer. It avoids the case law approach.

Krislov, Samuel, *et al.* (eds). *Compliance and the Law: A Multi-Disciplinary Approach.* Beverly Hills, Calif : Sage Publications, 1972. A composite of behaviorally oriented articles that focus on the societal goal of compliance to standards established in law and the impact of criminal law toward reaching that goal.

Perkins, Rollin M. *Perkins on Criminal Law.* Mineola, N.Y.: Foundation Press, 1969. One of the more comprehensive textbooks on criminal law with primary emphasis on common law but with an adequate coverage of statutory law to identify the differences.

Weinreb, Lloyd L. *Criminal Law.* Mineola, N.Y.: Foundation Press, 1969. A casebook approach to criminal law and the inherent problems associated with administering the law. Several problems are posed the reader by the author along with case commentary. Sample legal forms and several supportive articles are presented to provide depth to the topic and some direct application of the criminal law, by use of legal forms and sample data.

The study of this chapter will enable you to:

1. Describe the offense of trespass.
2. Identify the difference between trespass and malicious trespass.
3. Describe what the prosecution must prove to establish the elements of entry in burglary.
4. Define "reasonable" as used in criminal statutes.
5. Describe the requirement of malice when specified for the intent element.
6. List the elements of breaking and entering.
7. Describe the elements of burglary (common law) not required for the offense of breaking and entering.
8. Distinguish legal title from possession, in terms of maintaining a trespass action.
9. List the elements of arson.
10. Define "affirmative demand" as used in criminal trespass statutes.

7
Offenses Against Habitation and Occupancy

Introduction . . . .

This chapter will deal with that group of offenses whose purpose it is to provide security against invasion of a man's home or property at common law. It will discuss the primary offenses against the right of a person to be secure in his home and on his property.

All state legislatures have deemed it necessary to enact criminal statutes and impose appropriate sanctions in varying degrees for the offenses against habitation and occupancy, commonly known as trespass, breaking and entering, burglary, and arson. The crimes vary in seriousness and thus in severity of sentence: from the least serious criminal trespass, which is the infringement upon another's property rights, to the more severe crimes of burglary and arson, which are considered offenses against the security of the household.

The criminal offenses against habitation and occupancy will be covered in their general order of severity and seriousness, beginning with trespass and following with the two closely related offenses of breaking and entering and burglary, and concluding with arson. First degree burglary is often considered the most serious of this class of offenses and usually carries the heaviest sanctions.

As in many statutory crimes, these criminal offenses are often broken down by statute into a number of degrees. In addition, statutes are usually grouped to allow offenses that are related to each other to have compatible sanctions. The sanctions and penalties that can be imposed increase in stepladder fashion depending upon the comparative severity of the crimes. There are numerous variations throughout the states with respect to the degrees or breakdown of the offenses and even to the

137

existence of statutory prohibitions. The student should become familiar with the statutory breakdown of offenses within his own state. Although the penalties and definitions of the degrees may vary considerably, the concepts and elements of the crimes remain generally constant throughout all jurisdictions.

The common law background of the general offense will first be discussed. Then, because statutes of each state have enlarged upon the common law definition of trespass, breaking and entering, burglary, and arson; a review will be made of the offenses in their various degrees. The review will center upon the elements of the crime, both at common law and by statute, and the elements will then be defined and discussed in some detail Sample statutes will be used to illustrate those complex and severe offenses that contain many elements and variations.

Trespass

Any direct interference with the possession of the property of another is a *trespass*. Trespass is generally considered to be an injury to another's possession of his property. The purpose of the trespass law is to prevent the unlawful and forcible invasion of an owner's possession of property, and to prevent the occasion for violence. A trespass may give rise to a right of the possessor to bring civil action for damages, or a trespass may give rise to a criminal prosecution. A trespass may be against another's possession of either real estate or personal property. Criminal trespass will be the subject of this section.

Although any unlawful physical invasion of another's property will constitute a civil trespass, those acts that are criminal in nature are limited by the extent and definition of the acts proscribed by the criminal statutes of each jurisdiction. Therefore, when one refers to an act as being a "trespass," there is a distinction between civil trespass and criminal trespass and, unless statutorily proscribed, a particular act will not constitute a criminal trespass.

Under the common law there could be no criminal responsibility for trespass unless the act was accompanied by violence and force of arms or tended to create a breach of the peace. At the present time a tendency to violence is not required to maintain the criminal action, and whether certain acts or conduct constitute criminal trespass depends upon the particular statute involved.

Although all of the offenses discussed in this chapter are trespassory in nature, the offenses, with the exception of trespass itself, are accompanied by aggravated circumstances They are generally subject to more severe penalties than the crime of trespass unaccompanied by violence or motives that do no more than threaten the owner's right to the undisturbed possession of his property.

A simple trespass, where criminally proscribed, is generally categorized as a misdemeanor and carries a possible sentence of a discretionary fine of not less than $1 and not more than $50, to which may, but need not, be added imprisonment for up to six months. The more serious offenses, such as first degree burglary, because of the frightening and often heinous nature of the offense by being a crime against the sanctity of the dwelling and the greater requirement of criminal intent, are classified as felonies. The defendant may be subject to fines of up to $1000 and mandatory prison terms of up to 20 years.

Because of the broad definitions of trespass, this section of the chapter will be devoted entirely to the review of those particular acts or conduct that are typically proscribed by statutes as "criminal trespass," and to related offenses that are generally categorized in the least serious category of crimes; namely, misdemeanors that are unaccompanied by aggravating circumstances or intent, which might change the offense to one of burglary, arson, or theft.

Particular Actions

Trespass to Land. The most common form of trespass is the wrongful invasion of another's land or the wrongful refusal to leave upon demand after lawful entry. The elements of the offense are generally the entry upon the land of another after having been forbidden to do so by the owner or his agent, or the refusal to depart from the land of another after having been notified to depart therefrom by the owner or his agent. The required elements to show a criminal trespass are: (1) a wrongful act by the defendant that disturbs or contests an owner's possession of his property, and (2) some affirmative demand by the owner or his agent not to disturb the possession of the property. The requirement of the third element of criminal intent varies from jurisdiction to jurisdiction. In jurisdictions where a particular intent is mentioned as an element of the offense, that intent is essential to the conviction. Thus, where terms such as "knowingly," "willfully," or "maliciously" are used to describe the manner in which the wrongful act is carried out, the state must prove not only the affirmative demand and wrongful act, but also that the act was carried out in the manner described by the statute. In jurisdictions where criminal intent is not required, the mere showing of demand and wrongful act will support a conviction for criminal trespass. The underlying theory is that a person intends to do that which he in fact does, and the intentional or voluntary disregarding of the owner's demand indicates a criminal intent.

Another common statutory criminal trespass is the prohibition against entering onto another's farmland when a printed or written notice forbidding or prohibiting trespass in general has been conspicuously posted or exhibited at the main entrance to the farmland. Thus, under the language of these statutes it is not necessary to show a demand directed personally and specifically to the intruder. The intruder is held to the knowledge that the owner has prohibited trespassing and is considered to have received a demand to not disturb the owner's possession of his property, by the general act of the owner's posting the requisite sign at the entrance onto his farmland.

Because the offense of criminal trespass is generally considered to be one against possession, it is not necessary to show legal title or possession of the property in the complaining witness as long as that person is in possession of, and has a right to, the property. The possessor may be someone other than the owner, such as a tenant, renter, or lessee.

If the demand to leave the property is made while the trespasser is on the property and he fails to depart within a reasonable time after notice to do so, he is guilty of a criminal trespass. "Reasonable time" is the time and manner in which a reasonably prudent person with ordinary sensibilities and intelligence would leave the property. If the trespasser remains for an "unreasonable" period prior to leaving and after demand to do so, he is guilty under the statute.

Because an adjoining land owner is generally considered to own up to the middle of a public highway that abuts his property, an interesting situation occurs with respect to public highways. Therefore, refusal of a third person to depart from a public highway upon demand by the abutting property owner to do so, when that person is on the owner's side of the street, is a criminal trespass under most statutes.

Another unusual situation is presented with respect to an occupant's rental of an apartment where the lease contains no provision against subletting and the lessee sublets to a third person. The sublessee has committed no trespass when he fails to leave upon demand of the owner, because the sublessee is lawfully in possession of the property. Also, when one is allowed into the first lessee's apartment or residence by the occupant and over the objections of the title owner, that person is not a trespasser under the statute, because the offense is one against peaceful possession.

Insofar as intent is required under some statutes, it is a defense to an action of criminal trespass if the offender is upon the owner's property in the bona fide belief that he has a legal right to be there. Thus, if someone takes possession of land under a good faith claim of ownership, he is not liable to criminal prosecution for trespass (although he may be liable to a civil action in trespass). In addition, if there is no demand to leave or not to enter, a simple entry upon another's land without permission with nothing more is not a criminal trespass. However, if an individual is invited onto property by the owner and thereafter the owner demands that he depart, a refusal to do so will constitute a trespass. In addition to a good faith belief, and consent by the occupier, an accused person is not guilty of a trespass if he is justified in entering another's property, such as when one enters reasonably to remove a danger to a community (i.e., to fight a fire).

Malicious Trespass. The common trespassory crime of malicious trespass involves injury to either the land or personal property of another. The elements of the offense are: (1) a malicious or mischievous intent, (2) an injury to another's property, and (3) the injury caused by the wrongful act of the defendant. The offense is generally categorized as a misdemeanor, but it may involve a more severe sentence than that applicable to the simple trespass without malicious intent or injury to property.

"Malice" is an essential ingredient of this offense; it need only be shown that an act was committed wrongfully and intentionally and without just cause or excuse, to prove malice. The property that is injured may be either real estate or personal property. As animals are considered to be personal property, if one shoots another's dog, cat, cow, or horse wherever that animal may be located at the time of the shooting, a criminal action for malicious prosecution may exist. But, because malice is an essential element, an act that is performed in good faith or with justification cannot constitute a malicious trespass.

Miscellaneous Offenses. Various other acts have, by statute, been declared criminal trespass. These acts include the entering on land and removing or injuring products of the soil or structures on land; distruction of vines or trees; the removal of stone, timber, or other valuables; landmarks; the defacing or disturbing of graves or tombstones; the defacing of library books or public records; interference with utility meters; and so forth. The extent of the offenses, in terms of what acts are specifically prohibited, depends upon the legislature. In some areas, it has even been determined that anyone who gathers cranberries from any public land between the first day of May and the fifteenth day of September is guilty of a misdemeanor!

Summary
The group of criminal offenses related to criminal trespass encompasses a wide diversity of acts against peaceful possession of property: it defies a uniform definition. The most widespread and well known offenses are acts against real estate in spite of the demands of those rightfully in possession of it. However, a trespass may also be committed against personal property, as in a malicious trespass. The statutory laws of the student's particular jurisdiction should be referred to, to determine the specific offenses defined in his state.

Breaking and Entering

Unlike trespass, which is considered an offense against possession and (in the absence of aggravating circumstances or injury) is treated as a misdemeanor, the closely related offenses of burglary and breaking and entering are historically considered offenses against the security of habitation, which exact much heavier penalties. Under common law the prospects of a trespasser or felon breaking the security of one's household required much more severe treatment than the mere trespass to land. The elements of a burglary were (1) the breaking (2) and entering (3) of the dwelling house (4) of another (5) in the nighttime (6) with the intent to commit a felony therein.

Every jurisdiction now has statutorily broadened the crime and categorized it into degrees, with the penalties for the breach of the various degrees varying with the extent of the offensiveness of danger to the household. All six elements were required to prove a burglary at common law because the breaking and entering of another's house with the intent to commit a felony during the daytime was not as horrifying as such an act committed in the nighttime. At night the building would be invariably occupied by the sleeping members of the householder's family, and there would be greater prospects not only of crimes against the property, but also against the family members. This situation would require stricter penalties than those meted out to mere trespassers. The courts and, later, the legislatures therefore began to categorize the various crimes involving breaking and entering, not only of households, but other buildings and structures. The penalties generally depended upon the extent of the threat to the sanctity of the home and property and to the life and limb of the owners or occupants.

Today, categorization of these offenses, as in trespass, varies considerably from state to state. It is necessary to discuss the categorization in general terms, by using some examples, because of the many variations from jurisdiction to jurisdiction. But, the primary elements of the offenses remain the same and the variations relate to statutory definitions and penalties.

Because breaking and entering is often not only an offense of and by itself, but it also constitutes two elements of the crime of burglary and its various degrees, an analysis will first be made of this offense.

Definition

Breaking and entering is the act and crime of breaking and entering of the enclosed property of another. The property may be a dwelling house, shed, barn, business building, garage, or even an automobile—as long as it is necessary for the offender to break and enter in order to violate or offend its sanctity.

There are also further breakdowns of the offense into statutes that make it a crime only to enter certain structures with criminal intent, an act that makes the issue of breaking irrelevant. For example, many statutes provide for the offense of "entering to commit a felony" and provide that whoever enters any dwelling house or other place of human habitation, business house, outhouse, shop, office, storehouse, warehouse, mill, distillery, pottery, factory, barn, stable, schoolhouse, church, meeting house or any building used for religious worship, booth, tent, enclosed ginsing garden, boat, wharf-boat or other watercraft, car, factory, freight house, station house, depot, railroad car, interurban or streetcar, or any other erection or enclosure, with the intent to commit a felony therein will be subject to imprisonment of not less than one nor more than ten years.

The elements of this offense are (1) the entering (2) of an enclosure of any type (3) with the intent to commit a felony therein. The common law burglary element of breaking in the nighttime and the requirement that the structure is a household are unnecessary to the condition of this particular criminal act. Thus, the purpose of such legislation is to provide punishment for acts that fall short of being burglary under the common law, but that still require more deterrents and punishment than are provided under the misdemeanor trespass statutes.

When the further element of breaking is present, the penalty becomes more severe. For example, statutory law criminalizes housebreaking or breaking and entering in many states by providing that whoever, in the daytime, breaks and enters into any dwelling house, kitchen, smokehouse, outhouse, shop, stable, streetcar, and so forth, with intent to commit the crime of larceny shall be subject to imprisonment of not less than 1 nor more than 14 years. Other statutes provide the same penalties for related offenses of breaking and entering with the intent to commit other felonies, misdemeanors, or any personal abuse, force, or violence.

The elements of the offense of breaking and entering are generally (1) a breaking in (2) and entering (3) of an enclosure owned by another (4) with criminal intent.

Breaking

At common law, there had to be the creation of a breach, or opening, of a structure in order to constitute a breaking. Moreover, the owner or occupant of a structure or dwelling was not entitled to the protection of law if he himself had created the opening because he himself had not properly secured his structure of the dwelling. One should not be punished who had been invited in any way to enter the dwelling.

To constitute a breaking, the offender must make a trespassory entry involving the creation of an opening into the dwelling. There must be a breaking, putting aside, or moving of something material that constitutes a part of the building and is relied on as a security against intrusion. The breaking may be into any part of the building and need not be from the outside. It is sufficient if a door to an inner room is opened.

However, the breaking may be either actual or constructive. The breaking required must either involve the application of force or constitute a constructive breaking. In order to find an actual breaking it is only necessary to have any force at all, however minimal, that effects an entrance through any usual or unusual place of entry, whether open, partly open, or closed.

It is not necessary that a portion of the structure be physically broken to constitute a legal breaking The turning of a knob, the lifting of a latch, or the pushing aside of a partially open door or curtain is sufficient. The breaking of a door inside the building is sufficient, even though actual entry into the building was made without a breaking.

Employees, servants, or lodgers have committed a breaking if they exceed their rights with respect to the time or manner of entry, such as breaking into other parts of the building where they have no right to enter or conspiring to allow others into the building for the purpose of committing a criminal act.

Breaking does not imply actual injury to the building but includes the putting aside of any material part of the building intended as a security against invasions, such as removing a window screen, breaking a canvas shutter, or opening a closed door.

Constructive breaking may be found under circumstances in which force is not used to make way for an entry. One type of constructive breaking is through the use of trick or artifice, such as concealing one's self in boxes or furniture; entering under false pretenses, such as claiming to be a police officer; or conspiring with someone who has access to the dwelling to let another into the building. Thus, constructive breaking occurs where there is no actual forcible break of the enclosure but rather where entry is made by fraud, threats, or confederacy with someone who has a right to be in the building. The rationale behind the doctrine of constructive breaking is that an invasion for criminal purposes by one means or another is equally abhorred in the eyes of the law. Art, cunning, connivance, and circumvention imply a forcible breaking of the barrier erected for the security of the building.

Entering

Following the breaking there has to be an entry. Entering is the act of entering a building after a break has been completed. Any entry at all would be sufficient. Thus, if one inserts a hand, a foot, or any instrumentality (a hook, pipe, or gun), or sends a child or animal into the building with which it is intended to commit a crime, the act of entry is completed. The least entry of any part of the body or any instrumentailty is sufficient to constitute an entry. It is not necessary for the act of entry immediately to follow the breach of the structure, to constitute a breaking and entering. For example, one may cut a hole into a building one day and the entrance need not be made until the next day. The act would nevertheless consummate the offense of breaking and entering.

The essential entry is a trespass and generally must be into some part of the building. It is necessary that the person, some part of his body, or some instrumentality be put within the building; and that it be inserted for the purpose of committing or aiding in the commission of a crime.

Examples of entries are the boring of a hole into a granary for the purpose of removing the grain through the hole(s) bored with the aid of gravitation; the insertion of a gun through an open window to injure an occupant of the building; the operation of a pump handle to cause gasoline to be expelled from a tank; the entry into a chimney with the intent to steal in the building, although one does not get into any of the rooms. In some jurisdictions the discharge of a firearm into a building is a sufficient entry.

As in breaking, when someone with the right to be in a place enters at a time or place beyond his authority, or conspires with another to allow entry to commit a crime, that person may be guilty of breaking and entering.

Burglary

As noted earlier, burglary and related offenses are considered offenses against the security of habitation rather than against mere possession and, as in the offense of breaking and entering, stautory law has tended to categorize a number of degrees of burglary depending upon the presence, lack of, or variation of the various elements of the offense. Punishment is graded according to the circumstances.

The statutory definitions and categorizations vary substantially from state to state, and the diversity is chaotic. The student must realize that the law, as outlined in this text, can cover only the general elements of the variations and degrees of the crime of burglary. The examples cited may not be totally accurate in all jurisdictions.

At common law burglary was a breaking and entering of the dwelling house of another in the nighttime with the intent to commit a felony therein. Statutory enactment of burglary laws varies greatly: many states distinguish between first degree burglary and second degree burglary, based upon whether the act was committed in the nighttime or in the daytime. Other statutes make no distinction with respect to the time of the commission of the crime; instead they distinguish the degrees based upon the character of the building that is broken into or the intent of the defendant at the time of the breaking. For example, the statute defining the degrees of burglary may have the following provisions and penalties for first, second and third degree burglary.

Sample Statute

1. *Whoever breaks and enters into any dwelling house or other place of human habitation with the intent to commit any felony therein, or to do any act of violence of injury to any human being, shall be guilty of burglary in the first degree, and on conviction thereof shall be imprisoned not less than 10 years nor more than 20 years and be disfranchised and rendered incapable of holding any·office of trust or profit for any determinate period.*

2. *Whoever breaks and enters into any boat, wharf-boat, or other watercraft, interurban car, streetcar, railroad car, automobile, airplane, or other aircraft, or any building or structure other than a dwelling house or place of human habitation, with the intent to commit a felony therein, shall be guilty of burglary in the second degree, and upon conviction shall be imprisoned not less than 2 years nor more than 5 years and be disfranchised and rendered incapable of holding any office of trust or profit for any determinate period. Provided, however, that the court shall have power to suspend prison sentence and place the defendant on probation in accordance with existing law.*

3. *Whoever enters any dwelling-house or other place of human habitation, or any boat, wharf-boat, or other watercraft, interurban car, streetcar, railroad car, automobile, airplane, or other aircraft, or any building or structure, with the intent to commit a misdemeanor*

therein; or whoever enters or attempts to enter any enclosed lot,
parcel, or tract of land, with the intent to commit a felony thereon,
with intent to sever from the soil any crop or part of a crop, culti-
vated plant or plants, fruits, or any products growing thereon, or to
sever or remove any building, gate, fence, railing, or other structure,
shall be guilty of burglary in the third degree, and on conviction shall
be fined in any sum not exceeding $500, and may, at the discretion
of the court or jury, be imprisoned in the state farm for any deter-
minate period not exceeding 1 year. Provided, that the court shall
have the power to suspend sentence and place the defendant on
probation in accordance with existing law.

Under this statute burglary is broken down into three degrees of
varying aggravation with sentences varying from a mandatory imprisonment of 10 to 20 years for the offense of first degree burglary to a discretionary period of up to 1 year for third degree burglary. The categorization is dependent upon the type of structure broken into or entered
and the requisite intent at the time of the entry.

The elements of first degree burglary under this statute are (1)
breaking and (2) entering (3) any place of human habitation (4) with
the intent to commit a felony therein or do an act of violence to any
human being. The common law requirement that the offense be committed during the nighttime has been deleted from this statute although
many jurisdictions distinguish between first degree and second degree
burglary based upon the time of the offense. The time of the offense
under this statute is irrelevant. In addition, the sentence of imprisonment
is mandatory, cannot be suspended, and carries a severe penalty of 10 to
20 years.

Second degree burglary under the statute is defined as the (1)
breaking and (2) entering (3) of any building or structure other than a
place of human habitation (4) with the intent to commit a felony therein.
Again, there is no distinction as to when the offense must be committed,
and the primary distinction between first degree and second degree burglary under this statute is the type of structure that is being broken into.

The offense against familial habitation is classified as more serious
in nature because the home has always been more sacred than a building
where one does not keep his family; furthermore, the possibilities of
violence or violent injury are increased by the prospect of encountering
an occupant who might defend his home and family to a greater extent
than he would his business or personal property. Therefore, the potential
incarceration is two to five years for the lesser offense, and the court has

the power to suspend this sentence; but it may not suspend the 10 to 20 year term for the first degree burglary of a place of human habitation.

Under this statute there is a further classification of burglary into the third degree. The elements of third degree burglary are the (1) entering of (2) any building or structure (3) with the intent to commit a misdemeanor therein. An alternative offense is (1) the entry or attempt to enter (2) any parcel of land (3) with the intent to commit a felony thereon or to sever any part of a crop or products growing thereon or to sever or remove any structure or fence.

The statute also makes the time of the offense irrelevant and it omits the element of a breaking. It also distinguishes between the intent to commit a felony and the intent to commit a misdemeanor. Because the element of a breaking is absent and the offender intended to commit a crime in the far less serious classification of a misdemeanor, third degree burglary as defined here is considered a misdemeanor rather than a felony, as are its related offenses. The penalty imposed is a fine of up to $500 or imprisonment for up to one year, with the power to suspend sentence given to the court.

Definition

In general, in all jurisdictions the same elements are present in the prosecution for burglary, although the categorizations and requirements vary considerably. The primary elements now to be discussed are as follows: (1) breaking (2) entering (3) the dwelling house (4) of another (5) in the nighttime (6) with criminal intent or intent to commit a felony therein.

The definition of both breaking and entering in the offense of burglary remains the same as the separate, related offenses of breaking and entering in its various degrees. A breaking is sufficient if one moves or puts aside something material, an act that constitutes a part of the structure and is relied upon as a security against intrusion. An entry is made if any part of the body or instrumentality is inside the dwelling for the purpose of carrying out the criminal design Both the breaking and entering can be either actual or constructive as when accomplished through fraud, deceit, artifice, or conspiracy.

Dwelling House of Another. The dwelling house of another, or place of human habitation as it is often described, is a building habitually used as a place to sleep. These third and fourth requirements of the offense of common law burglary illustrate the fact that first degree burglary is an offense not merely against property, but against another's habitation and that the gist of the crime is the felonious invasion of a man's dwelling. Because the crime is primarily an offense against the security of the habitation, the character of the house is generally immaterial if it is occupied as a dwelling, but it must be actually occupied as such.

A dwelling house may therefore be defined as any kind of structure used as a place of habitation and occupied by persons other than the burglar. However, a temporary absence of the occupant does not deprive the dwelling house of its character as long as the occupant left the house with the intent of returning. An occupant need not remain constantly in the structure or be there at the time of the burglary. The length of his absence is unimportant if he actually intends to return. However, if one leaves a structure with the purpose of not returning, the structure loses its character as a dwelling house.

The following buildings or structures have been found to be dwelling houses under the statutes: an apartment, a room in a hotel, or a store or other place of business if someone regularly sleeps there. However, it is insufficient if someone, such as a night watchman, sleeps in the building only from time to time. If a building is regularly used as a residence during a certain time of the year, such as a summer cabin or home, it qualifies as a dwelling house even when not occupied, because the test is whether the occupant intends to return.

With respect to outbuildings, the test as to whether the structure qualifies as a dwelling house is if it is so directly and intimately connected with the habitation, and its use so essential to the enjoyment of the habitation, that every reason for protecting the one applies to the other.

Variations in statutes and the physical character of the outbuildings have led to varying results in the courts Structures that have been held not to be dwelling houses include stables, chicken houses, rabbit pens, smokehouses, and a tent. However, when these places are contiguous to the owner's habitation and there is a dwelling house to which the place belongs as a part thereof, they have also been held to constitute a dwelling house within the sense of the statute.

Generally, business or commercial buildings are not considered dwelling houses, nor are railroad cars, boats, and other structures not normally used as places of human habitation, unless someone regularly sleeps and lives there.

Occupancy rather than ownership controls the question as to whether the dwelling house is that of another. Although one could not commit a burglary against his own dwelling in the sense of the word occupancy, one could commit a burglary against his own dwelling in the sense of the term ownership. Thus, an owner of property could be found guilty of committing a burglary against his property when he rents it to a third person and the third person and his family make their household or dwelling in the rented property. If several people occupy the same building, none can commit a burglary against that building, because it is not the property of another unless portions of it have been set aside for one resident. In such a case any of the others can commit a burglary into that portion that has been set aside. As noted in the sample statute, the requirement that the structure be that of another has largely disappeared from the wording of burglary statutes. However, no court has ever ruled that a man can be convicted of burglary for entering his own home.

Nighttime. The term "nighttime" is subject to varying definitions, but it is the simplest of the elements of the offense of burglary to define. Although this element is not necessary under many state statutes, it was an essential element of the crime of burglary at common law and remains so in many jurisdictions. At common law nighttime was that period between sunset and sunrise when there was insufficient daylight to discern a man's face. If there was sufficient daylight to discern a man's face, the offense was not burglary, but the rule did not extend to artificial light or the reflection of light from the snow or the moon.

Although under statutes "nighttime" may be defined as the period between sunset and sunrise or dispensed with altogether, in the absence of provisions "nighttime" within the burglary definition remains the same as at common law.

Criminal or Felonious Intent. The final element required in any burglary prosecution is intent to commit some criminal act in the building. The intent required must be held at the time of the breaking and entry. At the time of breaking and entering, if the offender intends only to commit a simple trespass, he is not guilty of burglary, although he in fact commits a felony after he enters so long as the felonious intent was not held at the time of the breaking and entering. The offenses are graded in parts based upon the nature of the criminal intent possessed at the time of the breaking and entering. Because felonies constitute the most serious category of crimes, penalties for breaking and entering with felonious intent are more severe than are those for the intent to commit a crime that is categorized as a misdemeanor. The criminal intent must be to commit the contemplated crime within the building. Therefore, if one intended to pass through the building and commit an offense elsewhere, there would be no burglary.

There are only two means to determine whether one possesses criminal intent at a particular point in time. One may determine another's intent from what that person says he intends to do, or from what he, in fact, does. Therefore, one can judge another's intent only through his words and/or actions. At law an individual is presumed to have intended the natural consequences of his actions if proof to the contrary is absent.

If intent required substantive proof it would be almost impossible to convict without a showing of the completion of the crime, and the combination of the intent or the complete cooperation of the accused in acknowledging his intent. Therefore, the requisite criminal intent may be inferred from an offender's acts, conduct, and all other circumstances surrounding the breaking and entering.

Generally an unexplained breaking and entering into another's structure gives rise to an inference or even a presumption that the acts were done with the intent to commit larceny or some other felony. The fact that the offender was caught prior to completion of the crime is of no importance. An intent to commit theft may also be inferred from a showing that a defendant broke the window of a store after midnight and was partially through the window when apprehended, or that he broke and entered another's house although, at the time of apprehension, he had not taken or moved any property. Therefore, criminal intent to commit a felony or misdemeanor may reasonably and justifiably be inferred from an unlawful and forcible entry, although the mere breaking and entering is not itself burglary where the requisite intent is lacking.

Consummation of the crime is not necessary in order to complete the offense of burglary since the person has committed a burglary if, at the time of the entry into the structure, he possessed the intent to commit a felony in it. It is the act of breaking and entering with the intent to commit a felony that is a crime and it is irrelevant whether the defendant fails to complete his purpose or changes his mind. The crime has already been completed without further action on the part of the defendant.

Distinctions have been made between the state of mind of intending to commit a felony or the intent to commit a misdemeanor. There are, as always, variations from state to state as to what act constitutes a misdemeanor or felony, although in all jurisdictions felonies are the more serious of the two classifications and entail heavier sentences.

There are generally three categories of crime: (1) treason, (2) felonies, and (3) misdemeanors. Felonies are generally those offenses that are punishable by penitentiary sentence, which is usually a sentence for one year or more. Misdemeanors are those state crimes that are punishable by imprisonment of less than one year or by fine instead of prison. Misdemeanants are generally incarcerated in a county jail and not in a state penitentiary.

Therefore, when one enters a structure with criminal intent, the intent to commit a felony or a misdemeanor depends upon his purpose in entering and upon the classification and penalty given to that crime by the state legislature. If one enters to steal anything he can get, he is generally presumed to have intended to commit a felony.

Arson

Arson at common law was the malicious or willful burning of the dwelling house or outhouse within the courtyard of another person. As with the offenses against property and habitation, state legislatures have frequently divided the crime of arson into degrees and have provided heavier penalties for arson committed under certain circumstances. More severe sanctions are imposed for the burning of a dwelling house than for the burning of other structures or personal property, or for burning with the intent to defraud an insurer.

Because arson at common law was an offense against the security of habitation rather than against the safety of the property, the offense was considered aggravated in nature. It was felt that the offense illustrated a greater wantonness and contempt for human life than did a mere offense against the property itself. Arson thus warranted harsher penalties than acts of simple trespass or acts not against the security of the habitation and the safety of the person; the act was against a person's life and safety in his own place of habitation. Statutory law has broadened the offense by including buildings and structures that are not places of human habitation, and by enumerating other offenses, such as burning one's own insured structure with the intent to defraud the insuror.

As in the offense of burglary, statutes generally divide the offense of arson into separate degrees and the distinction between the degrees is generally based upon the use of the property (as a dwelling house or some other use), whether the dwelling house was occupied at the time of the arson, and the value of the property at the time of the offense. The statutes generally proscribe a more severe punishment when the offense is directed against a dwelling house or against property that is valuable, or when it is committed in the nighttime. The purpose for a heavier penalty for the offense against the dwelling house is quickly apparent, and the reason for distinguishing between a daytime and nighttime arson is that persons more probably will be occupying the dwelling house and sleeping in the nighttime, thereby creating a greater likelihood of injury or death as a result of the burning.

Statutes have broadened the common law definition of arson and divided it into degrees. Statutory law also generally adds the offense of burning one's own building or any building with the intent to defraud an insurer or defines the offense as a degree of arson. The elements of this latter offense generally are (1) the willful and malicious (2) burning of (3) insured property (4) with the intent to injure or defraud the insurer. The structure must have been burned for a specific reason to defraud an insurer, and the charge thus differs from arson because arson does not require that its property be insured or burned with the specific intent of defrauding an insurer. Therefore, although one may be guilty of arson in burning insured property, he is not guilty of burning insured property with the intent to defraud an insurer unless he possesses the specific intent and purpose to defraud the insurer.

The following are sample statutes defining the elements of first degree arson, second degree arson, and burning personal property offenses; and defining the usual penalties.

Sample Statutes
Arson in the First Degree.
Any person who willfully and maliciously sets fire to or burns, or causes the setting of fire to or the burning, or who aids, counsels, or procures the

setting of fire to or the burning of any dwelling-house, roominghouse, apartment-house, or hotel, finished or unfinished, occupied or unoccupied; or any kitchen, shop, barn, stable, garage or other outhouse, or other building, that is part or parcel of any dwelling-house, roominghouse, apartment-house or hotel, or belonging to or adjoining thereto finished or unfinished, occupied or unoccupied, such being the property of another; or being insured against loss or damage by fire and such setting of fire to or burning, or such causing, aiding, counseling, or procuring such setting of fire to or such burning being with intent to prejudice or defraud the insurer, shall be guilty of arson in the first degree and, upon conviction thereof, shall be imprisoned in the state prison not less than 2 nor more than 14 years.

Arson in the Second Degree.
Any person who willfully and maliciously sets fire to or burns, or causes the setting of fire to or burning, or who aids, counsels, or procures the setting of fire to or the burning of any barn, garage, stable, or other building, finished or unfinished, occupied or unoccupied, not a part or parcel of any dwelling-house, roominghouse, apartment-house, or hotel, or any shop, storehouse, warehouse, factory, mill, or other building, or any church, meetinghouse, courthouse, workhouse, school, jail, or other public building or any bridge, finished or unfinished, occupied or unoccupied; such being the property of another, or being insured against loss or damage by fire and such setting of fire to or burning, or such causing, aiding, counseling, or procuring such setting of fire to or such burning being with the intent to prejudice·or defraud the insurer, shall be guilty of arson in the second degree and shall, upon conviction thereof, be imprisoned in the state prison not less than 1 nor more than 10 years.

Arson of Miscellaneous Personal Property.
An person who willfully and maliciously sets fire to or burns, or causes the setting of fire to or the burning, or who aids, counsels, or procures the setting of fire to or the burning of any barrack, cock, crib, rick, or stack of hay, corn, wheat, oats, barley, or other grain or vegetable product of any kind; or any hay, straw, grass, or grain of any kind, cut or uncut; or any pile of coal, wood, or other fuel; or any pile of planks, boards, posts, rails, or other lumber; or any streetcar, interurban car, railway car, boat, wharf-boat, water-craft or vessel, dirigible balloon, airplane of any kind or character, automobile or other motor vehicle, finished or unfinished; or any reaping machine, mowing machine, threshing machine, separator, clover huller, plow, cultivator, or any other agricultural or farming implement, vehicle, or machinery, finished or un-

finished; or any other personal property of any kind or character whatsoever not herein specifically named, such property being the property of another; or being insured against loss or damage by fire, and such setting of fire to or burning, or such causing, aiding, counseling, or procuring such setting of fire to or such burning being with the intent to prejudice or defraud the insurer, shall be guilty of a felony and shall, upon conviction thereof, be imprisoned in the state prison not less than 1 nor more than 3 years.

The required elements of the offense of first degree arson are the (1) willful and malicious (2) burning (3) of any building such as a part or parcel of any dwelling house (4) of another; or (1) burning (2) insured property that is a part or parcel of any dwelling house (3) with the intent to damage or defraud the insurer. The penalty prescribed for first degree arson is imprisonment for 2 to 14 years. As in the sample statute of first degree burglary, the offense need not be consummated in the nighttime (as in some jurisdictions) nor the building be occupied at the time (as in some jurisdictions).

The lesser offense of second degree arson carries a prison term of 1 to 10 years and contains the same elements as first degree arson with the exception that the property to be burned is not a part or parcel of any dwelling house. The burning to defraud the insurer of a structure that is not a part or parcel of the dwelling house is also defined as second degree burglary.

The final statute covers the full gamut of arson to personal property or burning to defraud the insurer of personal property. The seriousness of the crime is diminished, as is the severity of the penalty which provides for imprisonment of 1 to 3 years.

There are numerous other statutes that should be mentioned, and there are many variations of the above legislation from state to state. For example, there is legislation against burning goods, wares, merchandise, or chattels, and against the placing of combustibles or explosives to burn or to destroy certain property whether or not the act is accomplished. Specific statutes cover attempted arson, first degree murder where death results from arson, and many other specified offenses, although the general elements remain the same but merely vary in terms of severity.

Definition

Arson is generally defined in common law as the (1) malicious (2) burning (3) of the dwelling house (4) of another. It resembles burglary in that it was an offense against habitation at common law and the same conditions that relate to "the dwelling house of another" of burglary also apply to arson. Thus, an owner in possession and a person in sole lawful occupancy could not be guilty of simple arson, although an owner out of possession could be guilty, because common law arson was an offense against habitation and possession.

The Malicious Element. Criminal intent is an essential element of the crime of arson. The burning must be malicious to constitute arson. Although an accidental or negligent burning lacks the requisite malice, it is not essential that the offender intend the destruction of the dwelling or that ill-will exist. It is sufficient if an intent is shown to commit an unlawful act, the probable consequence of which is a burning, if the act is committed without regard to, or in reckless disregard of, the consequences. Thus, a specific intent to burn a structure is not required if, for example, a prisoner attempts to burn a hole in the door of a guardhouse and the entire structure subsequently burns, as long as it is shown that the offender set the fire willfully rather than negligently or accidentally.

However, it has been held that when a defendant lit a match in order to see while attempting to steal rum from the hold of a ship, and the rum caught fire, which started a blaze that destroyed the ship, the requisite malice was not present. It is arguable, however, that the act was committed without regard to, or in reckless disregard, of the consequences—if the defendant was aware of the inflammability of rum. Malice is found if the burning is accomplished with a design to do a wrongful act toward another without legal justification or excuse, such as if an offender sets out to burn another's building. There must be an intent to burn some building or structure. Sufficient intent is shown when it is found that the offender intended to burn any structure. Thus, particular malice toward a particular building or person is not required as long as the intent is to burn a building. The offender is guilty of arson with respect to each structure if the fire that he sets spreads beyond the immediate building. The offender is guilty of arson as the natural and probable consequences of his wrongful act.

The Burning Element. Arson is not committed unless some part of the structure is actually destroyed by fire. Thus, any charring of wood whereby the fiber is destroyed is sufficient, although the mere fact that the wood is discolored or scorched without ignition is not sufficient. The fiber of some part of the structural material must be slightly damaged;

mere blackening or discoloration is insufficient. An intent to burn and even an attempt do not constitute arson in the absence of burning. There must be a *corpus delicti*, or proof that the crime was consummated.

Some perceptible change must take place in the composition of the building. It is sufficient if any part of the structure, however small, is consumed; it is not necessary that the entire building or even a substantial part of it be materially altered. Thus, if a prisoner in a fireproof building sets fire to a door, there is a sufficient burning. However, when the fire is set against, near, or inside a building and no part of the building is damaged, there is no burning although a fire is created. The act proscribed is the act of burning, and as long as the result is accomplished, the method used to bring it about is irrelevant.

Student Checklist

1. Can you describe the offense of trespass?
2. Are you able to identify the difference between trespass and malicious trespass?
3. Can you describe what the prosecution must prove to establish the elements of entry in burglary?
4. Do you know how to define "reasonable" as used in criminal statutes?
5. Can you describe the requirement of malice when specified for the intent element?
6. Can you list the elements of breaking and entering?
7. Do you know how to describe the elements of burglary (common law) not required for the offense of breaking and entering?
8. Are you able to distinguish legal title from possession, in terms of maintaining a trespass action?
9. Are you able to list the elements of arson?
10. Can you define "affirmative demand" as used in criminal trespass statutes?

Topics for Discussion

1. Discuss the common law offense of criminal trespass.
2. Discuss the offense of burglary and its lesser-included offenses.
3. Discuss the offense of conspiracy.
4. Discuss the offense of attempt.
5. Discuss the common law crime of arson.

ANNOTATED BIBLIOGRAPHY

Hall, Jerome. *General Principles of Criminal Law*. Indianapolis, Md.: Bobbs-Merrill, 1960. A major textbook covering the basic underlying principles of our criminal law. It provides a good balance between common law and statutory law.

Inbau, Fred E., James R. Thompson, and Claude R. Sowle. *Criminal Justice*. 3rd ed. Mineola, N.Y.: Foundation Press, 1968. A thorough, two-volume treatise of criminal law and criminal justice. The authors' extensive experience is competently demonstrated in a broad, comprehensive coverage of the foundation topics as well as the contemporary issues facing the field today.

Kalven, Harry, Jr., and Hans Zeisel. *The American Jury*. Boston, Mass.: Little, Brown, 1966. An exhaustive study of the American jury system and its role in criminal law in practice. To study criminal law without looking at how juries apply it provides an incomplete picture.

Schwartz, Louis B., and Stephen R. Goldstein. *Law Enforcement Handbook for Police*. St. Paul, Minn.: West Publishing, 1970. A recruit-level handbook of criminal law from a layman's perspective. It attempts to be a nonlegal approach to a study of the criminal law. Numerous realistic field problems and examples are used to illustrate points.

The study of this chapter will enable you to:

1. Describe the offenses that are most commonly used to control the abuse of alcoholic beverages.
2. List three acts involving narcotics that are usually defined as crimes.
3. Describe the potential implications of *Robinson* v. *California* for narcotics addiction offenses.
4. Contrast the decision of *Robinson* v. *California* with *Powell* v. *Texas*.
5. Define the offense of adultery.
6. Describe the social utility of the adultery prohibition in early common law.
7. Identify the criteria frequently used to test obscenity.
8. Define riot and civil disorders.
9. Contrast perjury and subornation.
10. Describe the firearms and gun control acts enacted since 1930.

8
Miscellaneous Offenses

There are several offenses covering a wide range of acts deemed appropriate for control by society that do not fit into the classification categories of offenses against the person, property, and habitation and occupancy. These miscellaneous offenses include traffic law violations, game and wildlife control violations, offenses against public decency, health and safety code violations, and acts that are injurious to public order.

Narcotics

Society is experiencing the ever-increasing problems of narcotics addiction and is responding with more and more legislation to counteract this trend. The fact that we still search for the ultimate answer is indicative of the overall lack of success of these efforts. Defining the proper approach requires an adequate identification of the problem. Should the law be concerned with addiction or with the distribution channels? Are there underlying reasons for narcotics use, such as poverty or criminal association, that deserve attention? And, if elimination of narcotic traffic and rehabilitation of the user are goals of the law, does current legislation facilitate or retard achievement of these objectives?

Based on religious and moral values, society has dictated that non-medical narcotic use is wrong. It is generalized that the use of narcotics makes for weak members of society. But it is equally appropriate to generalize that those who use or are addicted to narcotics are inherently weaker in the first place, so that addiction is not a cause but rather a

161

manifestation of their social problems. These social attitudes are typically the product of middle- and upper-class standards, yet addiction, at least historically, has been a concern primarily in the lower social, economic, and educational levels of society.

Legislation

Legislation has reflected the social attitude that narcotics addiction is an evil to be eradicated by whatever means possible. The approach chosen in the last 50 years has been a series of enactments, both at the national and state levels, each with increasingly severe penalties aimed at discouraging narcotics use. The attempt to regulate narcotic traffic has generated elaborate schemes to control legitimate use, so that the illegitimate use is more readily identifiable. Penalties have been increased for the distribution and use of narcotics so that deterrence would weigh more heavily. But addiction continues as a major problem, and, probably of even more serious social consequences, the crimes that support the high cost of the drug habit continue to spiral.

In 1914 Congress enacted the basic federal narcotic legislation, the Harrison Act, which established a system of control for the manufacture, sale, possession, and prescription of narcotics. Those who professionally dealt in narcotics were required to be registered; containers of narcotics had to have federal stamps; and a restrictive tax was paid by those who manufactured and dealt in drugs. The Harrison Act remained the law until 1970, when Congress enacted the Comprehensive Drug Abuse Prevention and Control Act. This latter statute regulates the manufacture, distribution, and dispensing of specified controlled substances through registration with the U.S. Attorney General. The enactment also allows the Attorney General to establish production quotas of controlled substances. This latter provision is an attempt at matching the actual volume of drug production with the known use for legitimate purposes. The content and strength of federal legislation is important to effective narcotics control, because state provisions can easily be avoided by moving the narcotic traffic to another, less restrictive jurisdiction.

The vast majority of states have enacted, with modification, the Uniform Narcotic Drug Act, which was adopted in 1932. The amendments (1942 and 1958), however, are generally limited to the penalty provisions so that state substantive laws are to some extent similar. Typically, the major narcotics offenses provided for by state legislatures are *sale* and *possession*.

Sale. Section One of the Uniform Narcotics Drug Act defines the term "sale" very broadly. It includes barter, exchange, gift, or offer; each transaction made by any person, whether as a principal, proprietor, agent, servant, or employee is a punishable offense. The courts have also tended toward broader interpretations of the term, which give it meaning far beyond that normally understood in the general commercial context. These interpretations are apparently pursuant to the general legislative intent that all transactions in illicit drugs carry the threat of potentially severe punishment.

It is interesting to note the scope of transactions that are encompassed within this definition of sale. No exchange is necessary—a barter or a gift is sufficient to be termed a sale. There is frequently no gradation in punishment based on the amount of illicit drugs involved in the transaction, and the threat of punishment exists regardless of the capacity in which a person acts. By a strict interpretation of the statute, a deal between major suppliers of substantial proportions is treated the same as is a mere gift of a single unit between two casual users. There is, however, a recent trend toward recognizing gradations in transactions, which will do much toward preserving integrity in the criminal narcotics laws.

Possession. The next nearly universal narcotics offense is illegal possession of a narcotic drug. Because legislative techniques have been established to regulate the legal distribution and consumption of narcotics, any control exercised over drugs outside the legal regulatory process may subject the possessor to criminal liability.

Usually a possession charge must show that the defendant was aware of the nature of the substance he possessed, and that he intentionally and consciously possessed it. The easiest case to prove is that in which the defendant has actual physical possession, giving him control over the substance. But the defendant need not have actual or exclusive control or physical possession to be liable. He may be equally liable if he is sharing possession with one or more others or he may be shown to have only constructive possession, which is established when the drugs, although not physically in the defendant's possession, were, in fact, subject to his dominion or control. Mere proximity of a narcotic to persons is by itself generally insufficient to sustain a conviction for possession. Failure to prove that the defendant had knowledge of the presence of the illicit drugs is usually fatal to the state's prosecution of the case.

Quantitative differences are also of concern in possession situations. Arguments have been advanced that possession of quantities sufficient only for personal use are outside the scope of these statutes. However, courts have been reluctant to approve such a provision, because it would create a loophole in the narcotics regulations, and is usually contrary to expressed legislative intent. The enforcement problems that would be generated by such a provision outweigh its benefits. Distinctions between offenses based on addiction or nonaddiction or personal or nonpersonal use tend to complicate enforcement of narcotics control laws.

Changing Concepts of the Addict

Narcotics laws have emphasized the eradication of the drug traffic by removing both the distributors and the users from the street. Historically, little concern has been demonstrated for the causes of addiction or the physiological plight of the addict. In this context, there would be no apparent limit to the severity of punishment that could be applied to the offenders. In fact, the severity of the criminal sanction is often used merely to get the user to provide officials with information about supply channels, in return for reduced or suspended sentences.

In 1962, the U.S. Supreme Court decided a case that was to have major implications in the application of the criminal law to the narcotic addict. In *Robinson* v. *California*, the Court held that narcotics addiction is a disease and, therefore, that criminalization was cruel and unusual punishment, contrary to the Eight Amendment of the Constitution.[1]

The California statute that had been in question was not one that punished use, purchase, sale, or possession; but one that made the status of narcotics addiction a criminal offense. The importance of the Court's opinion is the recognition that addiction itself is a medical, social, and psychological problem and not one that can be eradicated through exercise of the criminal sanction. As a result of the *Robinson* decision, a few jurisdictions, most notably New York and California, have instituted civil commitment programs. These techniques, which have supplemented

[1] 370 U.S. 660 (1962).

a similar federal program, are aimed at providing needed institutionalized care and therapy, while avoiding the social stigma of criminalization and penal confinement. Such provisions should be the modern trend in narcotics addiction legislation.

Finally, it would be valuable to recognize the current British approach to the addiction problem, for it may well have future impact on the legislative alternatives available in this country. The British system regards addiction as a disease and the problem is treated accordingly. The addict need not resort to illegal sources for his supply but may obtain his drugs from regulated medical channels. This technique has the advantages of (1) minimizing the reliance on criminal sources, thereby reducing a lucrative market for illegal drugs; (2) introducing the addict to competent medical care and guidance; and (3) providing authorities with an accurate picture of the scope, location, and characteristics of the drug traffic. England has experienced a reduction in both the number of known addicts and in the volume of crime that addicts commit to support their addiction. These achievements have eluded equivalent programs in the United States.

An additional troubling aspect of the enforcement of narcotics laws is the practices that police are forced to use to expose and to apprehend violators. Because of the necessarily clandestine nature of the drug culture, police are compelled to engage in equally surreptitious techniques in order to be at all effective. A quick review of the revolution in criminal procedure that has occurred in the past decade will indicate the extent of judicial concern with these questionable and frequently illegal practices. Consequently, narcotics offenses are among the hardest to enforce today because of procedural attack by defense counsels. Because of the conflict between society's demands for enforcement and the questionable practices of enforcement now in use, reforms must be forthcoming so that acceptable enforcement techniques may be developed.

Sample Statute
Narcotic Drug Licenses.
It is unlawful for any person to manufacture, possess, have under his control, sell, prescribe, administer, dispense, or compound any narcotic drug, except as authorized herein.

No person shall manufacture, compound, mix, cultivate, grow, or by any other process, produce or prepare narcotic drugs, and no person shall dispense, nor shall any person as a wholesaler supply the same without first having obtained a license so to do from the state board of health. Provided, that the provisions of this section shall not apply to the dispensing, administration, giving away, mixing, or otherwise preparing any of the drugs mentioned in this chapter by a registered physician, dentist, or veterinarian in the course of his professional practice, where such drugs are dispensed, administered, given away, mixed, or otherwise prepared for legitimate medical purposes.

Alcohol

There is no doubt that the abuse of alcohol generates social problems that require legal solutions. Although complete prohibition was found to be an excessive remedy and too difficult to administer, some measure of control is desirable, because the abuse of alcohol is recognized as a source of concern in traffic safety, domestic relations, and physical and mental health programs. It is the distribution channels that are subject to extensive control for both regulatory and revenue purposes.

The offenses of public intoxication and driving while under the influence of alcohol are directed at those who have consumed excessive amounts of alcohol and who are performing in a manner likely to cause harm to others. Enforcement of these two offenses not only protects other members of society, it may, in fact, have a protective effect on the intoxicated person until his normal physical and mental capabilities are restored.

Public intoxication merely involves being found in a public place (any place where all people have a right to go) in a state of intoxication. Driving under the influence is similar except that the accused must have operated a motor vehicle upon a highway while under the influence of alcohol.

By applying the reasoning of the *Robinson* decision it would seem that public intoxication, particularly when the defendant is a chronic alcoholic, would be a crime of status, and that any criminal penalty would be contrary to the Eighth Amendment's cruel and unusual punishment provision. However, the United States Supreme Court saw otherwise in *Powell* v. *Texas*.[2] Powell, a chronic alcoholic, was arrested and

[2] 392 U.S. 514 (1968).

convicted of being drunk in a public place. Four Justices joined by the concurring opinion of a fifth Justice held that the defendant was not being punished for his status as an alcoholic, but for being in a public place while intoxicated. Powell was unable to show that his presence in public while drunk was compelled by his status as an alcoholic. It is not a criminalization of status to restrict a chronic alcoholic's public presence, and the *Robinson* rationale generally does not void public intoxication laws.

Use of alcohol is also restricted for certain classes of individuals. Frequently, states will have statutes making illegal the sale of alcohol to an intoxicated purchaser. The most typical prohibition is that of minors who may not purchase, possess, or loiter in places where alcohol is served. A frequently related offense is misrepresentation of age in order to obtain alcoholic beverages. Although the exact substance of these statutes will vary among jurisdictions, the policy of close control of the sale and consumption of alcohol is universal.

Sample Statutes
Selling, Giving or Serving Alcoholic Beverages to Minors Prohibited.
1. *It is unlawful for any person, firm, or in the case of a corporation, the officers, agents, and employees thereof, to sell, give, serve, or permit to be served alcoholic beverages, including wines and beer, to persons under 21 years of age or to permit a person under 21 years of age to consume said beverages on the licensed premises. Anyone convicted of violation of the provisions hereof shall be punished by imprisonment in the county jail for not more than 6 months or by fine of not more than $500.*
2. *It is unlawful for any person to misrepresent or misstate his or her age or the age of any other person for the purpose of inducing any licensee, his agents or employees, to sell, give, serve or deliver any alcoholic beverages to a person under 21 years of age.*

Moonshine Whiskey; Ownership, Possession or Control Prohibited; Penalties.
1. *Any person who owns or has in his possession or under his control less than one gallon of liquor, as defined in the beverage law, which was not made or manufactured in accordance with the laws in effect at the time and place where same was made or manufactured shall be guilty of a misdemeanor and, upon conviction, shall be punished*

by imprisonment in the county jail not exceeding 6 months or by fine not exceeding $500 or both.

2. Any person who owns or has in his possession or under his control one gallon or more of liquor, as defined in the beverage law, which was not made or manufactured in accordance with the laws in effect at the time when and place where the same was made or manufactured shall be guilty of a felony and, upon conviction, shall be punished by imprisonment in the state prison not exceeding 5 years of by fine not exceeding $5000, or both.

3. In any prosecution under this section, proof that the liquor involved in what is commonly known as moonshine whiskey shall be prima facie evidence that the same was not made or manufactured in accordance with the laws in effect at the time when and place where the same was made or manufactured.

Drunkenness.
Whoever shall be or become drunk from the voluntary use of intoxicating liquors or drugs shall be punished by a fine of not more than $25, or by imprisonment in the county jail for not more than 3 months; but no prosecution shall be instituted after 6 months after the commission of the offense.

Morality and Decency

Although the criminal law reflects society's general concept of morality, it is not the function of government to set sanctions that enforce violations of nonstatutory morality standards. The government's obligation is to protect members of society and their possessions from unnecessary harm by other members of society. This concept prevails through most of the criminal law as a constraint on the scope of criminal prohibitions and their sanctions. For example, when Connecticut sought to prohibit the use and distribution of contraceptives, the Supreme Court found the prohibition an unconstitutional invasion of the right of privacy. To make behavior criminal, the behavior must be harmful to society or destructive of social order—it cannot simply be morally offensive to a particular person or group.

In that subset of the criminal law that may be loosely categorized as "offenses against morality," the same immediate lack of social wrong seems to exist. Yet these crimes are among the oldest known to man, many having their origin in the common or ecclesiastical law. Adultery, incest, prostitution, bigamy, and obscenity typify the offenses against morality. A modification in certain of these offenses may be forthcoming. The recent reshaping of this country's abortion laws exemplifies the real possibility of reformation.

The Offenses

The crime of adultery is an appropriate place to begin an analysis of these offenses. It has historical roots reaching back to canon law, the influence of which is still very apparent in current adultery statutes. Although some statutes merely forbid "cohabitation with another in a state of adultery," the definition of adultery does deserve some attention. In canon law, adultery meant sexual relations by a married person with a person other than his or her spouse. The repugnancy in the eyes of the Church resided in the violation of the marital vows.

The common law definition of adultery was an act of sexual intercourse between a married woman and any man other than her husband. The offensiveness was thought to be the exposure of the wronged husband to the possibility of maintaining another man's children or to have them become heir to the wronged husband's estate. This definitional difference is important because it is reflected in existing statutes and alters the exact nature of the crime. It is generally agreed that a married woman who engages in sexual intercourse with a male other than her husband is guilty of adultery, but there is not yet complete agreement on whether a husband who has sexual intercourse with a single woman is guilty of adultery.

Adultery is distinguished from fornication, which is usually defined as sexual intercourse by any man regardless of marital status with a single female.

Prostitution is the practice of a female's offering her body for sexual intercourse with men for monetary or other gain. A single act does not constitute prostitution and, depending on statutory requirements, receipt of compensation may not be a requirement to be classified as prostitution. Prostitution legislation is allied to several other offenses, such as: (1) inducing a female to become a prostitute; (2) placing or keeping a female in a house of prostitution; (3) living with or accepting the earnings of a prostitute; (4) pandering; and (5) soliciting a female for the purpose of prostitution.

Enforcing these provisions against prostitution is often at the discretion of local police officials and may, in fact, be pursued only to control and to centralize the prostitution activity rather than to eliminate it. Similarly, statutes that seek to penalize the male for patronizing places of prostitution are often used to secure his cooperation in the prosecution of the female. Prostitution has been identified as a "victimless crime" and one that generally receives reduced attention when law enforcement resources are limited.

Prostitution is distinguished from rape by the fact that rape requires that the act of sexual intercourse be against the will of the female. Sexual intercourse with a female under a certain age, generally in the area of the mid-teens, is often statutorily defined as rape, regardless of whether the female consented to the act. Lack of consent and proof of penetration are the only elements needed to be shown, generally, to establish statutory rape.

In most jurisdictions the uncorroborated testimony of the victim is sufficient by itself for conviction. Because of this, the alleged rapist can only refute the victim's testimony with his own, in which case the determination of guilt is a question of believability. The alternative is that the alleged rapist attack the character of the victim. This attack is designed to establish the lack of chastity on the part of the prosecuting witness (though an unchaste woman can be raped), and to shake the credibility of her testimony before the judge or jury. Because of this potential embarrassment, as well as the indignities of prosecuting a rape case, many victims do not even report the crime to authorities.

Other morals offenses include incest and public indecency. Incest is sexual intercourse between persons who would be unable to marry legally because of their blood relationship (for example, brother-sister, father-daughter). Unlike rape, the character of the parties is not an issue, but knowledge or an awareness of the relationship must be shown. Public indecency laws prohibit indecent exposure of one's person in a public place where there are other persons present who may be annoyed.

Whoever, after having entered into a valid marriage, weds another without the legal dissolution of the first marriage or the death of the first spouse is guilty of bigamy. In some jurisdictions, an honest, reasonably held belief that a valid divorce has been granted dissolving a previous marriage, when that is not the case, does afford a defense. But this is not generally the position taken: remarriage is at the risk of a bigamy conviction if the divorce proves invalid. This is usually a problem only in transient divorce situations, in which one of the parties has established a temporary domicile to secure a divorce more readily.

Most sodomy statutes prohibit sexual activity that is generally described as against nature, and the specific practices that are prohibited are often listed within the statute. Any person participating, unless under duress, is guilty of the offense; and the consent of either party does not constitute a defense for the other party.

Enforcement of obscenity statutes presents two immediate problems: What is obscene? What violates the statute? The definition of obscenity and the legal tests to determine obscenity have plagued jurists for a long time, and still no truly universal resolution has been established. Among the latest and most definitive of the Supreme Court decisions is the following three-part analysis:

1. The dominant theme of the material taken as a whole appeals to the prurient interests.
2. The material is potentially offensive because it affronts contemporary community standards relating to the description or representation of sexual matters.
3. The material is utterly without redeeming social value.

Resolution of the obscenity question can be treated only on a case-by-case basis, in each instance weighing the inherent values of the materials against its social offensiveness. The Court's three-pronged test merely directs attention to relevant considerations in making the determination of what is or is not obscene.

Private possession of obscene material without any intention of public distribution is not a crime. The state has no legitimate interest in regulating the content's of a man's personal library, and no other member of society can demonstrate a need for protection. It is that activity which seeks to distribute offensive material, regardless of how extensively, that is within the legitimate concern of criminal obscenity statutes.

Public Order

Riots and Disorders

Not only is the individual protected by numerous criminal sanctions and prohibitions, so too is the social structure. And concern arises when a social institution is endangered. The laws of preservation of self and society are designed to protect against change by undesirable techniques. Riots and disorders are considered undesirable techniques.

Whenever a large group of persons collectively engages in unpredictable and uncontrollable disorder, a riot exists. Frequently, the participants are otherwise law-abiding citizens.

To preserve the peace, certain practices have been defined and criminalized in breach-of-the-peace statutes. These prohibitions may exist for disorderly conduct, vagrancy, unlawful assembly, or riot. In 1968 Congress passed the Anti-Riot Act, which outlawed activities that were intended to incite, organize, promote, encourage, participate in, or carry on any riot.[4]

State breach-of-the-peace statutes have their historical origin deeply embedded in the common law. Unlawful assembly is the meeting of a minimum number of persons, usually three or more, to carry out an unlawful purpose. Riot was a common law misdemeanor involving three or more persons engaging in the execution of a public disorder. Most contemporary statutory definitions of riot are identical to the historical concept.

Sample Statute
Affrays and Riots.
1. *All persons guilty of an affray shall be punished by imprisonment not exceeding twelve (12) months, or by fine not exceeding $500.*
2. *All persons guilty of a riot, or of inciting or encouraging a riot, shall be punished by imprisonment not exceeding 2 years in the state penitentiary, or by imprisonment not exceeding 12 months in the country jail, or by fine not exceeding $500 or by both fine and imprisonment.*

Disorderly conduct statutes are designed and defined in the broadest manner possible, so that they apply to a multitude of social problems, particularly those on the individual level. The following is an example:

Whoever shall act in a loud, boisterous, or disorderly manner so as to disturb the peace and quiet of any neighborhood or family, by loud or unusual noise, or by tumultuous or offensive behavior, threatening, quarreling, challenging to fight or fighting, shall be deemed guilty of disorderly conduct.

[4] 18 U.S.C. 2101 (1968).

The statute is so comprehensive that enforcement officials can find a suitable provision for almost any socially undesirable conduct. As a consequence of this broadness they are under constitutional attack, because they may criminalize conduct that is constitutionally protected. In the future, disorderly conduct statutes may have to be restructured by limiting judicial construction or legislative redrafting to make them more specific. Yet the offense does provide enforcement officials with a useful misdemeanor statute that can be helpful in handling a small disorder situation before it escalates to violence or riot.

Vagrancy
Another crime against public order is vagrancy. Modern vagrancy statutes are designed to support preventive enforcement techniques and the temporary detaining of individuals when necessary. Typical elements of vagrancy include lack of visible means of support, idleness, and the lack of a regular place of residence. These elements clearly make vagrancy a crime of status because they criminalize certain personal conditions. Another weakness in this offense is the vague statutory language that will often provide little guidance on enforcement policies and leave much discretion in the hands of the police. Yet this discretion, although legally questionable, does give vagrancy its real utility. Although it may be used to menace "undesirables," it can also be used to remove individuals from the streets who, because of their destitution, may be likely to engage in some criminal conduct to secure resources. Additionally, the charge of vagrancy can be used to give police custody of a destitute individual and provide him with a place to sleep and a meal.

Sample Statute
    Vagrants.
    Rogues and vagabonds, idle or dissolute persons who go about begging, common gamblers, persons who use juggling, or unlawful games or plays, common pipers and fiddlers, common drunkards, common night walkers, thieves, pilferers, traders in stolen property, lewd, wanton and lascivious persons, keepers of gambling places, common railers and brawlers, persons who neglect their calling or employment, or are without reasonably continuous employment or regular income and who have not sufficient property to sustain them, and misspend what they earn

without providing for themselves or the support of their families, persons wandering or strolling around from place to place without any lawful purpose or object, habitual loafers, idle and disorderly persons, persons neglecting all lawful business and habitually spending their time by frequenting houses of ill fame, gaming houses or tippling shops, persons able to work by habitually living upon the earnings of their wives or minor children, and all able bodied male persons over the age of 18 years who are without means of support and remain in idleness, shall be deemed vagrants, and upon conviction shall be subject to a fine not exceeding $250, or by imprisonment not more than 6 months.

Perjury

The structure of our legal system relies on the foundation of getting to the truth. Because a false oath undermines the judicial system, it must rank as a crime against the state and be subject to the criminal sanction. Perjury is defined as follows: Whoever having sworn or affirmed shall willfully, corruptly, and falsely testify in substance shall be guilty of perjury. Proof of criminal intent may be inferred from the giving of willfully false testimony that is reasonably expected to be misleading. If anyone procures another person to commit perjury, he is guilty of the crime of subornation of perjury. The combined threat of these two crimes, perjury and subornation, seeks to inhibit any collusive practices designed to make the discovery of perjured testimony more difficult.

Sample Statutes
Perjury.

(a) A person commits perjury when, under oath or affirmation, in a proceeding or in any other matter where by law such oath or affirmation is required, he makes a false statement, material to the issue or point in question, which he does not believe to be true.

(b) Proof of Falsity.

An indictment or information for perjury alleging that the offender, under oath, has made contradictory statements, material to the issue or point in question, in the same or in different proceedings, where such oath or affirmation is required, need not specify which statement is false. At the trial, the prosecution need not establish which statement is false.

(c) Admission of Falsity.

Where the contradictory statements are made in the same continuous trial, an admission by the offender in that same continuous trial of the falsity of a contradictory statement shall bar prosecution therefor under any provision of this Code.

Subornation of Perjury.

(a) A person commits subornation of perjury when he procures or induces another to make a statement in violation of the perjury statute (above) which the person knows to be false.

Perjury Otherwise than in Judicial Proceedings.

Whoever, being duly authorized or required by law to take oath or affirmation, not in a judicial proceeding, willfully swears or affirms falsely in regard to any material matter or thing, respecting which such oath or affirmation is authorized or required, shall be deemed guilty of perjury, and shall be imprisoned in the state prison not exceeding 20 years.

Perjury in Judicial Proceedings.

Whoever being lawfully required to depose the truth in any proceeding in a court of justice, commits perjury, shall be punished if the perjury is committed on the trial of an indictment for a capital crime, by imprisonment in the state prison for life or any term of years; and if committed in any other case, by imprisonment in the state prison not exceeding 20 years.

Subornation of Perjury.

Whoever is guilty of subornation of perjury, by procuring another person to commit perjury, shall be punished in the same manner as for perjury.

Bribery

Just as perjury seeks to preserve the integrity of the judicial forum, the offense of bribery seeks to avoid the corruption of anyone who holds a power in trust for the good of the community. Bribery is defined as follows: Whoever corruptly gives, promises, or offers any public official any money or valuable thing, or corruptly offers or promises to do any act beneficial to any such person, to influence his action, and whoever being a public official, solicits or accepts any such money, promise, or valuable thing to influence him with respect to his official duty shall be guilty of bribery. Both the offering of a bribe and the acceptance thereof are punishable offenses. Mere offer is sufficient; there is no need that there be an acceptance. The policy is to remove the temptation entirely, not just to punish those endeavors that are actually successful in corrupting a public official.

Sample Statutes

Bribery.

Any person who shall corruptly give, offer, or promise to any public officer, agent, servant, or employee, after the election or appointment of employment of such public offier, agent, servant, or employee and either before or after he shall have been qualified or shall take his seat, any commission, gift, gratuity, money, property, or other valuable thing, or to do any act beneficial to such public officer, agent, servant, or employee, or another, with the intent or purpose to influence the act, vote, opinion, decision, judgment, or behavior of such public officer, agent, servant, or employee on any matter, question, cause, or proceeding that may be pending or may by law be brought before him in his public capacity, or with the intent or purpose to influence any act or omission relating to any public duty of such public officer, agent, servant, or employee, or with the intent or purpose to cause or induce such public officer, agent, servant, or employee to use or exert or to procure the use or exertion of any influence upon or with any other public officer, agent, servant, or employee in relation to any matter, question, cause, or proceeding that may be pending or may by law be brought before each other public officer, agent, employee, or servant, shall be guilty of the crime of bribery.

Accepting Bribe.

Any public officer, agent, servant, or employee who, after his election, appointment, or employment and either before or after he shall have been qualified or shall take his seat, corruptly requests, solicits, or accepts for himself or another any commission, gift, gratuity, money, property, or other valuable thing or a promise to pay or give any commission, gift, gratuity, money, property, or other thing of value or to do any act beneficial to such public officer, agent, servant, or employee, or another, under an agreement or with an understanding between such public officer, agent, servant, or employee and any other person to the

effect that such commission, gift, gratuity, money, property, other thing
of value, or promise will influence the act, vote, opinion, decision judg-
ment or behavior of such public officer, agent, servant, or employee on
any matter, question, cause, or proceeding that may be pending or may
by law be brought before him in his public capacity or will influence his
act or omission relating to any of his public duties or will cause or
induce him to use or exert or procure the use or exertion of any influ-
ence upon or with any other public officer, agent, servant, or employee in
relation to any matter, question, cause, or proceeding that may be pend-
ing or may by law be brought before such other public officer, agent,
servant, or employee, shall be guilty of the crime of accepting a bribe.

U.S. Criminal Code

Title 18 of the United States Code contains the basic federal criminal
law statutes, and is divided into many subdivisions, each dealing with a
specific criminal conduct. The nature of the federal criminal law is similar
to that of the states. Many of the substantive offenses are the same; Title
18 forbids arson, assault, bribery, conspiracy, gambling, homicide, kidnapping, narcotics use, obscenity, perjury, rape, and riots. But the federal
criminal law also contains offenses that are more suitably federal, such
as protection of civil rights, counterfeiting, mail fraud, sabotage, and
treason.

Although much of the federal criminal code is duplicative, its
existence is necessary and justifiable. The Federal Bureau of Investigation must have statutory authority to charge suspects after apprehension.
As the primary investigative agency for the federal jurisdiction they must
have a criminal code to enforce. In a modern, mobile society much crime
involves activities ranging beyond the jurisdictional confines of single
states. Therefore, the federal criminal code must contain provisions for
crimes that are normally of state concern but that become interstate
because they have involved more than a single jurisdiction. Finally, the
federal criminal law offers the national government the power to prosecute a defendant if the state has, for one reason or another, failed to
successfully pursue or to obtain a criminal conviction. When the Southern states were slow to enforce violations of civil rights, the federal
district attorneys could move under the federal civil rights laws to prosecute the alleged offenders.

Title 18 has several faults that result from our mostly piecemeal legislative development. As circumstances change and Congress becomes motivated to modify the criminal law, new legislation alters, deletes, or adds criminal provisions. Years of this process have produced ambiguities and inconsistencies that can be corrected only by comprehensive revision of the federal criminal code. One major change needed is the clarification of each crime's elements. Because the federal criminal code must justify its presence in matters that are reserved to the states, most federal criminal substantive provisions contain some allegation of interstate activity as an element of the crime. The effort to establish the federal jurisdiction often complicates the proof of the offense, making prosecution difficult. It may be necessary to charge under a federal conspiracy statute because all of the actual conduct of the criminal offense except the planning took place within a single state. If Congress ever sees fit to revise Title 18, it should define each crime by identifying substantive elements, such as state law, and in a separate section specify the necessary jurisdictional requirements. This untangling would eliminate proof difficulties while maintaining the necessary jurisdictional distinctions between state and federal criminal law.

Health and Safety

A major function of government is the protection of public health and safety. The ordinary means of accomplishing this protection is through monetary penalties, injunctions, abatement of nuisances, and license revocations. But the criminal sanction may be exercised when it is deemed to be an appropriate remedy for wrongful conduct. Those types of health and safety regulations that are likely to involve criminal sanction might include the practice of certain professions without a license, littering, exposing another person to venereal or a communicable disease, false and misleading advertising of drugs, and maintenance of unfit dwelling places.

Public nuisance statutes may also involve the criminal law when conduct is particularily offensive. A public nuisance is a practice that is injurious to health, or indecent or offensive to the senses, or an obstruction to the free use of property.

Most of these provisions are, at least initially, likely to be handled by means other than the criminal law. Administrative actions of fines and suspension of license may be the more usual approach. But, where required, the state does have the right to criminalize conduct injurious to public health and safety.

Fish and Game

For the preservation and propagation of fish and game, legislatures have the power to enact provisions regulating and licensing hunters and fishers. The state may also allow minor criminal sanctions for violation of certain of these regulatory provisions. Typical game laws that may have criminal penalties are restrictions on the amount or size of fish or game taken; violation of season provisions; illegal methods of taking fish or game, such as with seines, nets, or illegal traps; use of explosives or certain firearms to hunt or fish. Recently, legislation outlawing use of snowmobiles for hunting and criminalizing certain pollution practices that may endanger the lives of fish or game have appeared.

Although the powers differ from jurisdiction to jurisdiction, game wardens often have expanded search and seizure powers in the execution of their duties. Because securing a warrant would usually involve much transportation and loss of time, the warrant requirement is relaxed if not, in fact, abandoned. It is possible to justify this approach under traditional search and seizure law as an exception because of the circumstances of the remoteness of ordinary hunting and fishing locations, which makes securing a warrant impractical.

With modern ecological concerns increased, criminalization of fish and wildlife preservation statutes may be anticipated. Penalties and sanctions are increasing for violations of these statutes, for society is viewing these acts as more harmful than they had previously considered them to be.

Weapons Control

Do we have the right to bear arms? The Second Amendment to the Constitution certainly suggests an affirmative answer:

A well-regulated Militia, being necessary to the security of a free State,
the right of the people to keep and bear arms shall not be infringed.

But almost a century ago the Second Amendment was interpreted by the Supreme Court as protecting the right to maintain and to equip a militia, not the individual's right to bear arms.

State gun control is at best inadequate in efforts to curtail crimes involving use of firearms. Some states have licensing provisions before purchase, but most states require only that licenses be obtained if the weapon is going to be carried on the person after the sale. Others merely require a notice to police of the fact of the weapon sale. A better approach would require registration and licensing both before the sale and in the event that the purchaser desires to carry the weapon on his person. The registration before sale would allow officials to prevent certain potentially harmful persons—the intoxicated, minors, incompetents, or convicted felons—from purchasing weapons. The burden of proof could be established at a high level for those seeking permission to carry their own weapons. But today's legislation generally falls far short of affording police the control and access to information that stricter registration provisions would offer. The Uniform Firearms Act pertains only to the commission of any crime while armed, which is a felony, and forbids possession of a pistol without a license.

The National Firearms Act of 1934 restricted trade in machine guns and short-barrelled shotguns and rifles by using the national taxing power and levying a prohibitive tax on their manufacture and transfer. Prompted by political shootings and assassinations, Congress enacted a Gun Control Act in 1968. This provision made it unlawful to import, transfer, manufacture, or deal in firearms or munitions unless licensed or unless permitted to acquire or to possess a firearm under state law. It also made the sale or delivery of a weapon to a minor or a convicted felon illegal. Finally, it has restricted to a small degree the mail-order sale of weaponry, which has been blamed for much of the unregulated traffic in handguns.

Gun control legislation should identify those weapons that have no legal use in the hands of private persons, and the type of persons who should be denied the right to purchase or bear arms because of some infirmity. It must provide the police with adequate registration information before the sale, so that an informed decision can be made as to whether the sale should be allowed.

Preventive control measures could certainly yield returns far beyond the burdens of inconvenience and universal cost that accompany a registration system. The opportunity for greater police input as to whether certain sales should be allowed at all is worth the infringement on the personal freedoms of those seeking to buy weapons. It has always been recognized that personal freedoms are secure, but are nonetheless subject to the legitimate functions of society. Regulation of deadly weapons is certainly a legitimate exercise of the state's protective powers.

Student Checklist

1. Do you know how to describe the offenses that are most commonly used to control the abuse of alcoholic beverages?
2. Are you able to list three acts involving narcotics that are usually defined as crimes?
3. Are you able to describe the potential implications of *Robinson* v. *California* for narcotics addiction offenses?
4. Can you contrast the decision of *Robinson* v. *California* with *Powell* v. *Texas*?
5. Are you able to define the offense of adultery?
6. Are you able to describe the social utility of the adultery prohibition in early common law?
7. Can you identify the criteria frequently used to test obscenity?
8. Can you define riot and civil disorders?
9. Can you contrast perjury and subornation?
10. Are you able to describe the firearms and gun control acts enacted since 1930?

Topics for Discussion

1. Discuss the social and legal issues involved in vagrancy statutes.

2. Discuss the social wrongs that are usually the subject of morality laws.

3. Discuss the acts involving narcotics that are controlled by criminal statutes.

4. Discuss the firearms and gun control acts at the federal level.

5. Discuss the *Robinson* and *Powell* cases in terms of the trend toward treating intoxication and addiction as illnesses instead of crimes.

ANNOTATED BIBLIOGRAPHY

Chamelin, Neil C., and Kenneth R. Evans. *Criminal Law for Policemen.* Englewood Cliffs, N.J.: Prentice-Hall, 1971. An introductory-level coverage of criminal offenses for the new or practicing officer. It avoids the caselaw approach.

Inbau, Fred E., and James R. Thompson. *Criminal Law and Its Administration.* Mineola, N.Y.: Foundation Press, 1970. An excellent casebook approach to criminal law with adequate commentary and analysis to serve the nonlegal student of the administration of justice.

Klotter, John C., and Jacqueline R. Kanovitz. *Constitutional Law for Police.* 2nd ed. Cincinnati: W. H. Anderson, 1971. A major resource for constitutional law issues associated with police practices. Emphasis is obviously on procedural law, but the textbook serves also as a foundation for substantive criminal law.

Lindesmith, Alfred R. *The Addict and the Law.* Bloomington, Ind.: Indiana University Press, 1965. A behavioralist's view of the drug problem and its relationship to criminal law. Reform and suggestions for new approaches provide a climax for the text.

The study of this chapter will enable you to:

1. Define a principal in the first degree.
2. Identify the elements required to establish the offense of attempt.
3. List the elements of the offense of conspiracy.
4. Define what is meant by a "wheel conspiracy."
5. Illustrate a principal in the second degree.
6. Describe the crime of solicitation.
7. Describe how the Wharton Rule guides conspiracy cases.
8. Contrast an accessory before the fact with an accessory after the fact.
9. Explain what is meant by a "chain conspiracy."
10. Provide an illustrative example of what is meant by taking a substantial step toward committing an offense.

9

Parties to a Crime

Those persons and/or groups who participate in the commission of a crime by playing specific and affirmative roles before, during, and after the offense are generally known as the parties to the crime. The following five sections of this chapter will deal with the two principal categories of parties—that is, principals and accessories—and will examine the three collateral areas relevant to a discussion of this subject —solicitation, conspiracy, and witnesses.

Principals

At common law, the concept that the commission of one offense may radiate guilt to several parties was illustrated by the recognition of four distinct categories of circumstances that identified a person as a culpable party to a felony:

1. Principal in the first degree.
2. Principal in the second degree.
3. Accessory before the fact.
4. Accessory after the fact.

Modern statutes have largely abolished the distinction existing between three of the four categories, recognizing that the accessory after the fact was not a true accomplice of the original completed offense and should therefore be punished differently from the other three, who would be subject to the same penalty specified for a particular felony.

Under the common law classification, a person may be a principal in an offense in either the first or the second degree. The distinction between both degrees, however, is one largely without a difference, because the penalty authorized for the commission of any felony is the same for both the first and the second degree principals.

A principal in the first degree is the criminal actor, the immediate or absolute perpetrator of the crime. He is the one to whom all substantive criminal offenses are written, the one who possesses the requisite mental intent and has caused a socially harmful occurrence—whether by his own hands or through some instrumentality or other nonhuman agency, or by means of an innocent agent.

When two or more participants jointly inflict bodily injury upon another, all involved are joint principals in the first degree to a charge of assault and battery. Joint principals in the first degree are distinguishable from situations where other actor(s) are merely aiding, such as physically confining a murder victim while the principal inflicts the fatal wound. They are guilty as a principal, but in the second degree. In cases where the single crime consists of several separate but essential acts, all of the parties involved in any of these acts are joint principals in the first degree (for example, when two persons forge separate portions of the same negotiable instrument).

An exception to the general rule that the actor who uses an intermediary to commit the offense is not a principal in the first degree involves those situations where the crime is accomplished by the use of an innocent or incompetent agent acting under the direction, influence, or control of the principal. For example, if a defendant persuades a mentally retarded patient to kill another, the controlling and originating party is the principal in the first degree, and the retarded patient is regarded as a mere instrument. In this example, the principal would be accountable for the acts of his intermediary.

Thus, a principal in the first degree need only be "constructively" present at the moment of perpetration. That is, it is unnecessary that he be present in person at the commission of the offense as long as he has caused the socially harmful occurrence without the assistance of any guilty or mentally culpable agent. For example, if an individual wires a bomb and activates a timed trigger mechanism with the intent to kill another when the victim starts his car, the perpetrator is guilty as a principal in the first degree, even though he was not physically present at his victim's death. Similarly, if one places poison for another person who takes it in his absence, or if an individual obtains money by false pretenses by sending a letter through the mail, each originating perpetrator is considered the principal in the first degree.

As far as legal consequence is concerned, no difference exists between principals in the first and second degrees. Both of them share the same guilt and penalty, except in those cases where aggravation or mitigation divides their respective guilt. The principal in the second degree differs from the principal in the first degree because he plays a secondary role of "aiding and abetting" the first degree actor by "counseling, commanding, or encouraging" him to commit the felony. And the principal in the second degree is distinguished from the accessory before the fact only in that he, the principal, must be present at the commission of a crime.

The principal in the second degree need not be at the crime in order to fulfill the presence requirement. He may fulfill the presence requirement by being constructively present; that is, if he is physically absent from the site of the crime but continues to cooperate with the perpetrator, and he is located in such a position so as to provide that assistance that will ensure the success of the criminal accomplishment. For example, a principal in the second degree is constructively present when he serves as a sentinel for the primary actor while the primary actor is involved in a breaking and entering.

Unless the accompanying mental state is present, the specified acts or omissions by themselves will not render the abettor guilty of the crime. It is not the perpetrator's state of mind, but rather the abettor's, that determines the abettor's guilt. In other words, if the aider renders aid or counsel without knowing or having reason to know of the criminal intentions of the perpetrating actor, he will not be guilty. For example, if a burglar enlists the assistance of a passerby to help him open a locked window and enter a victim's house, under the pretense that it was the burglar's home and he had inadvertently locked himself out, the bystander could not be considered a principal in the second degree because he lacked the requisite mental state or intent to commit burglarly.

Under certain circumstances, an abettor may escape liability for the crime and be relieved of responsibility for the subsequent acts of the perpetrator by withdrawing from the offense, even after he has given aid or counsel to a criminal scheme. Such withdrawal can erase his culpability only when he communicates a repudiation of his prior assistance to the originating actor, or when he countermands his prior aid to the best of his ability. But his acts of repudiation must be completed or communicated before the chain of events has become irretrievable. In cases where the act of abetment has gone beyond mere words, such as the supplying of materials to be used for the commission of the offense, effective withdrawal may require that such materials themselves be retrieved or at least rendered nonusable by the perpetrator.

Mere flight from the crime scene or fear and change of heart at the final moment are insufficient for exculpation (clearing from blame). However, some courts have accepted a timely warning communicated to the police as evidence of an effective withdrawal. Moreover, in most cases, the success of a legitimate and timely withdrawal is not jeopardized merely because a crime is committed, notwithstanding that withdrawal.

Accessories

The modern approach to identifying parties to a crime has been to blur the distinction between three of the four categories of parties. Consistent with today's view, the two principals (first and second degree) and the accessory before the fact are all accomplices in the felony.

The accessory before the fact differs from the principal in the second degree only in the requirement of presence. He has aided and counseled in the commission of a crime without being present at the time of perpetration, either actually or constructively. Here, absence is required in order to make him an accessory. However, if an individual provides both prior counseling and aid at the crime scene, he may become both a principal and accessory.

The accessory before the fact does not render aid at the time of committing the crime, but he may render aid in advance. And, although the aid may be far removed in time from the perpetration of the crime, it still must have retained some measure of influence in causing or assisting the offense, in order to qualify the actor as an accessory. In one case, it was held that it was no defense that an accessory had delivered his assistance and counsel more than a year prior to the commission of the offense. Thus, the courts have made it clear that, although time may be a factor, influence is the more important ingredient in determining the relationship of the accessory to the principal.

Even though the perpetrator changed the method of committing the crime (for example, if the solicited assistance called for robbery by stealth and the actor instead attempted a daylight effort), the accessory is still guilty of the felony as an accessory before the fact. Moreover, the assistance may come through an agent or intermediary without immunizing the accessory from guilt. Nor can the counselor or accessory escape guilt if reasonably foreseeable consequences result from the intended offense. The general rule seems to be that liability will be extended to the accessory where the principal's acts were a "natural and probable consequence of the original crime." For example, it is reasonably foreseeable that the commission of arson might result in injury or death to innocent victims trapped in the arsonist's target structure. However, if the perpetrator completely disregards the original wrong and commits another, the accessory is free of guilt for the actor's own crime.

A special issue involves those cases in which the aider's actions do not qualify as intentional assistance or encouragement in promoting the offense, but operate more as knowing assistance—such as the doctor who refers his patient to a competent abortionist, or the sale of liquor by an authorized dealer to a buyer intending an illegal resale.

The legal resolution of the problem posed by those cases where the alleged accomplice has no direct interest in the criminal scheme is still in doubt. But the trend seems to indicate that mere knowledge by one party that the other party intends to make an unlawful use of the service or property involved is not enough cause to place the guilt of the contemplated offense on the assisting party, if the criminal scheme involved is not serious or capital in nature. This approach seems desirable because it recognizes the need not unnecessarily to restrain lawful business by requiring a merchant or practitioner to concern himself with the affairs of his customers; yet it also seeks to preserve the social interest in preventing major crimes. Other criminal codes have recommended that knowing assistance or encouragement be treated as a distinct and separate criminal offense apart from accomplice liability for the crime aided.

As indicated earlier, the accessory after the fact is generally not treated as a party to the felony and is therefore not subject to the same penalties assigned to the felony. He is the one with knowledge of the commission of a felony who renders assistance and comfort to the felon to prevent his detection, apprehension, trial, or punishment. Without a statutory provision to the contrary, one cannot be an accessory after the fact by aiding a misdemeanant.

In order to qualify as an accessory after the fact, one must satisfy four requirements:

1. A completed felony must have been committed by the one assisted, although it is unnecessary that the perpetrator have been identified or arrested as the defendant. Therefore, if the victim of a murder attempt dies *after* aid has been rendered to the felon, the aider cannot be said to be an accessory after the fact to murder.
2. The aider must not be principal to the felony involved.
3. The aider must have more than mere suspicion that a felony has been committed—only real knowledge will suffice.
4. The aider must intend his acts of assistance to aid the felon in his efforts to elude apprehension, conviction, or punishment. In other words, if a felon was innocently harbored and nursed back to health by a charity organization unaware of his crime, an accessory charge will not lie without evidence of intent to impede law enforcement efforts.

Typical examples of acts qualifying as accessory after the fact offenses include concealing, destroying, or altering evidence; giving false testimony at a coroner's inquest; performing a surgical operation for the purpose of altering a felon's fingerprints; or supplying a fugitive with money and transportation.

It was recognized at common law that a wife could not be an accessory after the fact by providing her husband assistance, and today nearly half of the states have extended the exemption to include other close relatives.

Most state statutes today depart somewhat from the common law by dropping the traditional "accessory" terminology when referring to those involved after the fact. The modern approach has been to establish distinct penalties unrelated to the principal offense (usually five years, more or less) and to refer to the subject by creating such offenses as "obstructing justice," "hindering prosecution," or "concealing or aiding a fugitive."

If one receives some kind of consideration for his agreement not to prosecute or to inform on another who has committed a crime, he is said to have "compounded the crime." Key to the compounding laws is the agreement not to prosecute or to inform, and this agreement must be understood and shared by both parties. The mere unilateral delivery of consideration from the offender to the victim will not suffice. Consideration, of course, consists of anything of value or advantage, and only the party accepting the consideration is criminally liable.

The crime of solicitation permits the criminal justice system a basis on which to intercept and to prevent a specific criminal design from realizing fruition. Solicitation of a criminal offense is defined as the use of words or any other device by an actor to entice, advise, incite, order, urge, request, counsel, tempt, command, or encourage another person to commit a crime. Although only a handful of state jurisdictions operate with comprehensive solicitation statutes that make solicitation of *any* crime unlawful, and a few other jurisdictions cover only the solicitation of certain crimes, most criminal law scholars agree that the crime of solicitation is an important statutory tool for law enforcement.

Since the decision rendered in the leading case of *Rex* v. *Higgins* (1801), the offense of soliciting a felony has been recognized as a common law crime punishable as a misdemeanor. Leading cases further recognize that it is also indictable at common law to solicit another to commit a serious misdemeanor—one that might breach the peace, obstruct justice, or otherwise be injurious to the public welfare. The misdemeanor solicited must be a grave one. Again, although most state criminal codes have included a general attempt clause (an atttempt to commit any indictable offense), the solicitation of crime has received only scattered statutory treatment. The tendency has been to limit the punishability of solicitation to specified felonies; for example, soliciting bribery and inducing women to take interstate trips for immoral purposes.

Under the Model Penal Code, Section 5.02, solicitation would be defined broadly, including the solicitation of any crime, generally providing the same penalty for soliciting as that authorized for the complete offense. Critics of this position argue that such a stance is extreme and fails to recognize the difference in gravity between the mere solicitor and the perpetrator of the offense.

The crime of solicitation is no different from all other crimes. It requires both an act and the requisite mental state or intent that whatever criminal conduct was solicited will eventually be completed. The gist of criminal solicitation is that one person asks a second person to commit a crime. However, such a definition fails to adequately describe or define the mental element or act that is necessary in order to establish solicitation.

Although the usual common law definition and the typical solicitation statutes are silent with regard to the necessary intent for the solicitor, most modern codes specify and clearly describe the intent requirement. Several sample statutes contain the following language: ". . . with intent that another person engage in conduct constituting a felony"; ". . . with intent that a felony be committed"; and ". . . with intent that another person engage in conduct constituting kidnapping." The *Higgins* case refers to the "criminal intent" that is required in order to establish solicitation.

Most soliciting cases consist of a solicitation made by person A, the solicitor, to person B, generally the principal in the first degree, to engage in certain conduct that will bring about an *intended* criminal result. For example, if A solicits B to kidnap C and B cannot locate C and instead kidnaps C's brother, A is not guilty of criminal solicitation, because he did not intend that result. He did not possess the requisite mental state necessary to constitute the crime of solicitation. Soliciting requires no commensurate agreement to the action by the solicited one and is complete when the solicitor, acting with the necessary intent, communicates the request.

Although it is usually the person solicited to commit the crime who is the principal actor, it would seem sufficient to satisfy the intent requirement if the solicited one engages one or more intermediaries to accomplish the criminal purpose, even though it was the solicitor's intention that the person solicited commit the offense. Moreover, if the solicitation involves a successive series of other solicitations initiated and guided by the original solicitor, the actor could not escape guilt by concealing behind such an approach.

Intent alone is insufficient to round out the crime of solicitation; the *act* of soliciting is required. The mere communication of the solicitor's intent to another (either by written or spoken word) is sufficient. Legal commentators are prosaic in their choice of affirmative action verbs that describe the required acts for solicitation, and a good sample of these is included in the definition cited at the outset of this section. Some critics reject the use of the word "solicits," believing that its common law history has made it too vague; they prefer specific verbs such as "commands, enduces, entreats, or otherwise attempts to persuade."

Solicitation does not necessarily have to involve a personal communication from the solicitor to the intended actor; indeed, in cases in which the audience was solicited en masse from a public platform to commit robbery, the act and intent were deemed sufficient to constitute the crime of soliciting. However, a general solicitation by publication to a large indefinable audience, such as the attempts by brochure to persuade "dispossessed workers" to rise up and kill their "capitalistic masters," would be considered too impersonal for purposes of constituting solicitation.

The receipt of the intended communication by the intended receiver is not a necessary element in establishing solicitation. For example, if a drug distributor mails a written inducement to a local dealer urging him to accept a certain shipment of illicit narcotics for resale and that letter is intercepted, the solicitor's act is nevertheless indictable. The supporting rationale seems to be that the drug distributor's letter was an unmistakable manifestation of his threat to society, and by punishing such conduct law enforcement can deter the basis of cooperation between lawbreakers. Indeed, in this example, the solicitation can accurately be described as an attempt to conspire.

Because the crime of solicitation is complete as soon as the solicitor makes the request or command, will the courts recognize subsequent change of mind and affirmative effort to dissuade or to halt the solicited actor from committing the crime as a lawful defense?

The voluntary renunciation of criminal purpose by the solicitor is recognized as a statutory defense in only one state jurisdiction (Hawaii), and no appellate courts have ever decided the validity of renunciation as a defense. However, the Model Penal Code, Sec., 5.02 (3), provides that "it is an affirmative defense that the actor, after soliciting another person to commit a crime, persuaded him not to do so or otherwise prevented the commission of the crime, under circumstances manifesting a complete and voluntary renunciation of his criminal purpose." The mere furnishing of an opportunity to commit an offense to a willing subject offered by law enforcement officials does not constitute solicitation, providing that the subject is not "entrapped" or compelled beyond his own volition to commit the offense.

Soliciting a crime is a completed offense once the request has been communicated by the solicitor. Therefore, merely because the soliciting party was unaware that the person solicited was incapable of committing the offense, the solicitor cannot claim that incapacity as a defense. For example, if A solicits B to purchase illicit narcotics, it is no defense to the crime of soliciting that B was an undercover agent and a sworn police officer who had no intention of committing the crime solicited.

The legal arguments seem equally divided between those who

believe that soliciting is not dangerous because of the distance existing between mere talk and committed action and those who adopt the view that solicitation should remain forbidden conduct because it spawns cooperation between lawless elements in our society. However, the most persuasive advocates point out the necessity for retaining the crime of solicitation because it affords the criminal justice process an opportunity to deal with individuals who have indicated their dangerousness; and it gives law enforcement a basis for timely intervention to prevent an intended crime.

Conspiracy

Like all other crimes, conspiracy requires that there exists both an act and an accompanying mental state. The conspiratorial act consists of (1) an agreement between two or more persons (2) for the specific purpose of committing an unlawful act or a lawful act by unlawful means. The intent and purpose (to achieve the objective) constitute a mental state. It is the act of agreeing—the agreement itself—that is the essence of the crime of conspiracy rather than the means or the object of the criminal effort. For example, if two or more people agree to collect insurance proceeds by committing the act of arson, it is conclusive that both the means and the object are unlawful acts and that the combination between those involved, the agreement with intent, is the act of conspiracy.

The doctrine of conspiracy, founded in fourteenth-century English common law, was expanded in the seventeenth century into an inchoate crime, that is, an incompletely formed crime, or one where the conduct is punishable before it has realized fruition. Conspiracy survives today as a so-called common law crime, although most jurisdictions clearly define conspiracy by statute.

Most legal scholars agree that the act of agreeing to commit a crime is forbidden because it inspires the climate for further crimes either related or unrelated to those specifically contemplated. It was felt that in such a secretive, insulated environment, not only did the potential exist for other antisocial behavior, but evidence indicated that the people attracted to the original purpose were psychologically "locked in" to the group effort and could only extricate themselves by overcoming intense resistances and pressure. The action reduced the probability that the single defendant could stop the process that he himself had activated. In addition, the unlawful means or unlawful acts inspired by the instigating conspiratorial agreement tend to be conceived and consummated more efficiently and competently and with more specialization through a division of labor, which makes possible the attainment of criminal goals that are more ambitious and sophisticated than the efforts of a single perpetrator. Because group activity compounds the danger of criminal activity, the conspiracy doctrine is supported to prevent such activity in the inchoate state.

The conspiracy offense recognizes the need to allow preventive law enforcement intervention before the conspirators are permitted to initiate or complete the contemplated criminal act. Thus the question becomes: At what time in the process of preparation for a crime is the crime of conspiracy complete? Note that conspiracy differs from the offense of *attempt*. Under attempt law it must be shown that the defendant has undertaken a "substantial step" toward committing the offense; any act short of actual overt movement toward the criminal end will not satisfy the attempt requirement. Reaching further back than attempt, conspiracy recognizes criminal conduct at an earlier stage, where immediate achievement of the objective is less likely. However, the crime of conspiracy requires the existence of certain key elements, the first of which is knowledge by the defendant that the object or the means to accomplish the object is unlawful. So, although it is unnecessary for the prosecution to prove, in a heroin sale case, for example, that the single defendant was aware of the existence of such a statute (ignorance of the criminality of one's own act is no defense), in a like conspiracy case, the prosecutor *must* establish beyond a reasonable doubt that the conspirator knew that the sale of heroin was an unlawful act.

Closely aligned to the knowledge element is the requirement not only that a defendant–conspirator intended to agree, but that he intended to achieve an unlawful result or a lawful result by unlawful means. The prosecution must also show that each alleged conspirator alone possessed the requisite intent, because there must be common purpose or design between at least two persons in order to establish conspiracy. Thus, if defendants A, B, and C agree to take certain property from D, and C believes that such property is rightfully his, only A and B can be convicted of the conspiracy to commit the crime of theft or larceny. If only A has the necessary intent to steal, he can be convicted only of the crime of theft and conspiracy cannot be shown to have occurred.

At common law, it was unnecessary to show any further act beyond the mere agreement itself in order to prove conspiracy. But more and more state jurisdictions are requiring that an overt act in furtherance of the unlawful plan be proved. This third element of the conspiracy offense is required to demonstrate that the conspiracy is workable. And the so-called overt act need be committed by only one of the conspirators. It is not even necessary that such act be criminal in itself. However, if the single overt actor is found not guilty, his acquittal will affect the other alleged co-conspirators.

Once it can be shown that an agreement existed, any number of acts advancing the agreement will satisfy the overt act requirement, even though the object of that agreement has yet to be attained. For example, placing a phone call, delivering money, having a meeting, attending a preestablished rendezvous, and buying quantities of explosives have all been held to suffice as overt acts in the furtherance of the alleged criminal object.

It is useful at this point to examine two classic multiple conspiracies in which there may exist several conspiracies sponsored by the same conspirators, or a single conspiracy to accomplish several illegal acts, or any number of variations of these multiple groups and/or persons.

Identified most closely with the systematic distribution of certain contraband, the "chain" conspiracy consists of a successive flow of information, goods, or communication between several "links," and to the ultimate destination or conclusion. This type of conspiracy requires continuous cooperation and implies knowledge by all of the participants of the existence of the remote links of the chain, and is analogous to modern methods of obtaining and converting raw materials into marketable goods and then distributing them. The majority rule is that, if there is sufficient evidence to infer that a community of interest exists between all of the participants, the courts will consistently identify a conspiratorial arrangement. It is unnecessary that the parties know the identity of their fellow conspirators; they must only be aware of their existence. It is not even necessary that the details or size of the conspiratorial operation be known to the others

An arrangement most notably characteristic of organized criminal operations is described as the so-called wheel conspiracy, wherein an individual or group (the "hub") deals individually with at least two other persons or groups ("spokes") on an individual basis. A typical example might be a centralized syndicate that operates and manages separate and unrelated loansharking, vice, and narcotics activities. However, a single agreement to commit several crimes is punishable as but one conspiracy, and those involved in the "spoke" operation would not be indictable in a mass conspiracy.

As mentioned earlier, conspiracies are made punishable because collective or concerted action toward an unlawful end magnifies the risk to society by increasing the likelihood of success and by maximizing the available labor and resources. It is said that the conspiracy is harmful because of this added danger; there are, however, certain unlawful combinations wherein the added element of danger is absent. Such crimes as gambling, bribery, dueling, bigamy, incest, and adultery are illustrative of the Wharton Rule, which states that, "If only a minimum number of parties logically necessary to commit the substantive offense are involved, conspiracy indictments will not lie." If the offense can be committed by a single person or involves more persons than necessary to commit the crime, the rule will not apply. But, if, for example, several defendants were indicted for conspiring and agreeing to gamble, courts have held that a "plurality of agents" was necessary in order to commit the crime of gambling, and therefore no conspiracy occurred. The Wharton Rule is admirable because it avoids cumulative punishment (for conspiracy) in those offenses that necessarily require a plurality of agents, and in which the harm to society is not aggravated by such a combination.

The rule established at early common law that husband and wife, being considered one person for many purposes, could not be guilty of conspiring with each other if no third person were involved, has been rejected by nearly every jurisdiction considering the issue. The modern thinking seems to embrace the notion that a husband-wife combination can just as successfully increase the antisocial effect because of the plurality of persons involved as can any other union for unlawful purposes. There is little question that a corporation may be criminally indicted for participating in a conspiracy. Questions are raised, however, when the parties involved consist of the inanimate corporate entity and a single participant. The more convincing rule seems to be that a corporate conspiracy requires a plurality of *human* minds, and where only one exists, conscious agreement or mutual encouragement are impossible.

As with most substantive criminal offenses, several prominent defenses are available to conspiracy. In order for a co-conspirator to employ successfully the defense of *withdrawal,* he must satisfy the following three-pronged test:

1. He has completed an affirmative and convincing act demonstrating to his co-conspirators that he has withdrawn.
2. His act was timely, permitting his confederates time enough to abandon their plans.
3. His act was communicated to his companions in such a way that a reasonable man could not have been mistaken with regard to his purpose.

Moreover, it is necessary that such notice of abandonment be communicated to all members of the conspiracy.

Courts have generally been more receptive to the defense of impossibility of success when the charge was attempt rather than conspiracy, and as a uniform rule the courts have held that it is no defense to a charge of conspiracy that the defendant could not have been convicted of the substantive crime itself. To permit that defense would do violence to the essence of conspiracy law; namely, that it is the grouping for the purpose of making a criminal agreement and therefore the specific target of conspiracy law, that is dangerous, not the separate danger of attaining the criminal objective.

It is also a recognized defense to a charge of conspiracy that if two persons are tried together for conspiracy, an acquittal or similar disposition of one co-conspirator will bar the conviction of the remaining confederate. However, if numerous co-conspirators are charged, an acquittal of one or more will not bar the prosecution of others. In addition, whenever the offense and the act are one and the same, an acquittal of the offense operates to bar a conspiracy conviction (in the appropriate jurisdiction), because the completion of the act was necessary to establish the conspiracy. Conspiracy endures as an offense until the conspiratorial combination has achieved success or demonstrated abandonment, and the statute of limitations begins to run not from the formation of the agreement, but from the time of the last overt act.

Because the conspiracy laws enable the prosecution to get at the managers or overlords of a criminal enterprise without the necessity of proving an actual physical participation in the offense or proving specific knowledge of the details, conspiracy is viewed as an effective weapon against organized crime. Again, all that the prosecution need establish for conviction are the agreement and criminal purpose and some contribution to the criminal design.

The conspiracy sanction has been the recent target of constitutionally based criticism. Its advocates argue that conspiracy does not embrace a balance between the protection of society and the rights of the accused conspirators. Other critics contend that any indiscriminate and unthoughtful use of the conspiracy indictment threatens the fabric of First Amendment freedoms (freedom of speech). One answer to these and other issues has been introduced by the American Law Institute in the Model Penal Code section on Criminal Conspiracy (Tentative Draft No. 10, Section 5.03, 1960). Its acceptability by state legislatures and its adaptability to the conflicts arising within enforcement have yet to be determined.

Student Checklist

1. Can you define a principal in the first degree?
2. Are you able to identify the elements required to establish the offense of attempt?
3. Can you list the elements of the offense of conspiracy?
4. Are you able to define what is meant by a "wheel conspiracy"?
5. Can you illustrate a principal in the second degree?
6. Can you describe the crime of solicitation?
7. Are you able to describe how the Wharton Rule guides conspiracy cases?
8. Can you contrast an accessory before the fact with an accessory after the fact?
9. Can you explain what is meant by a "chain conspiracy"?
10. Are you able to provide an illustrative example of what is meant by taking a substantial step toward committing an offense?

Topics for Discussion

1. Discuss the Wharton Rule of conspiracy.
2. Discuss accessories to crimes and how criminal liability attaches.
3. Discuss voluntary renunciation of criminal purpose as a defense to the crime of solicitation.
4. Discuss solicitation as a criminal offense.
5. Discuss conspiracy.

ANNOTATED BIBLIOGRAPHY

Belli, Melvin. *The Law Revolution.* Volume One: *Criminal Law.* Los Angeles, Calif.: Sherbourne Press, 1968. The famed attorney presents a tour of American criminal law as viewed by a colorful practitioner. He contends that we are in a major revolution of the law and attempts to identify the trends of change.

Kalven, Harry Jr., and Hans Zeisel. *The American Jury.* Boston, Mass.: Little, Brown, 1966. An exhaustive study of the American jury system and its role in criminal law. In short, the jury system is criminal law in practice. To study criminal law without looking at how juries apply it provides an incomplete picture.

Krislov, Samuel *et al.* (eds). *Compliance and the Law: A Multi-Disciplinary Approach.* Beverly Hills, Calif.: Sage Publications, 1972. A composite of behaviorally oriented articles that focus on the societal goal of compliance to standards established in law, and the impact of criminal law toward reaching that goal.

Perkins, Rollin M. *Perkins on Criminal Law.* Mineola, N.Y.: Foundation Press, 1969. One of the more comprehensive textbooks on criminal law with primary emphasis on common law, but with an adequate coverage of statutory law so that the student can identify the differences.

The study of this chapter will enable you to:

1. Define the doctrine of self-defense.
2. Explain the operation of *ex post facto* prohibitions in criminal law.
3. Describe how entrapment serves as a positive defense to criminal liability.
4. Explain the doctrine of diminished capacity.
5. Describe how statutes of limitations operate.
6. Describe how voluntary intoxication may operate as a successful defense against criminal liability.
7. State the American Law Institute's Model Penal Code test for insanity, known as the "substantial capacity" test.
8. Distinguish the "Durham Rule" test from the "irresistible impulse" test for insanity.
9. Describe how the doctrine of immunity acts as a shield from prosecution.
10. Explain the purpose of the doctrine of immunity.

10

Defenses:
Capacity and Responsibility

This chapter deals with the most frequently employed substantive defenses to a charge of criminal conduct. These defenses are usually specified in terms of the circumstances that will excuse the offense.

Diminished Capacity

In earlier chapters we discussed the fact that conviction for a crime requires proof of a certain mental state that exists as an element of the offense. However, under the doctrine known as *diminished capacity,* or *partial responsibility,* proof of a lack of criminal intent, evidenced by insufficient mental and legal capacity to commit it, is a complete defense. The theory is that if the state of mind necessary for guilt is lacking, the crime has not been committed.

This defense generally arises in those cases where the defendant's alleged abnormal mental condition may have lacked the substance to afford him a successful insanity defense, but it is of sufficient character to be relevant in a final determination of guilt based on his intent.

The doctrine of diminished capacity is justified on the grounds that, if evidence concerning the requisite mental state necessary to prove the crime were inadmissable, most proscribed offenses would be nothing more than so-called strict liability crimes, with the commission of the act the only necessary proof of guilt.

Diminished capacity is distinguished from an insanity defense. A successful insanity defense generally results in a verdict of not guilty and subsequent commitment, but an approved showing of diminished capacity can result in a not guilty verdict to the specific defense charged. However, guilt on lesser included offenses is not barred.

Criminal incapacity does not necessarily include ignorance, stupidity, or illiteracy. Nor are being deaf and dumb or "shell-shocked" sufficient to constitute a lawful defense of diminished capacity.

Malice

Malice may be simply defined as the criminal intent that inspires a person to do grave injury to another. Malice in the legal sense connotes predetermination and a lack of any excuse or justification for the conduct that is purposely intended to cause the particular harm, or that is so wanton and reckless that knowledge by the perpetrator of the likelihood of some resultant harm is clearly evident.

As a general rule, if the harm intended occurs to another besides the intended victim, the perpetrator's malice is not diminished or mitigated. In other words, where A aims at B and misses, and instead kills C, it is no defense to a charge of homicide that A intended to kill B rather than C. In addition, if the manner of causing the intended harm is unintended in character, such as the victim dying not from the intended bullet wound in the heart, but from complications arising from a bullet in the stomach, malice can still be inferred from his acts.

However, if the harm resulting is not the harm intended, such as the poison left for a neighbor's cat but consumed instead by the neighbor's child, the general rule is that the malice is not transferable from the intended harm to the actual harm. The major exception is the·so-called felony-murder rule, where the intent to commit certain kinds of felonies will be considered adequate to convict for murder if a homicide is an unintended result.

The existence of malice may be legally established by inference gained from showing acts or conduct that lack justification or excuse, or that betray a reckless or wanton disregard of the inevitable results of such conduct.

Motive

The discussion of motive raises the issue of its appropriateness and relevance in criminal proceedings. Motive can never be considered an element of a crime and it is unnecessary in the support of a successful conviction; however, if the evidence of guilt is largely circumstantial, the value of motive as a procedural vehicle is highly important.

In criminal law, motive is defined as the spirit, or desire, that inspires a person to commit the intended offense. Even though the motives involved in any given offense are commendable, such motives, by themselves, can never be a defense to the crime committed. Similarly, the darkest and most sinister motives cannot, by themselves, be the basis for conviction if the act committed is not itself a crime.

Motive is distinguished from malice or intent in that malice or intent consist of the purpose or design with which the act is done, and motive supplies the moving cause inspiring the action. For example, if A murders B because of B's adulterous relationship with A's wife, A's intent was to kill, and his motive was retribution. In short, motive answers the question: Why?

Motive, where narrowly defined, does not include the defenses discussed in this chapter. However, motive can be relevant in the precharge decision-making conducted by the prosecutor. Also, motive may be considered as relevant by the judge in determining the severity within the allowable sentence.

A close examination of motive can be a crucial force in determining guilt or innocence when no direct evidence has been introduced. For example, if a defendant's business partner was discovered murdered and only circumstantial evidence linked the defendant to the murder, evidence of a strong hatred and prior hostile acts may supply the needed element to gain a conviction.

Intoxication

Most modern criminal codes provide that intoxication, whether it be voluntary or involuntary, or whether it be the result of alcohol or drugs, is a defense to a crime when it nullifies or fully dilutes some mental element upon which that crime depends. For example, A would not be guilty of burglary, even though he committed a breaking and entering into another's home, if his intoxication would negate his capacity to intend to commit a felony while inside.

However, if no particular motive, purpose, or intent is a necessary element of the offense charged, intoxication will not bar conviction. Also, the defense of intoxication is not available to that defendant who has already formed the intent to commit a crime, and who consumes alcohol or drugs in order to give himself courage, even though at the moment of the criminal act he was too intoxicated to entertain the requisite intent necessary to establish the crime.

The preceding discussion has generally referred to self-induced or voluntary intoxication. Involuntary, or "innocent," intoxication also exempts the individual from criminal responsibility. In order that voluntary intoxication operate as a successful defense, it is not enough that the defendant be put in a state of mind resembling insanity. Also, it is not necessary that the defendant be intoxicated to the point of unconsciousness. Involuntary intoxication, on the other hand, can successfully bar prosecution in many jurisdictions on a showing that the defendant could not understand the nature and quality of his acts or know the difference between right and wrong.

Involuntary intoxication includes those cases in which, as a result of an innocent mistake by the defendant as to the nature of the substance ingested, he becomes intoxicated and commits a criminal act. The leading cases involve drug overdoses, induced by fraud or trickery. However, it is not the trickery of the second party that establishes the defense, but rather the genuine mistake of fact by the recipient.

Other instances of involuntary intoxication include intoxication from medicine and intoxication under duress, the latter requiring a show of physical force or irresistible pressure in coercing the intoxication before exempting the intoxicated person from liability.

Contrary to the procedure established for raising the insanity defense, the defense of intoxication is raised by a plea of not guilty and a subsequent affirmative assumption of the burden by the defendant, who must present evidence demonstrating his intoxication.

Sample Statute
Intoxicated or Drugged Condition.
A person who is in an intoxicated or drugged condition is criminally responsible for conduct unless such condition either:
(a) Negatives the existence of a mental state which is an element of the offense; or
(b) Is involuntarily produced and deprives him of substantial capacity

either to appreciate the criminality of his conduct or to conform his conduct to the requirements of law.

Former Jeopardy

There is no more basic principle of criminal jurisprudence than the long-enduring public policy that seeks to protect a man from repeated attempts by the state to convict him for an alleged offense and to force him to endure ordeal, embarrassment, anxiety, expense, and insecurity after being once found innocent. This policy is embodied in the doctrine of former, or double, jeopardy, which provides that one may not be prosecuted a second time for the same offense.

In the strictest sense, this doctrine is not considered one of the recognized defenses to criminal liability. However, the doctrine does operate to protect and then to defend an individual from being subjected to the hazards of trial and possible conviction more than once for an alleged offense.

Former jeopardy applies to the offense and not to the set of circumstances or acts that spawned the offense. Therefore, the doctrine does not bar multiple prosecutions when a given situation may produce more than one offense. For example, a plea of not guilty to a charge of burglary would not necessarily bar prosecution of the same defendant on a charge of assault and battery arising out of the same situation. Nor does protection against former jeopardy bar prosecution by both the state and federal governments for the same offense. For example, if A is found innocent in a state trial court of violating a state dispensing-narcotics statute, he may nonetheless be tried and found guilty of violating a federal law that prohibits the same act of dispensing. The underlying rationale is that because separate sovereignties are involved (federal and state) the policies barring two prosecutions for the same offense do not apply.

The doctrine of former jeopardy, however, applies in those cases where conviction and sentence are followed by an attempt to increase the sentence, or where the accused is tried again after the original trial ended in mistrial.

There are no exceptions to the constitutional guarantee against double jeopardy. Nor can any court or state legislature limit or restrict the right in any way.

Capacity to commit a crime is presumed in most jurisdictions at roughly the age of 13 or 14, but that limit is not conclusive and may be overcome by a sufficient showing of lawful incapacity. Two forms of such incapacity, diminished capacity and intoxication, have already been discussed. But the most widely disputed and controversial form of incapacity revolves around the insanity defense.

"Insanity" is a word with many meanings, depending upon the setting and situation, but in a criminal law, nonmedical sense, it usually connotes a mental disorder resulting from deterioration or damage existing with the defendant at the time of an alleged offense, which robs him of the ability to know or to choose right from wrong. Other slight variations of this definition will be discussed in the following paragraphs.

It seems quite clear that if one lacks the criminal capacity to commit a criminal offense, he is also not criminally responsible for his acts. And the general test of criminal responsibility in over one-half of the jurisdictions is not only whether the individual possesses the capacity to understand the nature and consequences of the alleged act, but whether he has the ability to distinguish between right and wrong with regard to the act. This is the brief statement of the so-called M'Naghten Rule, or "the right-wrong test," as it is sometimes called.

Long the subject of controversy, but nevertheless the predominant rule in the United States, M'Naghten prescribes a broad and general definition of the elements necessary in order successfully to raise the insanity defense. The rule requires that there must first be a disability; that is, the defendant must at the time of the offense have been suffering "a defect of reason, from a disease of the mind." This disability must have resulted in one of two conditions: either the inability to know and to understand the nature and quality of his act, or the fact that what he was doing was wrong.

A minority of jurisdictions have adopted one of three other tests or "definitions" of insanity:

1. The so-called Durham Rule, which states that an accused is "not criminally responsible if his unlawful act was the product of mental disease or mental defect." Criticism of the Durham Rule chiefly focuses on the ambiguity of the word "product," and as a result appellate courts have uniformly declined to accept the Durham test.
2. A second test provides that even though the person knows the nature

and quality of his act and knows that it is wrong, he should be found not guilty by reasons of insanity if it can be conclusively demonstrated that he was unable to control his conduct because of mental disease. This situation is known as the "irresistible impulse" test, which has been criticized on the grounds that it represented an unwise and unnecessary broadening of the criteria for determining criminal responsibility.

3. A growing number of jurisdictions have adopted the American Law Institute's Model Penal Code approach, or "substantial capacity" test, which seeks to expand the concepts embodied in M'Naghten and the "irresistible impulse" tests. As set out in Model Penal Code Section 4.01, the test provides that:

A person is not responsible for criminal conduct if at the time of such conduct as a result of mental disease or defect he lacks substantial capacity either to appreciate the criminality of his conduct or to conform his conduct to the requirements of law.

As used in this Article, the terms mental disease or defect do not include an abnormality manifested only by repeated criminal or otherwise anti-social conduct.

The insanity defense, although occasionally criticized, is nonetheless consistent with the generally accepted theories of punishment and is supported because it separates from the criminal justice system those individuals who should not be subjected to the regular penal sanctions. As stated in the explanatory comments to Model Penal Code Section 4.01:

To put the matter differently, the problem is to discriminate between the cases where a punitive-correctional disposition is appropriate and those in which a medical-custodial disposition is the only kind that the law should allow.

Sample Statute

Insanity.

(a) A person is not criminally responsible for conduct if at the time of such conduct, as a result of mental disease or mental defect, he lacks substantial capacity either to appreciate the criminality of his conduct or to conform his conduct to the requirements of law.

(b) The terms "mental disease or mental defect" do not include an abnormality manifested only by repeated criminal or otherwise anti-social conduct.

A criminal offense has been defined as an offense against the public, pursued by the state. In other words, a criminal act is a wrong affecting more than the victim, indeed, the whole of society. Therefore, as a general rule, even though the party directly injured by the offense consents to the criminal act, such approval will not ordinarily operate as a defense in a criminal prosecution involving that act. Court decisions have emphasized that it is beyond the power of the individual who is harmed to license the criminal act.

In those cases where the lack of consent is, itself, an element of the crime, the victim's consent would provide a lawful defense. The crime of rape, for example, requires that carnal knowledge of a woman occurs without her consent. Therefore, the woman's consent to sexual intercourse bars a conviction for rape, because "without consent" is an element of the offense of rape.

It is well to note here the crimes that involve conduct that takes place because the "victim" had given some degree of consent. An embrace between lovers might be transformed into an act of assault and battery, in the absence of the necessary element of the victim's consent. In these cases, the element of consent determines the complexion, character, and lawfulness of an act.

We have mentioned that consent to sexual intercourse is a lawful defense to a charge of rape. But what if the victim is threatened with bodily harm if she refuses, and fearing for her safety, she accepts or acquiesces to the sexual act? The law holds that, if force or fear generates a genuine belief that failure to submit to the criminal act will result in great bodily injury or other heinous acts, such submission is not legally recognized as consent.

Fraud, or assent by deception in consent cases, is best discussed in terms of the two kinds of fraud—fraud *in factum* and fraud *in the inducement*. If the deception causes a misunderstanding as to the fact of the defendant's conduct (that is, fraud *in factum*), there exists no basis for effective consent. However, if the deception is concerned with some collateral matter (that is, fraud *in the inducement*) and not to the thing done, there does exist a legally recognized consent.

The most illustrative examples of the distinction between these two types of fraud are in the opinions dealing with prosecutions for physician-rapes. In those cases where a physician engaged in sexual intercourse with a female patient under circumstances in which she did not realize what was happening assumed that she was only submitting to an examination or operation, and believed also that penetration was being made by an instrument, it can be said that there was no lawful consent by the victim, because intercourse was obtained by fraud in the factum. Conversely, consent obtained by fraud in the inducement—for example, a physician has sexual intercourse with a female patient under the fraudulent pretense that such an act would cure her illness—is considered lawful and effective consent.

Other related consensual acts, such as condonation (the forgiveness of a criminal offense by the victim), are no defense. Nor will ratification (a formal sanction of the act) have the effect of barring a prosecution. Even voluntary restitution by the defendant and acceptance of the restitution by the victim is not a defense. Once again, the underlying rationale is that the principal injury resulting from the commission of a crime is not to the victim involved but to society.

Mistake of Law

"Ignorantia legis neminem excusat" (ignorance of the law excuses no man) is a rule that is deeply rooted in Anglo-American law. The popular conception of the maxim is a portrayal of a stern and inflexible rule devoid of any exceptions. It would seem that the contrary is more accurate, for the proposition that knowledge of the law is presumed is subject to numerous exceptions and qualifications.

The underlying rule with regard to mistake is that ignorance, or mistake, of law is not a defense to a crime except: (1) when a specific intent is essential to constitute the crime charge, and ignorance or mistake negates the existence of that mental state: or (2) when the mistake resulted from authorized reliance, or where the law is obscure, unsettled, or capable of multiple, reasonable interpretations.

The first exception has been prolifically discussed in those cases involving prosecution for larceny. Honest mistake of law is a defense when that mistake negates a required mental element of the crime. Therefore, if A enters another's home in an effort to retrieve property he believes to be his own in the honest belief of a lawful right to do so, A would not be guilty of theft because he does not have the mental state (intent to permanently deprive another of that person's property) required for theft. He is saved from conviction simply because one of the elements necessary for guilt has been negated—that of intent to deprive. Conversely, if A took the property knowing that it belonged to another but (for argument's sake) honestly believed that such conduct was not against the law, the intent to steal would nonetheless be present. In other words, it is not the intent to violate the law that is proscribed, but rather the intentional doing of the act, which is a violation.

If a defendant reasonably believes that his conduct is not unlawful and his understanding is based on an official statement of the law, or if the law was not reasonably made available to him, the government's actions or lack of action will bar him from prosecution for offenses committed in ignorance of that law. Also, until a statute or court decision has been declared invalid, a person is entitled to rely on it as being law. One cannot be held criminally liable if the law is declared void after his conduct that relied on a statute or court decision. The reliance, however, must be reasonable. If, for example, a lower court decision goes up on appeal and is later reversed, some courts have argued that reliance should fail as a defense because of the tenuous nature of the lower court's judgment.

In addition, reasonable reliance upon an official but erroneous interpretation, such as a state attorney general's opinion, can operate as a defense to later determined criminal conduct. However, reliance upon advice of private counsel will not constitute a defense to criminal acts, apparently because of the danger of collusion between attorney and client.

Mistake of Fact

Ignorance, or mistake of fact, will operate as a bar to conviction if the mistaken belief is based on reasonable grounds, honestly conceived, and of such a nature that, had the facts existed as they were conceived, the conduct would have indeed been lawful. As with mistake of law, the controlling logic is that mistake of fact results in the absence of a requisite element of criminal intent, thus rendering the criminal charge invalid. Typical examples include the patron who mistakenly leaves the restaurant with a coat he reasonably believes is his own and is therefore innocent of theft; or the man who honestly, but erroneously, believes a passing stranger to be an approaching assailant and strikes the victim in an effort to thwart the anticipated attack and is thus not guilty of assault and battery.

The test for a lawful defense because of mistake of law is the same for mistake of fact. First, the mental state required in the statute is conclusively determined, and then the question as to its existence in view of the defendant's mistake of fact is considered. On a charge of theft, the critical mental element is the intent to permanently deprive the *owner* of his property. Therefore, if A was aware that the property was not his but believed it to belong to C instead of B (the rightful owner), the mental element of depriving the owner is still present, and mistake of fact will not succeed as a defense. However, if by reason of mistake or ignorance of fact A believes the property to be his own, he does not possess the requisite intent to commit the offense and is thereby defended by his reasonable error in fact.

This logical progression becomes increasingly complex, however, under the questions raised by the requirement that the mistake not arise from a want of proper care on the part of the defendant—in other words, "reasonable grounds"—and, also, because imprecise legislative drafting has often blurred the definition of exactly what mental element is actually required.

In those cases where the violated statute is one that punishes a prohibited act without regard to the existence of a mental element (the strict liability statutes), ignorance or mistake of fact is not a lawful excuse for violation. Typical of these laws are the offenses making it unlawful to sell liquor to a minor. Even though the owner has exercised reasonable care in checking proof of age and in good faith believes the minor to be an adult (a technical mistake of fact), he will nonetheless be unable to claim successfully a mistake of fact defense. Today, most reviewing courts have softened the impact of the strict liability acts by inserting the added element of negligence as necessary to invoke the bar to the mistake of fact defense. Thus, the person accused of a strict liability offense could use the mistake of fact defense unless the state establishes an element of negligence by the accused in commiting the prohibited act.

Sample Statute

Ignorance or Mistake.

(a) A person's ignorance or mistake as to a matter of either fact or

*law, except as provided in Section 4–3(c) above, is a defense if it nega-
tives the existence of the mental state which the statute prescribes with
respect to an element of the offense.*

*(b) A person's reasonable belief that his conduct does not constitute an
offense is a defense if:*

1. *The offense is defined by an administrative regulation or order which
   is not known to him and has not been published or otherwise made
   reasonably available to him, and he could not have acquired such
   knowledge by the exercise of due diligence pursuant to facts known
   to him; or*
2. *He acts in reliance upon a statute that later is determined to be
   invalid; or*
3: *He acts in reliance upon an order or opinion of an Illinois Appellate
   or Supreme Court, or a United States appellate court later overruled
   or reversed;*
4. *He acts in reliance upon an official interpretation of the statute, regulation, or order defining the offense, made by a public officer or
   agency legally authorized to interpret such statute.*

Entrapment

Entrapment is a positive defense to criminal charges, but unlike most of
the defenses discussed in this chapter, entrapment presumes or admits the
guilt of the defendant in the first instance. The general definition of the
entrapment defense is that, if the defendant is instigated or lured by a
law enforcement official into the commission of a criminal act for the
purpose of prosecution and if the defendant otherwise had no intention of
committing the criminal act, the defendant may raise the affirmative defense of entrapment.

The elements of an entrapment defense, assuming or admitting the
completion of the crime and the defendant's guilt, are (1) the initial
planning of the offense by a law enforcement officer; (2) the procurement or instigation of the commission of the offense by the law officer;
and (3) the original lack of intent to commit the offense by the defendant. The defendant must have been otherwise "innocent" and would not
have otherwise committed the criminal act. Thus, if the officer originates
the idea to commit the crime and then instigates or induces the defendant
to commit the act when the defendant was not otherwise disposed to do

so, the defendant has an affirmative defense to criminal charges arising out of the act.

The term "entrapment" is an inaccurate description of the defense, however, because law enforcement officers clearly have the right and duty in fighting crime to make use of deception, subterfuge, or trickery to obtain evidence of a crime, as long as they do so in good faith. The more accurate terms for the defense would be "instigation" or "inducement," rather than "entrapment," because it is perfectly proper for law officers to set traps for wrongdoers as long as the idea for the crime has originated in the wrongdoer himself and not in the mind of the police. If the police merely furnish an opportunity for the defendant to commit the crime and do not take steps to instigate or to induce the commission of the crime, the defense is not available. The defense is also not available if someone not connected with law enforcement induces the defendant to commit the act.

There are a number of reasons suggested for the entrapment defense. One rationale is that of deterring police from such reprehensible conduct. Another is that the conviction of an otherwise innocent person would be contrary to public policy because it is less evil that some criminal should escape than that the government plan an ignoble part. Another theory of the defense is that the government is barred from convicting the defendant, because no one is entitled to judgment if his agent was the instigating cause of the harm, and the same reasoning applies to the government.

However, if the government merely provides an opportunity or lays a trap for the commission of the crime that the defendant habitually commits or is inclined to commit without suggestion, the defense is not available. For example, a policeman may pretend to be drunk and lie in the gutter with his wallet protruding and await the coming of a thief who is ready and willing to rob him. An undercover agent may approach a suspected narcotics peddler under the guise of being an addict. An officer may dress up in female clothing in anticipation of being attacked by and capturing a suspected rapist, mugger, or thief. If someone has telephoned another person on numerous occasions making indecent suggestions, and that person reports the fact to the police and, following their advice, agrees to meet the defendant; and if this results in the arrest of the defendant when he appears for the agreed meeting; the defense of entrapment is not available because the criminal idea had originated in his mind.

Sample Statute

Entrapment.

A person is not guilty of an offense if his conduct is incited or induced by a public officer or employee, or agent of either, for the purpose of obtaining evidence for the prosecution of such person. However, this section is inapplicable if a public officer or employee, or agent of either, merely affords to such person the opportunity or facility for committing an offense in furtherance of a criminal purpose that such person has originated.

Accessory

In crimes, parties are generally classed as principals (those present during the commission of the crime) and accessories. An accessory may be an accessory before or an accessory after the fact. The principal is the person who actually commits the crime. The accessory is one who aids or abets or procures the principal to commit the crime but is not present when it is committed; or who, after the commission of the crime, conceals or aids the perpetrator with knowledge of the crime and with the intent to aid the perpetrator in escaping capture.

An accessory before the fact is a person: (1) who was not present at the time when the crime was committed; but (2) who counseled, encouraged, or procured another to commit the crime, or otherwise aided or abetted in its commission; (3) with knowledge that the act to be committed was a crime and therefore with unlawful intent. The accessory before the fact renders aid in the commission of the crime in advance by drawing plans for the crime, procuring for the perpetrator the weapon or other means by which the crime is to be committed, or by otherwise making suggestions or giving encouragement to the commission of the crime. The act may be merely to induce another through threats or promises or by words or acts of encouragement. The purpose must be to encourage or to assist the perpetrator in the commission of the crime.

There must be an intentional lending of assistance or encouragement. It is therefore insufficient that one unintentionally engages in acts that give such assistance or encouragement to the perpetrator of the crime. The accessory must intend that the acts have the effect of assisting or encouraging the commission of the crime.

Four elements must be met to establish an accessory after the fact: (1) a crime must have been committed by another and completed prior to the act of the defendant; (2) the defendant must not himself be guilty of the crime as the principal; (3) the defendant must act in such a way so as to personally assist the criminal in his efforts to avoid capture; and (4) such assistance must be given with knowledge of the commission of the crime. Another requirement often found in statutes is that the defendant should not be related to the person who committed the crime within a certain degree, such as husband-wife or father-son.

Sample Statutes
Principal in the First Degree.
Whoever commits any criminal offense, against the state, whether felony or misdemeanor, or aids, abets, hires, or otherwise procures such offense to be committed, is a principal in the first degree and may be charged, convicted, and punished as such, whether he is or is not actually or constructively present at the commission of such offense.

Accessory After the Fact.
Whoever, not standing in the relation of husband or wife, parent or grandparent, child or grandchild, brother or sister, by consanguinity or affinity to the offender, maintains or assists the principal or accessory before the fact, or gives the offender any other aid, knowing that he has committed a felony or been accessory thereto before the fact, with intent that he shall avoid or escape detection, arrest, trial, or punishment, shall be deemed an accessory after the fact and be punished by imprisonment in the state prison not exceeding seven years, or in the county jail not exceeding one year, or by fine not exceeding $1000.

Ex Post Facto Laws

Our criminal philosophy is that the purpose of criminal law is to define socially intolerable conduct, and it does not permit a conviction for an act that was not clearly recognized as a crime at the time it was done. There should be no punishment for conduct unless it was considered criminal by some law in existence at the time the conduct was committed.

The U. S. Constitution and many state constitutions forbid legislative bodies from enacting any *ex post facto* law.

A law that creates a new crime and attempts to apply it retroactively to conduct that was not criminal at the time when the act was committed is an *ex post facto* law and is therefore prohibited. In addition, laws that attempt to inflict a greater punishment for the commission of a crime than was in existence at the time that the act was committed are *ex post facto* laws.

The following list of laws have been defined as *ex post facto* laws and are thus forbidden:

1. Every law that makes criminal an action done before the passing of the law (in which it was innocent when done), and punishes such action.
2. Every law that aggravates a crime, or makes it greater than it was when committed.
3. Every law that changes the punishment and inflicts a greater punishment than the law annexed to the crime, when committed.
4. Every law that alters the legal rules of evidence and receives less or different testimony than the law required at the time of the commission of the offense, in order to convict the offender.

A number of rationales have been suggested for the *ex post facto* prohibition. First, it would be unfair to apply retroactively to an individual a law of greater severity than the law in existence at the time that he committed the act. It is felt that the defendant is entitled to fair warning of the consequences of his conduct. Another reason for the rule is the fear of an unbridled use of power by public officials.

The rule against the enactment of *ex post facto* laws applies only to legislative acts of either the Congress or state legislatures and does not apply to judicial decisions. In addition, the rule applies not to civil matters but only to criminal actions.

Coercion

An act that otherwise constitutes a crime may be defended on the ground that it was done under coercion (often referred to as "compulsion" or "duress"). The elements that must exist for the defense of coercion to be used are that the committed act was the result of a threat by a third person that reasonably caused the defendant to believe that he must commit the act to avoid imminent death or serious bodily injury to himself or to another. However, the defense of duress is not available to the crime of intentionally killing an innocent third person.

If the defendant is being unlawfully threatened with bodily harm either to himself or to an innocent third party and commits the crime as a result of such threats, the act under the proper circumstances would be justified and the defendant would be not guilty of the crime in question. For example, if a third person with a gun threatens to shoot the defendant unless the defendant drives him to the scene of a robbery, which the third person then commits, the defendant is not guilty of the robbery because of the duress, compulsion, or coercion exerted over him.

The rationale of the defense is that public policy favors the commission of a lesser harm (the robbery) when it will avoid a greater harm (the death of the defendant). Therefore, the act is justified because it is better that the defendant choose the lesser of two evils in order to avoid the greater evil with which he is threatened. A further rationale would be that, because the purpose of the criminal law is to punish, there is little use in punishing when punishment cannot and does not serve as a deterrent to certain actions.

As noted, the defendant must make a choice of two evils and must choose to do the lesser evil. Thus, coercion is no defense to the intentional taking of life by the threatened person, although it is a defense to a killing committed by another during the commission of a crime in which the defendant is participating under coercion. In the example described, if the third party shoots a teller during the commission of the robbery, coercion is no defense. The coercion must produce in the mind of the defendant (1) a reasonable fear of (2) imminent (3) serious bodily harm or death. Threats of future harm or immediate nonserious harm or threats creating an unreasonable fear will not serve as a defense. Obviously, therefore, duress is not a defense if the accused is acting under order or the command of a superior.

Sample Statute
Compulsion.
(a) A person is not guilty of an offense, other than an offense punishable with death, by reason of conduct that he performs under the compulsion of threat or menace of the imminent infliction of death or great

bodily harm, if he reasonably believes death or great bodily harm will be inflicted upon him if he does not perform such conduct.

(b) A married woman is not entitled, by reason of the presence of her husand, to any presumption of compulsion, or to any defense of compulsion except that stated in Subsection (a).

Self-Defense

When one is unlawfully attacked by another and has no opportunity to resort to the lawful processes for his defense, it is proper for him to take reasonable steps to defend himself from physical harm. When he acts in a reasonable manner he has a complete defense to crimes against the person of another because he is said to be justified in taking such actions.

The self-defense doctrine is generally held to be that one who is free from fault may use nondeadly force in self-defense, or if additional conditions are present. The defendant must reasonably believe that he is in immediate danger of unlawfully bodily harm from his adversary. The defensive force used must not be unreasonable in view of the harm it is intended to avoid. The defendant must reasonably believe he cannot avoid the threatened harm without using defensive force or giving up some right.

The key factors to the doctrine of self-defense are therefore the use of a "reasonable" amount of force against another with a reasonable belief that it is necessary, and the fact that the amount of force must be reasonably related to the threatened harm that one seeks to avoid. A distinction is made between force that is intended or likely to cause death or great bodily harm, and force that is neither intended nor likely to cause such harm. If nondeadly force is sufficient to avert a threatened harm, deadly force would be unreasonable, and even nondeadly force may be found unreasonable if it is in excess of what is needed in a particular circumstance.

In addition to using reasonable force in self-defense, the defendant must have reasonable belief in the necessity for using such force to prevent harm to himself. One who honestly, though unreasonably, believes in the necessity of using force in self-protection is not entitled to the defense. One who honestly does not believe in the necessity of using force although it may appear reasonable to others is also not entitled to the defense. Mistake does not deprive the defendant of the defense of self-defense and, therefore, when his belief is reasonable although mistaken, the defendant may still avail himself of the defense of self-defense. Thus, if one has struck another in the reasonable belief that it was necessary to do so in order to avoid being stabbed, he is not guilty of an assault and battery, even though it is later determined that the other person was merely playing a joke with a rubber dagger. Likewise, when one is in impending danger from the third person but is unaware of the danger and slays that person in cold blood, he is not entitled to avail himself of the doctrine of self-defense.

There are two commonly stated rules with respect to the utilization of deadly force in self-defense. The first is the "no retreat rule," or the "true man rule." This majority view holds that one may stand his ground and use deadly force if such force reasonably seems necessary to save himself.

The second rule, adopted in a minority of states, is the "retreat rule," or the "retreat to the law." The position of this rule is that, even if the defendant was an innocent victim of a deadly assault he must take an obviously safe retreat if such a retreat is available, rather than resort to deadly force. Exceptions to the retreat rule are when the defendant is in his own home, or when the third person is one whom he is lawfully attempting to arrest, or who is a felon.

One may also be justified in the defense of another or in the defense of another's property. Briefly stated, it is generally held that one may use reasonable force in the defense of another person, even a stranger, when it is reasonably believed that the other person is in imminent danger of unlawful bodily harm from his adversary, and that the use of reasonable force is necessary to avoid the danger. Therefore, one who is himself free from fault may intervene and use force to protect an innocent victim of what appears to be intended crime. At common law, the household was regarded as a unit and any member of the household had the privilege to defend another member. It is held that one may defend his family, his servants, or his master whenever he may defend himself. This rationale has evolved to the extent that one has the privilege of defending another in a reasonable manner if the other person is the innocent victim of an unlawful attack. Thus, the privilege of self-defense appears to have merged with a privilege of crime prevention, and it forms the rationale for the present-day rule.

It is also generally held that one is protected when he acts reasonably under mistaken fact, although some jurisdictions adhere to the rule that when one goes to the defense of another he does so at his own peril and merely "steps into the shoes" of the third party whom he has assisted. He is entitled to no greater privilege than the defense of self-defense.

The general rule with respect to the defense of property is that one in lawful possession of property is justified in using reasonable force to protect it from trespass or theft when he reasonably believes that such action is necessary to prevent or to terminate an unlawful interference with his right to such property. Generally, deadly force is never authorized for the defense of property, and the amount of nondeadly force must be reasonable under the circumstances.

Sample Statutes

Use of Force in Defense of Person.
A person is justified in the use of force against another when and to the extent that he reasonably believes that such conduct is necessary to defend himself or another against such other's imminent use of unlawful force. However, he is justified in the use of force that is intended or likely to cause death or great bodily harm only if he reasonably believes that such force is necessary to prevent imminent death or great bodily harm to himself or another, or the commission of a forcible felony.

Use of Force in Defense of Dwelling.
A person is justified in the use of force against another when and to the extent that he reasonably believes that such conduct is necessary to prevent or terminate such other's unlawful entry into or attack upon a dwelling. However, he is justified in the use of force that is intended or likely to cause death or great bodily harm only if:
(a) The entry is made or attempted in a violent, riotous, or tumultuous manner, and he reasonably believes that such force is necessary to prevent an assault upon, or offer of personal violence to, him or another then in the dwelling, or
(b) He reasonably believes that such force is necessary to prevent the commission of a felony in the dwelling.

Alibi

The literal meaning of the word "alibi" is "elsewhere." In criminal law the term is used to describe the proof by which a defendant attempts to show that he could not have committed a particular crime, because he was "elsewhere" than the scene of the crime at the time of its commission, and it was therefore physically impossible for him to have committed the crime.

Although an alibi has been classed as an affirmative defense, it actually constitutes a rebuttal of the state's evidence that has identified the defendant as the person who committed the crime. It does not involve a denial that the crime took place; it merely constitutes a denial that the defendant committed the crime, or that he was able to do so, because of his physical separation from the scene. Thus, the defense is not available where the theory of prosecution is that the defendant acted through another person or with the aid of another person.

Because alibis are easily fabricated, the defense is looked upon with careful scrutiny. The defendant must show that he was at a place so distant from the scene of the crime that his participation in the crime was impossible. His alibi must cover the entire time when the presence would be required for the accomplishment of the crime. In addition, most states require the defendant to give notice to the prosecution of his intent to rely upon alibi as a defense, and they often require notice as to the place where the defendant claims to have been at the time of the crime and the witnesses who will testify in support of his alibi defense.

As to the effect of an alibi, if it establishes reasonable doubt in the minds of the jury, it is a good defense to particular charges.

Immunity

The term "immunity" refers to a doctrine that is not a defense to criminal charges, but merely a shield from being prosecuted for the commission of the criminal acts. Briefly stated, the government may enter into an agreement or a contract with a defendant for his exemption, or immunity, from prosecution in return for obtaining the defendant's honest and fair full disclosure of the crime on the trial of a confederate, whether or not the confederate is convicted. Agreements for immunity are generally made with the prosecuting attorney with the consent of the court, and the defendant must keep his part of the bargain if he wishes to retain the promised immunity. If a defendant's testimony is untrue or if a disclosure is only partial, the defendant loses his right to immunity and is subject to prosecution. In addition, the testimony elicited by the bargain must be testimony or evidence to which the privilege against self-incrimination applies. One becomes immune from prosecution for a particular charge only if he can properly refuse to testify because of self-incrimination, or if the testimony or evidence was otherwise privileged in nature, for example, protected by the attorney-client privilege.

The purpose behind the immunity doctrine is to aid the government to obtain convictions and evidence by inducing criminals to inform on each other, and at the same time to protect each person from being denied his constitutional right of self-incrimination.

No one has a right to immunity in any situation, and as a general rule the right of the government official to confer immunity upon the defendant is limited to recommendations by the prosecuting attorney or the district attorney for the granting of immunity and the ratification of immunity by the court.

Religious Beliefs

The religious doctrines or beliefs of a defendant are not recognized as a defense to a criminal charge. It is generally held that religious beliefs cannot be accepted as justification or excuse for committing a criminal act prohibited by statutes, for the crime is no less odious because it is sanctioned by what a particular sect may designate as religion.

Thus, acts of bigamy are not justified on the grounds that they are required or allowed by a defendant's religious beliefs. In addition, if a defendant is prosecuted for failure to furnish medical attention when it is his duty to do so or when it is designated a criminal offense not to do so by statute, the defendant cannot rely upon his religious beliefs in defense to such criminal charges.

Statute of Limitations

Statutes of limitations have been enacted in virtually all jurisdictions with respect to all criminal charges, with the usual exception of murder, and these statutes limit the time for a commencement of criminal proceedings. The statutes vary greatly from jurisdiction to jurisdiction, but as a general rule they state that, unless the criminal charges are commenced within a certain number of years after the commission of the crime, the state is thereafter prohibited from bringing such criminal charges against the defendant in the absence of unusual circumstances. Statutes of limitation are defenses against the bringing of the criminal charges and do not go to the issue of the guilt or innocence of the defendant with respect to the commission of the particular act. If the criminal charges are not brought within a certain period of time, the state is forever barred from filing such charges.

In the absence of statutes limiting the time in which a criminal charge must be brought against a defendant, the prosecution may be instituted at any time, no matter how long after the actual commission of the criminal act. In some jurisdictions there are periods of limitations defined according to the classification of the crime as a misdemeanor or felony. If the crime is in the less serious category of misdemeanors, for example, the statute may state that no criminal action may be brought for violation of the misdemeanor statute in question after two years following the commission of the crime. In the case of felonies, the statutes may provide that felony charges may not be brought against the defendant after a period of five years from the date of the commission of the crime.

As a general rule, statutes of limitations start to run from the time of the commission or completion of the crime, and not from the date the crime or the defendant is established. Unless the particular statute in question contains an exception that will stop its operation, such as if the defendant has fled the state, the running of the statute if not interrupted. However, some statutes provide that if the defendant has fled from justice or otherwise attempted to conceal his crime, the statute does not begin to run. The statute will run from the time the offense is committed until the criminal proceedings are commenced. Generally, the prosecution is begun and the statute tolled at the time that the charges are filed and an arrest warrant or summons is issued.

Student Checklist

1. Can you define the doctrine of self-defense?
2. Can you explain the operation of *ex post facto* prohibitions in criminal law?
3. Can you describe how entrapment serves as a positive defense to criminal liability?
4. Are you able to explain the doctrine of diminished capacity?
5. Do you know how to describe how statutes of limitations operate?
6. Can you describe how voluntary intoxication may operate as a successful defense against criminal liability?
7. Can you state the American Law Institute's Model Penal Code test for insanity known as the "substantial capacity" test?
8. Do you know how to distinguish the "Durham Rule" test from the "irresistible impulse" test for insanity?
9. Can you describe how the doctrine of immunity acts as a shield from prosecution?
10. Can you explain the purpose of the doctrine of immunity?

Topics for Discussion

1. Discuss the impact of coercion or duress on criminal liability.
2. Discuss the rule of law, "ignorance of the law excuses no man."
3. Discuss the use of entrapment as a defense to criminal liability.
4. Discuss the doctrine of self-defense.
5. Discuss the doctrine of immunity.

ANNOTATED BIBLIOGRAPHY

Fingarette, Herbert. *The Meaning of Criminal Insanity*. Berkeley, Calif.: University of California Press, 1972. A presentation of the key concepts associated with criminal insanity and criminal responsibility. The author attempts to develop root meanings of the concept of insanity and to relate theory and practice in the application of law.

Goulett, Harlan M. *The Insanity Defense in Criminal Trials*. St. Paul, Minn.: West Publishing, 1965. Written by a prosecutor acquainted with trial work for persons seeking a working knowledge of the use of insanity as a defense to criminal charges. An excellent view is also presented of prosecution strategy associated with trying cases where insanity defenses are used.

Kalven, Harry Jr., and Hans Zeisel. *The American Jury*. Boston, Mass.: Little, Brown, 1966. An exhaustive study of the American jury system and its role in criminal law. In short, the jury system is criminal law in practice. To study criminal law without looking at how juries apply it provides an incomplete picture.

Lindesmith, Alfred R. *The Addict and the Law*. Bloomington, Ind.: Indiana University Press, 1965. A behavioralist's view of the drug problem and its relationship to criminal law. Reform and suggestions for new approaches provide a climax for the text.

Silving, Helen. *Mental Incapacity and Criminal Conduct*. Springfield, Ill.: Charles C Thomas, 1968. Several essays on the status known as legal insanity. The primary theme is to discard old, seemingly useless concepts of law that undergird legal insanity for more useful and realistic principles that have evolved from psychology.

The study of this chapter will enable you to:

1. Define victimology.
2. Identify eight of the crimes commonly called victimless crimes.
3. Give an example for each category of Mendelsohn's classification of victims.
4. Describe the legal rights of a victim to use force in defending himself.
5. Describe the amount of force that a victim in possession of property may use in terminating a criminal trespass to the property.
6. Describe the differences between tort actions and victim-compensation programs in terms of providing relief for the victim of criminal acts.
7. Analyze the five basic methods for compensating victims.
8. Describe the trend of state legislation toward victim compensation programs.
9. Identify three early examples of victim compensation.
10. Analyze the rates at which crimes are underreported, based on the NORC survey.

11
Law and the Crime Victim

In novels, on the cinema and television screens, we avidly follow the activities of killers, experiencing a morbid thrill at their crimes, admiration for their ingenuity, and sometimes a sneaking regret at their capture. . . . We are terrified by the thought, but at the same time we are aware, that there is murder in all of us and that given the right (or wrong) circumstances we would also pull the trigger or bring down the hammer. Contemplating this we experience that slight, sometimes sickening, tremor of power. Another person's life in our hands. For a moment we are God. Then the feeling passes and we return to our normal, law-abiding lives—until we read about the next sensational murder.

Few would put themselves into the dead man's shoes. There is no sensation of power, no omnipotence. The thrill is in killing, not dying. So the victim is forgotten as soon as possible; buried under the huge pile of trial reports, newspaper articles, and murder books. Buried so that there is nothing to remind us of the frightening fact that each of us may be not only the potential murderer but also a potential victim.[1]

The victim of crime has been essentially ignored in most of the criminal justice literature. However, written accounts indicating concern for the welfare and rights of the victim are centuries old. In the last hundred years, scientific study of the victim's personal characteristics, as well as his rights, duties, and precipitating influence in criminal activities, has become increasingly popular, and a new science of "victimology" is beginning to emerge. New terminology has been proposed for studying criminal–victim relationships. Mendelsohn suggests "penal-couple" as

---

[1] Jack Gratus, *The Victims* (London: Hutchinson and Co., Ltd., 1969).

the criminal and his victim and "potential of victimal receptivity" as the aptitude of becoming a victim.[2]

There are three basic categories of victims: (1) the individual victim; (2) an organization, such as a business corporation or church group; and (3) society as a whole. Each category is subject to specific types of offenses. Although all crimes can be viewed as disruptions to the social order and therefore as offenses against the public, for our purpose we shall deal with offenses against society as those having no victim other than public morality and the social order.

An organization can be victimized in several ways. A criminal can stage a daring daylight armed robbery or burglarize an establishment at night. A customer may be overly tempted by store displays and shoplift or write a bad check. An employee can steal from the company or tamper with the books. In each case, the organization has a special problem. It must have a varied and sufficient stock of goods to attract clientele, but this abundance also attracts criminals. It must maintain its patronage or the enterprise will fail; therefore many, if not most, shoplifters go unpunished even if apprehended. After a warning, the shoplifter is asked to show good faith by remaining a customer. An employee is unlikely to be

Table 11–1. **Victimization by Race**
(Rates per 100,000 population)

Offenses	White	Nonwhite
Total	1,860	2,592
Forcible rape	22	82
Robbery	58	204
Aggravated assault	186	347
Burglary	822	1,306
Larceny ($50 and over)	608	367
Motor vehicle theft	164	286
Number of respondents	(27,484)	(4,902)

Source: Philip H. Ennis, "Criminal Victimization in the United States: A Report of a National Survey" (Field Survey II President's Commission on Law Enforcement and Administration of Justice (Washington: U.S. Govt. Printing Office, 1967), adapted from table 14, p. 31. Hereinafter referred to as the NORC study.

[2] B. Mendelsohn, "Victimology," *Etudes Internationales de Psycho-Sociologic Criminelle* (July–September 1956).

discovered. If he is caught he may be so valuable to the organization that they may hesitate to fire him or to press charges because of the ensuing bad publicity.

The individual victim is the most widely studied category. Most research concerns specific variables, such as age, sex, social class, ethnic group, and residence location. Most offenses are committed against people in the lowest income group, and the frequency of offenses declines as income increases. Exceptions to this are vehicle thefts and larceny of $50 and over, which increase sharply in higher income groups. Nonwhites are victimized in a disproportionately higher degree than are whites, but they are more liable to be members of the low income group where crimes are most common. Men are victims three times as often as women, but mutually held property in the husband's name may be the cause of this high

Table 11–2. **Victimization by Age and Sex**
(Rates per 100,000 population)

Offense	Male						
	10-19	20-29	30-39	40-49	50-59	60 plus	All ages
Total	951	5,924	6,231	5,150	4,231	3,465	3,091
Robbery	61	257	112	210	181	98	112
Aggravated assault	399	824	337	263	181	146	287
Burglary	123	2,782	3,649	2,365	2,297	2,343	1,583
Larceny ($50 and over)	337	1,546	1,628	1,839	967	683	841
Motor vehicle theft	31	515	505	473	605	195	268
	Female						
Total	334	2,424	1,514	1,908	1,132	1,052	1,059
Forcible rape	91	238	104	48	0	0	83
Robbery	0	238	157	96	60	81	77
Aggravated assault	91	333	52	286	119	40	118
Burglary	30	665	574	524	298	445	314
Larceny ($50 and over	112	570	470	620	536	405	337
Motor vehicle theft	0	380	157	334	119	81	130

Source: NORC survey.

Table 11–3. **Victimization by Income**
(Rates per 100,000 population)

Offenses	Income			
	$0 to $2,999	$3,000 to $5,999	$6,000 to $9,999	Above $10,000
Total	2,369	2,331	1,820	2,237
Forcible rape	76	49	10	17
Robbery	172	121	48	34
Aggravated assault	229	316	144	252
Burglary	1,319	1,020	867	790
Larceny ($50 and over)	420	619	549	925
Motor vehicle theft	153	206	202	219
Number of respondents	(5,232)	(8,238)	(10,382)	(5,946)

Source: NORC survey.

Table 11–4. **Victim-Offender Relationships by Race and Sex in Assaultive Crimes Against the Person (Except Homicide)**

Victim rate for each 100,000:[a]	Offenses attributable to—				
	White offenders		Negro offenders		All types of offenders
	Male	Female	Male	Female	
White males	201	9	129	4	342
White females	108	14	46	6	175
Negro males	58	3	1,636	256	1,953
Negro females	21	3	1,202	157	1,382
Total population[1]	130	10	350	45	535

Source: Special tabulations from Chicago Police Department, Data Systems Division, for period September 1965 to March 1966.

[a] The rates are based only on persons 14 years of age or older in each race-sex category. The "total population" category in addition excludes persons from racial groups other than Negro or white.

Table 11–5. **Victimization by Sex and Place of Occurrence for Major Crimes (Except Homicide) Against the Person (in percent)**

Place of occurrence	Victims of major crimes against person	
	Male	Female
School property	3.2	2.4
Residence	20.5	46.1
Transport property	1.4	.4
Taxis and delivery trucks	2.6	—
Businesses	3.2	1.1
Taverns and liquor stores	5.7	2.8
Street	46.8	30.7
Parks	.8	.5
All other premises	16.0	16.0
Total percent	100.0	100.0
Total number	(8,047)	(5,666)

Source: Special tabulations from Chicago Police Department, Data Systems Division, for period September 1965 to March 1966.

proportion. Women are most likely to be victimized in the 20 to 29-year age group, and men have their highest victimization rate between the ages of 30 and 39.[3] (See Tables 11–1 to 11–5.)

Other factors influence who is likely to be a victim of certain offenses. Robberies and burglaries are less frequent in smaller communities than in larger ones. Bars are common sites for aggravated assaults but are not popular locations for murder. Crime tends to be lowest in the morning and increases at night, especially in residential areas. Crime varies with the season. Spring and summer tend to be associated with crimes against the person, such as assault and rape, whereas fall and winter are noted for fraud, theft, and larceny. The bedroom has been found to be the most dangerous room in the house, with the kitchen a close second.[4] There are many proposed explanations for these phe-

[3] Task Force of Assessment, The President's Commission of Law Enforcement and Administration of Justice, *Task Force Report: Crime and Its Impact—An Assessment,* U.S. Govt. Printing Office, Washington, D.C., 1967).

[4] Stephen Schafer, *The Victim and His Criminal* (New York: Random House, 1968), pp. 92–97.

nomena, but they are merely interesting theories and as yet remain un-proved. Henri Ellenberger alleges that individuals, as potential victims, should know these relationships in order to assess their own situations for potential victim risk. The emerging field of crime prevention is also dependent on a recognition of these relationships.

The majority of offenders are known by their victims. Murders and aggravated assaults are much more likely to be committed by spouses, parents, estranged lovers, or relatives, rather than by an unknown stranger. Married persons are the most common combination of offender-victim.[5] These findings appear to be closely linked to the motive for the offense. The offender is most likely to react violently toward the people with whom he has the most frequent, intensive, and involved contact. The offender is most likely to view these people as the cause of his difficulties or anxieties.

Many authors have discussed a psychological tendency to become a victim. Von Hentig wrote of a "disease" that evidenced itself in a weariness of life and a tendency toward self-destruction. He divided victims into four groups: (1) the apathetic group that has lost its instinct for self-preservation; (2) the conniving group that plots its self-destruction; (3) the cooperative group that helps the offender; and (4) the instigating group that provokes the attack.[6] There are many examples of these behaviors: husbands who think their wives are trying to poison them and do nothing, wives who take repeated extreme physical abuse, a man who, after starting a quarrel, hands his opponent a gun and dares him to shoot. These victims "have asked for it," and are also therefore criminals, even though they may have been totally unaware of the causal or contributory nature of their behavior.

Victimless Crime

A victimless crime is a willing exchange among adults in private of strongly demanded, but legally proscribed goods or services.[7] These

---

[5] Ibid., pp. 66–68.

[6] Hans Von Hentig, *The Criminal and His Victim* (New Haven, Conn.: Yale University Press, 1948).

[7] Edwin M. Schur, *Crimes Without Victims* (Englewood Cliffs, N.J.: Prentice-Hall, 1965).

offenses are often called exchange crimes because of the transfer of goods and services. There is no victim involved except the social order or public conscience, unless the participants themselves are considered victims of their own actions. Examples of victimless crimes include gambling, prostitution, drug addiction, homosexuality, masturbation, drunkenness, abortion, suicide, and pornography. These offenses are differentiated from other types of crime in several ways.

First, there is a marked lack of consensus on whether these activities are truly criminal. They are common occurrences, generally ignored by the public. Thurman Arnold stated that these laws are unenforced because we want our conduct to go unchecked and unrepealed to satisfy our sense of morality.

Furthermore, these laws are difficult to enforce. Because the transactions are of a "willing" nature, there is rarely a complainant to bring the offenses to the attention of the authorities. And the acts usually occur in secret, in private places. This difficulty places enforcement officials in an unpleasant dichotomy: either they can stop enforcement of these laws altogether or enforce them only sporadically; or they can adopt aggressive tactics, such as repressive or borderline searches and seizures, electronic surveillances, or decoys. To enforce these laws at election time or to conduct intermittent vice drives usually places the police in a hypocritical, compromising, and therefore uncomfortable position. If enforcement officials use aggressive means they must degrade and demean both themselves and law enforcement. This leads to cynicism and disrespect by the public and encourages discriminatory enforcement and influence peddling within the policing agency.[8]

Finally these offenses are distinguished by the unintended consequences of the proscribing laws. The goods or services being exchanged are wanted almost desperately in many cases, and the illegality of procurement lowers the available supply of the commodity. In effect, this interaction of supply, demand, and prohibition places a "crime tariff" on the transaction, greatly increasing the price of the goods to the consumer.[9] This enormous profit encourages further deviance and under-

[8] Sanford H. Kadish, *The Crisis of Overcriminalization.*
[9] Herbert Packer, *The Limits of Criminal Sanction* (Stanford, Caiif.: Stanford University Press, 1968).

world organizational activity to supply the demand. The high prices in turn force the deviant consumer into secondary crime to obtain money to procure the goods. A second underworld is also created—a deviant subculture. This group functions to provide freer access to the desired substance or activity, as well as an acceptance of the deviant's life style.

In the case of drunkenness, law officers provide an extra social service by using their facilities for the "drying out" process. Statistics indicate that 40 to 50 percent of all arrests are for public intoxication, drunken and disorderly conduct, or related offenses. These "offenders" are taken off the streets and out of the public eye, are jailed overnight and released, or run through an assembly-line pseudo-court. This process is detrimental to the alcoholic and the agency. The alcoholic may need medical help, counseling. or other assistance that the police cannot provide, and the police need to spend their time in more vital law enforcement activities.

The public rationalizes these statutes by pointing out other "victims" involved in the crimes associated with the victimless crimes. The prostitute, in addition to the act of prostitution, may steal from her client, commit an indecent act in a public facility, encourage the sexual assault of a child, or contribute to the neglect of the hungry children of an inveterate gambler. These secondary or derivative crimes thus produce the real victims. The definition of victimless crime, however, excludes these offenses. The prostitute may be guilty of theft, larceny, or fraud, depending on the nature of the secondary offense, and the victimization is viewed as being from that offense, not the sexual behavior. The hungry children are victims of neglect and abuse; the illegality of gambling does not prevent the neglect of the children.

No suggestion has been made to legalize activities involving the use of force or coercion, or acts involving a minor. These offenses have definite victims, even if the minor is a willing participant, and should be prohibited and punished. Citizens have the right to expect public decency and should be protected from indecent and offensive public acts. However, a line must be drawn between what the public can expect in open facilities and what an individual has the right to do in the privacy of his own home with other consenting adults.

Victim-Precipitated Crime

Whenever a crime occurs, the entire blame is placed on the offender without taking a dynamic view of the crime from every angle, and without considering, among other things, any precipitative or causative behavior by the victim that may have eventually effected the development or concept of crime.[10]

During the last century, criminologists recognized the importance of studying the entire criminal sequence. The complicated interactions between the criminal and the victim indicated that the responsibility for the criminal behavior did not always belong solely to the offender. Several classes of victims were found to have taken a participatory or causative role in their own victimization. Mendelsohn classified victims by their contribution to the crime and obtained the following categories:

1. The completely innocent victim. This can be a child, an unconscious person, or an innocent bystander who is injured by accident.
2. The victim with minor guilt or a victim due to ignorance. This would include people who unwittingly place themselves in a victim-risk situation.
3. The voluntary victim, or the victim who is as guilty as the offender. This category includes:
   a. Suicide.
   b. Suicide by adhesion: remaining in a situation or with a person who is known to be dangerous.
   c. Euthanasia: the victim asks to be killed to escape pain or an incurable disease.
   d. Suicide committed by a couple.
4. The victim who is more guilty than the offender. This includes:
   a. The provoker-victim who instigates the violence.
   b. The imprudent victim who induces the criminal behavior.
5. The most guilty victim or the victim who is guilty alone, referring to the aggressor who is the victim of self-defense.
6. The imaginary victim: includes mental illness and hysteria where there is no actual crime.[11]

Several cases serve as typical illustrations of victim-precipitated homicides.

[10] Schafer, *The Victim and His Criminal*, p. 247.
[11] Ibid., p. 42.

A drunken husband, beating his wife in their kitchen, gave her a butcher knife and dared her to use it on him. She claimed that if he should strike her once more, she would use the knife, whereupon he slapped her in the face and she fatally stabbed him.[12]

The victim was the aggressor in a fight, having struck his enemy several times. Friends tried to interfere, but the victim persisted. Finally, the offender retaliated with blows, causing the victim to fall and hit his head on the sidewalk, as a result of which he died.[13]

A woman went to live with her son-in-law in response to his constant nagging to live with him. She commented to her friend, "I know I shall not live a fortnight." She was right, within two weeks she was dead.[14]

A young soldier borrowed a gun and returned with it a short time later. Only now it was loaded, though the armourer could not have known this. The soldier handed the rifle back, butt end first, and told his friend to pull the trigger. The gun fired and the soldier fell dead.[15]

Schultz lists four ways that a victim may contribute to an offense. They are:

1. By provoking or initiating a hostile reaction in the offender. For example, during a heated argument one party hands the other a gun and, knowing the other's hostile mood, accuses him of not having "the guts to shoot."
2. By direct invitation or incitation. For example, a female engages in heavy petting and mutual sexual preludes and, at the last moment, begins to resist the man's advances that are by that time, uncontrollable.
3. By omission of normal preventative measures. For example, the auto-theft victim parks his car unlocked with the engine running while he does some shopping.
4. By unconsciously inviting the offense through his emotional pathology. For example, a wife has masochistic needs that are gratified by her assaultive husband.[16]

Other behaviors may also lead the offender to perform violent acts. But infidelity, vile language, and failure to pay a debt are not generally included in a list of victim-precipitated crimes.

---

[12] Marvin E. Wolfgang, "Victim-Precipitated Criminal Homicide," in Bruce Cohen, *Crime in America,* (Itasca, Ill.: F. E. Peacock, 1970).

[13] Ibid.

[14] Gratus, *The Victims,* p. 18.

[15] Ibid.

[16] LeRoy G. Schultz, "The Victim-Offender Relationship," *Crime and Delinquency,* 14, 2 (1968), p. 137.

There are several problems in the study of victim precipitated crimes. Police files do not always include appropriate data-and tend to picture the victim as innocent of criminal behavior. Many crimes are never reported to the authorities: victim precipitation might be the cause of the failure to press charges. Finally, because the victim is the plaintiff, an admission of his role in the offense, may be contrary to his own self-interests in the case. Because of these data problems, almost all victim research deals with personal violence and usually concerns aggravated assaults and homicides where data are more carefully and fully obtained and people are likely to be prosecuted.

Wolfgang studied homicides in Philadelphia (see Table 11-6), and reports that 26 percent were victim-precipitated cases. He researched selected variables in the victim-precipitated and nonvictim-precipitated crimes and found several significant associations. Nearly 80 percent of victim-precipitated cases, versus 70 percent of nonvictim-precipitated cases, involved blacks. Males comprised 94 percent of the victims in victim-precipitated homicides, as against 72 percent for nonvictim-precipitated homicides. Females were less likely to be the victims but twice as frequently to be the offenders (29 percent) in victim-precipitated cases. Stabbings were significantly common, but blacks and women were more likely to employ this method; therefore, the method used may be a dependent rather than an independent variable. Age, location, and motive were not significantly different, but alcohol abuse and the previous arrest record of the victim seemed to be statistically contributory.[17]

Von Hentig uses a different victim typology based on psychological, social, and biological factors. He contends that the young, old, female, mentally defective, immigrants, minorities, dull-normals, depressed, acquisitive, wanton, lonesome and heartbroken, tormentors, and the blocked, and fighting are especially prone to becoming victims.[18] Several of these categories fit the victim-precipitated schemata. The very dependent, such as the young and the old, cause additional pressures on their family group and tend to be demanding and unpleasant. Immigrants, minorities, and mentally defectives offer easy marks to a potential criminal and usually live and work in high-risk areas. The acquisitive are subject to theft, fraud, and swindles because of their interest in an easy

[17] Wolfgang, "Victim-Precipitated Criminal Homicide."
[18] Von Hentig, *The Criminal and His Victim*, pp. 43–48.

Table 11–6. **Victim-Precipitated and Nonvictim-Precipitated Criminal Homicide by Selected Variables Philadelphia, 1948–1952**

	Total victims		Victim-precipitated		Nonvictim-precipitated	
	Number	Percent of total	Number	Percent of total	Number	Percent of total
Race and sex of victim						
Both Races	588	100.0	150	100.0	438	100.0
Male	449	76.4	141	94.0	308	70.3
Female	139	23.6	9	6.0	130	29.7
Black	427	72.6	119	79.3	308	70.3
Male	331	56.3	111	74.0	220	50.2
Female	96	16.3	8	5.3	88	20.1
White	161	27.4	31	20.7	130	29.7
Male	118	20.1	30	20.0	88	20.1
Female	43	7.3	1	0.7	42	9.6
Age of victim						
Under 15	28	4.8	0	—	28	6.4
15–19	25	4.3	7	4.7	18	4.1
20–24	59	10.0	18	12.0	41	9.4
25–29	93	15.8	17	11.3	76	17.3
30–34	88	15.0	20	13.3	68	15.5
35–39	75	12.8	25	16.7	50	11.4
40–44	57	9.7	23	15.3	34	7.8
45–49	43	7.3	13	8.7	30	6.8
50–54	48	8.2	11	7.3	37	8.5
55–59	26	4.4	6	4.0	20	4.6
60–64	18	3.1	7	4.7	11	2.5
65 and over	28	4.7	3	2.0	25	5.7
Total	588	100.0	150	100.0	438	100.0
Method						
Stabbing	228	38.8	81	54.0	147	33.6
Shooting	194	33.0	39	26.0	155	35.4
Beating	128	21.8	26	17.3	102	23.3
Other	38	6.4	4	2.7	34	7.7
Total	588	100.0	150	100.0	438	100.0
Place						
Home	301	51.2	80	53.3	221	50.5
Not home	287	48.8	70	46.7	217	49.5
Total	588	100.0	150	100.0	438	100.0
Interpersonal relationship						
Relatively close friend	155	28.2	46	30.7	109	27.3
Family relationship	136	24.7	38	25.3	98	24.5
(Spouse)	(100)	(73.5)	(33)	(86.8)	(67)	(68.4)
(Other)	(36)	(26.5)	(5)	(18.2)	(31)	(31.6)

Table 11–6. **Continued**.

	Total victims		Victim-precipitated		Nonvictim-precipitated	
	Number	Percent of total	Number	Percent of total	Number	Percent of total
Acquaintance	74	13.5	20	13.3	54	13.5
Stranger	67	12.2	16	10.7	51	12.8
Paramour, mistress prostitute	54	9.8	15	10.0	39	9.8
Sex rival	22	4.0	6	4.0	16	4.0
Enemy	16	2.9	6	4.0	10	2.5
Paramour of offender's mate	11	2.0	1	.7	10	2.5
Felon or police officer	6	1.1	1	.7	5	1.3
Innocent bystander	6	1.1	—	—	6	1.5
Homosexual partner	3	.6	1	.7	2	.5
Total	550	100.0	150	100.0	400	100.0
Presence of alcohol during offense						
Present	374	63.6	111	74.0	263	60.0
Not present	214	36.4	39	26.0	175	40.0
Total	588	100.0	150	100.0	438	100.0
Presence of alcohol in the victim						
Present	310	52.7	104	69.3	206	47.0
Not present	278	47.3	46	30.7	232	53.0
Total	588	100.0	150	100.0	438	100.0
Previous arrest record of victim						
Previous arrest record	277	47.3	93	62.0	184	42.0
Offenses against the person	150	25.5 (54.2)	56	37.3 (60.2)	94	21.4 (50.1)
Other offenses only	127	21.6 (45.8)	37	24.7 (39.8)	90	20.5 (49.9)
No previous arrest arrest record	311	52.7	57	38.0	524	58.0
Total	588	100.0	150	100.0	438	100.0
Previous arrest record of offender						
Previous arrest record	400	64.4	81	54.0	319	67.7

Table 11–6. **Continued.**

	Total victims		Victim-precipitated		Nonvictim-precipitated	
	Number	Percent of total	Number	Percent of total	Number	Percent of total
Offenses against the person	264	42.5 (66.0)	49	32.7 (60.5)	215	45.6 (67.4)
Other offenses only	136	21.8 (34.0)	32	21.3 (39.5)	104	22.1 (32.6)
No previous arrest record	221	35.6	69	(46.0)	152	32.3
Total	621	100.0	150	100.0	471	100.0

Source: Marvin E. Wolfgang "Victim-Precipitated Criminal Homicide" in: Donald R. Cressey and David A. Ward, *Delinquency, Crime, and Social Process* (New York: N.Y.: Harper & Row, 1969). Reprinted by special permission of the *Journal of Criminal Law, Criminology and Police Science,* Copyright © 1957 by Northwestern University School of Law, Vol. 48, No. 1.

profit, while the lonesome and heartbroken are victims of the same offenses because of their desire for companionship and happiness. The tormentors and the blocked and fighting victims are subject to the consequences of the atmosphere and situation they have created.

The victim–criminal relationship is a dynamic one, and their behaviors are not separate entities, but rather interactions. In precipitating a crime the victim actually takes the actor's role and is functionally responsible for the crime himself. There is little legal basis for taking the victim's behavior into account except in lessening the degree of the offense; for example, lowering the charge from murder to manslaughter. The victim is exempt from punishment for precipitatory behavior unless he has also violated the law. However, now that victim compensation laws are being enacted, several countries have exempted victim-precipitated crimes from partial or total payment.

Fooner suggests that:

> If society should assume some responsibility for making the victim
> whole, it should also require victim behavior that will diminish the num-
> ber of temptation-opportunity situations for offenders. Such behavior
> could be encouraged through educational programs on citizen defenses
> against criminality, plus legislative provisions which make victim com-

pensation contingent upon the victim's actions not being contributory to the crime.[19]

The subject of victim compensation will be dealt with as a separate topic later in this chapter.

Legal Force

In some instances, the law condones or excuses actions that would be criminal in nature if not for mitigating circumstances. The use of force in self-defense in defense of others or of property, and in making an arrest are examples of such instances. In each category definite regulations concern the amount of force and the circumstances under which it may be employed. These limits are especially strict regarding the use of lethal force by either a citizen or a police officer.

> *Force intended to invade the legally protected interests of another may, within limits, be met with a similar force by the person threatened to protect his own interests against impending harm. When the harm is directed against the person the privilege to repel the invasion is called self-defense.*[20]

Self-defense was unknown in early laws. Harms inflicted in defense of one's person were not privileged, and the defendant had to seek a pardon to avoid legal penalties. By 1400, however, self-defense was recognized as legal action, and it is presently treated as a conditional privilege.

Self-defense cannot be used as an excuse for assault or battery; the individual must believe that he is actually threatened by invasion of interest or negligent conduct. Danger does not, in fact, have to exist; the actor must show only that he acted honestly and that his fears were reasonable under those circumstances. If the danger is past, the privilege

[19] Michael Fooner, "Victim-Induced Criminality," in Simon Dinitz and Walter Reckless, *Critical Issues in the Study of Crime* (Boston, Mass.: Little, Brown, 1968), p. 206.

[20] F. V. Harper, *A Treatise on the Law of Torts* (Indanapolis, Ind.: Bobbs-Merrill Company, 1938), p. 91.

is also terminated. There is no immunity for revenge or retaliation, but only to avert impending harm.[21]

The amount of force used is generally judged by the "reasonable man" test, stating that the force used was not greater than that which would be employed by a reasonable man in that situation. In general, only the *amount* of force renders the actor liable. Deadly force is justifiable if the individual reasonably believes that this amount of force is necessary to prevent his death or great bodily harm. State regulations on the use of lethal force vary widely. In some states lethal force may be used to prevent one's being the victim of a violent forcible felony (e.g., rape), even though the felony would not result in the victim's death. Most states allow the use of force to resist an unlawful arrest by a police officer or citizen, but few states allow lethal force in resisting arrest. A police officer may use lethal force when a felon is resisting arrest, escaping (in some states), or endangering the lives of the officer or innocent bystanders, but the officer must not endanger the lives of others in the use of this force.[22] In other jurisdictions, a person being attacked must avoid the use of deadly force by attempting to escape, if retreat is possible with safety, unless he is in his own home or another place in which he has a legal right to be.

Defense of a third person is viewed in a manner similar to self-defense and states usually apply the same yardstick to both actions. The person defending a third person is responsible for his actions in the situation as he sees it, even though the third person would not be privileged to defend himself in the situation as it actually exists. The defender is not required to retreat before using deadly force unless he believes that he can ensure the third person's safety by doing so. Also, he may defend the third person without retreating in the victim's dwelling as if it were his own. In early law, this privilege was applied only to members of the victim's household, or those under his legal protection. Today, the privilege covers anyone whom the defender reasonably believes requires his protection.[23]

A person is also permitted to use force in the prevention or termination of an unlawful trespass of property in his possession or in the

[21] Ibid., pp. 91–95.
[22] Hazel B. Kerper, *Introduction to the Criminal Justice System* (St. Paul, Minn.: West Publishing Co., 1972), pp. 83–90.
[23] Harper, *Treatise on the Law of Torts*, p. 95.

possession of another in whose interest he acts. Five conditions exist to the privilege for use of force in defense of property: (1) that the defender is in possession of the property or (in some states) is acting in behalf of the owner; (2) that the intruder was not himself privileged; (3) that a request was made to cease the intrusion, unless such a request would be dangerous or futile; (4) that the force used was reasonable or necessary to prevent or terminate the intrusion; and (5) that the force employed was not excessive.

Deadly force is rarely condoned even for protection against arson or other property destruction unless the nature of the intrusion is such that it threatens death or severe bodily harm. A device may be used to protect property only if: (1) It is not designed to cause death or severe bodily harm; (2) the use of the device is reasonable under the circumstances as the defender sees them; and (3) the device is one customarily used for such a purpose, and/or reasonable care is taken to make its existence known to probable intruders.[24]

In some states a private citizen may make an arrest without a warrant for a felony if (1) he has reasonable grounds for believing the arrested person is guilty, and (2) the arrestee is, in fact, guilty. In many states a citizen may arrest for a felony if (1) he has reasonable grounds for believing the arrestee is guilty, and (2) a felony has been committed. In about five states a private individual has the same power as a police officer in arresting a person or reasonable grounds for believing (1) that a felony has been committed, and (2) that the arrestee committed it. Under common law neither the police nor a citizen could make an arrest without a warrent unless there was *positive* knowledge that a felony had been committed and reasonable grounds for believing that the arrestee was the guilty party.[25] For a misdemeanor, an officer and an individual may make an arrest for offenses committed in their presence if the arrest is made immediately or in prompt and unbroken pursuit. The only exception is the case of a fray or riot, where an officer may arrest all who are apparently engaged in the offenses, although they may turn out to be innocent. An officer or a citizen may arrest an insane person if it is necessary to prevent harm to himself or others.[26]

[24] Kerper, *Introduction to the Criminal Justice System*, pp. 94–95.
[25] Edwin H. Sutherland and Donald R. Cressy, *Principles of Criminology*, 7th ed. (Philadelphia, Pa.: J. B. Lippincott Co., 1966), p. 389.
[26] Harper, *Treatise on the Law of Torts*, pp. 122–126.

The person making the arrest is privileged to use reasonable force, if necessary, to effect an arrest. He may not use deadly force unless the offense is a felony threatening death or serious bodily injury. The general rule is that no more force can be used to prevent an escape than is lawful to make the arrest in the first place. Some states specify felonies where deadly force is authorized. Basically, the rules for the use of force in self-defense apply, except that the individual may stand his ground without retreating. LaFave, in his book *Arrest*, presents an interesting view of the problems that the officer faces in deciding what force is necessary and legitimate in apprehending and arresting a suspect.

Tort Actions

A tort is a legal wrong committed upon a person or property which is redressed in civil court. A crime is a *public* injury; a tort is a *private* injury. A single act may violate both criminal and tort law and the perpetrator would be the defendant in two suits. The state would be the plaintiff for the criminal suit (for example, *State of Maine* v. *A.*) and seek punishment for the public injury in the form of a fine or imprisonment. The victim would be the plaintiff in the tort action (for example, *A.* v. *B.*) and would seek damages or reparation.[27] The purpose of tort law is to lend assistance in obtaining redress for the individual who believes that he has been injured in some way. Torts may be classified according to the interests violated:

1. The physical body and freedom from confinement (false arrest or personal injury).
2. Property or property rights.
3. Honor and reputation.
4. Economic relations and transaction.
   a. Protection from fraud.
   b. Contract integrity.
   c. Advantageous economic relations.
5. Domestic relations.
   a. Marital interests.
   b. Parental interests.
   c. Filial interests.

[27] Kerper, *Introduction to the Criminal Justice System*, pp. 30–31.

6. Miscellaneous interests.
    a. Freedom from annoyance.
    b. Privacy.
    c. Reputation of goods and title to property.
    d. Political interests.[28]

Any illegal violation of these interests may be the subject of a civil suit for damages. Responsibility for invasion of these interests occurs not only by specific intent of the perpetrator, but also if the perpetrator is negligent toward those interests or if his conduct is extrahazardous with respect to such interests. Liability is confined to harms actually resulting from the actions and includes only those kinds of harm that are reasonably anticipated from the conduct. In other words, there is no liability for harm to persons or property not of the type that would be generally endangered. Also, the perpetrator is exempted for harm caused in such an extraordinary manner or involving such a peculiar sequence of events that is was not a forseeable result of his actions.

Other factors also nullify the perpetrator's liability. If the victim freely agreed to the act with full knowledge of the risks involved, he has no claim. A privileged situation exists where the social desirability of the action takes precedence over the threatened harm. A person who consents to an invasion has no claim. Also, a privileged invasion may be made for a socially desirable goal. Finally, the defendant is not liable if the plaintiff engaged in actions of the same nature, and the harm resulted from his own actions as well as those of the defendant.

Victim Compensation

Through civil court procedures, a victim should theoretically be able to recover any loss or damages he suffered from the perpetrators of the crime. However, this is often not the case. In a great number of crimes the criminal is never caught. When he is apprehended, he rarely has any money or property to cover the damages he has caused. Senator Mike Mansfield reported to a Senate subcommittee that recent surveys have indicated that, although 74.2 percent of the victims of violent crimes suffered economic losses in addition to physical and mental damages and

---

[28] Harper, *Treatise on the Law of Torts*, p. 5.

suffering, only 1.8 percent of these victims ever collected anything from their attackers.[29]

> Consider the plight of the victim of crime: He goes happily about his business, secure in the knowledge that the state will protect him. But it fails in its obligation, and mayhem strikes. After he is picked up off the pavement and delivered to the handiest hospital (where, of course, responsibility for his repair is his own), he slowly mends and resigns himself to any permanent impairments. He also resigns himself to the loss of pay he suffers during his recovery. Finally, he can return to work—if the job is still there. But the state is not satisfied; there must be a trial. The victim is a key witness to a crime. He must give up more of his time, more of his pay, relive an unpleasant experience, and submit himself to questioning; the object of which can be to impugn his dignity, competence, and integrity. When it is finally over, he can watch the prisoner being led away to free room, board, and recreation—to which he contributes through his tax payments. The prosecutor, the police, and the judge then give him his recompense; a few words of praise for his public-spirited cooperation.[30]

The concept of victim compensation has the longest history of any victim-centered topic. The Code of Hammurabi (*c.* 2200 B.C. stated:

> If the brigand has not been caught, the man who has been despoiled shall recount before God what he has lost, and the city and governor in whose land and district the brigandage took place shall render back to him whatever of his was lost. If it was a life that was lost, the city and governor shall pay one mina of silver to his people.[31]

The law of Moses required fourfold restitution for sheep and fivefold for oxen. In Homer's *Iliad*, mention is made of a brother's death being appeased by a fine. Most ancient laws and religions deal in some way with repayment to the victim. Often these repayments were 20 or more times the original value of the property. The biblical "eye for an eye and tooth for a tooth" was one of the earliest attempts to reform the extremely severe recompensation laws.

As governmental powers increased and crimes became offenses

[29] *Victims of Crime*, Hearing before the Subcommittee on Criminal Laws and Procedures of the Committee on the Judiciary, United States Senate, 92nd Congress, September–March 1972, p. 127.
[30] Ibid.
[31] "The Code of Hammurabi," sections 23–24, Trans. C. Johns, *The Oldest Code of Laws in the World* (Edinburgh, Scotland: T. & T. Clark, 1903), pp. 6–7.

against the state, punishment was taken over by the society and the rights of the victim to compensation declined. The overlord claimed a commission for his help and protection. As time passed, the rulers increased the fines until a criminal had his lands and possessions taken away and was sold into slavery for an offense. The victim's share of this new source of wealth steadily diminished. Only recently has the victim again made himself heard by demanding adequate reparation and redress from his assailant or the government.

There are five basic systems for the payment of restitution or compensation to a victim:

1. Damages awarded in a civil court suit on the basis of tort law. They are entirely separate from any criminal procedures.
2. Civil compensation awarded through the criminal court proceedings.
3. Civil restitution intermingled with penal characteristics and awarded through criminal proceedings. This is a compensatory fine or monetary obligation imposed on the offender in addition to the ordinary punishment.
4. Civil compensation awarded in criminal proceedings and backed by the state. In this case the state pays the victim's claim and then seeks reimbursement from the offender.
5. Compensation awarded through a special procedure. This is a state-assistance program offered to those who have a definite need caused by a criminal offense.[32]

Each of these systems has implicit advantages and disadvantages, and each has been used in different parts of the world with a varying degree of success.[33] The United States has relied on tort law almost exclusively for redress of grievances against criminality. Some states do have statutes permitting assessment of damages to the offender in a criminal court, but these laws are rarely used. California does require restitution in some cases, and probationers pay family support and reparation through their probation officers.

Everyone seems to support the victim's right to compensation and redress. The problem seems to be that of designing an adequate system effectively to handle the problem. Several authors have cited the advantages of having the criminal be responsible for the damages he has

[32] Schafer, *The Victim and His Criminal*, pp. 105–109.
[33] For further information see Stephen Schafer, *Restitution to the Victims of Crime* (Chicago, Ill.: Quadrangle Books Inc., 1960).

caused. This additional punishment might make the offender realize that he not only has wronged society, but also has hurt his victim. Restitution would improve the criminal's self-image and lessen the stigma involved when he is released into society. There are several proposals for financing this project. Prisoners' salaries could be raised to a level commensurate with regular labor wages, and the funds could be withdrawn from these wages to pay fines, family support, and restitution. The criminal's property (if any) could be confiscated and used for restitution. Increased use of work-release programs, probation, or other income-producing activities could be encouraged. Offenders could be allowed to remain free on the basis of making payments on fines or compensation. The possibility of large-scale incorporation of these ideas seems remote. Also, the victims of uncaptured offenders would have no recourse; therefore many victims would still be left to absorb the financial burden of crime.

The criminal seems always to have understood the interests of the victim and to have used this knowledge to his own advantage. Victims are usually more interested in getting their property back than in punishing the criminal and supporting the social structure by adherence to a strict law-and-order stand. Therefore, if the criminal is caught, he may offer restitution and compensation to the victim in return for not being turned over to the authorities. If the offender has already been arrested, he (or his agent) will make a similar offer in return for having the charges dropped against him. This seems like a valid proposition to the victim who would otherwise have to absorb the financial loss. The ease of buying one's way out of criminal responsibility by paying restitution may destroy the social and penal value of punitive restitution.[34]

The current trend is that the social system take over the responsibility for compensation to the victim. The rationale for this policy is divided into six different schools of thought:

1. The social contract theory. This view is founded on the philosophies of Hobbes, Locke, and Rousseau, who contended that people come together and institute governments. In order to obtain personal protection, they relinquish legal enforcement to the state. The victim has given up his right to personal vengeance and restitution, but the state has not protected him from victimization. Therefore, the state

[34] Schafer, *The Criminal and His Victim.*

has an obligation to those individuals whom it fails to protect; it is the victim's social right.

2. The social welfare theory. As in assistance for the aged, the disabled, and the unemployed, the victims of crime should be supported or aided, not because of any obligation on the part of the state, but because our twentieth-century conscience cannot tolerate the suffering involved.

3. By the grace of government. The grace concept contemplates the states' dealing mercifully with individuals.

4. Crime prevention. Recompensation can be used to promote Good Samaritans, by covering any injury or loss they may incur in helping a victim or police officer. Also, knowledge of the cost of crime would bring about the adjustment of public measures to combat crime. The manner and degree of the victim's contribution to the crime might teach the public how to avoid crime-breeding situations.

5. Political arguments. The emphasis on the rights of criminals has brought the rights of the victim to the foreground.

6. Antialienation. This philosophy reflects the attitude that something must be done to support the people's belief in the democratic form of government.[35]

Dinitz and Reckless pose some of the basic problems and questions that must be dealt with in victim-compensation proposals:

Is compassion for the victim to be the basic guideline or the principle that a victim has a moral and legal "right" to compensation? Who is to be compensated—all victims or only those in financial need? If the latter, how is such need to be assessed? Finally, should the offender be obligated to help share or fully pay the compensation? Victim-compensation proposals also raise some additional and equally vexing problems. What if the victim instigates the crime against himself? Who then is responsible? Suppose, also, that a severely injured person reports a mugging, robbery, or aggravated assault and the police cannot find a suspect or be certain that the man was, in fact, a victim of crime. Is he entitled to compensation? Finally, will a system of victim compensation materially increase the temptation opportunity pattern in victim behavior comparable to carelessness in property crimes?[36]

---

[35] *The Case for Compensation*, The Commonwealth of Massachusetts, Report of the Special Commission on the Compensation of Victims of Violent Crimes, Resolves of 1966, pp. 267–268.

[36] Dinitz and Reckless, *Critical Issues in the Study of Crime*, p. 202.

Both New Zealand's and Britain's compensation laws require the behavior of the victim to be taken into account. Whether an award is made and its amount are functions of the degree of responsibility attributable to the victim. Those who are eligible for compensation may include: the victim; the victim's dependents in the event of his death; anyone injured or killed in trying to prevent a crime and his dependents (Good Samaritan); anyone injured or killed in arresting or attempting to arrest a suspected offender; anyone injured or killed while giving aid to a police officer. An award for compensation is usually independent of a criminal verdict of guilty (to avoid perjury for purposes of obtaining a recompensation decree), although requirements are usually made regarding the notification of authorities and pressing charges. (See Tables 11–7 and 11–8).

Table 11–7. **Major States with Victim-Compensation Legislation**

State	Year enacted	Jurisdiction	Restrictions	Limit amount
California	1967	State Board of Control	Victim Dependents	$ 5,000
Hawaii	1967	Criminal Injuries Compensation Commission	Victim Dependent Other	$10,000
Maryland	1968	Criminal Injuries Compensation Board	Victim Dependent Other	$45,000
Massachusetts	1968	District Court	Victim Dependents	$10,000
New York	1966	Crime Victims Compensation Board	Victim Dependents Other	$15,000 Medical Unlimited
Nevada	1969	State Board of Examiners	Victim Dependent Other	$ 5,000
New Jersey	1971	Violent Crimes Compensation Board	Victim Dependent Other	$10,000

Source: United States Senate-Congressional Record, *Victims of Crime,* Hearing Before the Subcommittee on Criminal Laws and Procedures of the Committee on the Judiciary, United States Senate, 92nd Congress, 1st Session, September 29, November 30, 1971, and March 27, 1972, p. 723.

Table 11–8. States with Crime Victim-Compensation Acts: Contrasting Their Key Characteristics

State	Jurisdiction	Eligibility	Restrictions	Amount	Subrogation	Attorney fees	Loss of property	Determination
California: Cal. Gov't Code §§ 13960–13966 (1967); §§ 13970–13974 (1969).	State Board of Control (hearing)	1. Victim. 2. Dependents—in case of pecuniary loss from his injury or death.	Need basis.	Not in excess of $5,000.	State subrogated to rights of claimant against offender to the extent of payment of the claim. May intervene in claimant's action against offender or bring own.	Not in excess of 10%.	To private citizen preventing crime or apprehending a criminal, criminal, or rescuing a person.	May refuse to compensate for lack of cooperation with police in apprehension of offender.
Hawaii: Hawaii Rev. Law §§ 351–1, –351–70 (1967).	Criminal Injuries Compensation Commission (hearing)	1. Victim. 2. Dependents—in case of his death. 3. Other—person responsible for victim's maintenance, where pecuniary loss results from victim's injury.	General.	Not in excess of $10,000.	State may bring derivative action against the convicted offender in the name of the victim or dependents awarded compensation. Excess recovery given to claimant.	Commission as part of order may award reasonable attorney fees, not in excess of 15% of an award over $1,000—out of the award.	To private citizen in preventing crime or apprehending a criminal.	Reduce compensation to extent victim was responsible for the crime that caused his injury.
Maryland: Md. Ann. Stat. art 26A, §§ 1–17 (1968).	Criminal Injuries Compensation Board (single member with right to appeal to whole).	1. Victim. 2. Dependents—in case of his death. 3. Other—dependent on victim for their principal support. 4. Anyone injured or killed in attempting to prevent a crime, and his dependents.	Out-of-pocket loss of $100 or two weeks' earnings plus "serious financial hardship."	Art. 101, § 36 schedule used.	Subrogated to the extent of the award to recover payments resulting from the crime.			Reduce compensation to extent victim contributed to his injury. May be disregarded if victim attempted to aid a victim or prevent crime or apprehend a person after he committed a crime.

Table 11–8. Continued

State	Jurisdiction	Eligibility	Restrictions	Amount	Subrogation	Attorney fees	Loss of property	Determination
Massachusetts: Mass. Gen. Laws ch. 258A, §§ 1–7 (1968).	District Court	1. Victim. 2. Dependents—in case of his death.	Out-of-pocket loss of $100 or two weeks' earnings	Equal to loss up to $10,000.	....	"To the extent of compensation," any amount received by claimant from any source exceeding the actual loss to the victim may be recovered.	Court as part of order may award reasonable attorney fees, not in excess of 15% of an award over $1,000—out of the award.	Same.
New York: N.Y. Exec. Law §§ 620–635 (1966).	Crime Victims Compensation Board (single member with right to appeal to whole).	1. Victim. 2. Dependent—in case of his death. 3. Other—dependent on victim for their principal support. 4. Anyone injured or killed in attempting to prevent a crime, and his dependents.	Out-of-pocket loss of $100 or two weeks' earnings plus "serious financial hardship."	Not in excess of $100 per week earnings or support, nor an aggregate award of more than $15,000.	....	To the extent of the award to recover payments resulting from the crime.	....	Same.
Nevada: Nev. Rev. Stat. §§ 217.180– 217.260 (1969)	State Board of Examiners (hearing).	1. Victim. 2. Dependent—in case of his death. 3. Other—person responsible for victim's maintenance where pecuniary loss results from victim's injury.	General........	Not in excess of $5,000.	Subrogated to the cause of action of the applicant against the offender and may bring an action for the amount of damages sustained by applicant. Excess recovery paid to claimant.	Board as a part of order may allow reasonable attorney fees, not to exceed 10%—out of the award.	....	In determining whether to make an order for compensation, the board shall consider provocation, consent, or any other behavior of the victim.

254   *law and the administration of justice*

Table 11–8. Continued

State	Jurisdiction	Eligibility	Restrictions	Amount	Subrogation	Attorney fees	Loss of property	Determination
New Jersey: N.J. Session Law Oct. 1971.	Violent Crimes Compensation Board (hearing).	1. Victim. 2. Dependent—in case of death. 3. Other—person responsible for victim's maintenance where pecuniary loss results from victim's injury.	Out of pocket loss of $100 or two weeks earnings.	Not in excess of $10,000.	Subrogated to the cause of action of the applicant against the offender and may bring an action for the amount of damages sustained by applicant. Excess recovery paid to claimant.	Board as part of order may allow reasonable attorney fees, not to exceed 15% of the award—not out of award.	....	Reduce compensation to extent victim contributed to his injury. May be disregarded if victim attempted to aid a victim or prevent a crime or apprehend a person after he committed a crime.
Victims of crime act of 1972 (Title I).	Violent Crimes Compensation Board (hearing).	1. Victim. 2. Dependent—in case of his death. 3. Other—person where pecuniary loss results from victim's injury. 4. Anyone suffering pecuniary loss.	$100 minimum plus undue financial hardship.	Not in excess of $50,000.	Attorney General may maintain action against offender for recovery of the whole or specified amounts of the compensation.	Attorney fees allowable as under 18 U.S.C. 3006A.	....	In determining whether to make an order, the behavior of the victim is considered.

Source: United States Senate—Congressional Record; *Victims of Crime*, Hearing Before the Subcommittee on Criminal Laws and Procedures of the Committee on the Judiciary, United States Senate, 92nd Congress, 1st Session, September 29, November 30, 1971, and March 27, 1972, pp. 684–685.

In some countries the crimes covered by compensation laws are listed while in others any personal injury resulting from a criminal act is applicable. Usually there are both minimum claims and maximum benefits available. Several types of injury are considered, but property losses are not subject to restitution by the state. Claims may be made (depending on the jurisdiction) for: expenses actually and reasonably occurred; financial loss resulting from incapacity to work or for the dependents of a victim who is killed; pain and suffering; loss of reputation; and any other expenses that might reasonably occur. No double payment is allowed; therefore, insurance settlements and other reimbursement are subtracted from the award. Victim compensation in the United States tends to be based on need of the victim, but this is not universally true. When compensation is considered a right, everyone, regardless of need, should have access to the funds. Many of these problems have not been definitely resolved, but no longer are the victim and his rights being ignored by our social systems.

Special Victim Topics

There are several categories of victim that are not often considered. The families of criminals may be the victims of our social order. If a member of the family is labeled as a criminal, the entire family may be branded with a similar social stigma. If the offender provides the financial support of the family, they are victimized by his forced absence. With new legislative proposals being drafted to use the offender's property to give restitution, his family may be subject to even more victimization. Because they are, in most cases, innocent of any wrongdoing, should they be penalized for the offender's actions? Does society owe them support or aid of some sort other than welfare?

The criminal may be a victim in his own right. Schafer points out that little thought is given to the punishment dealt to an offender brought to justice for a crime precipitated by his victim.[37] Criminals, and even the public, may be victims of the police. Instances of "third-degree" tactics are not uncommon; a Michigan study reported that one out of

[37] Schafer, *The Victim and His Criminal*, p. 136.

ten officers used "improper" or "unnecessary" force. Police brutality may be divided into three categories: (1) brutality against sex criminals and "cop fighters"; (2) brutality inflicted by police officers who enjoy hurting people; (3) brutality that ensues when an officer is afraid or is under great physical or mental stress.

> (The policeman) . . . regards the public as his enemy, feels his occupation to be in conflict with the community and regards himself to be a pariah. The experience and the feeling give rise to a collective emphasis on secrecy, an attempt to coerce respect from the public and a belief that almost any means are legitimate in completing an important arrest.[38]

There are other types of victims of the police. Vice offenders are likely to be "rousted" with no intention of making an arrest. Many people are literally kidnapped by the police in the form of an illegal arrest and confinement. These offenses are often overlooked by the public because the victims are unlikely to press charges and because our social system so strongly condones the use of legalized violence.

> American society has always endorsed legitimate violence. In fact, most of us do not consider it violence at all. Respect for the law has become one of the nastiest features of American character. Anything we can get legitimated passes without question. . . . And any disruptive social group to which lawlessness can be imputed is a fair target for violent suppression.[39]

Although they are seldom used, there are tort laws that cover these offenses.

The United States government commissioned a victim survey research to determine the frequency of reporting crimes to the authorities and the subsequent bias of criminal statistics. The study was conducted by the National Opinion Research Center (NORC) from a sampling of 10,000 households. The findings indicated that forcible rapes were 3.5 times more frequently committed than the reported rates, burglaries were three times more frequent, aggravated assaults and larcenies were more than double, and robberies were 50 percent greater. Only car theft was reported at a lower rate. The most frequent reason given for not reporting an offense was that it seemed to be a private

---

[38] Westley, "Violence and the Police," *American Journal of Sociology*, Vol. 35, 1953.

[39] Edgar Z. Friedenberg, "Legitimate Violence," *The Nation*, June 24, 1968, p. 822.

matter, or that the victim did not want to harm the offender. Fear of reprisal was the motive given in the case of assault and family crimes: the feeling that police could not or would not do anything was also a common reason. Considering the percentage of convictions for offenses in comparison to complaints made to the police, it is easy to understand why victims place so little faith in law enforcement and court agencies.

> *To some extent we are all victims. We submit to injury from others which, if we really wanted to, we could avoid. We provoke by our acts and our works retaliation from people close to us in our families and our work. We see danger from others and pretend it does not exist. We cooperate with our friends—or enemies disguised as friends—in schemes which cause us injury or loss. We go through life hurting and being hurt. Fortunately—and it may be simply that we are lucky in not meeting potential killers—only very few of us end up as victims of homicide.*[40]

Student Checklist

1. Can you define victimology?
2. Are you able to identify eight of the crimes commonly called victimless crimes?
3. Are you able to give an example for each category of Mendelsohn's classification of victims?
4. Can you describe the legal rights of a victim to use force in defending himself?
5. Can you describe the amount of force that a victim in possession of property may use in terminating a criminal trespass to the property?
6. Do you know how to describe the differences between tort actions and victim-compensation programs in terms of providing relief for the victim of criminal acts?
7. Are you able to analyze the five basic methods for compensating victims?

[40] Gratus, *Victims*, p. 47.

8. Can you describe the trend of state legislation toward victim compensation programs?

9. Do you know how to identify three early examples of victim compensation?

10. Can you analyze the rates at which crimes are underreported, based on the NORC survey?

Topics for Discussion

1. Discuss the legal rights of victims of various types of crimes.
2. Discuss victim-compensation programs.
3. Discuss the use of force in repelling criminal acts.
4. Discuss the history of victim compensation in common law.
5. Discuss three rationales describing why society should provide compensation to victims.

ANNOTATED BIBLIOGRAPHY

Kerper, Hazel B. *Introduction to the Criminal Justice System.* St. Paul, Minn.: West Publishing Co., 1972. A basic introduction into the nature of crime and criminal responsibility, the criminal justice process, and professionals in the criminal justice field. Designed for the beginning student, this book deals with the model penal code and, through a series of footnotes, explains the differences encountered among the states in the United States. Appendixes include "How to Find and Cite the Law," a glossary of legal terms, and others.

Schur, Edwin M. *Crimes Without Victims.* Englewood Cliffs, N.J.: Prentice-Hall Inc., 1965. The introduction of this short volume covers the basic concepts of victimless crime, including definitions, theories, and the personal and social import of this field. The specific crimes of abortion, drug addiction, and homosexuality are dealth with in depth. Schur discusses the history of the offense, the subcultures involved, the effects of labeling, the crime tariff, and other specific effects of the crimes' illegality.

Schafer, Stephen. *Restitution to Victims of Crime.* Chciago, Ill.: Quadrangle Books, Inc., 1960. A short introduction including a historical background of victim compensation throughout the world. The author divides the topic into global areas, cites individual countries in each area, and discusses the etiology, current laws, and social attitudes toward victim compensation in each country.

————. *The Victim and His Criminal*. Random House, 1968. Covers the historical background of victimology including the basic theories of the criminal–victim interaction. The topics covered include the propensity for becoming a crime victim, victim research, the criminal's attitudes toward his victim, and other victim-related topics. The author presents his ideas in an easily readable and understandable format for a beginning student in this area.

Von Hentig, Hans. *The Criminal and His Victim*. New Haven, Conn.: Yale University Press, 1948. Von Hentig is concerned with the biological, sociobiological, and geophysical implications of crime and criminality. He deals with the contribution of the victim to the crime and divides victims into general classes of the young, the female, the old, the mentally defective and deranged, immigrants, minorities, and dull normals. Psychological types of victims are also theorized. This book represents the first major work in the field of victimology that is readily available to the student.

The study of this chapter will enable you to:

1. List five practices that would be considered in violation of the "cruel and unusual punishment" prohibition found in the Eighth Amendment to the U.S. Constitution.
2. Describe the current provisions for a convicted offender's rights to rehabilitation.
3. List the six standards or safeguards generally applicable to administrative proceedings to meet due process requirements.
4. Describe the changing attitude of the courts toward their review of confinement facilities in terms of the "hands-off" doctrine.
5. Describe how dress, hair length, and personal hygiene may be regulated by prison or confinement officials.
6. Give five typical incidents in which deadly force may be legally justified by a prison official.
7. List five occasions when the use of force against persons in confinement is justified.
8. Explain how the "clear and present danger" test is utilized for the censorship of reading material for confined persons.
9. Identify three administrative or security problems for confinement officials in providing inmates' rights to exercise religious beliefs.
10. Describe the right of convicted offenders to receive and send mail while they are in custody.

262

12

Substantive Rights of the Confined

Introduction

There is no standardized form of correctional law today. The few states that have codified their laws governing correctional facilities and the rights of the confined deal mainly with administrative procedures concerning the criminal process. Traditionally, courts have refrained from review or intervention in the management of correctional facilities, adhering to a "hands-off doctrine." The courts felt that, because penal institutions were created as extensions of our executive branch of government, their administration could be altered or regulated only by an exercise of executive power. Since the adoption of the Civil Rights Act, there have been numerous cases regarding prisoners' rights and a substantial body of law has arisen from these. Thus, the old policies are being replaced by judicial decisions regarding the constitutional rights of the confined.

Most of the civil rights cases of prisoners involve the denial of the due process requirements provided by either the Fifth or the Fourteenth Amendments of the Constitution. The Supreme Court has determined that due process has two facets, substantive and procedural. Substantive due process involves the fundamental rights of prisoners of life, liberty, property, and certain other specific rights that protect prisoners from governmental action. Some of these specific rights are outlined in the first eight amendments to the Constitution.

Due process, applied procedurally, requires that the procedures involved be fair to all parties. Much of our prison due process requirements have come from our administrative laws and procedures. These due process provisions have been created to protect the individual's right to be treated with fundamental fairness. Correctional due process has

263

been derived from cases involving social welfare agencies. The decision in these cases have been applied by the courts to prison disciplinary proceedings as well as to parole and probation revocation hearings, and the emerging requirements are the same in most cases. Generally, the standards applicable to an institution's quasi-judicial or administrative proceedings are:

1. Reasonable notice of the nature of the complaint.
2. A fair hearing before an impartial official or panel of officials.
3. Representation by counsel or counsel substitute.
4. Presentation of evidence (or witnesses) in one's behalf.
5. Cross-examination of witnesses.
6. Administrative review.

Some states do not recognize some of these due process safeguards as protected rights, and the cases providing the law on prisoners' rights are not clear. Prison disciplinary hearings are usually conducted informally and involve administrative questions. Thus, courts are reluctant to impose standards that might turn these informal hearings into formal adversary proceedings. The time and expense necessary to convert and to formalize such hearings, in addition to the logistic and financial problems of providing inmates and prison administrations with legal counsel, would be prohibitive. Courts have had additional reason to refrain from interference with these administrative hearings because the public has had little knowledge of the actual administration of correctional facilities. But, because of an increasing public awareness of prison conditions, the inmates' awakening realization of their legal rights as prisoners, and the resulting public pressure calling for judicial review of social welfare agencies, the courts have been given the impetus to investigate some of the issues surrounding prison due process. The trend seems to be toward increased judicial intervention, which will provide a clearer standardization of our laws concerning correctional institutions and prisoners' rights.

In probation and parole revocation hearings, the general due process requirements that have been outlined previously are almost uniformly applied in most states. After an arrest has been made and the criminal process is underway, these same due process standards are applicable.

The issues presented in this chapter are concerned with prisoners' substantive rights as provided by the Constitution and as reviewed by federal and state courts. Correctional law is presently in a state of flux and some of the court decisions supporting or minimizing the rights of prisoners may be overruled. Accordingly, the statements made in this chapter may not reflect the current state of the law. However, the general trends in the scope of prisoners' rights are demonstrated in the statements and decisions made recently by the courts, some of which are presented here.

The Right to Physical Safety, Humane Treatment, and Rehabilitation Programs

Courts have recognized the duty that prison administrators have to protect the inmates in their custody from physical assault and abuse. This duty includes protecting the inmate from abuse from prison personnel, from other inmates, and from himself (that is, suicide, starvation diet, and the like). The courts require only reasonable precautions and steps on the part of prison administrators to fulfill their duty. A court will not usually interfere in cases where the abuse was considered an isolated incident. However, class action suits brought by inmates seeking injunctive relief (a court order requiring the abuse to cease) have usually been effective means to obtain judicial review of existing prison conditions and their reform.

Prisoners have a qualified right to humane treatment while incarcerated. Incarceration itself may constitute a violation of the Eighth Amendment as being cruel and unusual punishment, if a facility lacks sanitation, adequate protection from assaults, and is severely overcrowded. Inmates have a right to have the things that are necessary to sustain their existence. They have a right to reasonable medical treatment: any negligent failure or deliberate refusal to give necessary medical treatment may constitute a deprivation of an inmate's civil rights. A correctional official cannot withhold medical treatment because of its expense or for discipline purposes. The problems with cases involving the lack or withholding of medical treatment result because of the requirement that the treatment in question must be "necessary." The attending physician and the prison officials must determine whether the requested medical treatment is necessary or not. Many cases of inadequate medical treatment have not been examined by the courts because of the courts' reluctance to interfere with administrative bodies and their discretionary power to make administrative decisions.

As with cases involving questions about prisoners' physical safety or humane treatment, the courts have adopted the "cruel and unusual punishment" test. This test provides that a court will intervene in the prisoner's behalf if the conduct in question is so gross or cruel as to "shock the conscience" of a civilized society.

Medical facilities and services in penal institutions are generally inadequate in providing inmates with basic preventive medical needs. However, with the increase of court actions on this question and the investigations of prisoners' complaints by governmental and other agencies, prisons are now beginning to recognize that adequate medical treatment is a fundamental right of prisoners, and that such facilities and services must be provided.

Presently, rehabilitation programs (education, job training, and the like) are not required by any statutory or constitutional right. However, the courts will consider the presence or absence of rehabilitative programs in determining whether conditions in a prison meet constitutional standards. If a rehabilitation program exists in a prison, prisoners may not be arbitrarily denied access to it. If a prisoner is denied access to such programs, the denial must be related to reasonable penal aims.

Use of Force

In discussing the inmates' right to be free from the fear of physical assault or offensive bodily contact, it is necessary to define the term "force" as it is used legally. Prisoners have the right to be free from the fear of offensive bodily contact as well as from actual assault. Force is defined as any physical force directed toward another, either by direct physical contact or by the use of a weapon. Prison officials have a privilege to use force against inmates in a correctional facility when such force is used:

1. In self-defense.
2. In defense of third persons.
3. For enforcement of prison rules and regulations.
4. In the prevention of an escape.
5. In the prevention of a crime.

Although prison officials are privileged to use force in these five situations, the degree of force used must be reasonable for the circumstances surrounding the incident. When a prisoner brings an action against a prison official for use of excessive force (assault), the court will examine the degree of force used by the inmate, the inmate's possession or non-possession of a deadly weapon, the prison official's perception that he or a third person is in danger of death or serious bodily harm, and any alternative means of force available to the prison official at the time of the incident. The court or hearing officer determines whether the official's use of force, considering all these circumstances, was reasonable.

The test for "reasonableness" is: Would a reasonable man, under similar circumstances, be entitled to use the same or a similar amount of force? The reasonableness of the force is dependent upon the amount of force being used by the inmate, the reaction force of the official, and the circumstances of the incident (potentiality of injury). For example, deadly force is never justified unless the prison official is acting under a "reasonable" belief that death or serious bodily harm may be inflicted upon himself or a third person and that the use of deadly force is his last means available to control the inmate or to protect himself or another from injury.

The courts still adhere to a "hands-off" policy in dealing with prisoners' complaints of unnecessary force used by prison officials for purposes of discipline. Unless the force or punishment employed is so gross or cruel as to shock the conscience of a civilized society or it goes beyond the legitimate penal aims, the courts will not regulate or restrict a prisons' punitive or disciplinary policies. Hence, only if the circumstances are exceptionally cruel, will the court deem it necessary to interfere and to determine if the actions were violative of the prisoner's Eighth Amendment right to be free from cruel and unusual punishment.

The Right to Privacy and Personal Appearance

The right to privacy does not exist behind prison walls. Prisoners' mail is censored, and in many institutions visits with family, friends, and sometimes even legal counsel are monitored by prison officials. The usual due process requirements under the Fourth Amendment, requiring a search warrant or at least probable cause prior to searches and seizure, do not apply in prisons. For security reasons, inmates in most institutions may be searched at any time, for any reason, and in any manner the prison official chooses to use.

Regulations regarding dress, hair length, and personal hygiene exist in practically all penal institutions, and they are considered necessary health, safety, and disciplinary measures. Recent court cases concerning mens' hair length or the wearing of beards and mustaches have supported the health rationale given by prison authorities. However, there have been no cases examining these decisions in light of the Equal Rights Bill as to whether these decisions were discriminatory on the basis of sex. Future litigation on this issue may be forthcoming because of the current changes in dress and appearance in the larger society.

The Right to Use the Mails

Prisoners have the right to use the mail system, according to the Supreme Court's interpretation of Article I of the Constitution, which also gives Congress and the U. S. Postal Service the exclusive right to regulate the postal system. Historically, however, courts have given prison authorities the privilege to inspect and to read all incoming and outgoing mail. This censorship is considered necessary to maintain security (in regard to contraband), and to limit the drain on prison budgets for the handling of mail. Although inspection of inmate communications is allowed, mail going between courts, legal counsel, or nonjudicial public officials is considered privileged and may not be intercepted or censored. Until recently (1968), no protection was given to these types of communications. According to recent court decisions, prison officials may examine these communications only after establishing that there are reasonable grounds to believe that evidence of a crime will be found in the correspondence in question. Some of the recent court decisions require that the inspection must take place with the inmate present or must be done by mechanical means, such as by fluoroscope or metal detector. Prison regulations regarding all nonlegal letters usually prohibit or delete communications that are offensive to race, nationality, or religious faith; that criticize the rules or officials of the prison; or are sexually arousing. The rationale for these abridgments of prisoners' First and Fourteenth Amendment rights is that they are necessary to ensure the stability of prison life and the prisoners' rehabilitation.

Prior to 1971, prisons banned letters that complained of internal conditions in the institution, sent by inmates to the news media. Personal interviews by news agencies with inmates were also under this ban. But recent court decisions have treated such censorship as an infringement upon a prisoner's and the news media's First Amendment rights prohibiting governmental interference with freedom of speech and the press. Interviews and communications with news agencies are now permitted, unless it is determined that the communication would present a "clear and present danger" of upsetting prison security, discipline, or orderly administration of the institution. Because prison officials make the primary decisions as to whether a communication presents a risk, their decisions are upheld until an informal hearing takes place, which can occur only if either a news agency or an inmate contests that primary decision.

The "clear and present danger" test is also used to determine what reading material and publications are received by the inmate. This test puts the burden on prison officials to demonstrate a compelling state interest concerning prison security or discipline *prior* to any censorship. Because of this standard, prisoners may now read many publications that were not previously permitted behind prison walls.

As an extension of the prisoners' right to access to the courts, prisons must have libraries that are sufficient to allow an inmate to do legal research on the points of law and procedure applicable to his case. Prison regulations limiting the possession of legal materials must be reasonable, so as not to infringe on the inmates' right to access to the courts.

Both historically and presently, courts have maintained the position that control of inmate correspondence is an administrative matter in which they will not interfere, unless it is shown that some independent constitutional right is being infringed upon in that control. The areas in which the courts have interfered with prison mail rules are those in which another constitutional right was involved. Communication between an inmate and a court involves the right of access to the court system. Correspondence between an inmate and his attorney involves both the right of access to the courts and the Sixth Amendment's guarantee of legal counsel for criminals. The First Amendment right to petition the government for redress of grievances is involved in the correspondence to and from nonjudicial public officials, and the freedoms of speech and press are involved in restrictions governing access to the news media and reading materials.

Reasonable restrictions on an inmate's right to use the mail (except privileged correspondence) have been upheld by the courts as a necessary administrative function of correctional facilities, unless such restrictions show a clear violation of another federal right.

Visitation and Right to Counsel

The right of inmates to visitation during incarceration is limited by prison authorities in terms of frequency, time, place, and persons for the purpose of institutional security. The time and place of an inmate's consultation with his counsel may have reasonable restrictions imposed so long as such restrictions do not place a hardship on the inmate or his attorney. These reasonable restrictions also apply to visits with the attorney's assistants or experts concerning the inmate's case. Inmates must be given a reasonably private conference area in which to confer with their attorney or his assistants, subject to any restrictions imposed because the particular prisoner has abused this privilege on prior occasions. Punishment arising out of an inmate's assertion or attempt to assert any of his rights to access to the courts or to counsel is a violation of a prisoner's constitutional rights, unless a compelling state interest justifies such punishment.

The First Amendment guarantee of free speech applies to a prisoner's right to visitation. Hence, any restrictions placed upon visitation must be justified by applying the "clear and present danger" test. If the First Amendment's clear and present danger test is found to be inapplicable in a particular situation, the equal protection of law guarantee of the Fourteenth Amendment precludes an arbitrary application of any restriction on visitation.

The Right to Religion

The First Amendment guarantees the right of all persons to the free exercise of their religious beliefs, yet prison restrictions exist even with the more popularly practiced religions. Where security, safety, or prison discipline may be disturbed by the exercise of religion, the courts have upheld the restrictions. Most of the recent litigation over the right to the free exercise of religion has involved actions brought by Black Muslims requesting the same rights given to inmates of other faiths (that is, their own reading material, religious services, and special diets). The courts generally have supported the rights of Muslim prisoners to practice their religion, but some of the Muslim religious publications have been banned because such material poses a threat to prison order and discipline. Restrictions on such religious communications are examined by using the "clear and present danger" test employed by courts for other types of communications. Because prison officials are under an obligation to maintain security and discipline within the institution, courts examine restrictions of religious freedom in relation to that obligation. Thus, if there is any justification for the need for such restrictions, the courts will usually approve of them.

The equal protection clause of the Fourteenth Amendment has been cited as relating to the issues raised by minority religious groups in prisons, and the courts have given them equal protection of the law in cases where the clear and present danger is minimal.

Pork-free diets have usually not been provided to Muslims or other minority religious groups because of budget restrictions, and because most prison diets are sufficient in other foods to support a pork-free program if one is necessary for religious purposes.

In general, Muslim religious medals, as those of other religions, may be worn in prison, unless the prohibition of such can be justified. Possible justification would be if the prisoner shows a probability that he would use the medallion as a weapon. Such "potential use" alone is strong enough to warrant its prohibition.

Political Rights

Just as a prisoner's First Amendment rights to freedom of speech have been restricted, his expression of political beliefs is also restricted under the claim that it endangers prison security or discipline. Generally, an expression of unpopular political beliefs is punishable: Such punishments have been found to be justified, except in a few individual cases. The clear and present danger test is also employed by courts to determine whether this expression should be restricted. Again, prison officials need not wait until an actual disturbance has taken place but may act on a reasonable belief that the security and discipline of the prison, or the safety of the inmates or staff, might be jeopardized by any organization or assembly. As a result of the discretionary power of prison officials to restrict any activity with a potential of disrupting the institutional security, political activity in prisons is minimal, and cases relating to expression of political beliefs are few. The courts have dealt with each case on an individual basis. Thus, it is difficult to formulate any comprehensive standards for political conduct that would apply to prisons generally.

The only workable inmate organizations at present that could produce any model for legal trends in political expression are the prisoners' labor unions, which have found a qualified recognition by prison authorities. However, with the emergence of prisoners' rights and judicial protection of such, perhaps more organized prison politics will emerge.

Summary

"Once a person enters prison, he loses all his rights." Many people still believe that this saying is true. However, certain substantial rights are now recognized and upheld by the courts, and an emerging body of correctional law regarding prisoners' rights is being compiled.

An analysis of recent court decisions concerning the rights of the confined is important for a number of reasons. Such analysis provides the correctional officer, the prisoner, and the layman with an understanding of the criminal process, the administration of correctional facilities, and our society's penal aims. Of greater significance is that it provides us with an insight into the legal justice system and its protection and regulation of the prisoner's individual rights. Such regulation is an example of our system of checks and balances, which supports the expression of each person's rights as provided by the Constitution. This analysis should become more comprehensive as a clearer uniformity of our correctional law evolves.

Student Checklist

1. Can you list five practices that would be considered in violation of the "cruel and unusual punishment" prohibition found in the Eighth Amendment to the U. S. Constitution?
2. Are you able to describe the current provisions for a convicted offender's rights to rehabilitation?
3. Can you list the six standards or safeguards generally applicable to administrative proceedings to meet due process requirements?
4. Do you know how to describe the changing attitude of the courts

toward their review of confinement facilities in terms of the "hands-off" doctrine?

5. Can you describe how dress, hair length, and personal hygiene may be regulated by prison or confinement officials?

6. Can you give five typical incidents in which deadly force may be legally justified by a prison official?

7. Are you able to list five occasions when the use of force against persons in confinement is justified?

8. Can you explain how the "clear and present danger" test is utilized for the censorship of reading material for confined persons?

9. Do you know how to identify three administrative or security problems for confinement officials in providing inmates' rights to exercise religious beliefs?

10. Are you able to describe the right of convicted offenders to receive and send mail while in custody?

Topics for Discussion

1. Discuss the "cruel and unusual punishment" prohibition of the Eighth Amendment to the U.S. Constitution.

2. Discuss the security problems associated with the rights of inmates to receive and send mail.

3. Discuss the rights of inmates to exercise religious beliefs.

4. Discuss the legal guidelines available for prison officials in their use of force.

5. Discuss the rights of offenders to legal counsel.

ANNOTATED BIBLIOGRAPHY

Friend, Charles E. "Judicial Intervention in Prison Administration," *William and Mary Law Review*. 9, 1 (Fall 1967), 178–192. Until recently, the courts have had a noninterference attitude toward prisons, and only lately have the courts placed an emphasis on the rights of the accused. The individual convict's rights include: claims for injuries suffered while in custody, nonarbitrary rules of correspondence, the right to legal advice and materials, and the use of *habeas corpus* for protection of prisoners' rights and the discipline of prisoners. The article also identifies the difficult tasks of prison administrators, caused by the new judicial interest in prisoner complaints.

Palmer, John W. *Constitutional Rights of Prisoners.* Cincinnati, Ohio: W. H. Anderson Company, 1973. This book begins with a basic introduction to the legal system presenting a perspective through which individual cases and their effects may be measured. It deals with a discussion of the various areas of prisoners' rights, including the use of force, disciplinary procedures, visitation, correspondence, religion, legal services, medical treatment, parole, and civil and criminal liabilities of prison officials. A second section is composed of judicial decisions and cases relating to the subject of Section One. Included are "A Model Act to Provide for Minimum Standards for Protection of Rights of Prisoners (NCCD)" and "United Nations Standard Minimum Rules for the Treatment of Prisoners and Related Recommendations."

Rudovsky, David. *The Rights of Prisoners.* New York, N.Y.: Avon Books, 1973. A general guide that sets forth the rights of confined individuals under the present law and offers some suggestions as to procedures for protecting those rights. The various areas dealt with are disciplinary actions, religious and racial discrimination, privacy, personal appearance, speech, cruel and unusual punishment, political rights, and parole.

South Carolina Department of Corrections. *The Emerging Rights of the Confined.* 1972. The result of an in-depth research project, conducted by the South Carolina Department of Corrections, on correctional case law. The areas studied include: access to courts and counsel, religious freedom, correspondence and visitation, access to media, grievances, personal appearance, disciplinary methods, punitive isolation and administrative segregation, administrative investigation and interrogations, inmate safety, facilities, medical treatment and practices, administrators' liability, rehabilitation, classification and work assignment, transfers, and detainers and parole.

Spaeth, Jr., Edmund B. "The Courts' Responsibility for Prison Reform," *Villanova Law Review,* August, 1971, pp. 1031–1046. Jailhouse lawyers are those inmates who have read some legal material and who frequently advise other inmates on their legal rights, at a cost. An alternative to this is to use the sources of an individual from a defender's association who could counsel inmates professionally. Another approach is to bring law students in from nearby law schools to assist inmates in all phases of legal activity.

The study of this chapter will enable you to:

1. Contrast the ages at which presumptions were formed about criminal liability under the common law, and later by statute, for criminal acts performed by juveniles.
2. Describe the history of the separation of adjudication and confinement of juveniles from that of adults.
3. Identify the philosophy of the early juvenile court movement.
4. Describe the contributions of the *Kent* case in 1966.
5. Describe the impact of the *Gault* decision.
6. Explain how the Miranda Warning applies to juvenile offenders.
7. Contrast juvenile adjudication safeguards with the procedures used for adult adjudications.
8. Define *parens patriae*.

13
Criminal Law and the Juvenile

History and Philosophy

The roots of juvenile law lie deep in the British criminal law, under which children below the age of 10½ were not punishable for any crime; between 10½ and 14 they were punishable if found to be capable of mischief; and beyond the age of 14, they were subject to criminal law and punishment as an adult.

In the United States, the generally accepted common law rules for criminal prosecution of juveniles rendered them exempt if below the age of 7; presumptively exempt between the ages of 7 and 14, because of the child's presumed incapability of forming intent, or *mens rea;* and presumptively capable of forming criminal intent beyond the age of 14. Unfortunately, children in the 1880s were still being convicted and sometimes executed.

The foundations of juvenile law and juvenile courts nevertheless arose from these common law rules of criminal responsibility. The chancery (equity) courts contributed also by responding to the need for relief from the strictness of a rigid common law system of pleading and available relief.[1] In the thirteenth and fourteenth centuries, the Crown exercised jurisdiction over the estates of minors, on the assumption that children were wards of the state. In time this jurisdiction was enlarged to

---

[1] Chancery courts in England had broad authority over the welfare of children. However, their jurisdiction was exercised almost exclusively on behalf of minors whose property rights were jeopardized. The workings of the court of chancery were exceedingly ponderous. Charles Dickens's *Bleak House* documents them at great length.

include matters affecting the general welfare of children. The chancery origin of juvenile law and juvenile courts contributed to the philosophy of protection of young persons as wards of the state.

Throughout the 1800s in the United States, many legislations were enacted to soften the effects of criminal conviction on young persons. First, there was a separation of juveniles from adults in prisons. Later, separate institutions for juveniles were created, an act that led to probation provisions (1841).

Eventually, recognition of the potential for harm to youth in pretrial detention by contact with older, more seasoned violators, and the harm of the trial itself, resulted in separate trials for juveniles. By the close of the nineteenth century, segregation of children before and during trial led directly to the creation of the juvenile court movement. With the advent of the juvenile court movement what remained lacking, both in theory and practice, was a completely noncriminal system of treatment of juveniles in the courts and correctional institutions. Children in this period may have been jailed separately from adults prior to trial but they were jailed nevertheless; they may have been tried separately from adults but they were tried nevertheless; and if convicted they might be sent to a separate juvenile institution but sent they were for punishment. What this implied was a philosophy of retribution in which children were prosecuted criminally for their misdeeds.[2]

In 1899, the Illinois legislature created the first juvenile court. This act created no new courts but designated one of the courts' members to serve as a juvenile court judge whose jurisdiction covered the delinquent child. An important aspect of the act was the virtual elimination of all features of the criminal trial, including arrest and indictment, and substitution instead of informal proceedings and hearings for custody. The standard to be applied in formulating a disposition was that it should approximate as nearly as possible that which should be given by its parents (the concept of *parens patriae*). Broad use was to be made of probation officers in investigating cases before hearings, as well as in placing and supervising a child after the hearing. Children could be sentenced only to institutions created for their care or to an adult institution pro-

[2] Lewis Yablonsky, "The Role of Law and Social Science in the Juvenile Court," *Journal of Criminal Law, Criminology, and Police Science*, Vol. 53, No. 4, December 1962.

vided they were completely segregated from adult inmates. The juvenile court movement, in short, sought to treat the child not as a criminal to be punished but as a "delinquent" to be guided and corrected.[3] It provided for:

1. Separate detention and nonpublic hearings for juveniles.
2. Probation supervision.
3. Confidentiality of records.
4. Disposition within a broad range of alternatives.

Children were no longer to be treated as criminals nor dealt with by the process used for criminals, but instead were to be dealt with as a wayward child would be by a wise parent.

The juvenile court movement flourished, and within a decade nearly half of the states had established juvenile courts. By 1925 all but two states had done so. A significant development of that era was the bringing together under one jurisdiction not only delinquency cases but also neglect and dependency cases. This meant that the juvenile courts had jurisdiction over violation of criminal law by children and violation of laws that pertain only to children, such as dependency laws or neglect by parents (or other legally responsible persons). Some juvenile courts are now authorized to deal with other activities involving children, such as adoption, appointment of guardians, nonsupport by a parent, and contributing to the delinquency or neglect of minors on the part of adults.

Juvenile courts today are concerned with children up to the ages of 16, 17, or 18, with some exceptions. The juvenile court takes various organizational forms:

1. Independent courts with jurisdiction over children.
2. Family courts with jurisdiction over specified offenses and relations and specified types of family conflict, including jurisdiction over children.
3. Juvenile and domestic relations courts.
4. Juvenile courts as sections or parts of courts with more general jurisdiction.

Juvenile courts may range in number in any one state from 5 to 50, and each court is an autonomous operation. The juvenile courts in the United States are not, therefore, part of a juvenile court system as such. The variations among jurisdictions are as great as the number of separate

---

[3] Charles W. Tenney, Jr., "The Utopian World of Juvenile Courts," *The Annals,* May 1969.

courts. In only a small number of jurisdictions are there specialized juvenile courts and judges who give their full time to the juvenile court. The juvenile court is usually a branch or division of another court whose orientation is not that of individualized justice for the child. A question often raised is whether a judge who moves to the juvenile court hearing from another court can make the transition to this different role. There are few specialized juvenile courts with a full-time judge; perhaps 250 out of some 3000 to 4000 serve only the juvenile court. With the exception of these 250, judges serving the juvenile court do so on a part-time basis, serving other courts as well.

Definitions of Delinquency

Definitions of delinquency in juvenile law include violation of laws or ordinances by children, but the legal provisions extend considerably beyond these. A summary list of acts included in delinquency definitions is that the offender: (1) violates any law or ordinance; (2) is habitually truant; (3) (knowingly) associates with thieves, or vicious or immoral persons; (4) is incorrigible; (5) is beyond control of parent or guardian; (6) grows up in idleness or crime; (7) behaves in such a way as to injure or endanger self or others; (8) absents self from home (without just cause and without consent); (9) partakes in immoral and indecent conduct; (10) (habitually) uses vile, obscene, or vulgar language (in public places); (11) (knowingly) enters, visits house of ill repute; (12) patronizes or visits policy shop or gaming place; (13) (habitually) wanders about railroad yards and tracks; (14) jumps train or enters car or engine without authority; (15) patronizes saloon or dram house where intoxicating liquor is sold; (16) wanders streets at night, not on lawful business; (17) patronizes public poolroom or bucket shop; (18) immoral conduct around school (or in public place); (19) engages in illegal occupation; (20) places himself or herself in occupation or situation dangerous or injurious to self or others; (21) smokes cigarettes (or uses tobacco in any form); (22) frequents place whose existence violates law; (23) is found in place for which permitting adult may be punished; (24) is addicted to drugs; (25) is disorderly; (26) begs; (27) uses intoxicating liquor (28) makes indecent proposals; (29) loiters, sleeps in alleys, or is vagrant; (30) runs away from state or charity institution; (31) is found on premises occupied or used for illegal purposes; (32) operates motor vehicle dangerously while under the influence of liquor; (33) attempts to marry without consent, in violation of law; or (34) is given to sexual irregularities.

The Juvenile Court in Theory and Practice

The basic philosophy of juvenile courts reflects the sentiment that every child should be protected and rehabilitated rather than subjected to the harshness of the criminal system. Juvenile courts substitute procedural informality for the adversary system; emphasize investigation of the juvenile background in deciding upon dispositions; rely heavily on social science for both diagnosis and treatment; and, in general, are committed to the rehabilitation of the juvenile as their predominant goal. To meet the nonpunitive, rehabilitation philosophy of the courts, a new vocabulary was developed: trials became hearings, sentences were dispositions, punishment became treatment, and reformatories were training schools. Hearings were informal and nonadversary, and the guiding principle for the courts both in findings and in dispositions was "the best interest of the child."[4]

> Nationally, persons under 15 years of age made up 9 percent of the total police arrests; under 18, 26 percent; under 21, 39 percent; and under 25, 53 percent. . . . In 1972, 53 percent of the individuals arrested for violations of the Narcotic Drug Laws were persons under 21 years of age.
>   Of the 1,270,860 juvenile offenders taken into custody in 1972, 45 percent were handled within departments and released; 1.3 percent were referred to welfare agencies and 1.6 percent were referred to other police agencies; 1.3 percent were referred to criminal and adult courts; and 50.8 percent were referred to juvenile court jurisdictions.[5]

The heavy responsibility of the juvenile court is thus very clear. What had begun as a powerful idea in dealing with delinquents failed to mature properly. With little guidance or control, the juvenile court has

---

[4] Tenney, p. 107.

[5] Clarence Kelley, Director, FBI, *Crime in the United States: Uniform Crime Reports* (Washington, D.C.: U.S. Govt. Printing Office, 1972), pp. 34, 116.

become a kind of social agency with therapeutic responsibilities considerably beyond its potential.

As early as the 1920s some criticism of the juvenile court began to be heard. Lack of services and facilities hampered effective functioning of the court, just as in adult courts. But beyond this, the juvenile court began to reflect a serious disregard of due process for the child. This resulted in a disregard of children's rights in many situations. With a position of *parens patriae,* there was no need for due process to place a child under the state's protection and guardianship, just as there is no need for due process on the part of a parent who deprives his child of liberty to shield it from waywardness.

In the process of saving a child from becoming delinquent or from continuing in a life of delinquency and later a career of crime, the juvenile court, with the full force of state statute, was able to take under its jurisdiction children who committed certain acts (truancy, running away, or being "incorrigible") for which adults could not be legally held. In most courts these kinds of cases constituted the bulk of the cases. Furthermore, these children, whether committing these "children's" offenses or offenses that would have been crimes if committed by adults, were subjected to certain treatments whose effectiveness has been seriously questioned and that were often provided by persons unskilled and untrained to apply them. The question became: "Is this treatment causing more harm than good?" The high rate of repeat offenses and the number of those who continued in crime were serious reasons to think so. The promise of the juvenile court was beginning to pall. Serious adjustments were to come.

By midcentury, the social work agency concept of the court, in contrast to the legal view, began to be strongly favored. The foremost proponent of the need to look at the juvenile court was the late lawyer-sociologist Paul Tappan, whose text *Juvenile Delinquency* gave this critical question the attention that it demanded.[6] Tappan was concerned with:

1. The broadening of jurisdiction over delinquency in the name of prevention.
2. The abandonment of due process in the juvenile courts.
3. The failure of the courts to provide real rehabilitative approaches and instead their favor of older punitive practices.

[6] Paul Tappan, *Juvenile Delinquency* (New York, N.Y.: McGraw-Hill, 1949).

4. The many "tragedies" visited upon children because of real limitations of the courts.

Further criticism was leveled at a more procedural level. Juvenile statutes give judges broad powers over children's lives, yet the courts have a serious lack of published set procedures. In 1967, the President's Commission on Law Enforcement and the Administration of Justice stated:

> There is increasing evidence that the informal procedures, contrary to the original expectation, may themselves constitute a further obstacle to effective treatment of the delinquent to the extent that they engender in the child a sense of injustice provoked by seemingly all-powerful and challengeless exercise of authority by judges and probation officers.[7]

In the 1960s and early 1970s, widespread efforts throughout the country to assure civil liberties and individual rights contributed to a range of efforts to ensure fairness in children's cases by assuring procedural safeguards. Two landmark decisions by the U.S. Supreme Court reflect this concern in the nation. The first was the *Kent* decision, in which Justice Fortas wrote:

> While there can be no doubt of the original laudable purpose of juvenile courts, studies and critiques in recent years raise serious questions as to whether actual performance measures well enough against theoretical purpose to make tolerable the immunity of the process from the reach of constitutional guarantees applicable to adults. There is much evidence that some juvenile courts . . . lack the personnel, facilities and techniques to perform adequately as representatives of the State in a "parens patriae" capacity, at least with respect to children charged with law violations.
>
> There is evidence, in fact, that there may be grounds for concern that the child receives the worst of both worlds: that he gets neither the protections accorded to adults nor the solicitous care and regenerative treatment postulated for children.[8]

The *Kent* decision dealt with a specific issue; the procedures required of the juvenile court to waive jurisdiction over a juvenile suspected of a serious offense—generally an act that would be a felony if committed by an adult—to the adult criminal court for trial as an adult. The Court

---

[7] President's Commission on Law Enforcement and Administration of Justice, *The Challenge of Crime in a Free Society*. Washington: U.S. Govt. Printing Office, 1967, p. 85.

[8] Kent v. United States, 383 U.S. 541 (1967).

was emphatic that the waiver of jurisdiction was an important action to the juvenile because there are special rights and immunities that are not provided in the juvenile court hearing.

Kent led to Gault, a case in which procedural safeguards were further detailed.[9] In a sense, this decision led to a change in direction of the pendulum swing from the juvenile court as an administrative social service agency to the juvenile court as a legal judicial agency.

The Gault decision held that the juvenile code of the state of Arizona deprived allegedly delinquent children of the procedural safeguards guaranteed by the due process clause of the Fourteenth Amendment. The Court held that due process guarantees apply to all children alleged to be delinquent: the right to adequate notice of charges; the right to representation by a lawyer, either retained or appointed by the court; the right to confrontation and cross-examination of witnesses; and the right to be advised of the privilege against self-incrimination.

Gault led to Winship.[10] The result is a mandate reflecting the Kent decision assuring due process and the Gault decision providing for both due process and fair treatment Winship clearly rejected the "civil" humanitarianism of administrative parens patriae in favor of applying the safeguard of a criminal action. In Winship the issue was whether proof beyond a reasonable doubt is among the essentials of a juvenile hearing of adjudication. The direct implication of this decision was that the child is entitled to a jury trial with all of the procedural safeguards of the Constitution and the Bill of Rights. In the adjudication hearing the determining of guilt or innocence of the juvenile will be made if the child is afforded all the necessary safeguards. At the disposition hearing all of the juvenile court's social and psychological and other resources will be brought to bear. The distinction is that they will be applied only after adjudication of guilt.

Kent, Gault, and Winship have unlocked the constitutional door to

---

[9] In re Gault, 387 U.S. 1 (1967). Gault, a 15-year-old boy charged with making an obscene telephone call, had been committed to a state institution, where he might have been kept until he became 21. If he had been 18 at the time of the offense the maximum punishment would have been a fine of $5 to $50 or imprisonment in jail for not more than two months. See also: Norman Lefstein, Vaughan Stapleton, and Lee Teitelbaum, "In Search of Juvenile Justice: Gault and Its Implementation," Law and Society Review, 3 (May 1969), 491–562.
[10] In re Winship, 397 U.S. 358 (1970).

the full array of legal rights that apply in adult criminal trials. However, if the positive aspects of the juvenile court are to survive, it is imperative that judges keep their perspective and maintain a reasonable balance when considering any further "logical extensions" of Supreme Court rulings pertaining to juvenile rights. The ultimate consequence would be the establishment of an adversary, criminal court for children, with perhaps little or no attention to the special needs of the child. These special needs become the subject of the dispositional phase of the proceedings only. As one juvenile court judge stated, "We have become so hung up by the alarms over the procedural invasion of *Gault* that we have forgotten that a minor fraction of our time is spent on *Gault*-controlled proceedings, and that most of this can be reduced to the routine of a check-off list. We have forgotten that *Gault* does not enter into the disposition process, except for its commendable rule of fairness. We have forgotten that the 'disposition is the heartbeat of the juvenile court,' and deserves what it has not received: the best of our thinking, the best of our discussions, the best of our efforts." [11]

The Substantive Law of Juvenile Deviancy

In recent years considerable concern has been exhibited over the informal procedures and lack of due process prevalent in the juvenile courts. This focus on the courts was stimulated by a series of appellate court cases in which legal technical rights were sought. In providing appropriate legal safeguards, the controversial issue is whether the child's needs are relegated to a lesser priority. Also implied in this question is the degree of concern necessary in law enforcement, which precedes adjudication; and the degree of concern necessary in corrections, which follows. It is only when the process is considered totally that a child's rights may be truly protected and his needs considered.

A properly operated juvenile justice system that includes enforcement, adjudication, and corrections manifests three important concerns:
    1. Protection of individual rights. The juvenile justice system cannot interfere in the life of a child unless the case is clearly within the

[11] Lindsay G. Arthur, "The Forgotten Focus," *Juvenile Court Journal*, 21, 3 (Fall 1970), p. 71.

authority granted. Children must be protected from the mistaken, the vicious, the prejudiced, and the cynical use of enforcement, adjudication, or corrections.

2. Protection of the public through imposition of external controls, namely, arrest, the determination of delinquency, and application of corrective techniques.

3. Help for each child to achieve his fullest potential as his right and society's expectation.

All segments of the juvenile justice system are equally involved; the first issue—the protection of juvenile rights—presses so heavily at this time that it almost obscures the other two. This need not be so. In what follows, an attempt is made to consider all three concerns in the process of enforcement, adjudication, and corrections.

Enforcement

Arrest and detention of the juvenile are the first steps in activating the juvenile justice system. The basic question to be asked in terms of children's rights is: When may police arrest a child?

Packer considers the basis for the use of police discretion in arrest as follows: "I do not think that the police can any longer have it both ways. They cannot enjoy the discretion which it is argued they need and, at the same time, insulate themselves from effective outside scrutiny of how they exercise that discretion. As long as the criminal process in the courts has to serve as the only effective vehicle for its correction of abuses, through the reversal of convictions, the courts will go on policing the police." [12] Discretion in arrest and detention of a juvenile has four dimensions: (1) release of the youth, with or without a warning, but without making an official record or taking further action; (2) release of the juvenile, but writing up a brief field report for the juvenile bureau, or a more formal report referring the matter for possible action; (3) turning the matter over to the juvenile bureau immediately; (4) referring the case directly to juvenile court.

An instance in which discretion of the police officer to arrest or not to arrest was argued took place in the following Ohio case. A minor was taken into custody after alleged use of obscene language and inter-

---

[12] Herbert Packer, "The Courts, the Police, and the Rest of Us," *Journal of Criminal Law, Criminology, and Police Science*, No. 238, 1966, p. 57.

ference with the lawful use of a playground. Counsel for the minor argued that the officers had no right to arrest because they had no warrant and the juvenile was not committing a misdemeanor in their presence (as is necessary in arrest of an adult). The Ohio code, said the court, "does not forbid any . . . officer or their person authorized by the juvenile judge from taking into custody any child who is found violating any law or ordinance, or who is reasonably believed to be a fugitive from his parents or from justice, or whose surroundings are such as to endanger his health, morals, or welfare."

The court ruled that a police officer may take a child into protective custody without due process if the officer has reasonable grounds to believe that the child is a delinquent, neglected, or dependent child.

How do confessions and admissions of a juvenile relate to the privilege against self-incrimination? Primary in this discussion is the concept of the "totality of circumstances" rule, well demonstrated in the following case. A 15-year-old youth was taken into custody late at night by a security guard and turned over to the police. Interrogation continued until 5:00 A.M., when the boy was released to the custody of his 18-year-old sister. During interrogation and until confession, no attempts were made to notify the parents. But this alone was not enough to make the confession inadmissible. It was argued that the arrest and detention by the security guard, coupled with the breach of the statutory requirement that juveniles can be questioned only "for a reasonable time," made the confession inadmissible.

The court, in considering the totality of the circumstances, ruled that "The failure of police to notify the child's parents that he had been taken into custody, coupled with other circumstances such as his age, the unlawfulness of his arrest by the security guard, the lateness of the hour, the duration of detention, and the absence of his parents, attorney, or friend established that his confession to the police was involuntary and inadmissible in a proceeding charging him with being a juvenile delinquent." [13]

The Miranda rule requires that a person in custody, and prior to any questioning, must be told that he need not answer any questions or make any statements that may incriminate him. The juvenile's understanding of the rule and the free will of admitting statements must be

[13] In re Williams, 49 Misc. 2d 154, NYS, 2d 91 (1966).

assessed in each case. The Miranda Warning (to an adult) must be simplified for a juvenile. The standard Miranda Warning for adults may be given as follows:

1. *You have the right to remain silent during any questioning now or at any time.*
2. *Anything you do say can and will be used in court against you.*
3. *You have a right to have an attorney present with you during this or any conversation, either an attorney of your own choosing or, if you cannot afford an attorney, one appointed for you prior to questioning, if you so desire.*

After the above warning, the arrested or detained person will be asked the following questions and his response will be noted where space is provided:

Question: Do you understand each of these rights that I have explained to you?

Answer:

Question: Having in mind and understanding your rights as I have told you, are you willing to talk with us?

Answer:

I hereby certify under penalty of perjury, that the foregoing is true.

Signed: _____ Date and Time _____

A simplified Miranda Warning, based on the San Diego Police Department form, devised for use with juveniles is as follows:

1. *You don't have to talk to me at all, now or later on, it is up to you.*
2. *If you decide to talk to me, I can go to court and repeat what you say against you.*
3. *If you want a lawyer, an attorney, to help you decide what to do, you can have one free before and during questioning by me now or by anyone else later on.*
4. *Do you want me to explain or repeat anything about what I have just told you?*
5. *Remembering what I've just told you, do you want to talk to me?*

It is also absolutely necessary that the person giving the warnings be in a position subsequently to demonstrate that the complete warnings were given and understood by the recipient. Any waiver by the latter must be shown to have been given willingly, with full understanding of the consequences.

Upon arrest, the next question at issue is: What constitutes the basis for detention and bail for juveniles? In brief, a decision for detention must be based on judicial findings of evidence, and questions of bail must be solved on a constitutional basis.

Standards that govern bail settings are relatively clear. The more serious the charge, the more extensive the prior record, the weaker the defendant's community ties; the greater is the chance for high bail or removal, and the lesser the chance for release.

These and other issues involved in enforcement are beginning to create a vast reservoir of decisions—a body of knowledge that points to the demand that law enforcement programs pay full heed to the rights of juveniles.

Adjudication

The *Gault, Kent,* and *Winship* decisions have revolutionized the juvenile courts in recent years. Procedural safeguards for children and the insuring of due process forcefully illustrated the need to give legal considerations the same high priorities as social/humanitarian concerns. Other legal concerns directly related to the adjudication phase of the juvenile justice system include intake, privacy of records, right to counsel *(Gault),* and transfer *(Kent)*.

Intake. The juvenile court intake process is a screening mechanism in which information about a case is reviewed or evaluated. The process should occur as fast as possible, because subjecting children and families to long periods of uncertainty increases their tension and anxiety.

From the outset, the following basic questions should be posed.
1. Does the court have jurisdiction over the complaint or the action?
2. Is there sufficient evidence to support the allegations?
3. Should the petition be authorized?

Intake also has a diagnostic element. It identifies those youngsters in whose lives the court should no longer be concerned. It can also recommend programs for those in the remaining group, those for whom the court can accept treatment responsibility. Cases can be assigned to certain treatment categories described in the following paragraphs.

The first is a minimal service based upon routine surveillance while the child is on probation. Major reliance is placed on the probationer himself and his family's ability to solve the problems, once having been formally confronted by law enforcement and the court process. Probationers are advised of the requirements of probation. They and their families are told that they should submit routine reports to their officers and that periodic reports would also be secured from their school, work, and other pertinent areas of social adjustment. They are also told that they are expected to demonstrate their own readiness to reside in the free community.

A second category is that of intensive service of youngsters who are assigned to social services, based upon their needs and an assessment of their ability to use available help. Such cases are carried by a staff, professionally trained in the behavioral sciences.

The gap in dispositional alternatives available to courts is wide. The judge may return a youngster to his own home as part of an intensively served caseload under probation supervision. If the child cannot accommodate to that degree of freedom, the alternative—and usually the only alternative—is complete removal from the community and commitment to a correctional institution.

The exercise of discretion during intake is necessary and desirable. But the haste with which such discretion is usually exercised often makes for unwise decisions that jeopardize the child's future. Inappropriate decisions made by intake workers are frequently the result of three conditions:

1. The lack of sufficient information upon which to base a decision.
2. The lack of clearly stated standards to guide the intake workers in making their decisions.
3. The lack of established procedures for determining whether to file a complaint or release.

Intake is faced with some difficult problems because of these lacks, which only more strikingly underline the need for sensitivity to individual needs and the desirability of individualized action. The intake worker must exercise the prerogative to refuse petitions filed by the police where appropriate and to make referral decisions immediately, whether to provide further court action or to release the child to the community without further involvement.

Privacy of Records. Since the beginning of the juvenile court movement, the confidentiality of juvenile proceedings has been under attack. The privacy of juvenile proceedings and records is generally respected. Publicity in the media is regulated by law in most states, and the laws do prohibit the publication of names of juveniles in delinquency cases. The issue is not easily resolved in the minds of citizens—it represents a delicate balancing of social goals with competing values. Publicity as a possible deterrent to others is pitted against the desire not to stigmatize the child.

Fingerprints of juveniles are usually regulated by statutes, rules, or regulations. However handled, the laws or rules are designed to attain maximum protection for the community. They must be designed to prevent indiscriminate, unnecessary fingerprinting and abuse of the prints, which might have a detrimental effect upon the individual's later life. The following procedures are widely accepted:

1. Police agencies should be allowed to keep a limited file of fingerprints of juveniles on a local basis.
2. Cards should be added to this file only when the offense is one in which police experience shows that prints are useful in solving future cases.
3. No fingerprints of children under 14 would be placed in the file.
4. The files would be kept separate from adult criminal files and under special security procedures limiting access to police personnel on a need-to-know basis.
5. Cards would be destroyed if the decision after investigation of the case is that no basis for juvenile court jurisdiction exists, or if a juvenile reaches the age of 21 and has no record of violation since the age of 16.[14]

Right to Counsel. In proceedings to determine delinquency, which may result in commitment to an institution, the child and his parents must be advised that the child has a right to be represented by a lawyer and that if they are unable to pay, counsel will be appointed.

In the *Gault* case in 1967, the right to counsel is presented in a powerful manner:

> *The juvenile needs the assistance of counsel to cope with problems of law, to make skilled inquiry into the facts, to insist upon regularity of the proceedings, and to ascertain whether he has a defense and to prepare and submit it. The child requires the guiding hand of counsel at every step in the proceedings against him . . . the probation officer cannot act as counsel for the child . . . nor can the judge.*[15]

In a similar strongly worded opinion, Chief Judge Murrah wrote in connection with a 1946 commitment of a mentally subnormal child:

> *Where, as in both proceedings for juveniles and mentally deficient persons, the state undertakes to act in parens patriae, it has the inescapable*

---

[14] *Standards for Juvenile and Family Courts* (U.S. Children's Bureau), Department of Health, Education and Welfare, 1966, pp. 50–52.
[15] In re Gault, 387 U.S. 1, 87 S. Ct. 1428 (1967).

duty to vouchsafe due process, and this necessarily includes the duty to see that a subject of an involuntary commitment proceeding is afforded the opportunity to have the guiding hand of legal counsel at every step of the proceedings, unless effectively waived by one authorized to act in his behalf.[16]

Right of Transfer. Transfer is usually used in waiver to an adult court of juveniles suspected of serious offenses that, if committed by an adult, would be considered felonies. Waiver is used routinely, but until the *Kent* decision, the procedure remained poorly defined.

The concept of transfer is well stated in a 1969 decision:

Since the presumption of the statutory framework of juvenile law is that juveniles are to be treated as juveniles, the "full investigation" required before waiver to the adult court must explore all the possible dispositions short of waiver by which the "welfare (of the child) and the best interests of the district," may be secured. Both counsel and the court have a vital role to play in this exploration. The child's advocate should search for a plan, or perhaps a range of plans, which may persuade the court that the welfare of the child and the safety of the community can be served without waiver. And the court itself cannot remain inert. It also has a duty to utilize its "facilities, personnel, and expertise for a proper determination of the waiver issue."

Any such hearing must, however, make a thorough examination of the juvenile's possible future as well as his distressing past. The previous history of the youth is relevant. But its relevance lies not in the justification it may provide for the juvenile court to abandon its statutory duty to help the young offender, but in the insight the past may contribute to the strategy for rehabilitation. For it is only after all rehabilitation possibilities have been canvassed that a decision to waive jurisdiction to the district court is ever proper.[17]

Inapplicability of transfer is the milestone decision in the *Kent* case. It has had a major role in reforming the juvenile court movement. In this case is was held that the juvenile court's original waiver was inappropriate in the first place, because the juvenile was afflicted with a serious mental illness and was amenable to commitment to a mental institution by determination of the juvenile court as early as 1961.

---

[16] In re Heryford v. Parker, 396 F 2d 393 (10th Cir. 1963).
[17] Haziel v. U.S., 494 F. 2d 1274 (D.C. Cir., 1969).

Such a waiver was not necessary for protection of society and was not conducive to juvenile's rehabilitation. Therefore, the error was in not committing the youth to a mental institution at the earliest date possible.[18]

Corrections

The greater problem for determination by the juvenile court is not whether the child committed a delinquency, but what must be done to help him avoid further delinquency. Rehabilitating juveniles by individualized sentencing includes a range of services, not excluding commitment to a correctional institution. Sentencing may raise a variety of issues that require relief in the appellate courts. These include issues of probation, probation revocation, and appeal. Once a child is found to be within the jurisdiction of the court after a finding of guilt or innocence, a disposition may very well include the return of the child to the family and community with the provision that the terms of his residence there should be subject to continued supervision of a probation officer. Or, it may be considered necessary to remove the child from the home to a correctional institution or other placement. Such decisions as these should rest upon sound probation department social study and diagnosis, with a careful consideration of the child's personality, attitudes, and characteristic ways of dealing with life problems. They must also include the family's resources and degree of acceptance of its responsibilities, as well as available community assistance to the child and family.

Conditions of probation may be imposed upon a child. These may vary widely, but they must not be in violation of constitutional guarantees. In *Jones* v. *Commonwealth*, the Virginia Supreme Court stated:

Jones and another were found guilty of throwing stones at a dwelling at nighttime and declared delinquent. The judgment against them imposed several conditions of probation, among these being that each boy "attend Sunday School and Church each Sunday hereafter for one year . . ."

No civil authority has the right to require anyone to accept or reject any religious belief or to contribute to the support thereof. The growth of religion is not made dependent on force or alliance with the State. Its support is left to moral and spiritual forces.[19]

[18] Kent v. U.S., 401 F2d 408 (D.C. Cir. 1968).
[19] Jones v. Commonwealth, 185 Va. 335, S.E. 2d 44 (1946).

In regard to the related issue of revocation of probation, the Maryland Court of Appeals asserted that:

A probationer is not expected or required to at once achieve perfection. If his conduct is that of the ordinary well-behaved person, with no more lapses than all people have, with no serious offenses charged against him, and without indication that he intends to pursue the course which led to his original conviction, the courts and probation officers should not seek for unusual and irrelevant grounds upon which to deprive him of his freedom.[20]

Most appeals that originate in the juvenile court usually treat the issue of disposition. Three procedures are used:

1. Direct appeal. The typical juvenile court act provides for this.
2. Review and rehearing. The procedure takes place before the same court that originally adjudicated the case, and new matter may be introduced.
3. *Habeas corpus.* Most statutes provide for this type of review any time after committal.

In addition to these categories of concern, there are numerous others that have been (and will continue to be) tested in the courts. These range from equality and discretion of sentence to social investigation abuses and the deletion of records. The body of juvenile case law will continue to grow in today's climate of equality and justice for all, including children.

Student Checklist

1. Are you able to contrast the ages at which presumptions were formed about criminal liability under the common law, and later by statute, for criminal acts performed by juveniles?
2. Can you describe the history of the separation of adjudication and confinement of juveniles from that of adults?

---

[20] Swan v. State, 200 Md. 420, 90 A.2d (1952). While on probation, Swan placed a political sign on the property of another. Others were doing the same and not being punished. He was found guilty of conspiracy to disturb the peace and his probation was revoked.

3. Can you identify the philosophy of the early juvenile court movement?
4. Are you able to describe the contributions of the *Kent* case in 1966?
5. Do you know how to describe the impact of the *Gault* decision?
6. Do you know how to explain how the Miranda Warning applies to juvenile offenders?
7. Are you able to contrast juvenile adjudication safeguards with the procedures used for adult adjudication?
8. Can you define *parens patriae?*

Topics for Discussion

1. Discuss the In re *Winship* decision.
2. Discuss the range of disposition alternatives available to a juvenile court judge.
3. Discuss the procedural safeguards generally followed for juveniles to protect them in the enforcement function of criminal justice.
4. Discuss the *Gault* case.
5. Discuss the concept of *parens patriae.*

ANNOTATED BIBLIOGRAPHY

Emerson, Robert M. *Judging Delinquents*. Chicago, Ill.: Aldine Publishing Co., 1970. Context and process in the juvenile courts is looked at closely and clearly. Its findings are related to the juvenile courts' projected image as well as to the other facets of the juvenile justice system. It is the reform-minded work of a scholar.

Fox, Sanford J. *The Law of Juvenile Courts in a Nutshell*. St. Paul, Minn.: West Publishing Co., 1971. One of the West Publishing Nutshell Series designed especially for law school course review and bar review purposes. A brief but thorough depiction of juvenile courts and the issues and law involved in jurisdiction, role of law enforcement, the judicial process, hearings, disposition, waiver, and appeal.

Hahn, Paul H. *The Juvenile Offender and the Law*. Cincinnati, Ohio: The W. H. Anderson Company, 1971. A fairly thorough treatment of the juvenile offender and the criminal justice system's response from the enforcement perspective. Emphasis is on the legal aspects rather than the behavioral.

Lemert, Edwin M. *Social Action and Legal Change: Revolution Within the Juvenile Court*. Chicago: Aldine Publishing Co., 1970. Based on a detailed analysis of change in the law and the administration of justice affecting juvenile offenders. It describes how a small group of reformers sought to make changes in the law, and their inquiries into the consequences of these changes on the courts and related agencies.

National Council on Crime and Delinquency. *Model Rules for Juvenile Courts*. Council of Judges, National Council on Crime and Delinquency, 1969. A detailed effort by and for juvenile court judges that studies every facet of the juvenile court process and outlines each facet's purpose and function in a model fashion.

Rubin, Ted, and Jack F. Smith. *The Future of the Juvenile Court.* Joint Commission on Correctional Manpower and Training, Washington, D.C., 1968. A consultant paper, commissioned by the Joint Commission, that seeks to provide an understanding of the juvenile court today in terms of both its judicial and correctional functions.

Task Force Report: Juvenile Delinquency and Youth Crime. U. S. Govt. Printing Office, Washington, D.C., 1967. An inquiry into the working of the juvenile justice system and recommendations on improving its effectiveness. Consists of surveys, consultant papers, and special position statements.

The study of this chapter will enable you to:

1. Describe the relationship between principles, assumptions, theories, and the practice of criminal justice administration.
2. Define the term "justice."
3. Contrast justice with the concept of jurisprudence.
4. Define the positive law theory.
5. List four examples of the positive law theory observable today in our criminal justice system.
6. Define the social good theory of justice.
7. List three examples of the social good theory of justice observable today.
8. Define the natural right theory of justice.
9. List five examples of the application of the natural right theory of justice.
10. Contrast the four basic methods of jurisprudence.

14
Justice and Jurisprudence

To the student, the study of theories of justice does not seem important, yet much practical knowledge can be gained from such a study. The student is confronted with a huge body of material that superficially appears to be so conflicting and contradictory that a total understanding seems hopelessly unattainable. This chapter cannot hope to untangle the web of controversy that has evolved over the course of 300 years. Its purpose, therefore, is to present, in a loose framework, the major theoretical underpinnings of our judicial system.[1] To do so requires some generalization, which the student must keep in mind while reading this chapter, which is merely an introduction to juristic theory.[2]

Although the study of theory is not simple, it is essential for any serious student of the administration of justice. The fact that our present legal and justice systems are founded and shaped by theory dictates that those involved must be familiar with these guidelines. The process of transforming theory to reality involves various interpretations and modifications. (See Figure 14-1.) Any attempt to function as a practitioner in criminal justice without knowledge of the antecedents of this reality will be ineffectual.[3]

---

[1] The phrase "judicial system" refers collectively to all courts empowered by federal, state, and local political subdivisions to determine the guilt or innocence of alleged law violators and to sentence according to the law. Generally, each state is considered to have a separate court system, as does the federal government.

[2] Juristic theory, in essence, is jurisprudence—the principles, values, assumptions, and so forth, that constitute the philosophy by which a court or judge applies the law.

[3] An antecedent is a preceding event, condition, or cause to something that follows. It is also the conditional element in a proposition, such as, "if A, then B."

Figure 14-1. The relationship between justice concepts, jurisprudence, law, and a legal decision.

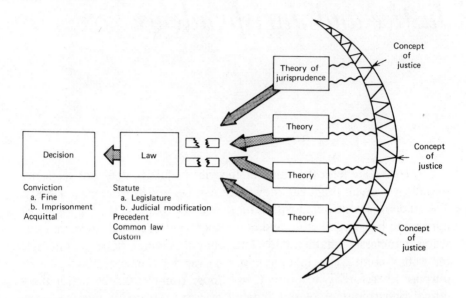

Theory is an often misused term in the administration of justice. Its misuse probably best indicates the split between the behavioral sciences and the practitioner in criminal justice agencies. Theory formulation is a first step to the orderly examination of a problem encountered by a practitioner. The proposal of a theory is simply the offering of an explanation of how or why the problem occurred. The theory is then tested, examined, and otherwise scrutinized to separate fact from fiction, to establish principles, and gradually to validate the theory. In essence, theory is the goal to which one's efforts should be applied. As will be demonstrated, the lack of *one* uniformly accepted theory of justice has continually and historically weakened criminal justice services by fragmenting change-oriented groups toward pursuing different ends. In addition, these separate political and juristic groups have failed to coordinate their efforts with their particular theoretical goals.

Consequently, we must first examine the major theories of justice and pinpoint their essential characteristics. This chapter will attempt to analyze these theories by examining their elementary components. A more intricate study into these areas can thereafter be completed by the student when the need arises. The chapter intends to open up your understanding of justice theory; it should not be considered the final word on the subject.

Major Theories

There are three major theories of justice that warrant examination. They are:
1. The positive law theory.
2. The social good theory.
3. The natural right theory.

The Positive Law Theory

The positive law theory, originally the work of Thomas Hobbes, has several unique positions that separate it from the other two theories.[4] The first major proposition is that justice and injustice are dependent upon positive law. There are two component parts to this premise. First, if there were no law (man's original state in nature), there could be no justice. Man must have an organized framework in which to operate before laws and justice can exist. Hence, justice depends on society, which has the power to enforce whatever its social order deems a basic norm. Thus, justice (and law) can vary from society to society because the agreements governing social principles, goals, and methods of effecting justice can differ. Every society has a concept of justice, but it need not, nor will it universally be the same. A second major principle of this theory is that justice consists of and depends on conformity to the positive law, because law and justice are socially defined and enforced concepts. A "just man" is one who observes the laws of his country. Such an individual has no inherent rights outside those defined by society. Hence, the positive law theory denies the existence of natural rights—those rights enjoyed by man in his original state of nature, most often labeled life, liberty, and the pursuit of happiness.

The theory's third major position is that justice is obligatory and

---

[4] Hobbes (1588–1679) was an English political theorist. His major contribution was his belief that absolutism in government is necessary to prevent the anarchy to which natural human selfishness and desires inevitably lead

must be enforced by legal sanctions. From this, it would appear that justice rests on might. However, justice is formulated by society or some representative of it. Therefore, what every man agrees to cannot, theoretically, be unjust. Although justice does rest on might, this obligation to adhere to rules is warranted because those who live under these rules have granted their approval to be so structured. The final principle of this theory is closely tied to the previous one, and holds that the virtue of justice is identical with obedience. If one thinks of law as a covenant (a solemn pact or agreement) to be maintained by society, this ideal is simpler to grasp. Societal members, upon agreeing to conduct themselves within the boundaries of law, are therefore obligated to do so. To be just, then, is to be obedient to the terms of the covenant.

The Social Good Theory

The social good theory takes issue with the previously described principles by refusing to identify justice with conformity to the positive law. Advocates of the social good theory state that justice is applicable in all areas of life, whereas the law is specifically applied only to certain areas of life. A father may be just or unjust to his children without being inconsistent with the law. Also, because the law does not always realize complete justice, it cannot be considered synonomous with it. Justice as an ideal sets the standard for laws that may or may not be accomplished by the law itself. Another important aspect of the social good theory is that it does not deny the existence of certain "natural rights" that form the concepts of justice. Indeed, the criteria found in "natural" justice are ways of judging the goodness of laws in the social theories. The second major premise of the social good theory is that all questions of justice must ultimately be decided in terms of social utility. This position holds that the ultimate decision as to what is just is determined by whether the application of such principles operates toward the betterment of society. If such a course of action runs counter to this "good," it must be considered unjust. Accordingly, justice makes no sense apart from its contribution to society.

Although not denying natural rights, social theorists claim that their discussion is unnecessary because we do not exist in a natural environment, but rather function in social groupings. The social good theory minimizes individual rights and proposes that rights and duties should function to serve the advancement of society. Thus, all questions of justice must be decided in terms of their ability to further the social good. Man's duty is not to function for his personal betterment, but to further his society—and thereby serve himself.

The Natural Law Theory

The natural law theory of justice is the third and the most complex theory with which we shall deal. Yet it is perhaps the most important set of principles thus far examined, because its principles are essentially the foundation of our system of government. The individual to whom we attribute these principles is John Locke, a seventeenth century political theorist. Locke based his philosophy on the premise that certain rights and privileges of action existed in man's original state of nature. He claimed that these rights are timeless and that they should be afforded to all rational and responsible human beings. Individuals should therefore be allowed the complete freedom to exercise these rights. The fact that man has ordered himself into societies should in no way prohibit his right to freedom. Man's government functions only to enforce these natural rights, labeled by Locke as life, liberty, and property. Because any further governmental action would serve to deprive individuals of their rights, all governments must have limited powers. The rights and freedoms that man has in nature must remain. All men are equal with regard to the law and the end it serves—justice.

Although Locke hinted at a division of governmental powers, it remained for the French nobleman Montesquieu to advocate a concise political system that would accomplish it. He believed that power tended to corrupt those to which it was given and that the safest way to deal with this problem was to check power with power. Toward that end, he proposed that the government be divided into three separate areas—legislative, executive, and judicial. By entrusting this power to three equal and independent groups, Montesquieu believed that undue governmental abuses of power could be avoided by counterbalancing one governmental function with another.

The United States legal system is philosophically based on the combined theories of Locke and Montesquieu. The constitutional division of power and the accompanying system of checks and balances owe its inspiration to Montesquieu. The Lockian theory of natural rights and the primacy of the individual over the state was a position strongly held by the founders of our country. A government that attempted to limit those rights was deemed tyrannical and intolerable, as described in the Declaration of Independence. Furthermore, the extreme care in indicating the right of individuals found in the Constitution and Bill of Rights is also attributable to Locke's precepts.

Analysis of the Theories

The first theory to be studied, the positive law theory, is by far the simplest of the three: It defines justice as conformity to the law. Justice in the objective sense is equal to legality. Thus, this theory demands that society obey the law and justice will be maintained.

The social good theory provides a more analytical vehicle for determining justice. Justice is, according to this concept, doing what is useful for the social good. The key problem that must be resolved with this theory is a determination of which acts provide for the greatest betterment of society.

The natural law theory is the most complex of the three theories. It holds that justice involves rendering to each individual what is his own by right. This right was man's in his natural state and should continue to be his in today's societal setting. This position is disputed by the other two theories. Both the positive law and the social good theories relegate the individual to a secondary position in the attainment of their goals. The natural right theory differs further because it does not equate justice with law. Natural theorists hold that the law may or may not reflect completely the principles of justice. The natural right theory tends to purport that justice is a larger concept than is law.

Attempts to understand the similarities and differences between the three theories are often blurred by the complexity inherent in this type of analysis. The fundamenal controversy between these theories centers around the relationship between justice and society. The natural rights theory advocates that society be broken down to its smallest denominator—individual numbers—and that these numbers be given all the rights due to man as a man. Justice, according to the natural rights theory, is what *man* is, not what society makes it.

The positive law theory and the social good theory dispute this contention. These theories hold that society determines the scope and dimensions of justice. Justice is portrayed as a compromise between what men would like to have and what they actually can obtain through their association with others. The needs and aims of society should be served by justice rather than by individual limits of freedom. The natural right theory holds that there is a universal law (law that should govern all men and should be based on providing man his natural rights); the other two theories state that law is relative to each society.

Although each theory has its unresolved differences with the others, each obliges us to do something that is good and that will benefit mankind. Briefly stated, the basic principles are:

1. Obey the law (held by all three theories).
2. Act toward the promotion of the social good (held by the social good and natural rights theories).
3. Render to each that which belongs to him as a natural right (held only by the natural rights theory).

Jurisprudence

Although it would seem that our three theories of justice could not effectively coexist within our government framework, especially because the foundations of our country seem so deeply rooted in one particular theory, all of these theories are observable in present-day practices in our formal judicial system. In the legal sphere these theories of justice are applied through the procedure known as jurisprudence. Although the concept of jurisprudence will be discussed in detail later, a preliminary definition is warranted. Jurisprudence can be loosely referred to as the process whereby legal jurists, or judges, determine how a point of law will be decided. It is the "science of law" with which those involved in legal questions ascertain the *principles* on which the particular legal rule in question is based. Subsequently, the specific finding should be parallel to the appropriate major principles involved. Jurisprudence flows from the general to the particular, and the particular must reflect and advance the concepts of the general theory.

We have seen that jurisprudence is based on a set of principles; the question now becomes: Where do these principles come from? The answer to this is found in our earlier discussion of the several theories of justice. Elaborated within those theories are the final ends that man and his government should strive to attain. We have also seen that each of these theories has a different goal and conflicting ideas as to what importance should be placed on individual liberty, governmental responsiblity, and other issues. Therefore, the decisions made by various judicial authorities depend upon what theory or combination of theories of justice is used as a foundation in the decision-making process.

Let us examine the types of approach used by legal jurists in the jurisprudence procedure. Although the methods can serve as indicators of the justice theory held by the decision-maker, it is an oversimplification to hold that jurisprudence approaches are strictly equivalent to one particular theory.

The four basic methods of jurisprudence are:
1. Analytical
2. Historical
3. Philosophical
4. Sociological

The Analytical Method

The analytical school of jurisprudence consists of the examination of the structure, subject matter, and principles of the legal system. From this analysis, the principles, theories, and conceptions of the particular legal system can be discerned. The analytical method also presupposes the legitimacy of the government to make authoritarian decisions, and the decisions can vary from nation to nation (no true international law) and still be legitimate. This method is linked to the positive law theory of justice.

The Historical Method

The historical method of jurisprudence centers upon the investigation of the historical origins and subsequent development of the legal system and its institutions. It includes the doctrines and precepts observable within this framework. Observation of the history of law reveals the principles used in the current legal thrust and thereby serves to organize the authoritarian actions of present judicial decisions.[5] Through this method

---

[5] "Authoritarian" is a frequently misused term in criminal justice. One use of the term is to apply it to the blind use of authority without concern to an agreed-upon guideline, such as a set of laws or a constitution. Another use of the term is simply the exercise of authority in a legal, orderly, or agreed fashion. The latter definition is used here.

a continuity of law is established that emphasizes the development of legal precepts from their origin to the present day.

The Philosophical Method

The philosophical approach to jurisprudence stresses the observance of the philosophical bases of present legal institutions and doctrines. It seeks to find the theoretical presuppositions of the legal system, and to thereafter understand and organize present operations towards the achievement of these "ideals." Through this examination of the goals of the law, present-day institutions and doctrines can be compared and criticized as to their contribution to the achievement of the goals contained within the observed philosophy.

The Sociological Method

All three of the previously discussed methods are founded on the notion of natural law (an ideal body of principles toward which the present legal system is working to achieve), or on a reality-based concept of the realization of a consistently observed idea. They strive to determine the origins of our legal structure and to further the advancement of these founding principles. However, the sociological method studies the legal system as a social instrument whose role is to function as a special agent of social control. Although this method studies present legal institutions and doctrines in the context of the social ends to be accomplished, its scope of inquiry is essentially in the present. It seeks to justify legal actions by their effects on current society. Although there is a final goal in mind, sociological jurisprudence is not primarily concerned with serving an abstract ideal. Rather, its aim is to further comparative achievements, with an improved contemporary situation as the desired result. This may seem to be a small distinction, but when it is applied, the sociological approach differs greatly from other methods of jurisprudence.

Applications of the Theories

The theoretical differences that we have discussed are not readily observable in actual legal procedures. Because our legal system is staffed by men and women, and not machines, the clear-cut distinctions of the various theories become blurred. No one individual can adhere to one strict approach, because theoretical definitions have a tendency to stress some phases of legal procedure and overlook or understress others, in attempting to present a complete argument. The individual jurist must interpret and include various ideas from several theories, thereby developing a complete decision-making method.

One must also remember that men cannot be isolated from their inherited instincts, traditional beliefs, and acquired convictions; all of which are dependent on environmental situations and societal positions. Thus, in viewing the actual mechanics of our legal system it must be remembered that the final decisions result from a synthesis of many inputs, both theoretical-and reality-based, and that in the final analysis the amount of justice contained within decisions depends on the individual decision-maker.

Theory versus Practice

Although it is impossible to establish the *one* theory of justice and corresponding method of jurisprudence that rules in our country, it is possible to view the overall legal system and make various comments about its substance. The founding precepts of our nation were derived from the natural law theory of justice—that the preservation and furtherance of an individual's liberties is the primary purpose of government. Contemporary events indicate that this nation has strayed from the main thrust of this principle.

The present form of legal operations seems to lie between this natural law theory and the social good theory. As observed previously, a primary part of the social good theory is rooted in the concept of utility, that decisions should be based on the doing of whatever will attain the greatest good for the largest number of society. Legal questions should be determined by a balancing process, in which the alternative that gives the entire society the most benefit would be selected. A jurist should therefore add up all the pluses (positive societal affects) and minuses (injustices that may result to some). The choice that has the most positive attributes to society should be chosen. Implied in this procedure is the fact that some members of society may, and indeed probably will, suffer inequities. This fact is justified by the benefits to the largest portion of society. Thus, the transaction can be considered an improvement for society as a whole. The utilitarian school advocates that injustice be forced upon a few so that the majority of society will advance. If scrupulously applied, this theory is valid; eventually the injustices to the minority would be systematically reduced. Society would eventually have no "minuses" to consider when weighing alternatives. At such a time, the "perfect" social grouping will at long last have been attained. However, in its present mode of application, this concept does not seem to be working toward its own defined goals.

Current practices seem intent on furthering the liberties of selected members of society to the greatest extent. This parallels a partial adherence to the natural rights theory. But we must remember that the original natural rights concept proposed that these liberties be afforded equally to *all* men, not to just a few. The rationale for this selected freedom of action is based upon the principles of utility and the theory of social good. This theory, suggests, therefore, that certain injustices are necessary for the greater advancement of society as a whole. This might be acceptable if an impartial observer existed who could objectively decide the questions of justice and injustice and the extent to which this imbalance should be carried in furthering the social good. Unfortunately, such a detached decision-maker exists only within the realm of theory. Therein lie the roots of our current problem.

An overview of our contemporary system of law, law enforcement, and corrections shows that most of our efforts in this sphere are concentrated on one particular section of the populace; namely, the poor, members of certain ethnic minorities, and others similarly disadvantaged. This emphasis is rationalized because within these groups lies the bulk of antisocial activities. For the "good of society," these elements must be controlled. Society's present demands for an economical labor pool has dictated that one section of the populace remain without the advantages afforded to the middle and upper classes. The theory of social good has consequently been modified and, in a sense, "frozen," so that this type of "necessary" injustice may be perpetuated. The legal function, most of whose members belong to the privileged classes, has willingly served its own vested interests. This effort has not necessarily been a conscious one, but the results remain the same. Perhaps the most glaring example of this judicial disinterest can be observed in the area of civil rights. The extent of social inequality forced upon black Americans cannot be justified by any of our concepts of justice or jurisprudence. Yet it was economically expedient and, for the most part, socially acceptable to maintain this imbalance. Only recently has headway in this area been made. However, we still believe, as documented by arrest records, that blacks are responsible on a percentage basis for most of the crimes committed in this country.

In the past ten years we have had a rapid rise in our nation's crime rate, and society's concern with the crime problem has accelerated. As a result, the privileged classes (who have the most to lose in a lawless society) have attempted, through the limitation of personal liberties and by increased authoritarian governmental action, to solve the problem. This solution has met with little success. The reasons lie in the following two general areas.

The first is the assumption that the lower classes are responsible for virtually all the crime. Therefore, efforts have intensified to patrol these malcontents more closely, to limit their actions—for the good of society. But crime is not exclusively a lower-class phenomenon, but a problem that can be found in all classes of society. Part of the reason that lower-class crime seems so prevalent is that most of our enforcement efforts are directed toward that group. In-depth studies now being made into the crimes of the middle and upper classes indicate that every class is guilty of widespread criminal activities. Middle-class delinquency, income tax evasion, political bribes, industrial negligence, price gouging, graft, and embezzlement are all manifestations of upper-class crime. Is the manufacturer of a negligently designed or constructed automobile that causes accidents and deaths any less guilty of murder than an individual who strangles his victim? Is not the landlord who owns a tenement building with substandard plumbing, heating, ventilation, and fire escapes just as socially harmful as the person who commits robbery? Our current brand of justice makes this distinction, largely based on an Americanized concept of utility.

The above examples bring us to the crux of the matter. Our current legal framework has allowed certain groups of individuals to gain almost unlimited amounts of liberties. This freedom was given because it was believed that to do so would serve the "public" interest. What has resulted is that the groups given this liberty have used it to command as much power as can be gained within the boundaries of this freedom. Consider the power wielded by such giants as ITT and the major oil companies. The Vietnam War demonstrated the influence held by those industries who had a vested interest in perpetuating the conflict. Most recently, we have witnessed another example of unrestrained freedom as exemplified by government and business in the Watergate affair and "related matters."

When the legal branch granted these liberties, they believed that they were furthering society's interests. What has happened is what the naturalist Montesquieu warned would occur when liberty (which can be transformed into power if manipulated properly, or improperly, depending on what side of the fence one stands) is not counterbalanced by another equal power. Excesses were, and are, the inevitable result.

Our present social utilitarianism must be reassessed. The selective granting of unlimited liberty to some, while hindering the freedom of others, should be reexamined. The realm of the social good theory provides us with a perfect method for basing this reevaluation. It holds that legal actions should be founded upon the principles of societal advancement. Is our present set of circumstances reflective of overall societal improvement? The answer appears to be "no." The excess allowed by the present policy of "selective freedom" have reached the point where society is being seriously hindered. The philosophy that advocates one goal is accomplishing an opposite goal. It must become evident that the liberties given to the "vested interests" are being used to further what is good for their interests and not what is best for society. The decade of the seventies will be the critical period in which this imbalance will be either readjusted or continued and increased to the detriment of this nation.

The Future

What can be done? Our governmental system has gained enormous freedom of action, as have large industrial interests, and neither seems willing to give up the liberties it has attained. Moreover, what plan of action should be instigated to overcome current injustices? Perhaps one answer lies in the concepts of justice proposed by the contemporary theorist John Rawls and his followers. This philosophy urges us to reassess the current structure of liberties and how they are dispersed, and rejects the attainment of the greatest net balance of satisfaction. Instead it seeks to reinject a system of equal liberties. Rawl's theory, referred to as the "justice as fairness" concept, advocates the redistribution of liberties so that each individual in society is given an equal right to the most extensive liberty that can be enjoyed *uniformly* by all members of society.

Conversely, inequalities to some shall be considered totally unjust. A limitation of liberty would be total only if this loss proves to be indispensable for the good of all society. In proposing these principles, Rawls does not wish to tear down our existing system and start afresh. Rather, he proposes guidelines to render our present society more just than it is now. A prerequisite is that societal man accept a larger share of the responsibility in making the new balance of justice and in maintaining it once it is made. Thus, rational thought and involvement are considered essential to the working of this system. Of course, not all men will freely agree to this type of plan. Therein lies the major stumbling block to the adoption of the "justice as fairness" doctrine.

Will it be possible to force some members of society to relinquish some of their freedom so that all others can benefit? Must we wait until we are overwhelmed by the inequities of the situation before we decide to act collectively? When this time comes, will we have sufficient freedom to do anything about it? These are the questions that must be dealt with in confronting the problem. Rawls and his theory present one possible answer. By advocating equal justice for all, utilitarian requirements are removed. Instead, a standard of liberty, a modern set of "natural laws," is substituted. *Total* societal responsibility is implied by this theory. All members of society must realize that an injustice is an injustice and a crime is a crime. The fact that we have ordered our list of criminal acts to place primary emphasis on the trespasses of the poor is a reality. This fact may be seen as an arbitrary manipulation of guilt by those who have the liberty and power to make such an assignment upon those who cannot do anything about it. We must recognize that the government is becoming controlled by those monied interests who wish to perpetuate the present system. These interests have also been seeping into our legal system at an alarming rate and threaten to undermine the relative objectiveness long held by this function. Jurisprudence philosophy may initiate a method of analysis based solely on serving these vested interests. The ITT antitrust case is perhaps a foreshadowing of this subservience. In this incident the government seemingly influenced the Justice Department into dropping the proceedings because they would be injurious to the company concerned. The interests of the majority were opposed by the excesses of a powerful minority and the latter's interests prevailed (at least in the preliminary stages).

Current disclosures of governmental and industrial misdeeds make an ideal situation for an immediate reassessment of our contemporary mode of legal operation. The legal sphere, charged with the question of maintaining the balance of justice, must take the lead in reinstating a more equitable system. We have examined various theories of justice and jurisprudence, any of which could, if faithfully applied, help remedy the present situation. Which theoretical path should be followed is open to question. It is proposed here that the legal function must regard the true pursuit of justice as primary. The particular theory of justice used is not of immediate concern; what is essential is that vigorous efforts be made to incorporate the essence of the chosen theory in contempory decisions. Parallelism between the advocated ends of the particular theory and the thrust of current legal actions is vital to the reinstitution of progressive movement within the law. Without such advancement, the future of our legal system, and of our nation as a whole, is uncertain.

Summary

This chapter has attempted to present the theoretical components used in our legal system. The most abstract of these concepts were the several theories of justice. The positive law theory, the social good theory, and the natural rights theory all reflect different ideas as to what justice should be. Despite their differences, each of these theories attempts to better order our society.

This ordering is, in part, the responsibility of the legal sphere. Its function is to translate the general principles of justice into specific rules of conduct. In so doing, the judiciary utilizes the concepts of jurisprudence, which are theoretical principles that apply specifically to the legal field. The theories of jurisprudence are derived from, and sometimes closely resemble, the particular "fathering" justice theory. Perhaps the best example of this is the relationship between the social good theory of justice and the sociological jurisprudence theory. In most cases, however, the connections between justice theory and jurisprudence principles are not easily distinguished. Moreover, although the concepts of jurisprudence are supposed to supply the basic foundation for legal decisions, we have seen many other factors become entrenched in this decision-making process. These other criteria have served to increase the intangibility of the jurisprudence process itself.

In our present time of crisis we need desperately to reinject the principles of justice and jurisprudence back into our government and legal system. The mechanisms and philosophies exist. What we need most are individuals who will follow the essence of these principles and reinstate them into our society.

Student Checklist

1. Can you describe the relationship between principles, assumptions, theories, and the practice of criminal justice administration?
2. Are you able to define the term "justice"?
3. Are you able to contrast justice with the concept of jurisprudence?
4. Do you know how to define the positive law theory?
5. Can you list four examples of the positive law theory in our criminal justice system today?
6. Do you know how to define the social good theory of justice?
7. Can you list three examples of the social good theory of justice observable today?
8. Do you know how to define the natural right theory of justice?
9. Can you list five examples of the application of the natural right theory of justice?
10. Are you able to contrast the four basic methods of jurisprudence?

Topics for Discussion

1. Discuss the differences between justice and jurisprudence.
2. Discuss the positive law theory of justice.
3. Discuss the social good theory of justice.
4. Discuss the natural right theory of justice.
5. Discuss the application of theories of justice to the American criminal justice and legal system.

ANNOTATED BIBLIOGRAPHY

Bird, Otto. *The Idea of Justice*. New York, N.Y.: Frederick A. Praeger, 1967. Provides a concise description of the theories of justice and the fundamental points of controversy between them.

Bodenheimer, Edgar. *Jurisprudence*. Cambridge, Mass.: Harvard University Press, 1962. Gives an historical development of the theories of jurisprudence and their actual application in today's legal field.

Perelman, Charles. *Justice*. New York, N.Y.: Random House, 1967. Treats the development of the various theories of justice in an easily understood manner.

Pound, Roscoe. *Jurisprudence*. Vol. I. St. Paul, Minn.: West Publishing Co., 1959. Perhaps the best book on jurisprudence available. Delineates the development of the various schools of jurisprudence as well as their current form and usage.

Rawls, John. *A Theory of Justice*. Cambridge, Mass.: The Bellknap Press, 1971. Proposes a modern approach to justice theory. The author suggests the "justice as fairness" philosophy as a viable alternative for current problems.

The study of this chapter will enable you to:

1. Contrast the role of the criminal justice agency administrator with that of the legislator and judge in developing law.

2. Identify the trend towards the courts' increasing adjudication of issues that have been traditionally within the administrators area of responsibility.

3. Define administrative law.

4. Describe the rule-making function that administrators of criminal justice agencies usually perform.

5. Describe how the impact of administrative law on the management of criminal justice agencies has been basically generated from judicial decisions.

6. Identify the manner in which policy formulation as an administrative function guides in the use of discretion in justice administration.

7. Describe how labor–management relations in criminal justice agencies are affected by administrative law.

15

Administrative Law for the Criminal Justice Administrator

Administrative law is not new in the American system of jurisprudence. Its rise as a recognized branch of the law has been due primarily to the increase in the complexity of government and the proliferation of governmental bureaucracies. The myriad of quasi-legal problems flowing from these bureaucratic units of government necessitated the assignment or delegation of quasi-judicial authority to nonjudicial persons, boards, or other bodies to render decisions on matters not entirely within the scope of the courts or not requiring court action. These quasi-legal decisions are subjected to judicial review in the final analysis, however. Although the title of this chapter draws its name from this conceptual practice in bureaucratic agencies, the impact of administrative law on the management of criminal justice agencies, including police, courts, and corrections, has basically generated from judicial decisions,

The 1950s and 1960s witnessed an upsurge of court cases applying both the Fifth and Fourteenth Amendments to the conduct of individuals. Partially as a result of this judicial trend, individuals in society as a whole have become more activistic. Historically, individuals in the criminal justice system have accepted their lot without question in the areas of employer–employee relations and the loss of rights and privileges by convicted offenders. Some, to the contrary, tried to bring about change, but usually found themselves powerless in their struggle "to fight city hall." No help was forthcoming from the courts, who refused to become involved in issues viewed as purely administrative in nature.

The courts have now become involved, and silent acceptance of conditions has been replaced by activism. Police officers have gone to the courts to air their grievances on selection and promotion criteria, employee discipline, and collective bargaining agreements. Inmates in correctional facilities have been seeking judicial interpretation on matters affecting their constitutional rights to due process and equal protection of the law. No longer do the courts accept these matters as being purely administrative.

The long-range impact of court decisions in the area of administration of criminal justice agencies cannot yet be determined. Many feel that we have just seen the beginning. One thing is certain: the effects of this judicial trend have drastically changed the thinking and functioning of criminal justice administrators. The following statement, which appears in a publication dealing with the impact of these judicial decisions on the corrections field, perhaps sums up best the effects on criminal justice:

> *This interest in an individual's basic constitutional rights is by no means unique to the correctional setting. Areas such as welfare, education, selective service, public housing, et cetera, are also being affected by the current trend in the judicial system. Administrators involved in these areas are beginning to realize that they can no longer be arbitrary or capricious with their decisions: the mere fact that an agency has followed a certain practice for many years is no longer a valid excuse for continuing to follow this practice. The burden has shifted from the affected person's having to establish why the practice should not be continued, to the administrator's having to justify why a particular practice should be followed. Because of the trend of recognizing these basic constitutional rights of individuals, the correctional administrator is becoming increasingly frustrated, as are administrators in various other areas such as welfare, education, selective service, public housing, et cetera. He is being told, as are these other administrators, that practices he has followed for years are in violation of the constitutional rights of those confined. The court decisions are being rendered so fast that it is most difficult, if not impossible, to keep abreast of these decisions, let alone understand them and foresee the trend set forth by the decision.*[1]

Rulemaking

The formation of policy and the initiation of procedures, rules, and regulations have long been an integral part of any criminal justice admin-

---

[1] South Carolina Department of Corrections, *The Emerging Rights of the Confined* (Columbia, South Carolina: The Correctional Development Foundation, Inc., 1972), pp. i-ii.

istrator's responsibility, but that responsibility has now become more pronounced. Not only must the administration attempt to conform to the rapid flow of judicial decisions and legislative enactments but he must, of necessity, attempt to second-guess what will become mandatory. Planning, studying, research, and preplanning are now essential.

The emphasis on rulemaking has been a result of judicial decisions, and it has also had an impact on those decisions. The absence of adequate rulemaking by criminal justice administrators has led to the grievances that, in turn, caused the judicial activism that resulted in decisions affecting the scope and necessity of rulemaking. Thus, those who would lay the cause for the development of this area of law solely at the feet of the courts, have not fully analyzed the atmosphere in which these changes have taken and are taking place.

A number of interesting phenomena in law are occurring as a result of these court decisions, not the least of which is that the courts have entered the arena of adjudicating issues that had traditionally been the responsibility of administration. One of the chief criticisms of the courts has been that, by their assumption of authority to declare policy invalid, they are indirectly—and sometimes directly—establishing agency policy. Thus, the courts are becoming the rulemakers! It would seem that the only way to avoid this is for the administrator to become aware of the trends and to establish a meaningful policy-making program in his own agency.

The range of court decisions making themselves felt upon the criminal justice administrator and his prerogative of rulemaking include matters as diverse as hair styles and hair length for police officers, residency requirements as a condition of employment for police, prohibitions on moonlighting, promotion policies, overtime pay for police officers on lunch hour, maternity leave policies, height and weight requirements as a condition of employment, visitation and correspondence privileges of correctional facility inmates, inmate access to news media, and availability of legal materials and assistance to inmates. The decisions have, by no means, been one-sided. The interesting point is that they have reached the courts. An example of judicial intervention in traditionally administrative matters might be useful at this point. In *Allen* v. *City of Mobile,* black police officers filed suit against the city on the basis of two federal civil rights statutes. The suit alleged racial discrimination in the assignment of duties and in the promotional testing procedure for sergeants. Specifically, the plaintiffs contended that (1) black officers were being assigned only to predominantly black areas of the city; (2) black detectives were assigned cases affecting only black citizens; (3) black officers and white officers did not work together as partners either in patrol or detectives; (4) black officers were systematically excluded from performing certain duties that white officers were assigned, such as the traffic court, docket room, and planning and training divisions; (5) promotional examinations were culturally discriminatory against blacks; (6) the seniority point system in the promotional process was discriminatory because past discriminatory hiring practices prevented blacks from accumulating seniority points; and (7) service ratings used in the promotional process were discriminatory because they were not rationally related to job performance and were so subjective as to permit supervisory prejudice to bear on the rating. The findings of the Federal District Court for the Southern District of Alabama supported some of the plaintiff's contentions and rejected others, but in its opinion the court required certain actions by the city of Mobile and particularly the police department, which clearly reflected its intervention in the administrative affairs of the agency. The court required the Mobile Police Department to implement a plan whereby only four black officers would be required to work on black beats at any one time. They also required that the remaining black officers be assigned to white areas and some white officers to predominantly black beats, and that black officers be rotated so that all of them would work in white areas. The court further ordered that in the area of patrol car assignments at least one out of every five white trainees must be assigned to a black officer and that in normal patrol assignments *no* officers of the same race were to be assigned to the same car. In situations where two detectives work together as partners, the court required that one black and one white officer be made partners as the number of available men permitted. With respect to the movement of black officers into divisions other than patrol, the court required the department to report to the court every six months on the progress made in assigning black officers to nonpatrol functions. In the case of those allegations attacking the fairness of the police department's promotional testing program, the court specified, among other things, how and when service ratings would be given officers, what must be contained in the ratings, and the method by which seniority would be be calculated for promotional purposes.[2]

[2] Allen v. City of Mobile, 331 F. Supp. 1134 (1971).

The wisdom or necessity of the federal court's ruling in the Alabama case is not in issue, but the decision clearly reflects judicial intervention in what were once considered purely administrative matters.

Law enforcement agencies are not alone in feeling the pangs of the abrogation of the "hands-off" doctrine by the courts. Administrators in the various subsections of corrections also have cause for concern. At an ever-increasing tempo, the courts have become more sensitive to issues involving the claim of the violations of constitutional rights of correctional inmates. What is permissible institutional discipline seems to be one of the main areas in which there is judicial intervention into administrative rulemaking. Inmates have long had the protection of the Eighth Amendment guarantees against cruel and unusual punishment, to avoid any arbitrary or capricious imposition of punishment by correctional administrators or their subordinates. More recently, courts have begun requiring the application of procedural safeguards before disciplinary measures are taken. Some of the procedures required include: (1) timely written notice of charges; (2) hearing by an impartial disciplinary board at which the inmate is entitled to the assistance of a classification counselor; (3) an opportunity for the inmate to present information and to rebut the charges; (4) a record of the hearing to be given to the inmate; (5) an explanation of the rationale of the decision; (6) the rights of confrontation and cross-examination; and (7) the right to call witnesses on behalf of the inmate.[3]

One of the major obstacles faced by the criminal justice administrator lies in the interpretation of these court decisions. Not all of the decisions handed down are as explicit in their guidelines as was *Allen* v. *City of Mobile*. It is not unusual to find court decisions leaving more questions unanswered than those that are answered in the holding. Consequently, the administrator is often confronted with a rulemaking problem in which the court orders the implementation of a particular procedure without defining how it expects the agency to comply or how far the administrator must go to reach a standard of compliance. To illustrate, refer to some of the procedural safeguards now applicable to inmate disciplinary proceedings. What constitutes an impartial disciplinary board? Must or may it be made up of correctional authorities? If so,

---

[3] South Carolina Department of Corrections, *The Emerging Rights of the Confined* (Columbia, S.C.: The Correctional Development Foundation, Inc., 1972), p. 109.

are they automatically presumed to be partial? If not, are other inmates or "outsiders" supposed to participate? Related questions can be posed *ad infinitum*. Coping with the answers to these questions will require procedural changes in the administration of the agency through the process of policy formulation, rulemaking procedures, or whatever name one wishes to call it. Whether appropriate procedures are established or not, the administrator's decision is again subject to judicial review. If he has properly performed his rulemaking task, he will be much better able to deal with the situation.

Policy-Making and Police Discretion

Law enforcement officers and agencies, particularly on the local level of government, are frequently and critically involved in the recognition, prevention, and resolution of sensitive social problems. The manner in which a situation is handled by the police; the daily decisions made by police officers on matters affecting the lives of citizens with whom they deal; the choices police officers must make in such matters as deciding whether to arrest, whether to intervene in a domestic disturbance, whether to break up a fight, or whether to stop and frisk—all may have dramatic and lasting effects upon the quality of life in his community. Every single police officer is, on numerous occasions, confronted with the necessity of making such important decisions. The wrong decision can be disastrous. Several recent national commission reports cite examples.[4]

Discretion

The police do exercise a great deal of discretion. Recognition of that fact, however, has not always existed. Failure to recognize and to accept

---

[4] President's Commission on Law Enforcement and the Administration of Justice, *The Challenge of Crime in a Free Society* (Washington, D.C.: U.S. Govt. Printing Office, 1967), pp. 104–106; President's Commission on Law Enforcement and the Administration of Justice, *Task Force Report: The Police* (Washington, D.C. U.S. Govt. Printing Office, 1967), pp. 24–25; *Report, National Advisory Commission on Civil Disorders,* Washington, D.C.: U.S. Govt. Printing Office, 1968), pp. 164–165.

the amount of police discretion that does exist has caused many of the shortcomings in the criminal justice system. The persistent misbelief that the duties of police officers are mechanical and always prescribed by law, and that *all* laws are enforced fully and impartially, deceives and misleads those within the criminal justice system as well as the general public. If there is any truth in the statement that a police officer in an average size city has the responsibility for the enforcement of 30,000 federal, state, and local laws, the belief that enforcement is full, with no opportunity for choice, becomes absurd.

Also contributing to the inability to enforce "all laws, all the time, against all the people" are the realistic factors of limited resources, ambiguous laws, obsolete laws, and unenforceable laws. But even these factors do not convince some of the diehards who firmly hold that controls over police actions are unnecessary and unwarranted. They maintain that the exercise of common sense by the officer on the street suffices to dispose of all situations successfully; and that the impositions of laws and policies controlling the discretion of police officers would create a lack of trust in law enforcement agencies by citizens of the community and bring embarrassment to the department. They further assume, in their arguments against the establishment of enforcement discretion guidelines, that even if a police officer does act improperly sufficient controls already exist through legislative enactments, the powers of prosecuting attorneys to override police actions, and the review power of the courts who may, and often do, sanction police behavior.

These contentions are misleading in two respects. First, they assume that a degree of control exists over matters falling within the criminal justice process when, in fact, the actual amount of control is less than adequate to guide a police officer in the performance of his duties. Second, much of what a police officer does falls outside the scope and control of others within the criminal justice system and therefore lacks the element of accountability. Eighty to ninety percent of an officer's time is spent in performing service to his community. Many of these problems are of such a nature that the police officer cannot cope with them on his own. He must be able to call on other community resources to help. Obviously, systematic planning and coordination are necessary on a community-wide basis and must be initiated on a department level.

The need for enforcement discretion policy and guidelines is becoming more apparent each day. In its 1967 report, the President's Commission on Law Enforcement and the Administration of Justice noted:

> In view of the importance, complexity, and delicacy of police work, it is curious that police administrators have seldom attempted to develop and articulate clear policies aimed at guiding or governing the way policemen exercise their discretion on the street. Many police departments have published "general order" or "duty" or "rules, regulations, and procedures" manuals running to several hundred pages. They deal extensively, and quite properly, with the personal conduct of officers on and off duty, with uniform and firearms regulations, with the use of departmental property, with court apearances by officers, with the correct techniques of approaching a building in which a burglary may be in progress. . . . What such manuals almost never discuss are the hard choices policeman must make every day: Whether or not to break up a sidewalk gathering, whether or not to intervene in a domestic dispute, whether or not to silence a streetcorner speaker, whether or not to stop and frisk, whether or not to arrest. . . .[5]

The absence of policy in this area places the lowest ranking officer in the agency—the patrolman—in a position of often having to make some of the most difficult and complex decisions. This situation is unique in government service, but it is not unavoidable.

The ramifications of all this are that the individual officer acts (1) without situational supervision and direction from his superiors; (2) by improvisation of solutions that may be influenced by his personal imagination, resourcefulness, or biases; and (3) with the development of informal and self-developed criteria that serve as the basis for the manner in which *he* perceives his duty and its performance. In many circumstances the results do little to improve the attitude of the citizenry toward the police and local government as a whole.

The need for control and direction of police discretion can best be summed up as follows:

> If the exercise of governmental authority is to be subjected to appropriate controls and if the citizenry, local governments, and even police administrators are to have an opportunity to influence police practices, it is clear that a much greater degree of structure and control must be

[5] President's Commission on Law Enforcement and the Administration of Justice, *The Challenge of Crime in a Free Society*, p. 103.

introduced into the whole area of discretionary decision-making on the part of police personnel.[6]

Police discretion is here to stay. It will not and should not become obsolete, but it does need guidance. Police administrators need to make policy that will assist the man on the street to perform his responsibilities more effectively and efficiently.

It has long been accepted by law enforcement that the quality of law enforcement in a community is directly proportionate to the quality of law enforcement desired by the citizens of that community. What has been neglected is that the citizenry generally has little or no say as to how their police departments should operate. We often admit that law enforcement and government as a whole are ultimately responsible and answerable to the public, but how often does the public have the opportunity to make input in the operations of its police agencies? Historically, the police have viewed their method of operation as being "top secret"— beyond the control or even the comprehension of the layman. The American Bar Association's Standards for Criminal Justice seem to reflect that it is now time to rethink and reevaluate citizen participation in the formation of police policy.[7]

The formation of enforcement discretion policy has many other advantages besides that of involvement of citizens. It can inform the public that the police are an administrative agency; it can help to convince legislatures to redefine crimes with consideration to the realities of practical enforcement; it can help to define and to control police powers; it can place the policy-making responsibility at the top echelon of the agency where it belongs, rather than by default with the policeman on the street; and it can take much of the guesswork and improvisation out of police work.[8]

---

[6] American Bar Association Project on Standards for Criminal Justice, *The Urban Police Function*, tentative draft (Washington, D.C.: American Bar Association, 1971), p,. 125. See also: Kenneth Culp Davis, *Discretionary Justice:A Preliminary Inquiry* (Baton Rouge: Louisiana State University Press, 1969); and Herbert Packer, *The Limits of The Criminal Sanction* (Stanford, Calif.: Stanford University Press, 1968).

[7] American Bar Association Project on Standards for Criminal Justice, *The Urban Police Function*, pp. 116–144.

[8] Ibid., pp. 127–128.

In those instances where the exercise of discretion by police involves matters within the responsibility of the criminal justice system, such as the protection of individuals' rights and the enforcement of criminal statutes, the actions of police are always subject to judicial review. If police administrators continue to take a "do-nothing" attitude concerning formulating administrative policies in these sensitive areas, the courts undoubtedly will continue to intervene.

> *By constantly awaiting court determination of policy issues (which typically flow from cases involving clearly improper police practices), the police take themselves out of constructive involvement in policy-making.*[9]

One need only read some landmark Supreme Court decisions affecting police procedures to see that the Court has long been involved in the establishment of police policy. The Supreme Court is not alone; many other courts are also involved in rendering decisions that make policy for the police. However, the decisions handed down by the Supreme Court provide only for the minimum protections that the states and federal governments must afford their citizens. Beyond this, courts and legislatures are free to impose even more restrictive standards. Many such harsher criteria have been imposed on the police generally by lower court interpretation of high court decisions. The many and varied interpretations have led to much confusion. Standards differ from jurisdiction to jurisdiction, and yet the police officer, without guidance from administrative policy, is always expected to make the right decisions. These complexities lead to an absence of consistency in enforcement, which is one of the prime purposes of policy. Administrative policy can bring about a greater degree of consistency, which, in turn, leads to equal justice and an impartial enforcement of laws.

At present, courts generally review only the propriety of the individual officer's conduct without examining his departmental policies. This limitation is due, in large measure, to the absence of any precedent in the courts, that is, policy to review. The formulation of policy on matters within the realm of the criminal justice process can relieve the officer of much responsibility, ease his decision-making burden, cause better cases to be made, and generally create a more favorable record in the judicial review of cases handled by the department.

[9] Ibid., p. 129.

Numerous judicial opinions in recent years have encouraged departments to create policies affecting the criminal process. This might have the effect of a judiciary influenced by police policy rather than the converse situation, which has been the only course open throughout the evolution of our criminal justice system. As an example, when the United States Court of Appeals for the District of Columbia had occasion to review a policy of the Washington Metropolitan Police Department pertaining to near-the-scene identification of a suspect, the Court said:

> We also note that, after this case arose, the Metropolitan Police Department put into operation a regulation restricting on- and near-the-scene identification confrontations to suspects arrested within 60 minutes after the alleged offense and in close proximity to the scene. We see in this regulation a careful and commendable administrative effort to balance the freshness of such a confrontation against its inherent suggestiveness, and to balance both factors against the need to pick up the trail while fresh if the suspect is not the offender. We see no need for interposing at this time any more rigid time standard by judicial declaration.[10]

Collective Bargaining

The labor movement is not new to law enforcement, but its role and impact have grown to tremendous proportions over the past decade and a half. During the late nineteenth and early twentieth centuries several police strikes occurred in the United States, which marked the beginnings of the organized labor movement in law enforcement. These strikes began as early as 1889 in Ithaca, New York, followed in 1918 by a strike in Cincinnati, Ohio, and culminating with the now infamous Boston police strike of 1919. The Boston police strike has been cited because of its negative effects on the labor movement.

More than 1000 striking police officers lost their jobs permanently. And the American Federation of Labor, which had sought to organize police departments during that period, was so severely criticized that its influence in the public sector lessened dramatically. The police strike

---

[10] United States v. Perry, 449 F. 2d 1026, 1037 (D.C. Cr. 1971).

also gave police administrators throughout the country a basis for opposing employee organizations to represent police officers in matters pertaining to working conditions, grievances, and other employee relations. Yet many of the factors precipitating the Boston police strike were partially resolved as a result of the strike, thus indicating that some benefit to the employees did accrue from the strike.

The police labor movement became dormant, and it was replaced by the formation of social organizations. Not until the 1940s did the American Federation of Labor begin again to concentrate its efforts on organizing law enforcement agencies. During that decade a number of police employee organizations did become affiliated with the American Federation of Labor. But it was not until the late 1950s that the attitudes of police officers and other criminal justice employees changed from passive to activistic or militant. This transition was triggered by the inadequacy of law enforcement officers' wages. No longer was law enforcement viewed as a desirable job because of its long-term security. Blue-collar workers were earning more money, had better working conditions, and had much better incidental job benefits. In addition, the long period of passive acceptance of working conditions created an absence of outlets for law enforcement officers to express grievances with their working conditions. A widespread frustration grew.

Perhaps the most significant contribution to the transition in attitudes began in 1959, when legislatures began enacting collective bargaining laws permitting public employees to negotiate formal written contracts on wages, hours, and terms and conditions of employment. Prior to 1959, court rulings had prohibited public employees from collectively bargaining with employers in the absence of legislative authority.[11] Today, more than 30 states have enacted collective bargaining legislation for public employees. Approximately one-half of these laws specifically provide for collective bargaining for police.[12] Although none of these laws permit public employees, including police officers, to strike because of their sensitive and crucial role in maintaining the welfare of society, the col-

[11] For example, see Weakley County Electric System v. Vick, 309 S.W. 2d 792 (1958).
[12] By 1972, those states having collective bargaining laws that included the right of police to bargain collectively were: California, Delaware, Hawaii, Kansas, Massachusetts, Michigan, Minnesota, Nebraska, New Jersey, New York, Oklahoma, Pennsylvania, Rhode Island, and South Dakota.

lective bargaining laws do require the employer to negotiate in good faith with the employee organizations. This good faith requirement should, in most instances, alleviate the necessity for concern about strikes. Because organized labor (with which many police employee organizations are affiliated) advocates the right to strike, police administrators have been reluctant to accept employee organizations. This contention is no longer valid. By judicial decree, public employees have the right to join any labor organization, even if it is an affiliate of organized labor.[13]

Local law and departmental policy are two means of prohibiting strikes by public employees. If these laws or policies conflict with the goals of the labor organizations, the employee must decide where his loyalties reside. Should he support the union in violation of policy and law, his employer has alternative means of handling the situation. If good faith is being exercised by both the employer and the employee organization, the issue may or must be submitted to arbitration for resolution, because, under many of the collective bargaining laws, arbitration is compulsory. Should arbitration fail, the injunctive powers of the courts may be called upon to prevent a strike. Rarely is this required.

The specific wording of local regulations prohibiting strikes is extremely important. If after-action disciplinary procedures or injunctive action are to be taken against employees, a broadly worded regulation that covers all types of work stoppages, such as strikes, slow-downs, "blue flu," or mass resignations, is more effective. John Burpo suggests the following as an illustration:

> No member of the department shall engage in the following activities: the concerted failure to report for duty, the willful absence from one's position, unauthorized holidays, sickness unsubstantiated by a physician's statement, the stoppage of work, or the absence in whole or in part from the purpose of inducing, influencing, or coercing a change in the conditions, compensations, rights, privileges, or obligations of employment.[14]

Arbitration is a procedure in which issues that are not resolved or resolvable by communications between employee organization and em-

---

[13] For example, see Atkins v. City of Charlotte, 296 F. Supp. 1068 (1969).

[14] John H. Burpo, "The Legal and Management Aspects of Police Strikes," *Public Safety Labor Report,* Gaithersburg, Md.: International Association of Chiefs of Police, November 1972, 1–169.

ployer are submitted to a third party or panel for decision. If an individual is to act as the arbitrator, he must be independent of any relationship to either the employees or the employer. An arbitration panel will often be composed of one representative from each side and an independent third party, chosen by mutual agreement. Which system is used will depend upon the terms of the collective bargaining contract. The contract will also specify whether arbitration is compulsory if an impasse is reached in communications, or if it is only an alternative solution. In addition, if arbitration is provided for in the agreement, the contract will specify whether the decisions of the arbitrator are final and binding or advisory only. If advisory only, either party may ignore a decision they deem unsatisfactory. However, compromise is usually the end result. Final and binding arbitration is generally complied with, but it is subject to judicial review, except in a few jurisdictions where the state public employee collective bargaining law contains a prohibition of appeal to any court from an arbitration board decision.

An injunction is a court order that either prohibits the employees from striking or orders them to go back to work if they have already struck. Going into court to obtain an injunction is, for the most part, an act of last resort, implying that the negotiations have failed. Once the injunction has been issued, the burden is on the court to enforce it, backed by the court's contempt powers. Usually, the injunction is a successful tactic, for, in the majority of cases, employees have no desire to go to jail.

With one or two exceptions, collective bargaining is a relatively new phenomenon in the field of correctional administration, dating back only to the mid 1960s. Individuals working for correctional agencies, be they institutions or community programs, adult or juvenile programs, also fall within the coverage of legislation regulating the rights of public employees to collectively bargain.

A survey was conducted in August 1972, in which 126 questionnaires were sent to state agencies throughout the country responsible for the administration of state level correctional programs in adult institutional care, probation and/or parole agencies, and juvenile correctional agencies. Of the 61 percent response, 18 agencies indicated that they had or were in the process of negotiating formal or informal agreements with employee unions or associations in the area of collective bargaining. At least one agency in each state responded.[15]

Strikes and work stoppages are infrequent in the correctional setting, although several significant incidents have occurred. Brushy Mountain State Prison in Tennessee was forced to close when 150 of the 170-man guard force refused to return to work after two guards were dismissed by the warden for disciplinary reasons.[16] The guards were members of the American Federation of State, County, and Municipal Employees Union (AFSCME). However, the state had no collective bargaining statute and the union was not recognized by states officials.

Following a riot in a Maryland correctional institution, guards staged a brief work stoppage to protest a promise made by the governor that there would be no reprisals against the rioting inmates who "ran the institution," according to the guards. The guards indicated that their protest was because of a concern for their own safety.[17]

In general, there appears to be a trend toward an increase in collective bargaining in corrections as there is in law enforcement, and it is anticipated that this activity will continue. What it will lead to or where it will end cannot be determined, but criminal justice administrators need to prepare themselves for dealing with this rapidly developing management responsibility. Administrators must become involved, not as a matter of choice, but out of necessity. The well-prepared administrator can do much to enhance the positive aspects of employer–employee relations. The ill-prepared manager can do much harm to himself, his agency, and his community.

Objective analysis of labor–management relations indicates a number of positive results that can be achieved from formalizing labor relations, including: the fostering of better communications within the organizational structure; more concern for improving employee working conditions; and the improved morale, discipline, and esprit de corps that

[15] The survey was conducted by Joann Morton, Director, Southeastern Correctional Management Training Council. Detailed analysis of the survey is soon to be published in a monograph entitled *Readings in Public/Management for Correctional Administrators,* on behalf of the Southeastern Correctional Management Training Council, by the Corrections Division, Institute of Government, The University of Georgia. The information used herein is with permission of the author.

[16] "Prison Fines 150 Striking Guards," *Atlanta Constitution,* July 22, 1972, page 18A; "Ray Moved in Dispute," *Atlanta Constitution,* July 23, 1972, page 2A.

[17] "Inmates End Rebellion, Guards Stage Protest," *Atlanta Constitution,* July 18, 1972, page 1A.

leads to increased effectiveness and efficiency in job performance. However, the success of the relationship rests, to a great extent, upon the shoulders of the criminal justice administrator.

Student Checklist

1. Can you contrast the role of the criminal justice agency administrator with that of the legislator and judge in developing law?
2. Are you able to identify the trend toward the courts' increasing adjudication of issues that have been traditionally within the administrators' area of responsibility?
3. Are you able to define administrative law?
4. Can you describe the rule-making function that administrators of criminal justice agencies usually perform?
5. Can you describe how the impact of administrative law on the management of criminal justice agencies has been basically generated from judicial decisions?
6. Do you know how to identify the manner in which policy formulation as an administrative function guides in the use of discretion in justice administration?
7. Are you able to describe how labor–management relations in criminal justice agencies are affected by administrative law?

Topics for Discussion

1. Discuss the use of administrative rules and guidelines to provide consistency in the use of discretionary authority in the administration of justice.
2. Discuss how administrative law complements statutory and case decision law.
3. Discuss the trend toward more involvement of the courts in administrative rulemaking.
4. Discuss the impact of administrative law on labor–management relations in criminal justice agencies.

5. Discuss the potential impact on correctional institutions of increased judicial review of administrative actions.

ANNOTATED BIBLIOGRAPHY

Public Safety Labor Relations Center of the Research Division, International Association of Chiefs of Police, *Public Safety Labor Reporter,* Gaithersburg, Md.: International Association of Chiefs of Police, 1971, 1972, 1973. This looseleaf service, which began publication in 1971, is the most up-to-date, authoritative source of information on labor management relations in law enforcement and the public safety area. It is supplemented monthly and covers materials in legislation, court decisions, collective bargaining agreements, arbitration awards, administrative law decisions, departmental rule and procedures, personnel forms, comparative labor data, negotiations and contracts, dispute settlements, discipline, and employment practices.

Southeastern Correctional Management Training Council, *Readings in Public/Management for Correctional Administrators,* Athens, Ga.: Corrections Division, Institute of Government, The University of Georgia. Publication pending. Publication is pending of this monograph, which will contain a number of readings on labor/management relations in the corrections area, including specific readings on the development of collective bargaining and its impact on correctional administrators.

South Carolina Department of Corrections. *The Emerging Rights of the Confined.* Columbia, S.C.: Distributed by the Correctional Development Foundation, Inc., 1972. This 223-page document is perhaps the most comprehensive study of the impact of judicial decisions on the rights of the confined written and researched to date. Text and case citations are excellent and are not confined to South Carolina. This is a truly national-scope project.

The study of this chapter will enable you to:

1. Define the concept of discretion in justice administration.
2. List the four stages in the exercise of discretion relating to an incident involving a violation of the criminal law.
3. Explain the phrase "Where law ends, tyranny begins."
4. Describe what is meant by the "ministerial" philosophy of law enforcement.
5. Contrast the statutory authority of police personnel, prosecutors, and judges in their use of discretion.
6. Illustrate four examples of how discretion is used by a police officer, a prosecutor, and a judge.
7. Describe how nonenforcement of the criminal law can be discretion.
8. Explain why Davis stresses "openness" as a key to the successful use of discretion by any governmental agency.
9. List the ten major objectives of a good rule-making procedure as a base for exercising discretion.
10. Write an essay on the compatibility of law and the exercise of discretion in the administration of justice.

16
Discretion and the Law

Discretion—its use and abuse—is one of the major contemporary topics of criminal justice administration, as evidenced by its prominence in the American Bar Association's Standards for Criminal Justice project report titled, "Standards Relating to the Urban Police Function," and the several reports of the National Advisory Commission on Criminal Justice Standards and Goals. The high priority being placed on discretion is not unexpected; the President's Commission on Law Enforcement and the Administration of Justice, as early as 1967, identified the use of discretion and its abuses as a major problem facing the administration of justice.[1] During the half decade that followed, the national spotlight began to focus on discretion as a cause of many of the problems of criminal justice and its three subsystems of enforcement, adjudication, and rehabilitation (corrections). This chapter attempts to identify and to define the role of discretion in the criminal justice system and to specifically examine the legal base for the use of discretion.

Discretion Defined

Discretion in criminal justice administration is present whenever a public official or representative of a criminal justice agency has the flexibility

[1] President's Commission on Law Enforcement and the Administration of Justice, *The Challenge of Crime in a Free Society* (Washington, D.C.: U.S. Govt. Printing Office, 1967), pp. 104–106. The report cited as particularly troublesome areas those involving the exercise of police discretion in resolving minor disputes, in protecting the right of free speech and assembly, and in dealing with street gatherings.

to make a choice among several possible courses of action or inaction. Discretion is also defined as the act or the liberty of deciding according to the principles of justice and one's ideas of what is right and proper under the circumstances, without willfulness or favor. Inaction, or a decision not to act, is considered one of the alternatives available to the criminal justice representative and should not be overlooked. Discretion, as discussed in this chapter, will be limited to its exercise by public officials, representatives, or employees of the criminal justice system or some segment of it; be they police officers, prosecutors, public defenders, judges,[2] probation officers, parole officers, juvenile officers, correctional guards, or treatment officers in a correctional setting. Regardless of their title, if they have the power to select a decision from among several possible decisions or indecisions, they have the power, whether lawful or not, to exercise discretion in the administration of justice.

Normally, we find persons exercising discretion doing so in a four-step process: (1) to determine or ascertain the facts; (2) to determine which laws are applicable; (3) to decide how the law is to be applied; and (4) to decide what course of action or inaction is appropriate based upon the facts in the law. Usually, the fourth step is of most popular concern because it focuses on the agent of the criminal justice system who actually makes a decision. Any of the preceding three steps, although subject to variations depending upon the individual's background, prejudices, biases, and training, may have a major effect upon the ultimate outcome.

Discretion may also be observed in (1) the finding of relevant facts, (2) the determination of the applicable law, and (3) the application or interpretation of the law. In summary, discretion is the power or right to decide or to act according to one's own judgment, or the freedom of judgment or choice.

[2] Judicial discretion is frequently viewed as a "special" level of discretion calling for a clear and trained mind of reason, courage, impartiality, and conscience to accomplish in a calm spirit a result in conformity to law and just and equitable to all parties. In short, it is deemed a high order of discretion that is consistently and uniformly applied.

Law, Tyranny, and Discretion

Exemplifying our concern with discretion and the law are the words etched in stone at the front entrance to the Department of Justice in Washington, D.C. Those words are, "Where law ends, tyranny begins." These brief words of William Pitt clearly depict an assumption of our legal system that has caused many problems within the administration of criminal justice. In contrast to Pitt's words, a basic foundation or assumption of this chapter is that, "Where law ends, tyranny does *not* need to begin." A society's concern for justice can begin to be measured when its justice beyond "where the law ends" is examined. Law, which is simply a standard, cannot be blindly administered, as is sometimes suggested by the blindfold on the figure of justice. Instead, discretion that is structured and based upon soundly developed policy can be used to balance the inequities inherent in any ministerial or blind enforcement of a law that cannot, in itself, consider all the conditions and circumstances that accompany a law violation and the subsequent enforcement of that law.

All agencies of criminal justice have historically exercised the use of discretion. During the past few decades, prosecution and judicial personnel have formally and openly recognized their authority and responsibility to exercise discretion, whereas personnel of the enforcement and rehabilitation subsystems of criminal justice have consistently maintained that they do not have the authority to exercise discretion and do not, therefore, exercise discretion. Law enforcement agencies are usually a major source of problems for their own communities by denying the use of discretion. The American Bar Association's report titled "The Urban Police Function" clearly recognizes, in Standard 4.1, the use of discretion by stating,

> The nature of the responsibilities currently placed upon the police, requires that the police exercise a great deal of discretion—a situation that has long existed, but is not always recognized.

Police personnel have been trained and conditioned to subscribe to the belief that they are merely ministerial officers, obligated to enforce the law without fear or favor, mechanically, as prescribed by the criminal law statutes. The criminal law statutes of most states support this latter belief: they leave no ambiguity whatsoever on the question of enforcement. They uniformly hold that a police officer has no alternative but to initiate a criminal prosecution once he has ascertained the facts and obtained adequate evidence of a criminal offense.

One such jurisdiction, the District of Columbia, makes it a specific criminal offense for a police officer to fail to make an arrest once he has determined that the facts justify an arrest.

> *If any member of the police force shall neglect making any arrest for an offense against the laws of the United States committed in his presence, he shall be deemed guilty of a misdemeanor and shall be punishable by imprisonment in the district jail or penitentiary not exceeding two years, or by fine not exceeding $500. . . .*[3]

Such statutes are not unusual. Some states do not have a specific statute, but those states generally provide for malfeasance, misfeasance, and non-feasance of office, which may be used to criminally charge police personnel not enforcing a law. In this section, we have attempted to define discretion followed by the recognition that it *does* exist in the criminal justice system.

It is essential to focus again on the components of the exercise of discretion. What makes a representative of a criminal justice system decide as he does? The elements that most readily have an impact on the decision-maker in each of the stages are his values, his perception of the facts of the situation, and the various environmental and social influences upon him. Therefore, a broad liberal arts and behavioral education is essential for the criminal justice practitioner. The complexity of the exercise of discretion requires that the system be staffed by personnel who have a capacity to recognize, to comprehend, and to tolerate the widely varying value structures among the clientele of the criminal justice system and who can assess and compensate for the various influences acting upon himself and his copractitioners.

The Need for Discretion

Of all the incidents that are socially harmful to someone, whether it be to oneself or some other person, a relatively small percentage are not covered by criminal law, and they are therefore excluded from being subject

---

[3] D.C. Code Ann. §4–143 (Supp. III, 1970). See also: Wisconsin Statutes §946.12(1) (1969); and, State v. Lombardi, 8 Wis. 2d 421, 99 N.W. 2d 829 (1959) where a sheriff was convicted as a public officer who "intentionally fails or refuses to perform a known mandatory, nondiscretionary, ministerial duty of his office."

to prosecution. Generally, these socially harmful incidences are covered under civil law providing for some redress of damages to the person wronged.

Figure 16-1 shows the relative number of incidents that are covered by the criminal law and the number of incidents that are brought to the attention of law enforcement personnel or agencies. The relative allocation of incidents are approximations: studies have shown that criminal offenses are commonly under-reported at rates of 3 to 10 times those that are actually reported. For those crimes actually brought to the attention of the law enforcement agencies, line D in Figure 16-1 shows the relative allocation between prosecution and nonprosecution enforcement actions. The nonprosecution enforcement area provides for a wide range of enforcement and nonenforcement activities that encompass a lengthy spectrum of discretion alternatives. "No action" is not included in the range as it is depicted by the difference between bar C and bar D. The enforcement action includes such alternatives as warnings, both verbal and written; informal juvenile probation; voluntary restitution or repayment of damages; station house adjustments; and other extralegal remedies. The relatively high percentage of these nonprosecution enforcement actions make it essential that we recognize in law the use of discretion and grant authority to use it in accordance with approved policies and guidelines. Obviously, these actions assume personnel educated and trained in the use of discretion.

The prosecutor usually has statutory authority to determine whether a complaint should be accepted and a warrant issued, but he also has latitude in determining whether a crime has been committed, whether adequate evidence is available, and whether extenuating circumstances exist to negate the state's interest in prosecuting. Just as law enforcement agencies tend to act as a sieve in retaining only those cases that they feel should go on to prosecution and court action, so does the prosecution, via plea-bargaining and other screening devices, in an attempt to reduce the number of cases going on into the courts. Court diversion programs are also being used by the prosecution and the courts to reduce the number of cases. This screening causes the criminal justice system to be like a funnel: the police agencies are at the top of the funnel, the widest part of which depicts the largest number of cases; and the funnel narrows down to the bottom, or the end of the criminal justice system. Those persons reaching the convicted stage in the criminal justice system are few in comparison to the number of incidents entering the

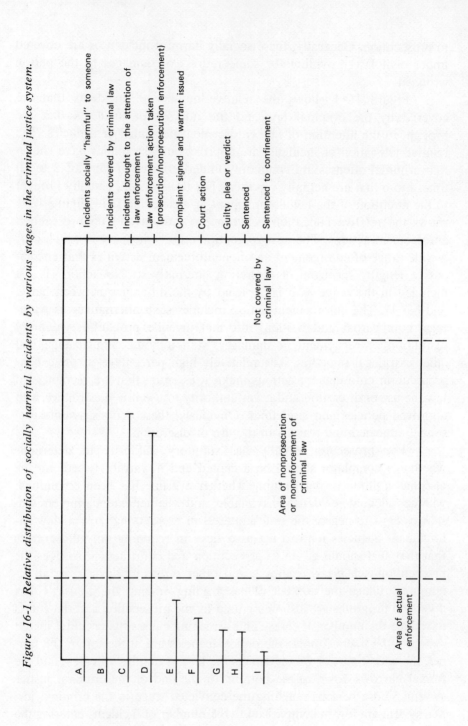

Figure 16-1. Relative distribution of socially harmful incidents by various stages in the criminal justice system.

A — Incidents socially "harmful" to someone
B — Incidents covered by criminal law
C — Incidents brought to the attention of law enforcement
D — Law enforcement action taken (prosecution/nonprosecution enforcement)
E — Complaint signed and warrant issued
F — Court action
G — Guilty plea or verdict
H — Sentenced
I — Sentenced to confinement

Not covered by criminal law

Area of nonprosecution or nonenforcement of criminal law

Area of actual enforcement

system at the law enforcement stage. The discretion exercised by each one of the major components of the criminal justice system should be obvious.

Subsequent to the sentencing stage of the criminal justice system, corrections introduces other examples of discretion in the daily operation of community-based treatment programs, institutional care in the form of county jails, city jails, work houses, prison farms, and state and federal prisons. A high proportion of the tasks performed by correctional personnel in each one of these facilities or on probation or parole requires a great deal of discretion. Correctional law is becoming increasingly complex in terms of the rights of people in confinement or on probation and parole. (See Chapter 12 for a fuller discussion.)

Discretion in Law Enforcement

The American Bar Association has favored open public recognition of the exercise of discretion by police. The ABA's major standard in the area of discretion centers around the need for structured control of the exercise of discretion. Their recommendation, Standard 4.2, is:

> Since individual police officers may make important decisions affecting police operations without direction, with limited accountability, and without any uniformity within a department, police discretion should be structured and controlled.

This standard recognizes that line personnel are relatively unsupervised and have only limited accountability for their enforcement decisions made on the street. Normally, the only material available to guide the police officer in his exercise of discretion are found in manuals covering general orders, rules, regulations, and procedures dealing with uniforms, firearms, use of police department property, court appearances, and other similar regulatory detail. The decision-making manuals seldom deal with the difficult choices that policemen must make every day as a part of their daily tour of duty; for example, deciding whether to and how to break up a sidewalk gathering, whether to conduct a stop-and-frisk, whether an arrest is justified, or whether to act in a family quarrel.

The American Bar Association Standard 4.2, recommends that officers be given some guidelines by which they can better make their routine decisions. Individual police officers, when left to make their own decisions, tend to develop their own criteria for disposing of incidents on their tour of duty. These influences may be appropriate, or they may be highly inappropriate or even contrary to the law. In effect, police officers are allowed to muddle their way through hundreds of types of incidents with little standardization of response from the criminal justice system. As described earlier, the majority of incidents brought to the attention of the criminal justice system are handled without going to the courts, therefore leaving the resolution to the police officer to be, in effect, a trier of facts, an advisor on law, a counselor, and a social worker.

The complexity of factors involved in most incidents requiring police attention or decisions involving criminal law suggests that comprehensive strategies must be developed to provide for a wide range of alternatives for remedying the encountered situations. Many criminal law violations involve problems with schools, hospitals, social service agencies, drug treatment programs, detoxification centers, and a wide range of other community institutions. As a result, the police should work with these other community agencies in developing guidelines for line personnel encountering the criminal law violations on the street. To encourage the various social institutions to cope with potential or real criminal law violators, obviously police must exercise more discretion in disposing of these incidents, which should be provided for by city councils, legislatures, and the courts.

Standard 4.3 of the ABA report, dealing with administrative rule-making, reads as follows:

Police discretion can best be structured and controlled through the process of administrative rule-making by police agencies. Police administrators should, therefore, give the highest priority to the formulation of administrative rules governing the exercise of discretion, particularly in the areas of selective enforcement, investigative techniques, and enforcement methods.

Supporting the above standard, Davis poses the question, "In our entire legal and governmental system, how can we improve the quality of justice for individual parties; how can we reduce injustice?" Professor Davis's response to the question is that, over the centuries, the main answer has been to build a system of rules and principles to guide decisions in individual cases. He contends that this answer is as good today as it has been through the centuries. Davis urges the police to use procedures that parallel the rule-making procedures of federal and state administrative agencies. The American Bar Association report paraphrases the objectives of a good rule-making procedure as described in length by Davis.[4]

The ten objectives of a good rule-making procedure to introduce reform into police practices should be:

1. To educate the public in the reality that the police make vital policy.
2. To induce legislative bodies to redefine crimes so that the statutory law will be practically enforceable.
3. To rewrite statutes to make clear what powers are granted to the police and what powers are withheld, and then to keep the police within the granted powers.
4. To close the gap between the pretenses of the police manuals and the actualities of police behavior.
5. To transfer most of the policy-making power from patrolman to the better qualified heads of departments, with the result of action on the advice of appropriate specialists.
6. To bring policy-making out into the open for all to see, except when special need exists for confidentiality.
7. To improve the quality of police policies by inviting suggestions and criticisms from interested parties.
8. To bring the procedure for policy determination into harmony with the democratic principle, instead of its running counter to that principle.
9. To replace the present police policies based on guesswork with policies based on appropriate investigations and studies made by qualified personnel.
10. To promote equal justice by moving from a system of *ad hoc* determination of policy by individual officers and particular cases to a system of central policy determination and a limitation of the subjective judgment of individual officers to the application of the centrally determined policy.[5]

[4] Kenneth Culp Davis, *Discretionary Justice: A Preliminary Inquiry* (Baton Rouge, La.: Louisiana State University Press, 1969, Chapter 8.

[5] American Bar Association, "Standards Relating to the Urban Police Function," American Bar Association Project on Standards For Criminal Justice, American Bar Association, 1973, pp. 127–128. See also Professor Davis' text, footnote 4; and The President's Commission on Law Enforcement and the Administration of Justice, *Task Force Report: The Police*, 1967, pp. 18–21 for a discussion of some of the same objectives.

Standard 4.4 of the ABA report asks the various legislatures and courts to require and to support local law enforcement agencies to develop rules and criteria guiding the use of police discretion. It also provides for the orderly review of these rules and criteria by the courts in relevant court cases. Courts are futher encouraged to keep the law enforcement agency administrators advised of violations involving the use of police discretion so as to permit a review of training needs, and to increase supervision and control where needed to ensure conformity to the rules. In 1973, the Task Force On Police of the National Advisory Commission on Criminal Justice Standards and Goals recommended a supporting standard, Standard 1.3, titled, "Police Discretion." That standard, in full, is as follows:

> *Every police agency should acknowledge the existence of the broad range of administrative and operational discretion that is exercised by all police agencies and individual officers. That acknowledgment should take the form of comprehensive policy statements that publicly establish the limits of discretion, that provide guidelines for its exercise within those limits, and that eliminate discriminatory enforcement of the law.*
>
> *1. Every police chief executive should have the authority to establish his agency's fundamental objectives and priorities and to implement them through discretionary allocation and control of agency resources. In the exercise of his authority, every chief executive:*
>
> *a. Should seek legislation that grants him the authority to exercise his discretion in allocating police resources and in establishing his agency's fundamental objectives and priorities;*
>
> *b. Should review all existing criminal statutes, determine the ability of the agency to enforce these statutes effectively, and advise the legislature of the statutes' practicality from an enforcement standpoint; and*
>
> *c. Should advise the legislature of the practicality of each proposed criminal statute from an enforcement standpoint, and the impact of such proposed statutes on the ability of the agency to maintain the existing level of police services.*
>
> *2. Every police chief executive should establish policy that guides the exercise of discretion by police personnel in using arrest alternatives. This policy:*
>
> *a. Should establish the limits of discretion by specifically identifying, insofar as possible, situations calling for the use of alternatives to continued physical custody;*
>
> *b. Should establish criteria for the selection of appropriate enforcement alternatives;*

c. Should require enforcement action to be taken in all situations where all elements of a crime are present and all policy criteria are satisfied;

d. Should be jurisdictionwide in both scope and application; and

e. Specifically should exclude offender-lack of cooperation, or disrespect toward police personnel, as a factor in arrest determination unless such conduct constitutes a separate crime.

3. Every police chief executive should establish policy that limits the exercise of discretion by police personnel in conducting investigations, and that provides guidelines for the exercise of discretion within those limits. This policy:

a. Should be based on codified laws, judicial decisions, public policy, and police experience in investigating criminal conduct;

b. Should identify situations where there can be no investigative discretion; and

c. Should establish guidelines for situations requiring the exercise of investigative discretion.

4. Every police chief executive should establish policy that governs the exercise of discretion by police personnel in providing routine peacekeeping and other police services that, because of their frequent recurrence, lend themselves to the development of a uniform agency response.

5. Every police chief executive should formalize procedures for developing and implementing the foregoing written agency policy.

6. Every police chief executive immediately should adopt inspection and control procedures to insure that officers exercise their discretion in a manner consistent with agency policy.

Implementing a Rule-Making Procedure

The objectives of a good rule-making procedure listed above form the foundation for a good progam to augment the use of discretion. Each one of the objectives will be dealt with at length with some recommendations on how to achieve them.

The Objectives

1. *To educate the public in the reality that the police make vital policy.*
To create a solid foundation for open use of discretion, the police agency

should mount an effort to educate the public to the reality that the police do, in fact, determine enforcement policy and are not simply blind enforcers of the law. Educating the public may take the form of a good public relations program; the use of a speakers' bureau to meet with social, civic and other groups in the community; and the acquaintance of students in local schools with law enforcement policy-making procedures.

2. *To induce legislative bodies to redefine crime so that the statutory law will be practically enforceable.* Effective working relationships should be established with city councils, village boards, and state legislatures to seek their support in redefining the criminal statutes so as to make them enforceable in a realistic manner. Frequently, outdated criminal statutes do not apply to current situations in the community. Also, many laws are passed as a reaction to a short-term problem or a problem that was sensational in nature in a response to a public demand for a statutory law that reflects a situation that no longer exists. Legislative bodies occasionally provide for periodic review of all criminal statutes so as to be more responsive to enforcement problems.

3. *To rewrite statutes to make clear what powers are granted to the police and what powers are withheld, and then to keep the police within the granted powers.* This objective calls for careful and open deliberation by legislative bodies to determine clearly and to state which powers are to be exercised by the police and which ones are to be withheld. In addition, it also calls for the creation of a mechanism to insure that the police stay within the powers granted by the legislature in their use of discretion. At first glance, this objective may appear to be unduly restrictive of police practices, but it actually intends to promote better relationships with the public, because both the public and the law enforcement representatives would know what to expect of each other in the performance of police duties. In addition, the present seeming murkiness of the police officer's powers would be communicated to new police personnel by a training and educational program.

4. *To close the gap between the pretenses of the police manuals and the actualities of police behaviors.* Police manuals are notoriously lacking in guidelines, policy, or rules for the use of discretion. Manuals that include policy, rules, and regulations are administrative decisions that should be comprehensive enough to assist the individual police officer in his encounters with incidents requiring the use of discretion. Many times, manuals are used to express "what should be," and do not represent what goes on in actual police behavior.

5. *To transfer most of the policy-making power from the patrol-man to the better qualified heads of departments, acting on the advice of appropriate specialists.* This objective asks that the administration of the department, using the services of trained specialists, establish and disseminate guidelines or standards to promote more uniformity and consistency among the field decisions made by law enforcement officers in daily tours of duty. If the decisions about guidelines are not made at the administration level, individual patrolman generally adopt their own criteria for exercising discretion. These individual standards tend to reflect the patrolman's background, biases, and prejudices and do not promote consistency.

6. *To bring policy-making out into the open for all to see, except when special need exists for confidentiality.* The term "open" is the key to this objective and calls for moving policy-making involving discretion into the open, so that the public can easily view the policy-formulation procedure and can provide input into it if they are interested in doing so. Traditionally, police administrators have found it easier to deny that discretion is exercised by police personnel. To admit that the discretion is used without some standardization of criteria for exercising the discretion invites criticism by the public affected by the discretion being exercised. Without clearly stated policy, the police administrator is in an awkward, if not legally indefensible, position. Occasionally, some enforcement problems become more aggravated by the open disclosure of nonenforcement, or the open exercise of discretion. In these cases, it is probably justifiable to treat policy formulation in a confidential manner. However, there should be some provision for review by representatives of the public, such as the city council, a specific board, or a commission.

7. *To improve the quality of police policy by inviting suggestions and criticisms from interested parties.* This objective is an extension of the preceding objective. It openly encourages the review of police policies by interested parties and various civic organizations who may be directly affected by police policy. They should have the opportunity to air their concerns about the development of relevant police policies. Admittedly, the open invitation for suggestions and criticisms tends to make more work for the administrators of a public agency. But the long-range benefits accrued by a police agency open to public review, would tend to offset the additional administrative burden.

8. *To bring procedure for policy determination into harmony with*

the democratic principle, instead of their running counter to that principle. By opening policy determination to review by all interested citizens, a police agency encourages participation by these persons or groups, thereby fostering an adherence to the democratic principles upon which our society is based.

9. *To replace the present police policies based on guesswork with policy based on appropriate investigations and studies made by qualified personnel.* This objective urges deviation from the prevailing police practice of determining policy based on intuition and experiences that may no longer be attuned to the community. Instead, the objective urges that prior to the formulation of policy the problem be analyzed and studied by personnel who are acquainted with the problem, and who have the qualifications to recommend policy that is truly reflective of community sentiment and law.

10. *To promote equal justice by moving from a system of* ad hoc *determination of policy by individual officers and particular cases to a system of central policy determination and a limitation of the subjective judgment of individual officers to the application of the centrally determined policy.* This objective urges that the policy be determined at the top of the organization and be disseminated in a fashion so as to encourage uniform application of the policies by all personnel. It also recognizes that the current practice of letting individual officers establish their own criteria and, in effect, muddle through without guidelines, does not promote equal justice for all.

In summary, the foundation of any discretion program is the presence of an open rule-making procedure that invites public scrutiny. A good rule-making procedure will also provide for the formulation of the rules and criteria by the administration of the organization with an effective dissemination mechanism, as well as a monitoring provision, to ensure conformity to the standards.

Student Checklist

1. Are you able to define the concept of discretion in justice administration?
2. Can you list the four stages in the exercise of discretion to an incident involving a violation of the criminal law?

3. Do you know how to explain the phrase "Where law ends, tyranny begins"?

4. Are you able to describe what is, meant by the "ministerial" philosophy of law enforcement?

5. Can you contrast the statutory authority of police personnel, prosecutors, and judges in their use of discretion?

6. Do you know how to illustrate four examples of how discretion is used by a police officer, a prosecutor, and a judge?

7. Are you able to describe how nonenforcement of the criminal law can be discretion?

8. Can you explain why Davis stresses "openness" as a key to the successful use of discretion by any governmental agency?

9. Can you list the ten major objectives of a good rule-making procedure as a base for exercising discretion?

10. Are you able to write an essay on the compatibility of law and the exercise of discretion in the administration of justice?

Topics for Discussion

1. Discuss the definition of discretion.

2. Discuss the abuses of discretion and the impact of these abuses on the administration of justice.

3. Discuss the legal base for exercising discretion in the three major functions of criminal justice.

4. Discuss the American Bar Association's standards on police discretion.

5. Discuss the ten objectives of a good rule-making procedure.

ANNOTATED BIBLIOGRAPHY

American Bar Association. *Standards Relating to the Urban Police Function.* New York, N.Y.: Institute of Judicial Administration, American Bar Association, March 1972. A comprehensive compilation of standards developed by an advisory committee for the Institute of Judicial Administration. The use of discretion appears as a major component of the Standards and is firmly recognized by the committee as a potentially positive force for improving the administration of criminal law.

Davis, Kenneth Culp. *Discretionary Justice: A Preliminary Inquiry.* Baton Rouge, La.: Louisiana State University Press, 1969. Covers the use of discretionary actions in applying justice to all forms of governmental control and regulation. It takes a positive approach to the social need for discretion, but it attempts to develop guidelines.

Dickinson, John. *Administrative Justice and the Supremacy of Law.* New York, N.Y.: Russell and Russell, Inc., 1959. One of the early works in administrative law recognizing the existence and role of discretion in law. It is not limited to criminal law and provides a broad foundation to the contemporary concern with discretion in criminal law and its enforcement.

Goldstein, Joseph. "Police Discretion Not to Invoke the Criminal Process: Low-Visibility Decision in the Administration of Justice," *The Yale Law Journal,* 69, 4 (March 1960), 542–594. A legalistically oriented analysis of the use of discretion by police personnel. The article does an excellent job of placing police discretion in its proper context with the use of discretion by the other subsystems of criminal justice. Extensive footnotes cite the other significant works on discretion.

Packer, Herbert L. *The Limits of the Criminal Sanction.* Stanford, Calif.: Stanford University Press, 1968. Focuses upon the gray area around the extremes of law, where law ceases to be the guide and individual discretion takes over. The impact of discretion on social control is relatively unknown.

Perelman, Charles. *Justice*. New York, N.Y.: Random House, 1967. An essay by a University of Brussels professor on his philosophy of justice. It is included here because of the need for a solid foundation in justice by anyone exercising discretion in the administration of justice.

Skolnick, Jerone H. *Justice Without Trial*. New York, N.Y.: John Wiley and Sons, Inc., 1966. Focus on the use of discretion as exercised in a range of enforcement situations. It vividly depicts the need for guidelines and control.

The study of this appendix will enable you to:

1. Describe the procedure for determining the current law on a legal issue considering statutory law, case law, and administrative rulings.

2. Using *Shepard's Citations*, select five current case decisions relevant to an issue of criminal law.

3. Locate a case decision in the National Reporter System starting with the case citation.

4. Using a legal encyclopedia, obtain a general statement of the law on an issue.

5. Locate relevant cases using the American Digest System.

6. Frame a legal question so that it may be researched.

7. Describe the "fluidity" of law:

8. Describe how law review articles may be used to provide an interpretation of a legal issue.

9. Identify the judicial circuits of the United States Court of Appeals.

10. Determine how administrative law is located in the Federal Register.

Appendix A
A Methodology of Law

Introduction

The purpose of this appendix is to outline for the student an orderly method for approaching the study of law and the search for law. Successful legal research requires no magic, only common sense and some background knowledge. The objective of legal research is to locate those authoritative statements that would be considered binding or persuasive to a court or other body that must make a final decision on the specific matter at issue.

There is no universally accepted definition of "law" in all its aspects. It is the sum of the rules by which men and women live. No society can endure without some kind of system or order or legal system. Under our Anglo-American system, laws are a restraint on both government and governed. Law reflects society. Law may emerge from any one of the three branches of government—executive, legislative, judicial. It may also arise from a hierarchy of multiple government units, and the law of one may not be binding upon a matter subject to the jurisdiction of another. Law coming from a superior government is controlling of lesser governments and their inhabitants. The law of the federal government, wherever it applies, is considered the supreme law of the land and cannot be contradicted by any state or local law. Similarly, the law of a state, not in conflict with an overriding federal law, is supreme throughout the state. The laws of one state are not considered binding on the citizens of another state, and the ordinances of one city are not applicable to the activities of individuals within another city.

Sources of Law

Under the Constitution of the United States, one branch of government—Congress—is designated as the legislative, or lawmaking, branch. Congress is authorized to make legal rules or laws for the guidance of the people of the entire country and these legislative enactments are called *federal statutes*. Similarly, the constitutions of each state provide for a legislative branch whose function it is to make legal rules or laws for the control of the conduct of the citizens of that state. These laws are called *state statutes*. This body of law is commonly called the *written law*. It is published in books called *Statutes* or *Codes*.

No system of administering order and justice can be entirely reduced to written rule. Situations calling for a decision of the courts are so varied in character that it is impossible to provide a written rule, or statute, for every case that may arise, and it is also necessary for the courts to interpret the statutes. There are, therefore, certain principles of law that have been gradually evolved by the courts through the years. Rules for dealing with new situations or with situations that are not specifically covered by a statute are derived by the courts from these principles. When such a case comes before the court, the court reaches a decision based upon an application of the principles of law to the facts in that particular case. This decision is written out, the reasoning of the judge or judges is shown, and it becomes a part of the record of the court. If the same question is again brought before that court, the court's tendency will be to decide it in the same way—to follow its previous decision. These decisions constitute what is known as the *common law*, or the *unwritten law*, or *case law*, as distinguished from the *written law* or *statute law*. The decisions of all federal courts and the courts of last appellate jurisdiction of the states are preserved in a book form, called *Reports*.

Legal Research Materials

Law books and legal research materials are classified as *primary authority; secondary authority;* and *index,* or *access, material.* Primary authority is either binding upon the courts or is highly persuasive. It originates from all three branches of government at federal, state, and local levels. The legislative bodies at federal and state levels enact statutory law (at the local level, statute law is termed *ordinances*), which is binding primary authority before the courts except when validity is constitutionally challenged. Statute law, as used here, also includes constitutions, charters, treaties, and compacts. The judicial branch of our government consists of federal, state, and local courts. Although all levels of courts determine the rights of the parties before them, usually only the published decisions of the appellate courts, as distinguished from the trial courts, are regarded as primary authority and serve as precedents in future cases.

Commentaries on law by legal experts and noted legal authors are referred to as secondary authority. Legal encyclopedias, legal textbooks, professional law journals, law reviews, and periodicals make up this classification of law books. This type of authority has no binding effect upon the courts; it is explanatory and argumentative only.

Index and access materials are used to search and to find the primary sources of authority. Actually, all the above listed secondary materials are law finders. However, the most commonly used index for searching for decisions of the courts is the legal digest. Because the decisions are of necessity arranged chronologically in the order in which they are decided and not alphabetically by subjects covered, it is necessary that some means be devised for finding the decision or group of decisions scattered through the reports, which involve the particular question in which the searcher is interested. This is the function of the digest. The alphabetical arrangement of topics of law is similar to that of an encyclopedia. Rather than text, however, the digest summarizes the points of law of each decision found in the reports and classifies them by topic and subtopics of law or by subject matter or questions of law in each topic.

Criminal law problems run the gamut of the whole body of law and involve laws emanating from all levels and branches of government. Accordingly the researcher must be familiar with the publications found in the law library and with the best methods for their use.

Source of the Materials

The nature of a particular problem to be resolved largely determines the books to be searched and the procedure to be followed. On questions involving the constitutional rights of an accused person, for example, the beginning point will be the Constitution of the United States and the court decisions construing its applicable provisions. In resolving questions relating to the search and seizure of game from a hunting camp as another example, a careful examination of the statutes of the state and the court decisions interpreting them would be the starting point of research, because the authority for such action is derived from the state legislature. Also, rules and regulations that may have been adopted by a state agency charged with enforcement or implementation would be searched. Other questions, such as the reasonableness of a stop-and-frisk, may not be governed by legislation. The research would then be confined principally to court decisions.

A constitution, whether state or federal, is the supreme law of the jurisdiction and, among other matters, defines the authority of its three branches of government. Frequently, the constitutionality of a statute, regulation, or other government activity will be questioned. Constitutions are usually found printed in the sets of books containing the statutes of the federal government or of the particular state. One of the best sources to consult for the United States Constitution is the *United States Code Annotated*. Each section of the text of the Constitution is followed by notations of court decisions construing the section. This set then provides an easy method for obtaining a list of the court decisions interpreting the sections of the Constitution. These notations take the form of summaries of the points of law of the court decisions and are called *annotations*. This features is common to all annotated codes or statute sets. Often, the annotations also contain citations and historical source references. Annotated sets of the constitutions and statutes exist for most of the states in this country.

Treaties and other international agreements to which the United States has become a party have the same effect and force as statutes. Treaties extend to all proper subjects of negotiation between governments. Until 1950, treaties to which the United States was a party were published in the *United States Statutes At Large*. Since then, treaties have been published in the *United States Treaties and other International Agreements Series*.

Legislation is the written expression of governmental policy. It is enacted by a legislative body such as the Congress of the United States; or a state legislature or general assembly; or a municipal council, commission, or board. The publication of legislation usually involves a number of steps. At the close of each legislative session, the enactments are published in books called *Session Laws*, *General Laws*, or *Public Acts*.

The session laws are printed and bound in the chronological order of their passage, without regard to subject content. On the federal level, the *United States Statutes At Large* contain the enactments of each session of Congress. The *Oregon Session Laws* contain the enactments of each session of the Oregon Legislative Assembly, and the *Public and Local Acts of Michigan* contain the enactment of each session of the Michigan Legislature.

Periodically, the laws of the sessions will be incorporated into sets compiling the session laws which are in effect at the time of the compilation. These compilations are called *Codes, Compiled Statutes*, or *Revised Statutes*. In these sets the laws are arranged in orderly form; all laws relating to a particular topic are usually grouped together in chapters and sections. These sets are indexed to assist the researcher in locating laws pertaining to a specific problem.

The *Statutes At Large* of the United States have been codified. The two most commonly used compilations are the *United States Code*, published by the U.S. Government Printing Office, and the *United States Code Annotated*, an unofficial publication published by a private publisher. The annotated set is of greater value in research because it contains historical notes and notations of court decisions and agency regulations construing each statute and constitution provision.

The codes or statutes of most states are also published officially by an agency of the state, and unofficially by a private publisher. The privately published sets are usually annotated. However, chapter and section numbering are identical and, in practice, a citation to the unofficial set is acceptable to the courts.

Ordinances are the legislation of the governmental units, such as counties, cities, or towns. The ordinances and administrative regulations of larger cities and counties are customarily published and known as *The Ordinances of* (name of city or county). These usually are organized and arranged in the same manner as state codes or statutes. In the smaller communities, the ordinances are not usually published but must be consulted in the office of the clerk of the city or town.

The administrative law of the executive branch of our government consists of the executive orders of the president of the United States and the various state governors, the rules and regulations promulgated by the boards and agencies, both federal and state, and decisions of such bodies. Orders issued by the president, and rules and regulations of federal departments and agencies, are published as they are issued daily in the *Federal Register*. At the end of each year, they are compiled into the *Code of Federal Regulations*.

Regulations of the state agencies may or may not be published. In some states, these rules and regulations are compiled into sets similar to the codes. Generally, they are simply called *The Administrative Rules and Regulations of* (name of state). When a compilation is not available, the office of the state agency must be consulted for a copy of its rules and regulations.

The United States Constitution and Congress have established a system of federal courts consisting of the Supreme Court of the United States; the 11 United States Court of Appeals; and 92 United States District Courts, which include the Bankruptcy Courts, the Tax Court, the Court of Claims, the Customs Court, the Court of Customs and Patent Appeals, the Temporary Emergency Court of Appeals, and the Court of Military Appeals. (See Figure A–1.) Decisions of the United States Supreme Court may be found in three different sets of books: the *United States Reports*, the *Supreme Court Reporter*, and the *Lawyers' Edition of the Supreme Court Reports*.

Figure A-1. The 11 federal judicial circuits, see 28 U.S.C. §41. (Reprinted with permission from West's Law Finder: A Research Manual for Lawyers, *Copyright © 1967 by West Publishing Company.)*

Decisions of the lower federal courts from 1789 to 1880 can be found in *Federal Cases*. Since 1880, decisions of the United States Courts of Appeals have been published in the *Federal Reporter*, and the decisions of the United States District Courts are published in the *Federal Supplement*. The *Federal Rules Decisions* report district court decisions involving the Federal Rules of Civil Procedure and the Federal Rules of Criminal Procedure since 1941.

The constitutions and legislatures of the states have also established a system of courts for the state level. The names and the organization of the courts vary from state to state. Usually, a state court system consists of a court of last appeal, a trial level court, and an inferior court level. The highest state court is usually called the supreme court or the court of appeals. It primarily hears and decides appeals from the trial courts. Its decisions are published and are considered binding upon the courts throughout the state. A number of states have established an intermediate court system. Most of the decisions of these courts are final. The decisions of these intermediate appellate courts are usually published, and they are considered the law of the state unless they are inconsistent with a later statute or a decision of the highest appellate court. The trial courts in a state are generally called circuit or district courts. They hear testimony, receive other evidence, conduct jury trials where appropriate, and decide the case in the first instance. They usually are courts of record. Inferior courts consist of police, small claims, traffic, and the like. The decisions of these lower and inferior courts are not published and are not regarded as binding precedent on other courts. These courts are not courts of record.

The National Reporter System. The decisions of the highest state courts, including the intermediate courts of appeals, are usually published in two places: in the official state printed state reports, as for example the *Wisconsin Reports,* and in the unofficial National Reporter System, begun in 1879, published by the West Publishing Company. The National Reporters contain the decisions of all state appellate courts. They are divided into nine regional reporters: the *Atlantic Reporter,* the *California Reporter,* the *New York Supplement,* the *North Eastern Reporter,* the *North Western Reporter,* the *Pacific Reporter,* the *South Eastern Reporter,* the *Southern Reporter,* and the *South Western Reporter.* (See Figure A–2.) The *New York Supplement* originally contained all of the lower appellate court decisions of the state of New York. It has been expanded to include

Figure A-2. The National Reporter System Map, showing the states included in each Reporter group. The National Reporter System also includes the Supreme Court Reporter, the Federal Reporter, the Federal Supplement, Federal Rules Decisions, the New York Supplement, and West's California Reporter. (Reprinted with permission from West's Law Finder: A Research Manual for Lawyers, Copyright © 1967 by West Publishing Company.)

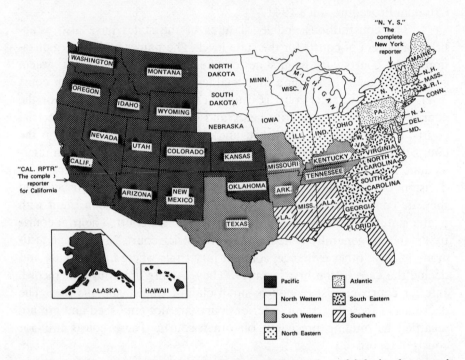

the decisions of the New York Court of Appeals, which is the state's highest court. The *California Reporter,* first published in 1960, contains the decisions of the California Supreme Court, District Courts of Appeal, and the Appellate Department of the Superior Court.

The complete National Reporter System also includes the *Federal Reporter,* the *Federal Supplement,* the *Federal Rules Decisions,* and the *Supreme Court Reporter.* The current decisions are published first in an advance service called advance sheets, which are eventually published in a hard-bound edition. The volume designation and the pagination of the advance service are the same as those of the bound edition. The text of the decisions is identical in the official reports and the National Reporters. The National Reporters feature headnotes or syllabi summarizing the holding of each decision and classifying each headnote with an appropriate topic and key number. As will be explained later, this topic and key number can be used to locate other decisions on the same point of law in the American Digest System.

The National Reporters cover all reported appellate courts in the United States. Other services publish court decisions of specialized or particular interest, which may be either annotated or unannotated.

The annotated-type reporter sets out each court decision in full and then follows it with an annotation, or commentary, which extensively reviews other court decisions and the statutory provisions dealing with the same points or principle of law. If such an annotation is available, the work of the researcher is simplified. The *American Law Reports* is such an annotated publication which reports and annotates significant decisions of a general nature. The *American Law Reports Federal* reports and annotates decisions of significant federal law.

The unannotated-type reporter sets out only the court decision in full and without commentary, but collects decisions dealing with a special subject area. *American Maritime Cases, American Federal Tax Reports, Labor Cases,* and *Trade Cases* are just a few examples of some of the specialized reporters.

Proper Citations

If a court decision is published in more than one reporter, it is customary to indicate all sources in a citation of the decision. A citation includes (in this order) the name or title of the decision, that is, the names of the plaintiff and the defendant; the number of the volume; the abbreviated title of the reporter; the page number; and the year in which the decision was decided. Examples of proper citations are given on the following pages.

A U.S. Supreme Court Decision. The full citation of an important background decision on the issue of the reasonableness of an arrest is *Terry* v. *Ohio,* 392 U.S. 1, 88 S.Ct. 1868, 20 L. Ed. 2d 889 (1968). The citation means that the parties in the case were Terry and the state of Ohio and that the decision may be found in three different places: (1) in volume 392 of the *United States Reports* at page 1; (2) in volume 88 of the *Supreme Court Reporter* at page 1868; and (3) in volume 20 of the *Lawyers' Edition of the Supreme Court Reports, second series,* at page 889. Finally, the year in which the decision was decided is shown in parentheses.

A State Supreme Court Decision. The complete citation of a 1971 decision of the Wisconsin Supreme Court holding that a custodial search of a suspect at the police station must bear a reasonable relationship not to the arrest, but to the jail custodial purposes, which includes the inventorying of possessions belonging to the suspect and placing them in safekeeping during custody in jail is *Warrix* v. *State,* 50 Wis. 2d 368, 184 N.W. 2d 189 (1971). This decision may be found in volume 50 of the second series of the official *Wisconsin Reports* at page 368; it also may be found in volume 184 of the second series of the unofficial *North Western Reporter* at page 189.

A pre-National Reporter State Decision. The citation to the early pre-National Reporter Oregon decision holding that firing a gun is not justifiable where the arrest can be made by less dangerous means is *Lander* v. *Miles,* 3 Ore. 35 (1868). This decision can be found only in the official state publication of the decision in the *Oregon Reports* because the unofficial publication *Pacific Reporter* had not yet been published. The decisions of state courts that were made before the publication of the unofficial regional reporter will have only the one citation and the date of the decision.

A State Decision Without an Officially Published Report. The citation to a 1960 Florida decision that an officer can never use more force than appears reasonably necessary to make an arrest, or subject the person arrested to unnecessary risk of harm, is *City of Miami* v. *Albro,* 120 So. 2d 23 (Fla. 1960). This decision can be found only in the unofficial publication *Southern Reporter* because the state of Florida, like a number of other states, has discontinued the official publication of the *Florida Reports.* Other states that have discontinued the publication of the official state reports are: Alaska (since 1958), Iowa (since 1968), Kentucky (since 1951), Missouri (since 1955), North Dakota (since 1953), Oklahoma (since 1953), Texas (since 1962), and Wyoming (since 1959). The name of the state is indicated in parentheses together with the year of the decision.

Standard Abbreviations. The standard abbreviations of the *National Reporters* are:
> Atlantic : Atl. (or A.) and A. 2d
> California ᵌ Cal. Rptr.
> New York Supplement : N.Y. Supp. (or N.Y.S.) and N.Y.S. 2d
> North Eastern : N.E. and N.E. 2d

North Western : N.W. and N.W. 2d
Pacific : Pac. (or P.) and P. 2d
South Eastern : S.E. and S.E. 2d
South Western : S.W. and S.W. 2d
Southern : So. and So. 2d
Supreme Court : S. Ct.
Federal : Fed. (or F.) and F. 2d
Federal Supplement : F. Supp.
Federal Rules Decisions : F.R.D.

Legal Encyclopedias

The legal encyclopedia is the most commonly used tool of the legal researcher. Its narrative text is a highly accurate statement of the law and is easily understood. Because of its footnotes, it is an excellent way to locate primary authority, such as court decisions, statutes, and government regulations. However, this text material is not binding upon judges or other ruling bodies.

There are two major general legal encyclopedias published in this country today: *Corpus Juris Secundum* and *American Jurisprudence,* which is in progress of revision into *American Jurisprudence, Second Series.* The textual material of both encyclopedias is comparable; both purport to cover all fields of law. They differ basically in the scope and coverage of the footnotes. *Corpus Juris Secundum* and its predecessors incorporate all court decisions in the footnotes, and list the decisions by jurisdiction. *American Jurisprudence* and *American Jurisprudence, Second Series,* purport to refer in the footnotes to only those court decisions that are considered leading decisions. They also footnote references to annotations in the *American Law Reports.* The accepted abbreviations of the encyclopedias are: *Corpus Juris Secundum—C.J.S.*; American Jurisprudence—*Am. Jur.*, and American Jurisprudence, Second Series— *Am. Jur. 2d.* A complete reference to an encyclopedia includes the volume number, the title of the encyclopedia, the topic, the section of the topic, and the date of the volume; for example, 35 C.J.S. *False Imprisonment* §8 (1960).

Legal Textbooks, Journals, and Digests

A law textbook or treatise normally deals in depth with a particular area of law. Like the legal encyclopedia, law textbooks and treatises are narrative treatments of the law by authorities and experts. They are helpful to the researcher because they bring together in one place the leading court decisions, pertinent statutes and government regulations, and other legal writings relating to the subject; and they discuss current problems and trends in the law. They may be a multivolume or single-volume work. A sizable number of textbooks and treatises relating to criminal law or a single aspect of criminal law have been published. A few noteworthy titles are: Anderson edition, *Wharton's Criminal Law and Procedure* (1957); Burdick, *The Law of Crime* (1946); Clark and Marshall, *Crimes* (7th ed. 1967); LaFave and Scott, *Handbook on Criminal Law* (1972); Perkins, *Criminal Law* (2d ed. 1969); LaFave, *Arrest* (1965); or Varon, *Searches, Seizures, and Immunities* (1961).

A *Restatement* is a particular type of textbook that is limited in coverage to a single field of law. The product of intensive joint study by scholars, judges, and practitioners of the American Law Institute, ten *Restatements* are currently in use. Each includes black letter rules, and explanatory comments and illustrative problems to which the rules would or would not be applied. To a very large extent, the black letter rules have been synthesized from decisions of the courts throughout the United States.

The law journals or legal periodicals published by law schools and bar associations contain professional articles of both general legal interest and special subject interest. Periodicals of special interest in the field of criminal law are: *American Criminal Law Review*; crime and delinquency—*Criminal Law Bulletin*; criminology—*Journal of Criminal Law, Criminology and Police Science*.

The legal digest contains short summaries of court decisions under alphabetically arranged topic headings similar to that of the encyclopedias. The American Digest System, published by West Publishing Company, is made up of several sets of digests which contain all of the court decisions, federal and state. The *Century Digest* covers the years 1658 to 1896. Court decisions for each succeeding 10-year period are found in the *Decennial Digests*, of which there are now seven: the *First, Second, Third, Fourth, Fifth, Sixth,* and *Seventh Decennial Digests*. The volumes of the *General Digest, Fourth Series,* cover the years since 1966, pending the publication of the *Eighth Decennial Digest*.

If only decisions of federal courts are sought, the *Federal Digest* may be used instead of the voluminous *American Digest*. Each state has a digest, which is more convenient than the *American Digest* for locating court decisions of a particular state.

Those digests published by the West Publishing Company preface each topic with a "key" number except in the *Century Digest* and the *First Decennial Digest*, where paragraph numbers are used. Once the "key," or paragraph number, is found, one can search throughout all of its digests for court decisions on the point of law.

"Key" Numbers. The appropriate "key" number or numbers may be located by using:

1. The descriptive word index to the digest.
2. The topical analysis at the beginning of each topic in the digest.
3. The headnotes to a decision in point appearing in the national or regional reporter.
4. The table of cases to the digest when the name of a decision in point is known.

To illustrate the method of ascertaining the "key" number or numbers, assume that we are researching the question of reasonable stop-and-frisk. Assume further that we know that one of the decisions in point is *Terry* v. *Ohio*, 392 U.S. 1, 88 S.Ct. 1868, 20 L. Ed. 2d 889 (1968). Locating the decision in volume 88 of the *Supreme Court Reporter*, at page 1868, (the reporter is published by the West Publishing Company and therefore also is "key" numbered), we search the headnotes to the decisions for the one that relates to our problem. This discloses that the point of law in which we are interested may be found under the topic "Searches and Seizures" and the "key" numbers that seem most applicable are key 3.3(1) and key 7(1). Key 3.3(1) refers to "circumstances justifying search and seizure" and key 7(1) refers to "unreasonable searches and seizures and violation of constitutional rights, in general." The same topic and key numbers can be obtained by finding the name of the decision in the table of cases and checking the various topics and key numbers given under the name of the decision.

If a decision in point by name is unknown, but the researcher is sufficiently familiar with the subject area to know that "Searches and Seizures" would be the appropriate topic, the key numbers may be located by looking through the analysis at the beginning of the topic in the most recent Decennial Digest. In this instance, we find "Searches and Seizures" in volume 27 of the *Seventh Decennial Digest*, 1956–1966. The analysis of the topic shows key 3.3(1), "Circumstances justifying search and seizure" and key 7(1), "Constitutional rights and violation thereof."

If the researcher does not have the familiarity with the subject to trust his knowledge to select the right topic, the Descriptive Word Index can be used. Terms such as "arrest," "stop and frisk," and "searches and seizures" all would make reference to the topic "Searches and Seizures" key numbers 3.3(1) and 7(1).

Techniques for the Use of Sources

The preceding section has described the various law books and sources in which legal principles and rules may be found. The basis techniques for their use in locating the principles and rules applicable to a given problem will be developed in the following section.

Every legal research project involves a number of steps. Each researcher has his own preferred methodology of search. However, any method should involve at least the following steps:

1. Ascertaining the essential facts.
2. Analyzing the problem.
3. Framing the question to be researched.
4. Identifying key words or the proper topical heading or headings.
5. Using an appropriate search method.
6. Studing the primary and secondary authorities found.
7. Checking the subsequent history and present status of the primary authorities in *Shepard's Citations*.

Analyzing the Problem

After the essential facts are ascertained, it is helpful to break down the situation in terms of (1) the parties or persons involved, (2) the subject matter or property involved, (3) the nature of the issue or claim, and (4) the object or remedy sought to be obtained.

1. The person or persons involved may be important because one or more may belong to a class governed by special rules, such as informers, or former convicts, or juveniles.
2. The subject matter or property comprises the essential things and places involved in the situation, such as gun, abandoned auto, narcotics paraphernalia, motel room, open field.
3. The nature of the issue or claim may consist of an act of commission, such as rape, assault with a weapon, homicide, or an act of

omission, such as failure to have a search warrant, or failure to give a Miranda Warning.

4. The object or remedy sought may be in a criminal case, the suppression of evidence, the impoundment of an auto, or—in a civil case—money damages.

As an illustration of the above analysis, assume that officers, armed with an arrest warrant for burglary of a coin shop but not a search warrant, were admitted to the suspect's home by his wife, where they waited until the suspect arrived. When he entered, he was served with the warrant. Although he refused the officers' request "to look around," they conducted a search of the entire house from attic to the garage, on the basis of the lawful arrest. A number of items, primarily coins, were found and at trial were admitted into evidence against the defendant. His attorney objected on the grounds the coins had been unconstitutionally seized.

Analyzing the facts of this situation:

1. Parties involved : suspect husband, wife.
2. Subject matter : confiscated coins without a search warrant.
3. Nature of claim : unconstitutional search.
4. Remedy sought : suppression of evidence.

Framing the Question to be Researched

Once the problem has been carefully analyzed, the next step is to frame the question to be researched or to identify the legal issue involved. If more than one issue is raised, a separate question should be framed on each. In stating the issue or framing the question, it may be helpful to assume that you are framing the question for someone else to do the research. It should be stated with clarity and sufficient fullness so that someone else will understand it, but it should be limited enough to confine the other person to the single issue involved. This does not mean that the issue or question as originally framed becomes final. Further research and discovery of more facts may require a restatement of the question.

Returning to the facts hypothesized in our illustration, the question to be researched may be stated: "May a warrantless search of the defendant's home be justified as incident to a valid arrest?"

Identifying Appropriate Catchwords or Topical Headings

The organization of the text and material in the basic legal research books (the digests, encyclopedias, and statutes) is alphabetically by

Figure A-3. Key Number System Law Chart. Digest topics are arranged by subject matter in the key number classification system. (Reprinted with permission from West's Law Finder: A Research Manual for Lawyers, *Copyright © 1967 by West Publishing Company.)*

KEY NUMBER SYSTEM LAW CHART

Digest Topics arranged by subject matter in the Key Number classification system.

1. PERSONS
2. PROPERTY
3. CONTRACTS
4. TORTS
5. CRIMES
6. REMEDIES
7. GOVERNMENT

---

1. PERSONS

RELATING TO NATURAL PERSONS IN GENERAL

Civil Rights
Dead Bodies
Death
Domicile
Food
Health
Holidays
Intoxicating Liquors
Names
Poisons
Seals
Signatures
Sunday
Time
Weapons

PARTICULAR CLASSES OF NATURAL PERSONS

Absentees
Aliens
Bastards
Citizens
Convicts
Drunkards
Indians
Infants
Mental Health
Paupers
Slaves
Spendthrifts

PERSONAL RELATIONS

Adoption
Apprentices
Attorney and Client
Executors and Administrators
Guardian and Ward
Husband and Wife
Labor Relations
Marriage
Master and Servant
Parent and Child
Principal and Agent
Workmen's Compensation

ASSOCIATED AND ARTIFICIAL PERSONS

Associations
Beneficial Associations
Building and Loan Associations
Clubs
Colleges and Universities
Corporations
Exchanges
Joint-Stock Companies and Business Trusts
Partnership
Religious Societies

PARTICULAR OCCUPATIONS

Agriculture
Auctions and Auctioneers
Aviation
Banks and Banking
Bridges
Brokers
Canals
Carriers
Commerce
Detectives
Druggists
Electricity
Explosives
Factors
Ferries
Gas
Hawkers and Peddlers
Innkeepers
Insurance
Licenses
Livery Stable Keepers
Manufactures
Mercantile Agencies
Monopolies
Pawnbrokers and Money Lenders
Physicians and Surgeons
Pilots
Railroads
Seamen
Shipping
Steam
Street Railroads
Telecommunications
Theaters and Shows
Towage
Turnpikes and Toll Roads
Warehousemen
Wharves

2. PROPERTY

NATURE, SUBJECTS, AND INCIDENTS OF OWNERSHIP IN GENERAL

Abandonment
Accession
Adjoining Landowners
Confusion of Goods
Improvements
Property

PARTICULAR SUBJECTS AND INCIDENTS OF OWNERSHIP

Animals
Annuities
Automobiles
Boundaries
Cemeteries
Common Lands
Copyrights
Crops
Fences
Fish
Fixtures
Franchises
Game
Good Will
Literary Property
Logs and Logging
Mines and Minerals
Navigable Waters
Party Walls
Patents
Public Lands
Trade Regulation
Waters and Water Courses
Woods and Forests

PARTICULAR CLASSES OF ESTATES OR INTERESTS IN PROPERTY

Charities
Curtesy
Dower
Easements
Estates
Estates Tail
Ground Rents
Joint Tenancy
Landlord and Tenant
Life Estates
Perpetuities
Powers
Remainders
Reversions
Tenancy in Common
Trusts

PARTICULAR MODES OF ACQUIRING OR TRANSFERRING PROPERTY

Abstracts of Title
Adverse Possession
Alteration of Instruments
Assignments
Assignments for Benefit of Creditors
Chattel Mortgages
Conversion
Dedication
Deeds
Descent and Distribution
Escheat
Escrows
Finding Lost Goods
Fraudulent Conveyances
Gifts
Lost Instruments
Mortgages
Pledges
Secured Transactions
Wills

3. CONTRACTS

NATURE, REQUISITES, AND INCIDENTS OF AGREEMENTS IN GENERAL

Contracts
Customs and Usages
Frauds, Statute of
Interest
Usury

PARTICULAR CLASSES OF AGREEMENTS

Bailment
Bills and Notes
Bonds
Breach of Marriage Promise
Champerty and Maintenance
Compositions with Creditors
Compromise and Settlement
Covenants
Depositaries
Exchange of Property
Gaming
Guaranty
Indemnity
Joint Adventures
Lotteries
Principal and Surety
Rewards
Sales
Subscriptions
Vendor and Purchaser

PARTICULAR CLASSES OF IMPLIED OR CONSTRUCTIVE CONTRACTS OR QUASI CONTRACTS

Account Stated
Contribution
Money Lent
Money Paid
Money Received
Use and Occupation
Work and Labor

PARTICULAR MODES OF DISCHARGING CONTRACTS

Novation
Payment
Release
Subrogation
Tender

4. TORTS

Assault and Battery
Collision
Conspiracy
False Imprisonment
Forcible Entry and Detainer

Fraud
Libel and Slander
Malicious Prosecution
Negligence
Nuisance
Seduction
Torts
Trespass
Trover and Conversion
Waste

5. CRIMES

Abduction
Abortion
Adulteration
Adultery
Affray
Arson
Bigamy
Blasphemy
Breach of the Peace
Bribery
Burglary
Common Scold
Compounding Offenses
Counterfeiting
Criminal Law
Disorderly Conduct
Disorderly House
Disturbance of Public Assemblage
Dueling
Embezzlement
Embracery
Escape
Extortion
False Personation
False Pretenses
Fires
Forgery
Fornication
Homicide
Incest
Insurrection and Sedition
Kidnapping
Larceny
Lewdness
Malicious Mischief
Mayhem
Miscegenation
Neutrality Laws
Obscenity
Obstructing Justice
Perjury
Piracy
Prize Fighting
Prostitution
Rape
Receiving Stolen Goods
Rescue
Riot
Robbery
Sodomy
Suicide
Threats
Treason
Unlawful Assembly
Vagrancy

6. REMEDIES

REMEDIES BY ACT OR AGREEMENT OF PARTIES

Accord and Satisfaction
Arbitration and Award
Submission of Controversy

REMEDIES BY POSSESSION OR NOTICE

Liens
Lis Pendens
Maritime Liens
Mechanics' Liens
Notice
Salvage

MEANS AND METHODS OF PROOF

Acknowledgment
Affidavits
Depositions
Estoppel
Evidence
Oath
Records
Witnesses

CIVIL ACTIONS IN GENERAL

Action
Declaratory Judgment
Election of Remedies
Limitation of Actions
Parties
Set-Off and Counterclaim
Venue

PARTICULAR PROCEEDINGS IN CIVIL ACTIONS

Abatement and Revival
Appearance
Continuance
Costs
Damages
Dismissal and Nonsuit
Execution
Exemptions
Homestead
Judgment
Jury
Motions
Pleading
Process
Reference
Stipulations
Trial

PARTICULAR REMEDIES INCIDENT TO CIVIL ACTIONS

Arrest
Assistance, Writ of
Attachment
Bail
Deposits in Court
Discovery
Garnishment
Injunction
Judicial Sales
Ne Exeat
Receivers
Recognizances
Sequestration
Undertakings

PARTICULAR MODES OF REVIEW IN CIVIL ACTIONS

Appeal and Error
Audita Querela
Certiorari
Exceptions, Bill of
New Trial
Review

ACTIONS TO ESTABLISH OWNERSHIP OR RECOVER POSSESSION OF SPECIFIC PROPERTY

Detinue
Ejectment
Entry, Writ of
Interpleader
Possessory Warrant
Quieting Title
Real Actions
Replevin
Trespass to Try Title

FORMS OF ACTIONS FOR DEBTS OR DAMAGES

Account, Action on
Action on the Case
Assumpsit, Action of
Covenant, Action of
Debt, Action of

ACTIONS FOR PARTICULAR FORMS OR SPECIAL RELIEF

Account
Cancellation of Instruments
Creditors' Suit
Divorce
Marshaling Assets and Securities
Partition
Reformation of Instruments
Specific Performance

CIVIL PROCEEDINGS OTHER THAN ACTIONS

Habeas Corpus
Mandamus
Prohibition
Quo Warranto
Scire Facias
Supersedeas

SPECIAL CIVIL JURISDICTIONS AND PROCEDURE THEREIN

Admiralty
Bankruptcy
Equity
Federal Civil Procedure
Insolvency

PROCEEDINGS PECULIAR TO CRIMINAL CASES

Extradition
Fines
Forfeitures
Grand Jury
Indictment and Information
Pardon and Parole
Penalties
Searches and Seizures

7. GOVERNMENT

POLITICAL BODIES AND DIVISIONS

Counties
District of Columbia
Municipal Corporations
States
Territories
Towns
United States

SYSTEMS AND SOURCES OF LAW

Administrative Law and Procedure
Common Law
Constitutional Law
International Law
Parliamentary Law
Statutes
Treaties

LEGISLATIVE AND EXECUTIVE POWERS AND FUNCTIONS

Bounties
Census
Customs Duties
Drains
Eminent Domain
Highways
Inspection
Internal Revenue
Levees and Flood Control
Pensions
Post Office
Private Roads
Public Service Commissions
Schools and School Districts
Social Security and Public Welfare
Taxation
Weights and Measures
Zoning

JUDICIAL POWERS AND FUNCTIONS, AND COURTS AND THEIR OFFICERS

Amicus Curiæ
Clerks of Courts
Contempt
Court Commissioners
Courts
Judges
Justices of the Peace
Removal of Cases
Reports
United States Commissioners

CIVIL SERVICE, OFFICERS, AND INSTITUTIONS

Ambassadors and Consuls
Asylums
Attorney General
Coroners
District and Prosecuting Attorneys
Elections
Hospitals
Newspapers
Notaries
Officers
Prisons
Reformatories
Registers of Deeds
Sheriffs and Constables
United States Marshals

MILITARY AND NAVAL SERVICE AND WAR

Armed Services
Militia
War and National Defense

topic. It is necessary at the beginning to gain a working knowledge of the main topics used in these sources and also the main index headings used. The latter are often referred to as *catchwords*. Before an index may be used effectively, the catchwords for the problem must be identified. Many indexes have a descriptive approach that refers the user to catchwords.

Using an Appropriate Search Method

There are four basic methods for legal research: (1) the analytical topic approach; (2) the descriptive word approach; (3) the table of cases approach; and (4) the words and phrases approach.

The Analytic Method. The analytical approach is the least mechanical of the four research methods. The law digests and encyclopedias classify and divide the law into more than 400 topics. These divisions are listed at the beginning of the first index volume of the encyclopedia, *Corpus Juris Secundum* and in the first volumes of the *Decennial Digests*. The seven grand divisions of law are: Persons, Property, Contracts, Torts, Crimes, Remedies, and Government. (See Figure A–3.)

In using the analytical method, the appropriate division of law must first be selected. In the above illustration of suppression of evidence obtained by a warrantless search incident to a valid arrest, it would appear that the proper grand division would be "Remedies." As we are concerned with proceedings that are limited to criminal cases, we find under the topic "Proceedings Peculiar to Criminal Cases" the subtopic "Searches and Seizures," which seems to be most appropriate to our problem.

Although these charts classify the law by grand divisions, the topics in the encyclopedias and digests are arranged in an alphabetical order. For example, volume 1 of *Corpus Juris Secundum* covers the topics "A" to "Adjective Law," and volume 101 covers the topics "Workmen's Compensation" to "Zoning," while volume 1 of the *Seventh Decennial Digest* covers the topics "Abandonment" to "Appeal & Error," and volume 34 covers the topics "Workmen's Compensation" to "Zoning."

To return again to our illustration, the topic "Searches and Seizures" is treated in volume 79 of *Corpus Juris Secundum*. Referring to the index for that topic at the end of volume 79, we find under "Warrants" the heading "Arrest" and the subhead "Necessity for Search Incident to Arrest" with a reference to section 67, pages 840–845. In this section appears the following:

*The officers may search the room where the arrest is made and any
other places to which they can get lawful access, but the right of search
does not extend to the entire premises, unless all parts of the premises
are used for an unlawful purpose.*

Many law books, including the set of *Corpus Juris Secundum*, are
kept up-to-date through supplements or pocket parts, so-named because
the upkeep supplements are published in a pamphlet that is inserted into
a "pocket" in the inside back cover of the volume. It is essential to refer
to the supplement or pocket part for any changes or recent developments
in the law since the publication of the main volume. Checking the pocket
part to volume 79 of *Corpus Juris Secundum* under the topic "Searches
and Seizures" section 67, page 844, we find:

Since the publication of Corpus Juris Secundum *the case of* Harris v.
U.S., *cited to the text has been disapproved. . . . A warrantless search
of defendant's entire house incident to a lawful arrest is unreasonable
as extending beyond defendant's person and an area from which he
might obtain a weapon or something that can be used in evidence
against him.* Chimel v. California, *Cal. 89 S.Ct. 2034, disapproving*
Harris v. U.S. *67 S.Ct. 1098 . . . and* U.S. v. Rabinowitz, *70 S.Ct.
430 . . ."*

A full reading of the *Chimel* decision reveals a similar situation to the
one in question.

Normally, research should not end until all of the available law
books have been examined on the point in question. *American Jurisprudence* and *American Jurisprudence, Second Series* should also be
consulted, especially because their footnotes contain references to annotations in the *American Law Reports*. Volume 68 of *American Jurisprudence, Second Series* included a comprehensive section on "Searches and
Seizures." Referring to this topic in the index at the end of the volume,
we find that under "Arrest, search incident to" we are directed to sections 92–98, where we read:

*The permissible scope of a search incident to an arrest is a question
recognized by the Supreme Court of the United States to have prompted
decisions "far from consistent." But in 1969, in* Chimel v. California,
*395 US 752, 23 L Ed 2d 685, 89 S Ct 2034, reh den 396 US 869, 24
L Ed 2d 124, 90 S Ct 36, the court discussed the history of its holdings
on the question . . . the court concluded that there is ample justification,
in a search incident to an arrest, for a search of the arrestee's person
and the area "within his immediate control," construing that phrase to
mean the area from within which he might gain possession of a weapon
or destructible evidence. On the other hand, the court stated, there*

is no comparable justification for routinely searching any room other than that in which the arrest occurs, or for searching through all of the desk drawers or other closed or concealed areas in that room itself, such searches, in the absence of well-recognized exceptions, being permissible only under the authority of a warrant.

Authority for the statement is given in the footnotes as well as a reference to an annotation in volume 23 of the *Lawyers Edition, Second Series, United States Supreme Court Reports*, at page 966. Going to volume 23, we find an annotation "Constitutionality of searching premises without search warrant as incident to valid arrest—Supreme Court cases." One is fortunate in his research whenever such an annotation is found on his problem, for it reviews and comments upon all the existing court decisions to the date of the publication of the particular volume. Periodically, these annotations are updated by supplemental annotations appearing in later volumes. More recent court decisions and annotations on the same general subject may be located by referring to the topic "Searches and Seizures" in *Lawyers Edition Index to Annotations*, or the *American Law Reports Digests*.

Descriptive Word Index Method. The descriptive word index approach involves an examination of the facts and issues to ascertain the outstanding words or phrases, commonly called catchwords. The descriptive word indexes, which comprise either the first or the last volume or volumes of most digests, list the numerous catchwords in alphabetical order. When the word is located in the index, reference is made to a particular volume and page, section, or key number wherein the matter is treated.

The use of the descriptive word index can be demonstrated by searching the index in an attempt to find the law applicable to the following problem. A son questions the right of his father to consent to a warrantless search of his room for stolen goods. The precise question to be researched may be framed as follows: "May a parent consent to a warrantless search of his son's room?" Appropriate catchwords must be selected. It would seem that either *parent* or *search* would be appropriate. A good beginning place is the descriptive word index to the *Seventh Decennial Digest* of the *American Digest*. When searching for law, it is wise to start with the most recent materials available. It saves the researcher much time in the long run, for it is the most recent decision that prevails in the courts.

The catchword "Parent" is found in the "J–Z" volume of the Descriptive-Word Index at page 383, but the reference indicates that the proper word to see is "Infants." Looking then to the "A–I" volume of the Descriptive-Word Index under "Infants," we find "Search and seizures, consent given by parent. SEARCHES 7(27)." If we had started with the word "search" in the "J-Z" volume, we find at page 735, "Parent and child, consent. SEARCHES 7(27)." Thus, if either "parent or "search" had been selected, the researcher would have been referred to the topic "Searches and Seizures" key number 7(27). Under the American Digest System, the researcher can now select any one of the digests in that system and locate all court decisions that have been classified under the topic "Searches and Seizures" key number 7(27) in the particular jurisdiction, if the digest is a state digest, such as the *California Digest*, or for a particular period of time if the digest is one of the Decennial Digests.

In the *Seventh Decennial Digest* the topic "Searches and Seizures" key number 7(27) is found in volume 27. Because we know the key number, it is not necessary to search the analysis at the beginning of the topic. The researcher may proceed directly to the proper key number. At page 1107, we find a 1965 decision from the Eighth Circuit Court of Appeals digested, which indicates that a parent with whom the defendant was living could consent to police officers' entry and search of defendant's room. The decision of *Maxwell* v. *Stephens*, 348 F.2d 325 (C.A. Ark.), is cited. For more recent decisions, we must search each volume of the *Fourth General Digest* under the topic and key number "Searches and Seizures" key 7(27).

If we wish to limit our search to a particular state, we may search the digest for that state. For example, we wish to know how the state of California has decided this question. The Descriptive-Word Index to the *California Digest* refers us again to topic and key number "Searches and Seizures" key 7(27). Volume 39A of the *California Digest* contains this topic and key number. Reading the digested decisions under key 7(27), we find at least two digested decisions that deal with the question in our illustration in the pocket part supplement. Both decisions are in agreement on the point of law. The most recent decision cited is the 1971 decision, *People* v. *Daniels*, 16 Cal. App.3d 36, 93 Cal. Rptr. 628, which held that a mother who owned the home in which the defendant lived rent-free was authorized to consent to a search of the bedroom in which the defendant slept, notwithstanding that the defendant was an adult child and was in an adjacent room at the time of the search. Items found in such a search were admissible.

Unless the research must be limited to a particular state digest or a particular Decennial period, an exhaustive search would require the examination of the topic and key number in all the Decennial Digests in the American Digest System.

Table of Cases Method. If the names of the parties to a court decision and its approximate date are known, the volume and page where it is reported may be found by using the appropriate volume of the digest containing the Table of Cases. Even if the citation of the report is known, the Table of Cases may be used to locate the topics and key numbers in the digest where it has been summarized. This method is a common one for locating decisions similar to the specific one that may be known to the researcher; that is, checking the topic and key number where the known decision has been classified and then locating like or similar decisions.

Words and Phrases Search Method. If the objective of the researcher is to ascertain the court decisions construing or interpreting a particular word or phrase, such as, *arrest, criminal negligence, mens rea,* or *police officer,* the simplest and most effective method is to refer to the set of books entitled *Words and Phrases.* This set alphabetically lists words and phrases that have been the subject of judicial interpretation, and it summarizes the holding of each decision with complete citation.

Searching the Statutes and the Legal Periodicals

The preceding sections have demonstrated the use of the legal encyclopedias, *Corpus Juris Secundum* and *American Jurisprudence,* and the legal digests. The use of the *American Jurisprudence* encyclopedia also revealed a method of locating annotations in the *American Law Reports.* However, in all criminal law questions, research should begin with a careful check of the statutes of the particular state. The state statutes relating to criminal law and criminal procedure will ordinarily have been assembled together in several chapters. The sections included in each chapter are shown in numerical order at the beginning of the chapter, similar to the analysis at the beginning of a topic in the encyclopedias or the digests. However, the detailed index to the statutes is consulted in normal circumstances. Suppose we wish to determine what action constitutes a valid arrest in the state of Illinois. An examination of the index to *Illinois Annotated Statutes* under the heading "Arrest" discloses that arrest is covered generally by Chapter 38, section 107, and following sections, and that the method of arrest is specifically covered by Chapter 38, section 107–5. Turning to this section we find:

> *Method of Arrest*
> *(a) An arrest is made by an actual restraint of the person or by his submission to custody.*
> *(b) An arrest may be made on any day and at any time of the day or night.*
> *(c) An arrest may be made anywhere within the jurisdiction of this state.*
> *(d) All necessary and reasonable force may be used to effect an entry into any building or property or part thereof to make an authorized arrest. (Laws 1963, p. 2836, § 107–5, eff. Jan. 1, 1964.)*

Following this section, we find Code Committee Comments, a historical note, cross-references, law review commentaries, digest and encyclopedia references, and notes of decisions. Looking to the current pocket part supplement, we find there has been no change in the section, but that there are a number of recent decisions interpreting the section in light of specific fact situations.

Studying the Primary and Secondary Authorities

By the time you have reached this stage of your research, you should have a reasonably sound doctrinal basis for an answer to the question you are researching. Doctrinal basis implies an understanding of how the courts have dealt with your problem, and an evaluation of an appropriate selection of court opinions in terms of the courts' reasoning and the validity of their discussion of precedents. The legal encyclopedias and textbooks may have suggested criticisms and approaches at variance with the existing precedents. Whether or not this is your experience, the next step in your research should focus on a search for such criticism and commentaries. Available to you as a starting point of search are the many legal periodicals and law journals which deal with every conceivable aspect of law, its development, its applications, its shortcomings, and its future. You will start your search for relevant materials in these journals and periodicals through the *Index to Legal Periodicals.*

The *Index* was begun in 1908 and is published monthly. The monthly issues are cumulated into hard-bound annual volumes, which in turn cumulate into three-year volumes. The periodicals and journals indexed are covered in a single subject and author alphabet. There is a special section in the *Index*, which covers decisions which have been the subject of articles. Therefore, the same search approaches used with the digests and encyclopedias may be used with the *Index to Legal Periodicals*; that is, the subject or topic search or the case search. In addition, if one is interested in the writings of a particular author, he may locate articles by the name of the writer.

To illustrate the use of the *Index*, suppose we wish to read some current articles on "Entrapment." A search of a recent issue of the *Index* reveals a 1972 article in volume 37 of the *Missouri Law Review* at page 633 entitled "Entrapment: A Critical Discussion," which may be helpful. A further search of the cumulative volumes shows a number of relevant articles. Suppose we wish to round out our search on the *Chimel* case. In the "Table of Cases Commented Upon" in the 1970-1971 *Index to Legal Periodicals*, we find eight articles listed which discuss the significance of the decision on American criminal law.

Checking the Subsequent History of Cases and Statutes: "Shepardizing the Case"

A court decision or statute cannot be relied upon with confidence unless its subsequent status has been checked to determine whether the decision has been overruled or modified, or whether the statute has been amended or repealed. This decision involves the use of the proper volume of *Shepard's Citations*. A separate *Shepard's Citation* volume exists for each reporter in the National Reporter System. Thus, federal decisions and statutes are covered by the *Shepard's United States Citations*; decisions reported in the *Atlantic Reporter* are covered by the *Shepard's Atlantic Citations*. There is a separate *Shepard's Citations* volume for each state's reports as well. For example, the decisions and statutes of the state of Oregon are covered in *Shepard's Oregon Citations*.

To illustrate the use of *Shepard's Citations*, assume that we wish to check the current status and history of the 1972 decision of *Adams* v. *Williams* reported in 407 U.S. 143, dealing with the constitutionality of a stop-and-frisk arrest where the officer had been advised by an informant that the person sitting in a nearby auto was carrying narcotics and had a gun. Consulting the "Case Edition" of *Shepard's United States Citations*, we first locate the volume number of the decision; that is, volume 407. The upper outside corner of the *Shepard's* page indicates the volumes included on the page. Second, we examine the columns below the volume number for the boldface-type number, which indicates the initial page on which the *Adams* decision is reported, that is, 143. The citations following the boldface-type number 143 indicates where the *Adams* decision has been subsequently cited. Letter symbols precede some of the citations. These symbols set out the history and status of the decision. The key to the symbols is found in the front of every *Shepard's Citations* volume. On the page referring to the *Adams* decision the first two lines cite additional or parallel reporters where the *Adams* decision may be found. We find that the *Adams* decision is reported in volume 32 of the *Lawyer's Edition of the Supreme Court Reports, Second Series* at page 612, and in volume 92 of the *Supreme Court Reporter* at page 1921. The next three citations, preceded by the letter "s," we find are cites to previous decisions in a lower court of the same case. We also find that the next citation, preceded by the letters "cc," refers to a case different from the *Adams* decision, but a case arising out of the same subject matter. Such a case is usually called a "connected case." Other symbols tell us that the listed citations have either explained, followed, or attempted to distinguish the *Adams* decision. There is also a small superior number in the listed citations which corresponds to the number of the paragraph or the headnote of the *Adams* decision which the citing case discusses. We will also find that the *Adams* decision has been commented upon in volume 59 of the *American Bar Association Journal* at page 65. This use of *Shepard's Citations* ("Shepardizing"), established that the *Adams* decision has not been overruled or modified and that it is still good authority. However, if there is more than one volume in *Shepard's* unit, each volume and each supplement must be searched.

Shepard's Citations is used in the same manner when one is searching for decisions that have cited specific sections of statutes. *Shepard's* indicates every instance in which a particular statute or constitutional provision has been cited, applied, construed, or changed by subsequent legislation. The symbols used in the Statute Edition are somewhat different, but the key to them is found at the beginning of the particular volume.

Suggested Guide to a Search

The following list is offered to the student as a suggested guide to a search:

1. Analysis of the problem. Separate into aspects involved; including parties, procedure, and substantive issues.
2. Preliminary review of the subject matter. When needed for orientation, through encyclopedias, textbooks, restatements, and the like.
3. Search of statutes and administrative regulations involved.
   (a) Federal statutes.
   (b) Home state statutes.
   (c) Other state statutes.
   (d) Administrative rule and regulations implementing statutes.
4. Search for cases in point.
   (A) Cases and references cited by textbooks, encyclopedias, annotated statutes, and the like.
   (B) Additional cases in digests.
      (a) Through key numbers in Reporter cases read.
      (b) Analytical or topical approach.
      (c) Descriptive word index approach.
      (d) Table of cases approach.
      (e) Words and phrases approach.
   (C) Search the Annotated Reports System.
5. Search of treatises. To refresh memory, to supply additional background and analysis.
6. Search of indexes for legal periodicals. For more detailed analysis of theoretical and controversial points and for discussion of individual cases.
7. Completion of the search. Making certain that the latest editions and supplements have been searched.
8. Appraisal of the status of the authorities found. "Shepardizing" the cases and statutes.

Student Checklist

1. Can you determine the current law on electronic eavesdropping by a federal investigative agency?
2. Can you determine if *Terry* v. *Ohio,* 392 U.S. I, 88 S.Ct. 1868, 20 L.Ed.2d 889 (1968) has been modified or overruled, using *Shepard's Citations*?
3. Do you know how to find a case report using the National Reporter System given the citation?

4. Can you contrast the current law on entrapment in eight different states using a legal encyclopedia?

5. Using the American Digest System, can you find five leading cases related to search and seizure in your state?

6. Are you able to analyze a legal problem and to frame the legal question(s) involved?

7. Can you describe how statutory law, case law, common law, and administrative law mold, shape, and change the law?

8. Do you know how to locate a law review article?

9. Can you generally describe the circuits of the United States Court of Appeals?

10. Do you know who "makes" administrative law and how it is located in the Federal Register?

Topics for Discussion

1. Discuss the various "sources" of law.

2. Explain the structure of the National Reporter System.

3. Describe the procedure for determining the current law on the elements of burglary in your state reflecting both case and statutory law.

4. Detail the steps for using the *Lawyers Edition Index to Annotations*.

5. Explain how to use *Shepard's Citations*.

Glossary

Perhaps the fastest way to gain a general knowledge of a particular profession is to acquire an understanding of the terminology used. The criminal justice system uses many unique words and phrases in carrying out its duties. Many of the most frequently used terms will be defined in this terminology guide. It must be emphasized that the definitions presented here are not intended to be complete interpretations of the words. For a complete explanation, consult a law dictionary or a textbook on criminal justice terminology.

Notations

Abet
To encourage or advise another
to commit a crime.

Accessory
One who aids or conceals the perpetrator of a crime
so that he may avoid arrest or
punishment.

Acquit
To find a person not guilty
of the crime charged.

Administrative Law
That branch of public law that deals with the various
agencies of government prescribing in detail the
manner of their activity. Several aspects of
administrative law involve criminal sanctions and
regulate several segments of the administration of
criminal justice.

Admission
A statement by a defendant tending
to prove his guilt. Not a complete
confession.

381

Adultery
Sexual intercourse by a married person
with one who is not a wife or
husband.

Affidavit
A written statement made under oath.

Alibi
The defense that the accused was in some
place other than that where the crime
was committed.

Appeal
The transfer of a case to a higher court,
in which it is asked that the decision
of the lower court be altered or reversed.

Appellate Court
A court that decides appeals from
lower courts.

Arraignment
A court proceeding in which the defendant
is informed of the charge against him and
advised of his constitutional rights, and
at which he may enter a plea or deposit
bail.

Arrest
Detaining a person in a manner authorized
by law, so that he may be brought before a
court to answer charges of having committed
a crime. Both peace officers and private
persons may make arrests.

Arson
Willful burning of property.

Assault
An unlawful *attempt* to hurt another
person physically. If the person is
actually struck, the act is called
"battery."

Attempt
A criminal offense requiring (1) an act toward a
punishable offense (2) that is capable of completion
(3) and coming close to completion, but (4) must
not succeed.

Bail
Security in the form of cash or bond,
deposited with a court as a guarantee
that the defendant, if released, will
return to court at the time designated
to stand trial.

Battery
The unlawful use of force or violence
against a person without his consent.

Blackmail
The extortion of money from a person
through threats of accusation or
exposure of an unfavorable nature.

Bribery
The offering or accepting of any undue
reward to or by a public official in
order to influence his official actions.

Brief
A summary of the law pertaining to a case,
prepared by the attorneys for submission
to the judge.

Burglary
The crime of entering a building with the
intent to steal or to commit some felony. Not
to be confused with robbery, which is a
theft from the immediate presence of the
victim through force or fear. In burglary,
the victim is seldom present at the time.

Capital Crime
A crime punishable by death.

Caption and Asportation
Generally, to prosecute for theft, it is
necessary that both taking (*caption*) and
carrying away (*asportation*) be proved.

Certiorari (Writ of)
An order by a higher court to a lower court
directing that a case be transferred
to the higher court for review or trial.

Change of Venue
A change of the place of trial in
a criminal or civil proceeding.

Circumstantial Evidence
Evidence tending to prove a fact through
a logical association of other facts,
but without an actual witness to the
act to be proven.

Citation
A formal summons issued by a court
or peace officer directing a person to
appear before the court for some official
action. Popularly referred to as a
ticket.

Civil Action
A law suit to recover damages or to correct
some wrong between two parties. Does not
usually involve a crime and is apart from
a criminal action. A person may be
convicted in a criminal court and also
sued in a civil court for the same act. For
example, a drunk driver may be sentenced
to jail in a criminal proceeding and then
sued in civil action by the owner of a car
damaged by the drunk driver.

Commitment
An official court order directing that
a person be taken to a jail, prison,
hospital, or other location (usually
a place of confinement).

Common Law
The basic, unwritten concepts of English
and American law. In many states there
are no so-called common law crimes.

For an act to be a crime, there
must be a specific, written statute so
declaring it.

Complaint
The formal accusation of crime presented
to the court, which acts as the formal
commencement of a criminal prosecution.

Compounding a Crime
The unlawful act of accepting money
or other reward for agreeing to refrain
from prosecuting a crime, either by concealing
it from the authorities or withholding
evidence.

Compromising a Crime (misdemeanors only)
The proceeding, in some states, by
a court whereby a person charged with a
misdemeanor may be discharged without
prosecution upon payment of damages to
the party injured.

Confidential Communication
Communications between a person and his
attorney or clergyman or between a
husband and wife that may be legally
concealed in court testimony.

Conspiracy
A secret combination or agreement
between two or more persons to
commit a criminal act.

Contempt of Court
Disobedience to the court by acting in
opposition to the authority, justice, or
dignity thereof. Punishable as a crime.

Corpus Delicti
Establishing that a crime has, in fact, been committed.

Criminal Procedure
The method prescribed by law for the
apprehension, prosecution, and
determination of punishment of persons
who have committed crimes.

Criminology
The science that deals with crimes, their
causes, and their prevention and punishment.

Degree
Some offenses are defined by degrees; such as
first degree homicide, second degree, and so forth. By
using degrees, provisions may be made for varying
the elements required, varying the punishment, or
recognizing that some acts constituting the
offense are less serious than others.

Deposition
The written testimony of a person who
(for some reason) cannot be present at
the trial.

Embezzlement
The crime of stealing property or money
that has been entrusted to one's care.

Evidence
Testimony, physical objects, documents,
or any other means used to prove the
truth of a fact at issue in a court
proceeding.

Extortion
Similar to blackmail.

Felony
In most states, a crime punishable by death
or imprisonment in the state prison. All
other crimes are called misdemeanors.

Fence
A person who makes a business of purchasing
or receiving stolen goods from criminals.

Forgery
Any of several crimes pertaining to the
false making or alteration of any
document with intent to defraud.

Fugitive
One who has fled from punishment or
prosecution.

Grand Jury
A group of men and women whose duty it is
to make inquiries and return recommendations
regarding the operation of local government.
They also receive and hear complaints in
criminal cases, and if they find them

sustained by evidence, they present an indictment
against the person charged. It is called a
grand jury because it is usually composed
of a greater number of jurors than a
regular trial jury.

Habeas Corpus (Writ of)
A court order directing that a person who
is in custody be brought before a court
in order that an examination may be
conducted to determine the legality of
the confinement.

Habitual Criminal
Many states have statutes providing that
a person convicted a certain number of
times may be declared an habitual criminal
and is therefore unsuited for attempts for
rehabilitation. A person so declared may
then be sentenced to life imprisonment for
the protection of society.

Homicide
The killing of a human being by
another human being.

Inchoate Crime
An incompletely formed crime that is in itself a crime;
such as conspiracy.

Indictment
An accusation in writing, presented by the
grand jury, charging a person with a crime.

Information
An accusation in writing, presented by
a prosecuting official (that is, district
attorney, city attorney, or an equivalent
official), charging an individual with a crime.

Injunction
A court order whereby a person is ordered
to do, or is restrained from doing, a particular
thing. Not enforced by the police without an
additional court order to that effect.

Inquest
An inquiry with a jury conducted by a
coroner to establish the cause of death.

Intent
In general, there must be a concurrence
between a person's acts and his intentions
in order to constitute a crime. A person
cannot be convicted of a crime if he
committed the act involuntarily, without
intending injury. If a person acts
negligently, however, without regard for the
rights of other people, his action is sufficient
in itself to establish criminal intent. Thus,
the drag racer who kills an innocent party
may be convicted of manslaughter even though
he did not intend the death or injury of
anyone.

Jail
A place of confinement maintained by a
local authority, usually for persons
convicted of misdemeanors or awaiting trial.

The terms apply prison or penitentiary to
such institutions operated by the state
or federal government, usually for more
serious offenses.

Jurisprudence
The science and philosophy of law
in social control.

Kleptomania
An abnormal desire to steal.

Larceny
Same as theft. The unlawful taking of the
property of another; divided into grand theft
and petty theft. Grand theft includes the
taking of money or goods in excess of an amount
fixed by law, usually $50 to $200; and the theft
of any item from the immediate possession of another
without force or threat of force. All other theft
is considered petty theft.

Libel
The circulation of written matter that tends
to discredit or to injure the character of another.
It is not necessary that the material be false.
The prime consideration is the motive under
which it was issued. Slander is of the same
nature except that it is verbal rather than written.
Note: There are few criminal prosecutions for
libel or slander, which have generally become
civil matters.

Limitations, Statute of
The statutory time limit within which a
criminal prosecution must be begun. For

felonies, this is usually three years
from the date the crime was committed. For
misdemeanors it is one year. There are some
crimes that have a longer time limit and a
few, such as murder, that have no time limit.

Maim
The crime of willfully disfiguring another.

Mala in Se and **Mala Prohibita**
A basic grouping of crimes according to the
nature of the act. *Mala in se* means "bad in
itself" and refers to those crimes, such as
murder, robbery, and rape, that are deemed
to be wrong in almost all civilized societies.
Mala prohibita means "bad by prohibition" and
refers to those offenses, such as building and
safety regulations and certain traffic violations, that are established by statute for the
public convenience and that are not immoral
or bad in themselves.

Mandamus (Writ of)
An order issued by a court, directed to a
government agency or to a lower court,
commanding the performance of a particular
act.

Mann Act
The federal statute relating to the
interstate transportation of females
for immoral purposes.

Manslaughter
The unlawful killing of a human being

without premeditation or intent to
take life.

Mens Rea
A guilty mind or wrongful purpose;
a criminal intent.

Misdemeanor
A crime punishable by other than
imprisonment in the state prison.

Modus Operandi
Literally, method of operation. Refers to
the habit of criminals to continue to pursue
a particular method of committing their
crimes. Through study of a criminal's
habits, or *modus operandi*, it is possible
to link several crimes committed by the
same person and even to determine where
he can be expected to commit his next
crime.

Murder
The unlawful, deliberate, premeditated
killing of a human being. It is not
required that the premeditation be of any
specific length of time. The instant of
time necessary to form a specific intent
to kill is sufficient.

Norm
A standard or average for a given group
of persons, such as the adults of a particular

city. Laws are, in effect, an approximation of
social norms at the time of the passage of the law.

Oath

Any form of attestation by which a person
signifies that he is bound to perform a
certain act truthfully and honestly. A
person making a false statement while
under oath to tell the truth may be
prosecuted for perjury.

Peace Officer

General term used to designate a member
of any of the several agencies engaged
in law enforcement.

Penal Code

A collection of statutes relating to crimes,
punishment, and criminal procedures. This
is the portion of the law most frequently
used by police officers.

Perjury

The crime of knowingly giving false
testimony in a judicial proceeding
while under oath to tell the truth.
Subornation of perjury is the crime of
procuring or influencing someone else
to commit perjury.

Posse Comitatus

The authority of the sheriff to assemble
all able-bodied male inhabitants of the
county to assist in capturing a criminal,

keeping the peace, or otherwise defending the county. Refusal to obey the summons is a criminal offense.

Precedent
A parallel court case in the past, the decision of which may be used as an example to follow in deciding a present case.

Prima Facie
"On its face" or "at first view." Refers to evidence that, at first appearance, seems to establish a particular fact, but that may be later contradicted by other evidence.

Principal
A person concerned in the commission of a crime, whether he directly commits the offense or aids in its commission. All principals to a crime are equally guilty; therefore, the driver who waits in the getaway car during a robbery is as equally guilty of murder as the accomplice inside the building who fires the fatal shot.

Private Person's Arrest
The authority granted to a private party to make an arrest under certain conditions. Sometimes referred to as a "citizen's arrest," although it is not limited only to citizens.

Proof
The establishment of a fact by evidence.

Prostitute
A woman who engages in sexual relations
for hire.

Pyromania
An unnatural, overpowering attraction to
fire.

Rape
Unlawful sexual intercourse with a woman
against her will, usually accomplished by
physical violence, but may be committed when
the woman is drunk, unconscious, feeble-
minded, or otherwise unable to resist.
Statutory rape is when the female is under
the age of 18, even though giving her
consent to the act.

Res Gestae (things done)
Facts and circumstances
surrounding a particular act. Refers
particularly to acts or exclamations
overheard by a third party, which would
be inadmissible in court under normal
rules of evidence but which, because
they occurred at the moment of the
particular act in question, are
admissible under the rules of *res
gestae* evidence.

Resisting an Officer
Any person resisting, delaying, or obstructing a public officer in the discharge of his duties is guilty of a misdemeanor.

Robbery
The unlawful taking of personal property in the possession of another, from his person or immediate presence, against his will, accomplished by use of force or fear.

Seduction
The offense of inducing a woman to engage in sexual relations under a false promise of marriage.

Social Control
A conglomerate of social and political institutions' efforts to keep individual and group behavior within certain limitations as generally prescribed by law and augmented by informal recognition of social norms.

Statute Law
A written law enacted and established by the legislative department of a government.

Stipulation
An agreement between opposing attorneys relating to certain portions of a case. Usually refers to minor points in a case which are accepted without demanding proof in order to shorten the time of trial.

Testimony
Oral evidence given by a witness under
oath.

Theft (*See* **Larceny.**)

Tort
A civil wrong; an invasion of the civil
rights of an individual.

Trial
That step in the course of a judicial proceeding which determines the facts. A
judicial examination in a court of justice.
May be held before a judge and jury, or before a
judge alone.

Waive
To surrender or to renounce some privilege
or right.

Warrant
A written order from a court or other
competent authority, directed to a peace
officer or other official, ordering the
performance of a particular act and
affording the civil protection for the
person executing the order. Examples
are a warrant of arrest and a search
warrant.

Witness
A person who has factual knowledge of a
matter. One who testifies under oath.

Case Index

Subject Index

401

in legal systems of world compared, 36, 37, 42, 43
for juveniles, 277, 278, 286
more than once, doctrine of double jeopardy and, 207
rights of the accused and, 31, 106, 212, 217, 218
Coroner, 190
Corpus delicti, 72-73, 158, 387; *see also* Criminal law, principles of
Corrections, 83, 263, 264, 331, 335
administration of, 264
collective bargaining in, 330, 331
community-based, 341
correctional officials, role of, 15, 265
security problems for, 99, 268, 269, 270, 271
discretion in, *see* Discretion
functions of, 11, 12, 13, 14-15
impact of court decisions on, 318, 319, 321
juvenile, 278, 285, 286, 290, 293-294; *see also* Juvenile courts
legal systems of world compared, 35, 36 42-44
theory of crime and punishment, 10, 42, 266, 309
see also Prisons; Prisoners
Corruption, 3, 75, 175, 176
Counsel, court appointed, 23, 284
defense, 165
French state, 38
for indigent defendants, 19, 23
private, reliance upon advice of, mistake of law, 212
right to assistance of, 18, 22, 23, 31, 32
civil law system of, 36
for juveniles, 284, 287, 288, 289, 291, 292
prisoner's right to, 264, 267, 268, 269, 270, 321
Sixth Amendment's guarantee of, 269
Counterfeiting, 128, 129-130, 177
Courts, 4, 13, 113, 124, 188, 277, 326, 330
of appeals, 294, 327
appellate, 193, 208, 382
juvenile, 285, 293
changing attitudes toward, adjudicating issues, 317, 318, 319, 320, 321, 322, 326
intervention in management of correctional facilities, 263, 264, 265, 266, 267, 268, 269, 270, 271
civil, 42, 81, 118, 246, 247
criminal, 41, 43, 81, 118, 249
criticisms of, 319, 321
discretionary power of, *see* Discretion, of court
family, 279
federal, 264, 320, 321
powers of, contempt power of, 329, 330, 387
limited by Constitution, 63, 64
reviewing powers of, 323, 326
role of in society, 56, 57, 328
interpretations of narcotic legislations, 163, 164
in law enforcement discretion, 81, 90, 188, 196, 197, 198, 210, 212, 213, 224, 269, 342, 344

state, 19, 264
systems of the world, compared, 35, 38, 40, 41, 42, 59
trial, 36, 38, 39, 207
see also Juvenile courts
Court appearances, 341
Crime, 31, 72, 73, 83, 190, 250
capital, 90, 175, 189, 384
causes of, 9, 11, 310
classification of, *see* Offenses, classifications of
common law, *see* Common law
definitions of, 4, 7, 23, 31, 50, 58, 64, 66, 67, 73, 81, 82, 178, 237, 246, 248
need for new, 325, 343, 346
see also Offenses, definitions of
degrees of, *see* Offenses, degrees of
element of, *see* Offenses of, elements of
fighting, 21, 215
without intent, 74, 75; *see also* Intent
narcotics related, 162; *see also* Narcotics
against nature, 93, 94, 105, 171
organized, 198
parties to, 185, 199, 216
see also Accessory; Principals
petty, 37
prevention of, 8, 9, 83, 84, 189, 194, 251
effects of privileges on, 221
see also Self-defense
significance of location and time on, 223, 225, 231, 233, 234, 239, 240
and punishment, 8-10, 14
rate, and blacks, 310
repetition of, 284
reporting problems of, 4, 13, 170, 239, 257, 339
scene of, 188, 223
against the state, 104, 174
of status, 164, 166, 167, 173
statutory, 137
substantive, 61, 71, 177, 178, 197, 198
upper-class, 310
without victims, 80, 81, 234, 235, 236
violent, 42, 255
see also Juvenile delinquency; Offenses; Victimization; and Victim
Criminal acts, *see* Acts, criminal
Criminal code, 7, 8, 40, 175, 205
accessory, 189
comprehensive, 62, 63, 64, 65, 66
European, 42
federal, 65, 177, 178
state, 191, 192
Criminal courts, *see* Courts, criminal
Criminality, citizen defenses against, 242, 249
Criminalization, 144, 179
of disorderly conduct, 172, 173
of narcotic addiction, social stigma of, 164, 165
see also Narcotics
of status, alcoholics, 167
of vagrancy offense, 173
Criminal justice system, 4, 67, 85, 194, 229, 339
adjudication, 11, 13-14
components of, 335, 337, 341

Deterrence, 144, 162, 219
theory of crime and punishment, 10, 84, 100
Diminished capacity, doctrine of, 193, 203, 204, 208
Discretion, in administration of justice, 44, 49, 50, 67
in early legal history, 62, 63
by criminal justice personnel, 12, 13, 14
correctional, 271, 341
of court, 109, 122, 148, 149, 150, 151
juvenile, 290, 294
legal rights of prisoners, 265, 266
in sentencing, 103, 294
definition of, 11, 335, 336, 337, 338
in Japanese system of law, 37, 38
of judges, 14, 17, 41, 205
police exercise of, 12, 13, 170, 173, 322-327, 336, 337, 338, 341-345
in arrest of juveniles, 281, 286, 287, 288
denying use of by law enforcement agencies, 337
implementing rule-making procedures, 345, 348
need for, 338-341
need for policies and guidelines, 323, 324, 325, 339, 341, 342, 348
prosecutorial, 13, 14, 38
statutory authority of, 36, 37, 339
Discrimination, racial, 319, 320
Disorder, public, 171, 172, 173
Disposition, 34, 37, 198, 209
juvenile disposition hearing, 284, 285, 293
District attorney, see Attorneys
Divorce, 170, 171
Domestic relations, impact of on crime, 95, 166, 279, 341
Dossier, 34, 35, 38
Double jeopardy, doctrine of, 32, 207
Driving, under influence of alcohol, juvenile delinquency and, 281
Drugs, 4, 15, 193
addiction to, crime classification of, 235, 280
advertising of, health and safety code violations of, 178
intoxication as defense to crime, 168, 205, 206
traffic, eradication of, 163, 164, 165
see also Narcotics
treatment programs, 342
Drunkenness, law enforcement of, 168, 235, 236; see also Alcoholism; Intoxication
Due process of law, 16-17, 18, 19, 23, 31, 85, 284, 318
in juvenile courts, lack of, 285, 287, 289
prison due process, 263, 264, 265, 267
procedural, 16, 17, 19, 263, 264
substantive, 16, 19, 263
under Soviet system of law, 32
Duress, defense of, 77, 206, 218, 219; see also Coercion
Durham Rule, 208; see also Insanity
Dwelling, 118, 134, 149, 178
of another, 149, 150, 151, 157
breaking and entering into, 139, 142, 143, 144, 145, 147
burning of, 153, 154, 155, 156

see also Arson
use of force in defense of, 222
see also Offenses, against property; Property

Eighth Amendment to the Constitution, 164, 166, 265, 267, 321
Embezzlement, 125, 126, 127, 310
defined, 124, 387
Entrapment, defense of, 214-216
Equal justice for all, 3, 4, 52, 303, 309, 311-313, 318, 326, 343, 348
concept of, 12, 16, 18
juvenile, 294
Equal Rights Bill, 268
Ethnic groups, crime victimization and, see Victim; Victimization
European law, 28, 29, 36, 40, 42; see also Civil law; Legal systems
Euthanasia, 237
Evidence, 19, 22, 36, 206, 215, 216, 223, 339, 388
altering, accessory after the fact, 190
circumstantial, 119, 205
examination of, in France, 34, 36
hearsay, 40
illegally obtained, 17, 20, 41, 268, 269
inadmissible, 203
physical, 39
presented at parole hearings, 264
presented at trials, 13, 14, 32, 33, 38, 39
prima facie, 168
privileged, immunity doctrine and, 224
rules of, 20, 39, 40, 130
corpus delicti, 72, 73
ex post facto laws and, 217, 218
search for, 33, 60
sufficiency of, 39, 196
see also Exclusionary rule of evidence
Evidentiary privileges, 40
Exclusionary rule of evidence, 17, 18, 20, 21
of legal systems of the world, compared, 39, 40, 41
testimonial, 40
see also Self-incrimination
Exculpation, 188
Excuse of justification, see Justification
Ex posto facto laws, 32, 53, 217, 218
Extenuating circumstances, 339
Extortion, 122-124, 388

False arrest, 111, 246
False imprisonment, 111-112
False pretenses, entering under, 145, 146
obtaining property by, 120, 127, 128; see also Forgery
principals in the first degree, 186, 187
Family courts, 279
Federal Bureau of Investigation, 177
Federal civil rights law, 177
Federal conspiracy, 178
Federal criminal code, 65, 177, 178; see also Criminal code
Federal criminal sanctions, 112
Federal District Court, 320, 321
Federal narcotic legislation, 162; see also Narcotics

Federal rule of exclusion, 20
Felony, 15, 23, 104, 152, 244, 245, 246, 283, 292, 388
  accessories to, 188, 189, 190
  crime classifications of, 61, 90, 119, 122, 133, 153, 156
    burglary, 139, 147, 149, 152, 153
    kidnapping as, under statutes, 112
    theft of property, 120, 124
  felons, 93, 142, 189, 190, 221, 241
    convicted, weapons control of, 180
  felony-murder rule, 76, 92, 93, 94, 96, 204
  guilty of, 103, 168, 191, 192, 222
  intent to commit, 98, 204
    breaking and entering with, 142, 143, 144, 151
    intoxication and, 205, 206
    see also Intent
  principals to, 185, 186, 187, 190
  statute of limitations and, 225
  suicide as, 96
  victims of, 244
  weapons control and, 180
"Fencing," 132, 388; see also Stealing
Fifth Amendment to the Constitution, rights provided under, 18, 21, 22, 40, 263, 317
  U.S. Supreme Court interpretation of, 19, 23
Fines, 6, 8, 167, 168, 174, 179, 246, 248, 249, 250
  monetary, 67
  for offenses against persons, 98, 100, 105
  for offenses against property, 121, 133, 134, 139, 149, 153
  for sex offenses, 105, 106, 108, 109
  Soviet system of, 43
Fingerprints, 190, 291
Firearms, legislation to control use of, 179, 180, 196
First Amendment to the Constitution, rights provided under, 199, 268, 269, 270, 271
Fish and games laws, 179
Folkways, observation of, 5, 6, 8, 10; see also Norms
Force, application of, in breaking and entering, 144, 145
  legal, 236, 243-246
  legal definition of, 266
  threat of, 77, 113, 121, 122, 210
  use of, against the confined, justification for, 266-267
    deadly, 220, 221, 243, 244, 245, 246, 267
    proof of, 102, 103, 104, 206
    reasonable amount of, 243, 244, 266, 267
    rules for, 246
    in self-defense, 220, 222
Forgery, 120, 128-129, 388
Former jeopardy, see Double jeopardy
Fornication, 107, 108, 169
Fourteenth Amendment, due process clause under, 18, 19, 20, 23, 263, 284, 317
  exclusionary rule of evidence and, 20
  prisoner's rights provided under, 268
Fourth Amendment to the Constitution, 18, 19, 20, 21, 267

U. S. Supreme Court interpretation of, 19, 23
Fraud, 125, 126, 127, 128, 233, 234, 246
  breaking and entering through, 145, 149
  mail, 177
  types of, 206, 210, 211
  victims, of, 239
Freedom, 23, 44, 51, 309
  of press, 269, 270
  right to, 305, 310, 311
  of speech, 55, 199, 269, 270, 271
French civil law, 28, 29, 33, 34, 38, 39, 43; see also Civil law; Legal systems
Fugitive, 190, 287, 388

Gambling, 173, 177, 197
  crime classification of, 13, 235, 236
Games, unlawful, 173
Gault decision, 289
German system of law, 42, 43
Government, authority and power of, 31, 50, 51, 52, 53, 54, 177, 215, 248
  civil, 53, 54
  function of, 55, 60, 168, 178, 306, 308, 310, 311, 317, 326
  legal systems and, worldwide compared, 27, 29, 30, 31, 35
  power of, abuse of, 312
    in criminal proceedings, 6-7, 8, 10, 11, 223, 224
    penal institutions as extension of, 54, 63, 263, 303, 305, 311
  "social contract" theory of law and, 53
Graft, 310
Grand jury, 9, 33, 35, 388
Grand larceny, 121
Grand theft, 130; see also Theft
Guardians, juvenile, 279, 280
Guilt of crime, 17, 18, 21, 53, 66, 76, 95, 98, 185, 187, 189
  confession, impact of, 72, 214
  determination of, 13, 38-41, 170, 203, 205
  "guilty mind," see Criminal law, principles of
  plea of, 14, 37; see also Plea bargaining
Gun, 180, 219, 238; see also Weapons
Gun Control Act, 180

Habeas corpus, 32, 294, 389
Habitation and occupancy, offenses against, 137, 146, 147, 148, 149, 150, 151, 153, 154, 157; see also Arson; Breaking and entering; and Trespass
"Hands-off" doctrine, 263, 267
  abrogation of by courts, 317, 319, 320, 321
Hard labor, punishment of rape offenses, 103
Harrison Act, 162; see also Narcotics, legislation to control use of
Health and safety code violations, 162, 166, 178, 179
Hearings, juvenile court, see Juvenile courts, hearings
Hearsay evidence, 40
Heroin, sale of, 195; see also Drugs; Narcotics
Hijackings, airplane, 7, 8
Hindering persecution, 190; see also Accessory, after the fact
Hobbes, Thomas, view of law as command of

Investigations, criminal, 22, 90, 177, 178
Irresistible impulse test, 209
Isolation, theory of crime and punishment, 10
Israeli courts system, 41
Italy, legal system in, 42, 43

Jails, *see* Prison
Japanese system of law, 37, 38, 41
Judge, 17, 65, 170, 248, 305, 336
 discretionary power of, *see* Discretion
 functions and power of in criminal justice system, 11, 12, 13, 14, 17
  in evolution of common law, 28, 59, 60,
   61, 64
  in issuance of search warrant, 20
  in legal systems of world, compared, 30,
   32, 33, 38, 43
  in sentencing, 43, 103, 205
  juvenile court, broad powers of, 278, 280,
   283, 285, 287, 290
Judicial process, 33, 175
Judicial system, 165, 174, 175, 305, 306
Judiciary, 30, 38, 327
 in civil law systems, 33, 35
 in common law system, 28
 role of, in discovery of law, 63, 66
Jurisdiction, 18, 64, 66, 90, 91, 101, 102, 130,
   156, 162, 164, 167, 170, 179, 206, 244,
   256, 326, 330, 337
 civil law, 44
 common law, 28, 40, 41
 criminal statutes, 138, 139, 140, 142, 143,
   146, 147, 149, 151, 153, 194, 208, 209,
   224, 225
 federal, 65, 177, 178
 over juvenile courts, 277, 278, 279, 280, 282,
   283, 284, 289, 293
 state, 191, 193, 196, 197, 198
Jurisprudence, 21, 44, 207, 306, 317
 analytical and historical, 55, 56, 306, 307,
   312
 basic methods of, 305-307, 308
 concept of, 305, 309, 391
 justice concepts and law, relationship between, 300
 philosophical approach to, 307, 312
 sociological approaches to, 56, 307
Jurists, legal, 53, 305, 306, 308; *see also* Jurisprudence
Jury, 3, 17, 38, 83, 170, 388
 grand jury, 9, 33, 35
 role of, in criminal proceedings, 103, 119,
   148, 223
 in legal systems of the world, compared, 30
Justice, administration of, 11, 12, 35, 49, 50,
   300, 302, 305, 337; *see also* Jurisprudence; Social ordering
 concepts of, 41, 301, 302, 304, 309, 313, 342
  as expressed by due process of law, 85
  jurisprudence, law and, relationship between, 300
  "justice as fairness" concept, 311, 312, 313
 equal, *see* Equal justice for all
 obstructing, 190, 191
 retributive, 27
 theories of, 299, 300

application of in legal procedures, 307, 311,
   313
 theory versus practice, 308-311
 jurisprudence and, 305-307
 natural law theory, principles of, 303-304,
   305, 308, 309, 311
 positive law theory, characteristics of, 301-
   302, 304, 306
 social good theory, characteristics of, 302-
   303, 304, 305, 308, 309, 311
 see also Criminal justice
Justices, of U.S. Supreme Court, 19, 129, 167
Justification and excuse, 75
 for commission of battery, 99
 for committing criminal act, religious beliefs
  and, 224
 homicide with, 91, 92, 93, 94, 95, 96; *see also*
  Manslaughter
 homicide without, 91, 92, 94; *see also* Murder
 legal, malice and, 157, 204
Juvenile courts, 43, 44, 336, 339
 adjudication, 285, 286, 289-293, 294
 appeal procedures, 293, 294
 criticism of, 282, 283, 284, 290, 292
 hearings, 281, 284, 285
 law, corrections, 285, 286, 293-294
  due process in, 282, 284, 285, 287
  enforcement of, 285, 286-289
  history and philosophy of, 277-280, 281-
   285
  procedural safeguards for, 283, 284, 285,
   289
  statutory law, 287
  substantive, of juvenile deviancy, 285-294
 movement, goal of, 278, 279, 290
 organization forms of, 279, 285, 286
 probation for, 278, 279, 283, 289, 290, 293,
   294
 social work agency concept of, versus legal
  judicial agency, 282, 284, 289
Juvenile delinquency, definitions of, 280, 281,
   286, 291
 incorrigible, 280, 282
 jurisdiction over, 277, 278, 279, 282
 juvenile delinquents, 37, 278, 279, 281, 283,
   284, 287, 330
 law enforcement of, 282, 285, 286-289

Kidnapping, 65, 93, 94, 112, 113, 177, 192,
   257
 aggravated, 113
 defined, 112
Koran, social ordering objectives of law in, 30

Labor movement in law enforcement, *see* Collective bargaining
Land, 133, 139, 140, 141, 142; *see also* Property
Larceny, 123, 127, 131, 211, 230, 231, 232,
   233, 236, 257, 391
 common law, 119-122, 130
 and embezzlement, difference between, 124,
   125, 126
 grand, 121
 intent to commit, 119, 120, 144, 152, 196
 from persons, 121-122

involuntary, 78, 91, 95, 96
voluntary, elements of, 91, 94, 95
Manual, police, 341, 343, 346
Marriage, 104, 105, 113, 114, 170
Masturbation, crime classification of, 235
Mayhem, 100, 248; see also Battery
Media, news, publicity of juvenile delinquency in, 290
Medical treatment, 265, 266
Menace, 220
Mens rea, 66, 277, 393
    actus reus and, relationship between, 76
    concept of, 71, 72, 73-76; see also Criminal law, principles of
    proof of, 79, 80
    see also Intent
Mental health agencies, 14, 42
Mental state, 186, 211, 213
    existence of, mistake of fact and, 213, 214
    mental capacity, existence of, 77, 103, 104, 203, 205, 206
    mental illness, insanity defense and, 208, 237, 291, 292
    proof of, criminal offenses and, 75, 191, 192, 194, 213
Mercy, jury recommended, 103, 113
Methodology of law, 353-380
Middle-class delinquency, 310
Minority, injustices forced upon, 41, 239, 309, 312; see also Injustices
Minors, 174, 180, 236, 279, 286
    alcohol, prohibitions for use of, 167, 213
    common law rules for criminal prosecution of, 277
    legal counsel for, 287, 288
    see also Age; Juvenile courts
Miranda warning, 22, 287, 288
    in West German system of law, 34, 41
Misappropriation, prohibition of, 133
Miscarriage, 105, 106, 107; see also Abortion
Mischief, malicious, 133, 141, 277
Misdemeanor, 15, 23, 104, 139, 141, 142, 144, 167, 168, 189, 191, 225
    arrest for, 245
    Class A, 120, 124, 133
    common law, 112, 122, 172, 173
    ,crime classifications of, 61, 90, 96, 153
    criminal intent, 144, 147, 149, 152, 153
    juvenile law, 287
Misfeasance, 338
Mistake, 119, 221
    of fact, lawful defense of, 206, 212-214
    of law, 211, 212
Mistrial, doctrine of former jeopardy and, 207
Mitigation, 187, 204
M'Naghten Rule, 208, 209
Model Penal Code, 65, 191, 193, 199, 209
Montesquieu, contribution to system of law, 54, 303, 311
Morality, offenses against, 55, 90, 168-171
Mores, observation of, 5, 6, 8, 10; see also Norms
Motive, for criminal offense, 76, 204, 205, 234, 239
Mugging, 215, 251
Murder, 42, 72, 95, 186, 205, 310

accessory principles, 96, 97, 190
definition of, 75, 91, 393
degrees of criminal offense for, 92, 93, 94, 156, 242
intent elements of, 76, 80, 82, 91, 92, 93
locations, significance of, 233, 234
self-assisting commission of, 94
statute of limitations and, 225
    see also Suicide

Narcotics, 161-166
    addiction, 177, 215
        changing concepts of, 164-165
    legislation to control use of, 161, 162-164, 166, 193, 197, 281
National Advisory Commission on Criminal Justice Standards and Goals, 337
National Conference of Commissioners on Uniform State Laws, 65
National Firearms Act of 1934, 180
National Opinion Research Center (NORC), 230, 231, 232, 257
Natural law theory of justice, 303-304, 305, 307, 308, 309, 312; see also Justice, theories of
Natural rights, justice and, 301, 302, 303
    Lockian theory of, 303, 304
Nature, crime against, 93, 94, 105, 171
Necessity, defenses of, 77
Negligence, criminal, criminal liability of, 73, 75, 80, 247
    death resulted from, 91, 95, 96
    defined, 78, 79
    lack of malice in, 157, 213
News media, 268, 269, 319
Nighttime, significance of, in occurrence of crime, 233, 234; see also Victim; Victimization
Nonfeasance, 338
NORC survey, *see* National Opinion Research Center
Norms, conformity to societal, 5, 8, 9, 10, 11, 12, 15
    definition of, 393
Nulla poena sine lege, 85
Nullem crimen sine lege, nulla ponna sine lege, 66

Oath, 174, 175, 396
Obscenity, offenses of, 171, 177, 280, 284
Obstruction of justice, 190, 191
Obtaining of property, offenses of, 120, 126, 127, 128; see also Embezzlement; theft
Occupancy, offenses against, 156, 157; see also Arson; Breaking and entering; Burglary; Habitation and occupancy; and Trespass
Offenses, classifications of, basis of, 54, 61, 73, 89-91, 129, 225
    "tort" and, distinction between, 60, 61, 62
    definition of, 89, 210; see also Crime, definition of
    degrees of, broken down by statute into, 137, 138, 143, 153, 242
    elements of, 204, 205, 211
    intent element of, 73, 74, 75, 77, 79, 80; see also Intent

miscellaneous, 75, 161-181
against morality, 168, 169, 170; *see also* Morality
against persons, 89, 90, 143, 153, 154, 241, 242
  abduction, 113-114
  assault and battery, 94, 97-100; *see also* Assault; Battery
  false imprisonment, 111-112
  homicide, 91, 101; *see also* Homicide
  infanticide and feticide, 96
  kidnapping, 112-113
  manslaughter, 93-96; *see also* Manslaughter
  mayhem, 100
  murder, 91-94; *see also* Murder
  robbery as, 121; *see also* Robbery
  sex offenses, abortion, 92, 96, 105, 106, 107
    fornication and adultery, 95, 107, 108
    incest, 104, 105
    indecent exposure, 108, 109
    prostitution, 109-111
    rape, 92, 93, 94, 101-104, 113
    seduction, 104
    sodomy, 105
  suicide, 96, 97; *see also* Suicide
against property, 79, 89, 90, 117-134, 143, 153, 178, 195, 251
  burning of, 153, 154, 155, 156
  counterfeiting, 128, 129-130
  definition of, 118
  destruction of property, 132, 133, 134, 157, 245
  embezzlement, 124-127
  extortion, 122-124
  false pretense, 127-128; *see also* False pretenses
  forgery, 128-129
  larceny, 119-121, 122; *see also* Larceny
  receiving stolen property, 130-131; *see also* Stealing; Theft
  robbery, 121, 122; *see also* Robbery
  theft, 130-131; *see also* Theft
  types of, *mala in se,* 73, 74
  mala prohibita, 73, 74
  see also Acts, criminal; Crimes
Omissions to act, 72, 76, 77, 78, 79, 187; *see also* Criminal liability; Negligence
Ordinances, violations of, 280, 287
Organized crime, conspiracy laws as effective weapon against, 198

Pandering, 109, 110, 169
Parens patriae, concept of, 278, 282, 283, 284; *see also* Juvenile courts
Parole, 14, 15, 264, 336, 341
  in legal systems of the world, compared, 42, 43
Partial responsibility, 193, 203, 204, 208
Patrol, 310, 320, 324, 343, 347
Peace, breach of, 97, 98, 172, 173
  public, 60, 61, 93
Peace officers, 99, 394
Penal institutions, *see* Corrections
Penalty, *see* Death penalty; Punishment
Penetration, proof of, 103, 104, 211

Penitentiary, state, 153, 172
Perjury, 174, 175, 177, 252, 394
Perpetrators of crime, 186, 187, 188, 189, 190, 195, 204, 247
  assistance to, 216; *see also* Accessory
Personal property, *see* Property, offenses against
Petit larceny, 121
Petty crimes, 37
Physical safety, right to prisoner's, 265-266
Pilferers, 173
Pimping, 109, 110
Plaintiffs, 239, 246, 247, 319, 320
Plato, his concept of law, 51
Plea-bargaining, 14, 37, 130, 277, 339
Pleas, 42, 206, 207
Police, 6, 7, 9, 90, 215
  administrators, role of on policing policy, 324, 325, 326, 328, 329, 343, 347
  authority and power of, 111, 245, 325
  brutality, 21, 22, 41, 257
  discretion, *see* Discretion
  impact of court decisions on, 19, 22, 317, 319
  labor movement in, *see* Collective bargaining
  manual, pretense of, 341, 343, 346
  promotion and selection policies, 317, 319, 320
  reform in, rule-making procedures, 343, 345, 346-348
  role of, in criminal justice system, 11, 12, 13, 323, 328, 337, 341, 342
    in criminal investigation, of legal systems of the world, compared, 33, 34, 35, 36, 41
    in prosecuting decision, 36, 37
  use of force by, 243, 246
Political rights, prisoner's, 271, 272
Poor, the, 161, 309, 312
Pornography, crime classification of, 21, 235
Positive law theory of justice, 301-302, 304, 305; *see also* Justice, theories of
Power, political, 303, 311; *see also* Government
Precedence, principle of, 59, 61, 68; *see also* Stare decisis
Predetermination, 204
Prejudices, of law enforcement officers, impact on criminal justice system, 336
Preliminary examination, Soviet system of law, 36
Premeditated killing, 92, 93; *see also* Murder
Presentence investigation report, 14
President's Commission on Law Enforcement and the Administration of Justice, 230, 233, 283, 322, 323, 324, 335
Presumption of innocence, 39
Pretense, fraudulent, 211
Pretrial investigation of crime, 33, 35, 36, 37, 38
Prima Facie, 168, 395
Principals, 190
  defined, 186, 187, 216, 217, 395
  in the first degree, 104, 185, 192, 217
    and in the second degree, differences in legal consequence, 187
    use of innocent agent, 186
  presence requirement, 186, 187, 188
  in the second degree, 185, 186, 188, 189

and accessory, difference between, 187
Prison, 4, 15, 109, 153, 167, 172, 330, 390
  federal, 341
  officials, 264, 265, 268, 270
    justifications for use of force, 266, 267
  reform, 265
  state, 168, 175, 341
    imprisonment in, for offenses against persons, 93, 95, 98, 100, 105, 106, 108, 112, 113
    for offenses against property, 121, 122, 130, 131, 132, 139, 155, 156
Prisoners, 158, 248, 250, 317, 319
  under European system of law, 42
  legal rights of, 263, 264, 265, 321, 341
    counsel, right to, 270
    free from assault, 266, 267
    human treatment, rights to, 265-266
    mails, right to use, 267, 268-269
    physical safety, rights to, 265-266
    political rights, 271, 272
    prison due process, 263, 267
    privacy, right to, 267-268
    procedural safeguards, 321
    rehabilitation, rights to, 265-266
    to religion, 270, 271
    visitation, right to, 270
    see also Due process of law, prison due process
  medical or psychiatric care of, 15
  separation of juveniles from adults, 278; see also Juvenile courts, law
Privacy, right to, invasion of, 21, 168, 247
  prisoners, 267-268
  of records, in juvenile courts, 289, 290-291
Private property, see Property; Offenses, against property
Private security, 11
Private wrong, social impact of, 82
Privileges, 40, 303
  for inspection of inmate communications, 268-269
  to use force, 243, 244, 245
  prison officials, 266, 267
Probable cause, 20, 33, 267
Probation, 15, 148, 249, 250, 336, 341
  American and European systems, compared, 42, 43
  functions of, 11, 12, 13, 14
  juvenile, 278, 279, 283, 289, 290, 293, 294
  revocation, 15, 264
Procuracy, Soviet, power and functions in criminal justice process, 35, 36, 38, 41
Prohibited acts, 213, 224
Project on the Minimum Standards for Criminal Justice, 65, 66
Proof, 38, 41, 98, 129, 158, 168, 174, 203, 395
  of age, strict liability acts and, 213
  alibi and, 222
  beyond a reasonable doubt, 284
  burden of, 38, 39
  difficulty of, 74, 75, 76, 109, 111, 163, 164, 178
  knowledge of facts, 73, 78, 129
  of intent, see Intent, proof of
  of penetration, in rape offenses,

103, 104, 175
  of threat of force, in rape offense, 102
Property, in defense of, 221, 222, 243, 244, 245
  personal, 117, 118, 120, 125, 141
    arson of, 153, 155, 156
    theft of, 131-132, 213; see also Stealing; theft
    trespass against, 138, 142
  offenses against, see Offenses, against property
  rights, 55, 117, 118, 130, 246
    infringement upon, 125, 126, 133, 137, 138, 139
    protection of, 122, 123, 131
    violation of, 114, 121; see also Robbery
  victims of crime against, 231, 233; see also Victims; Victimization
Prosecution, 13, 14, 17, 103, 130, 164, 168, 170, 174, 175, 195, 198, 206, 212, 214, 216, 236, 339
  civil law systems of, 39
  common law system of, 39
  criminal, 18, 76, 77, 119, 120, 127, 138, 141, 210, 211, 225, 337
    impact of immunity from prosecution, 223, 224
  criminal intent, importance of, 75, 149, 151, 152, 178
  decision for, 36, 37, 38, 205
  federal, 20, 23
  hindering, 190; see also Accessory, after the fact
  in legal systems of the world, compared, 35, 36, 37, 38, 39
  multiple, 65, 207
  state, 20
Prosecutors, 19, 195, 248, 336
  discretionary power of, see Discretion
  functions and power of in criminal justice, 11, 12, 13, 223, 323
    American system of law, 36, 37
  in criminal investigation, civil law system, 33, 34
  in legal systems of the world, compared, 35, 36, 37, 38
Prostitution, crime classification of, 235, 236
  provisions against, 109, 110, 111, 169, 170
Provocation, circumstances constituting, 94, 95, 96
Psychology, 9, 53
Public defenders, 336
Public indecency, 108, 109, 170, 215, 236, 280
Public nuisance, 109, 178, 179
Public officials, 122, 125, 129, 218, 268, 269
  corruption of, bribery offenses, 175, 176, 177
  rights of to collective bargaining, 329, 330; see also Collective bargaining
Public opinion, criminal justice system's responsiveness to, 16, 19, 24, 30
Public order, 171-174; see also Disorders; Riots; Vagrancy
Punishment, 167, 168, 170, 172, 175, 178, 189, 190, 191, 197, 199, 213, 217, 218
  concept of, 37, 52, 53, 60, 61, 66, 67
  crime and major approaches to, 5, 6, 7, 8-10,

14, 71, 72, 83-84; *see also* Criminal law,
  principles of
in juvenile courts law, 281
for narcotics violations, 162, 163, 164
for offenses against habitation and occupancy,
  144
for offenses against persons, 93, 94, 97, 98,
  100, 103, 104, 105, 106, 107, 108, 109,
  110, 111, 112, 113
for offenses against property, 120, 121, 122,
  126, 127, 130, 131, 133, 134, 142, 143,
  144, 148, 149, 153, 156
theories of, 10, 209, 219
  legal systems of world compared, 38, 42-44
  offender-oriented theories of, 83, 84
  socially-oriented theories of, 83, 84
victim compensation and, 249, 250
Soviet system of, 43, 44

Race, victimization by, *see* Victim; Victimiza-
  tion
Ransom, kidnapping for, 112; *see also* Kidnapping
Rape, 92, 93, 94, 170, 177, 215, 233, 396
  under common law, 101
  forcible, 102, 103, 230, 231, 232, 257
  by physicians, 210, 211
  proof of penetration, 103, 104
  statutory rape, 102, 170
  victim's consent, 102, 210, 211, 244
Ratification, of immunity, 211, 224
Reasonable doubt, beyond, 14, 18, 39, 223
Reasonable grounds, 213, 214, 268
"Reasonable man" test, 244, 245
Reckless acts, 96, 99, 133, 157, 204; *see also*
  Negligence
Recompensation laws, 248, 251; *see also* Vic-
  tim compensation
Reformatories, 281
Rehabilitation, 3, 4, 38, 83, 161, 335
  goals of, 10, 15
  of juvenile, 281, 293; *see also* Juvenile courts
  programs for prisoners, 265-266, 268
Release, 15, 43, 286, 287
Religious belief, and law, 27, 30, 55, 62
  prisoner's right to, 223, 224, 270-271
Renunciation, validity of, 193
Repeat offenses, juvenile, 282
Reporting of crimes, 4, 13, 170, 239, 339
Repudiation, acts of, 187, 188
Research, legal, *see* Legal research
Res Gestae, 396
Residential areas, significance of in occurrence
  of crime, 233; *see also* Victim; Victimi-
  zation
Responsibility, criminal, 208, 209, 237, 250
  partial, *see* Diminished capacity; Insanity
Restitution, 211, 248, 249, 250, 256, 339
Retribution, 10, 27, 37, 84, 205, 278; *see also*
  Punishment
Rights, of the accused, 18-23, 31-32, 199
  to assistance of counsel, *see* Counsel, right to
    assistance of
  to bear arms, 179, 180; *see also* Weapons con-
    trol
  of the confined, *see* Prisoners, legal rights of

of fetus, *see* Abortion
of the individual, *see* Individual rights
property, *see* Property, rights
to remain silent, 22, 31, 34, 35
"Right-wrong test," 208; *see also* Insanity
Riots, 171, 173, 177, 245, 331
  lawful, suppression of, 93
  statutory definition of, 172
Robbery, 92, 93, 94, 123, 189, 192, 219, 251,
  310, 397
  armed, 121, 122, 230
  reported rates of, 257
  victims of, 230, 232, 233
  see also Larceny, from persons
Roman system of law, 27, 28, 29; *see also* Civil
  law; Legal systems
Rousseau, Jean Jacques, 54, 55, 250

Sanctions, civil, 78, 79
  for conspiracy, 197, 199
  criminal, 79, 98, 137, 143, 153, 168, 171,
    174
    for health and safety code violations, 178,
      179
    severity of, narcotics addiction, 164
    for violation of fish and game regulations,
      179
    federal for kidnapping, 112
  penal, insanity and, 209
School property, victimization of, 134, 144,
  233
Screening, impact on criminal justice system,
  289, 339
Searches and seizures, protection against, 16,
  18, 179, 235, 267
  in Soviet system of law, 33
  unreasonable, 20, 21, 32
Second Amendment to the Constitution, 179,
  180
Seduction, 104
Self-defense, defense of, 220-222
  in defense of others, 221, 222, 243, 244, 266
  definition of, 243
  "retreat to the law" rule, 221, 245
  use of force in, 266
Self-incrimination, privilege against, constitutional right of, 40, 44, 224
  in French system of law, 35
  juvenile court law, 284, 287
Senate, United States, 248
Sentence, 3, 13, 23, 93, 94, 122, 124, 141, 153,
  341
  capital, 42, 91
  European systems, 42
  of fine, 141
  impact of double jeopardy on, 207
  judges' discretion in sentencing, 14, 17
  of juvenile delinquents, 281, 293, 294; *see*
    also Disposition; Juvenile courts
  motive as influencing force for, 76, 205
  perception of social harm reflected in, 81, 82,
    137
  suspended, 164
Sex offenses, 4, 94, 101-111
  crime victimization by, *see* Victim; Victimiza-
    tion

decision on regulations of postal system, 268
decisions on juvenile rights, 283, 284, 285
due process requirement, 263
interpretation of Fourth Amendment case, 20, 21, 22, 23
interpretations of Second Amendment, 180
power of, 19, 20

Taking, intent element of, 119, 120, 121, 122, 124; *see also* Larceny; Theft
Ten Commandments of the Bible, social ordering objectives in, 27
Testimony, 170, 218
  defendant's, immunity doctrine and, 223, 224
  perjured, 174, 190
  privileges, 40, 190, 217
  of witness, 14, 39, 40
Theft, 74, 215, 222, 233, 234, 236
  of auto, 230, 231, 232, 238, 257
  common law, 123, 124, 126, 127, 131
  grand theft and, distinction between, 130
  intent to commit, 152, 196
  mistake of fact, 211, 212, 213
  of property, 128, 131, 132
  statutes, 130-131, 132
  victims of, precipitative role of, 130, 230, 231, 232, 238, 239
Therapy, 10, 165
Third-degree tactics, 256
Threats, 131, 143, 145, 216
  defined, 123, 124
  of force, 220, 222
  written, 100, 123
Title 18 of the United States Code, 177, 178; *see also* Criminal code
Tort, 60, 61, 62, 246-247
  law of, 82, 97, 246, 249, 257
  liability, 78, 79
Traditions, evolution of law and, 56
Traffic law enforcement, 12, 23, 96, 161, 166
Traffic, narcotic, elimination of, 161, 162, 164, 165
  in stolen goods, 131, 132
  white slave, 109
Transferred intent, doctrine of, 75, 76, 82, 91; *see also* Intent
Treason, 153, 175
  high, 90, 129, 130
Trespass, civil, 138
  criminal, 138, 222
    breaking and entering, 143, 144, 145; *see also* Breaking and entering
    intent element of, 140, 141, 142
    of property, 139-141, 244
    simple, 141, 151, 153
  definitions of, 138, 139
Trials, civil, 40, 398
  of confederate, immunity and, 223
  criminal, 14, 17, 19, 32, 33, 37, 39, 40, 41, 207
    role of judges, in legal systems of the world, compared, 30, 34, 35, 36
  fair, 3, 4
  jury, right to, 32, 284
  for juveniles, 278, 281, 283, 284
  see also Juvenile courts

perjury statutes for, 174, 175
Trickery, 206, 215
Truancy, 280, 282

Underworld, victimless crimes and, 235, 236
Uniform Code of Military Justice, 75
Uniform Firearms Act, 180
Uniform Narcotics Drug Act, 162, 163
Uniform Rules of Criminal Procedure, 65
Uniforms, 341
Union, labor, 329; *see also* Collective bargaining
Unlawful act, 95, 157, 208, 209
  conspiracy, 194, 195, 196, 197
Unlawful assembly, 172; *see also* Disorder, public; Riots
Unlawful entry, 152; *see also* Breaking and entering
Upper-class crime, 310
U.S. Criminal Code, 177, 178; *see also* Criminal Code
Utilitarianism, social, 309, 310, 311, 312; *see also* Justice, theories of

Vagrancy laws, 172, 173-174, 280
Verdict, 103, 203, 204, 252
Vice laws, 197, 235, 257
Victim, 127, 190, 204, 211, 232, 310
  arrest record of, 239, 241, 242
  classification of, 230, 237, 239, 256
    individual, 231, 233, 234
    by their contribution to crime, 237, 238, 243, 251, 252
    see also Victim, precipitative and causative behavior of
  consent of, 210
  crimes without, *see* Crimes, without victims
  criminal liability and, 246, 247, 256
  criminals as, 256
  criminal-victim relationships, 229, 232, 234, 237, 242
  of false imprisonment, 111, 112
  plight of, 97, 106, 122, 248, 250, 251, 255, 257
  of police, 256, 257, 258
  precipitative and causative behavior of, 237-243, 256
  of property crimes, 118
  of rape, 101, 102, 103, 104, 170
  of violent crimes, 121, 186, 189, 190, 212, 221, 237, 247, 248
Victim compensation, 243, 247-256
  legislation, 242, 252
  right to, 229, 249, 251
Victim-compensation Acts, 253, 254, 255
Victimization, 233, 250
  by age and sex, 231, 233, 240
  of family of criminals, 256
  by income, 231, 232
  by race, 230, 240
Victimology, 229, 230
Violence, 42, 138, 198, 239
  act of, 77, 147, 148
  legalized, justification for use of, 222, 257
  provoker-victim and, 175, 237, 238
  use of, in criminal offenses, 97, 102, 103, 104, 121, 122, 144